JEPPESEN®
Sanderson Training Products

PRIVATE PILOT
FAA
AIRMEN KNOWLEDGE
TEST
GUIDE
for
COMPUTER TESTING

- **Questions, Answers, Explanations, References**
- **Coordinated with GFD Private Pilot Manual**
- **Explanations Adjacent to Each Question**
- **Organized by Topic, Includes Full-Color Charts**
- **Unique Sliding Mask for Self-Testing**
- **Perforated and 3-Hole Punched Pages**
- **Airplane and Recreational Pilot Questions**

JS312400-015
55 Inverness Drive East, Englewood, CO 80112-5498
ISBN 0-88487-306-4

PREFACE

Thank you for purchasing this *Private Pilot FAA Airmen Knowledge Test Guide*. This Test Guide will help you understand the answers to the test questions so you can take the FAA computer test with confidence. It contains all the FAA Recreational and Private Pilot airplane test questions. Included are the correct answers and explanations, along with study references. Explanations of why the other choices are wrong have been included where appropriate. Questions are organized by topic, with explanations conveniently located adjacent to each question. The three-hole punched, perforated pages provide flexibility so you can select and remove specific pages for effective study. Full-color charts identical to those on the FAA test are included, plus our unique sliding mask for self-testing. Please note that this Test Guide is intended to be a supplement to your instructor-led flight and ground training, not a stand alone learning tool.

THE JEPPESEN SANDERSON TRAINING PHILOSOPHY

Flight training in the developing years of aviation was characterized by the separation of academics from flight training in the aircraft. For years, ground and flight training were not integrated. There were lots of books on different subjects, written by different authors, which produced a general lack of continuity in training material. The introduction of **Jeppesen Sanderson Training Products** changed all this. Our proven, professionally integrated training materials include extensive research on teaching theory and principles of how people learn best and most efficiently. Effective instruction includes determining objectives and completion standards. We employ an important principle of learning a complex skill using a step-by-step sequence known as the **building block principle**. Another important aspect of training is the principle of **meaningful repetition**, whereby each necessary concept or skill is presented several times throughout the instructional program. Jeppesen training materials incorporate these principles in our syllabi, textbooks, videos, computer-based training (CBT), exercises, exams, PCATD Desktop Simulator, and this Test Guide. When these elements are combined with an instructor's class discussion and the skills learned in the simulator and airplane, you have an ideal integrated training system, with all materials coordinated.

Observation and research show that people tend to retain 10% of what they read, 20% of what they hear, 30% of what they see, and 50% of what they both hear and see together. These retention figures can be increased to as high as 90% by including active learning methods. Videos and textbooks are generally considered passive learning materials. Exercises, stage exams, student/instructor discussions, CBT, and practice in the simulator and airplane are considered to be active learning methods. Levels of learning include rote, understanding, application, and correlation. One of the major drawbacks with test preparation courses that concentrate only on passing the test is that they focus on rote learning, the lowest level of learning. Students benefit from Jeppesen's professional approach through standardized instruction, a documented training record, increased learning **and** increased passing rates. Our materials are challenging and motivating, while maximizing knowledge and skill retention. Nearly 3 million pilots have learned to fly using our materials, which include:

MANUALS — Our training manuals contain the answers to many of the questions you may have as you begin your training program. They are based on the **study/review** concept of learning. This means detailed material is presented in an uncomplicated way, then important points are summarized through the use of bold type and color. The best results can be obtained when the manual is studied as an integral part of the coordinated materials. The manual is the central component for academic study and is cross-referenced to video presentations.

VIDEOS — These motivating, high-quality ground school videos are professionally produced with actual inflight video and animated graphics. They allow you to review and reinforce essential concepts presented in the manual. The videos are available for viewing at flight and ground schools which subscribe to the Jeppesen Sanderson Guided Flight Discovery (GFD) Training System. Call **1-800-621-JEPP** for the names of our Training System dealers in your area.

SUPPORT COMPONENTS — Supplementary items include a training syllabus, stage and end-of-course exams, CBT, PCATD Desktop Simulator, FAR/AIM Manual, FARs Explained, airmen knowledge test and practical test study guides, test preparation software and videos, question banks and computer testing supplements, an aviation weather book, student record folder, computer, plotter, and logbook. Jeppesen Sanderson's training products are the most comprehensive pilot training materials available. In conjunction with your instructor, they help you prepare for the FAA exam and practical test; and, more importantly, they help you become a more proficient and safer pilot.

You can purchase our products and services through your Jeppesen dealer. For product, service, or sales information call **1-800-621-JEPP, 303-799-9090, or FAX 303-328-4153**. If you have comments, questions, or need explanations about any component of our GFD Training System, we are prepared to offer assistance at any time. If your dealer does not have a Jeppesen catalog, please request one and we will promptly send it to you. Just call the above telephone number, or write:

> Manager, Training and Courseware
> Jeppesen Sanderson, Inc.
> 55 Inverness Drive East
> Englewood, CO 80112-5498

Please direct inquiries from Europe, Africa, and the Middle East to:
> Jeppesen & Co., GmbH
> Frankfurter Strasse 233
> 63263 Neu-Isenburg, Germany
> Tel: 011-49-6102-5070
> Fax: 011-49-6102-507-999

UPDATES OF FAA QUESTIONS — You can obtain free updates for the FAA questions in this Test Guide by visiting Jeppesen's web site. These updates are generally valid within one year of book publication; if you are using an older Test Guide, the web site may not update all questions that have changed since the book was printed.

To find updated questions, go to **www.jeppesen.com**, click Online Publications and then click FAA Test Prep Updates. Due to improvements and ongoing reorganization of the web site, the exact location of the updates is subject to change.

Jeppesen Briefing Bulletin

The FAA is changing your test. We want you to be ready.

The FAA is concerned that many students are memorizing the answers to the FAA knowledge test. As a result, they are regularly shuffling around the answer choices to most questions in the FAA databases. This means if you have learned the answer to a question based on the letter of the correct answer, or based on the correct answer's position below the question, you will likely miss the question when you take the test. We believe the shuffle will continue on a regular basis, and it will not be possible for test preparation courses to match the sequence of the answer choices.

Jeppesen has never encouraged its students to memorize answers to FAA questions. We provide comprehensive, no-nonsense study material that teaches you what you need to know to determine the correct answers to the tests. And our test prep materials always tell you why the correct answer is correct and if it is not obvious, why the other answers are incorrect. We want you to know the material, not memorize it.

So, be careful how you study this material. While it is possible to memorize the letter and position of the correct answer, it is not in your best interest, either when taking the test, or further in your flight career when this knowledge will be tested in the cockpit. When answering an FAA question, carefully read and evaluate each answer choice and choose the correct answer based on what you know from your study, not from that answer's position.

Jeppesen thanks you for choosing our test preparation materials, and we are confident you are more than prepared to pass the FAA test.

TABLE
OF CONTENTS _____

PREFACE iii

INTRODUCTION viii

CHAPTER 1   Discovering Aviation 1-1
   Section A   Pilot Training 1-1
   Section B   Aviation Opportunities 1-3
   Section C   Introduction to Human Factors 1-4

CHAPTER 2   Airplane Systems 2-1
   Section A   Airplanes 2-1
   Section B   The Powerplant and Related Systems 2-2
   Section C   Flight Instruments 2-10

CHAPTER 3   Aerodynamic Principles 3-1
   Section A   Four Forces of Flight 3-1
   Section B   Stability 3-5
   Section C   Aerodynamics of Maneuvering Flight 3-8

CHAPTER 4   The Flight Environment 4-1
   Section A   Safety of Flight 4-1
   Section B   Airports 4-7
   Section C   Aeronautical Charts 4-15
   Section D   Airspace 4-29

CHAPTER 5   Communication and Flight Information 5-1
   Section A   Radar and ATC Services 5-1
   Section B   Radio Procedures 5-6
   Section C   Sources of Flight Information 5-13

CHAPTER 6   Meteorology for Pilots 6-1
   Section A   Basic Weather Theory 6-1
   Section B   Weather Patterns 6-3
   Section C   Weather Hazards 6-11

CHAPTER 7   Interpreting Weather Data 7-1
   Section A   The Forecasting Process 7-1
   Section B   Printed Reports and Forecasts 7-1
   Section C   Graphic Weather Products 7-13
   Section D   Sources of Weather Information 7-21

CHAPTER 8   Airplane Performance 8-1
   Section A   Predicting Performance 8-1
   Section B   Weight and Balance 8-11
   Section C   Flight Computers 8-21

CHAPTER 9   Navigation 9-1
   Section A   Pilotage and Dead Reckoning 9-1
   Section B   VOR Navigation 9-8
   Section C   ADF Navigation 9-13
   Section D   Advanced Navigation 9-17

CHAPTER 10 Applying Human Factors Principles 10-1
   Section A   Aviation Physiology 10-1
   Section B   Aeronautical Decision Making 10-5

CHAPTER 11 Flying Cross-Country 11-1
   Section A   The Flight Planning Process 11-1
   Section B   The Flight 11-2

CHAPTER 12 Federal Aviation Regulations 12-1
   Section A   14 CFR Part 1- Definitions and Abbreviations 12-1
   Section B   14 CFR Part 61- Certification: Pilots, Flight Instructors and Ground
            Instructors 12-3
   Section C   14 CFR Part 91- General Operating and Flight Rules 12-16
   Section D   NTSB 830- Aircraft Accident and Incident Reporting 12-31

APPENDIX 1   Subject Matter Knowledge Codes C-1

APPENDIX 2   Legend Information L-1

INTRODUCTION

The *Private Pilot FAA Airmen Knowledge Test Guide* is designed to help you prepare for the Recreational Pilot or Private Pilot Computer Test. It covers FAA exam material that applies to airplanes, including pertinent Federal Aviation Regulations (FARs). Questions and answers pertaining to rotorcraft, gliders, balloons, powered-lift, and airships have been omitted.

We recommend that you use this Test Guide in conjunction with the Guided Flight Discovery (GFD) Pilot Training System. The Test Guide is organized like the GFD Private Pilot Manual, with eleven chapters and distinctive sections within each chapter. Questions are covered in the Test Guide in the same sequence as the material in the manual. References to applicable page numbers in the manual are included along with the answers. A separate chapter (Chapter 12) in the Test Guide is devoted to FAR questions and answers.

Within the chapters, each section contains a brief introduction. FAA test questions appear in the left column and answers and explanations are in the right column. Below is an example of a typical reference for a question.

[1]   [2]   [3]   [4]   [5]   [6]

4-59.   **J11**   **4-59.** **Answer C. GFDPPM 4-47 (AIM)**

(FAA Question)   *(Explanation of FAA Question)*

[1] Jeppesen designated test guide question number. The first number is the chapter where the question is located in the Test Guide. In most cases, this corresponds to the chapter in the GFD manual. The second number is the question number within the chapter. This number may or may not be in sequential order. In this example, the question is in chapter 4 of the Test Guide and it is the 59th question.

[2] FAA subject matter knowledge code. The reference to this code can be found in the appendix of the Test Guide.

[3] The Jeppesen test guide number is repeated in the right hand column above the explanation.

[4] Correct answer to the question, in this case answer C is correct.

[5] The location where the question is covered in the GFD manual. In this case, the question is covered on page 4-47 in the GFD Private Pilot Manual.

[6] Abbreviation for the FAA or other authoritative source document. In this case, the reference is the Aeronautical Information Manual (AIM). Abbreviations used in the Test Guide are as follows:

AC	—	Advisory Circulars
A/FD	—	Airport/Facility Directory
AIM	—	Aeronautical Information Manual
AW	—	Aviation Weather, AC 00-6A
AWS	—	Aviation Weather Services, AC 00-45
FAR	—	Federal Aviation Regulation
AFH	—	Airplane Flying Handbook, FAA-H-8083-3
IAP	—	Instrument Approach Procedure
IFH	—	Instrument Flying Handbook, FAA-H-8083-15
GFDICM	—	Guided Flight Discovery Instrument/Commercial Manual
GFDPPM	—	Guided Flight Discovery Private Pilot Manual
NAVWEPS	—	Aerodynamics for Naval Aviators

PHB	—	Pilot's Handbook of Aeronautical Knowledge, AC 61-23
WBH	—	Aircraft Weight and Balance Handbook, FAA-H-8083-1
TERPS	—	U.S. Standard for Terminal Instrument Procedures

Below the reference line is the FAA question in the left column and the explanation in the right column. The explanation includes the correct answer followed by an explanation of why the answer is correct and why the other answers are wrong. In some cases, the incorrect answers are not explained. Examples include instances where the answers are calculated, or when the explanation of the correct answer obviously eliminates the wrong answers.

The answers in this Test Guide are based on official reference documents and, in our judgment, are the best choices of the available answers. Some questions which were valid when the FAA test was developed may no longer be appropriate due to ongoing changes in regulations or official operating procedures. However, with the computer test format, timely updating and validation of questions is anticipated. Therefore, when taking the FAA test, it is important to answer the questions according to the latest regulations or official operating procedures.

Two appendices from the FAA test materials are included in the back of the Test Guide. These are Appendix 1, Subject Matter Knowledge Codes, which also lists reference material, and Appendix 2, which consists of legend information from the National Aeronautical Charting Office (NACO) Airport/Facility Directory (A/FD). You will need to refer to this legend to answer some questions concerning A/FD information. Appendix 3 in the Test Guide contains a numerical listing of all airplane questions. Included in this listing is a tabulation with the Jeppesen test guide question number, FAA question number, correct answer, and the page number where the question appears in the Test Guide.

Figures in the Test Guide are the same as those that are used in the FAA Computerized Testing Supplement. These figures, that are referred to in many of the questions, are placed throughout the Test Guide as close as practical to the applicable questions. When a figure is not on the same page or facing page, a note will indicate the page number where you can find that figure. In addition, pages in this Test Guide are three-hole punched and perforated to allow you to easily remove any figure for reference while answering a specific question.

HOW TO PREPARE FOR THE FAA TEST
It is important to realize that to become a safe, competent pilot, you need more than just the academic knowledge required to pass a test. For a comprehensive ground training program, we recommend a structured ground school with a qualified flight or ground instructor. An organized course of instruction will help you complete the course in a timely manner, and you will be able to have your questions answered. The additional instruction will be beneficial in your flight training.

Regardless of whether or not you are in a structured ground training program, you will find this Test Guide is an excellent training aid to help you prepare for the FAA computerized test. The Test Guide contains all of the airplane questions as they are presented in the FAA computerized test format. By reviewing the questions and studying the Guided Flight Discovery Pilot Training materials, you should be well equipped to take the test.

You will also benefit more from your study if you test yourself as you proceed through the Test Guide. Cover the answers in the right-hand column, read each question, and choose what you consider the best answer. A sliding mask is provided for this purpose. Move the sliding mask down and read the answer and explanation for that question. You may want to mark the questions you miss for further study and review prior to taking the exam.

The sooner you take the exam after you complete your study, the better. This way, the information will be fresh in your mind, and you will be more confident when you actually take the FAA test.

WHO CAN TAKE THE TEST

When you are ready to take the FAA computerized test, you must present evidence that you have completed the appropriate ground instruction or a home study course. This proof may be in the form of a graduation certificate from a pilot training course, a written statement, or a logbook entry by a certified ground or flight instructor. Although you are encouraged to obtain ground instruction, a home study course may be used. If you cannot provide one of the above documents, you may present evidence of a completed home study course to an FAA aviation safety inspector for approval.

You also must provide evidence of a permanent mailing address, appropriate identification, and proof of your age. The identification must include a current photograph, your signature, and your residential address, if different from your mailing address. You may present this information in more than one form of identification, such as a driver's license, government identification card, passport, alien residency (green) card, or a military identification card.

WHAT IS A RECREATIONAL PILOT

The recreational pilot certificate is intended for those who are willing to limit their flying to a basic, single-engine aircraft with no more than 180 horsepower. Specific provisions (privileges and limitations) that apply to this certificate are listed in Title 14 of the Code of Federal Regulations (CFR) Part 61. Recreational pilots, with additional knowledge, proficiency, and experience, may upgrade their certificates to the private or higher level.

While this Test Guide is primarily intended for private pilot applicants, it does contain all the study questions for the FAA's Recreational Pilot Computer Test. Those questions which are specific to the recreational pilot can be identified by the words "recreational pilot" in the stem of the question.

GENERAL INFORMATION — FAA COMPUTER TESTS

Detailed information on FAA computer testing is contained in FAA Order 8080.6B, Conduct of Airmen Knowledge Tests. This FAA order provides guidance for Flight Standards District Offices (FSDOs) and personnel associated with organizations that are participating in, or are seeking to participate in, the FAA Computer-Assisted Airmen Knowledge Testing Program. You also may refer to FAA Order 8700.1, General Aviation Operations Inspector's Handbook, for guidance on computer testing by 14 CFR Parts 141 and 142 pilot schools that hold examining authority.

As an applicant, you don't need all of the details contained in FAA Orders, but you will be interested in some of the general information about computer testing facilities. A **Computer Testing Designee (CTD)** is an organization authorized by the FAA to administer FAA airmen knowledge tests via the computer medium. A **Computer Testing Manager (CTM)** is a person selected by the CTD to serve as manager of its national computer testing program. A **Testing Center Supervisor (TCS)** is a person selected by the CTM, with FAA approval, to administer FAA airmen knowledge tests at approved testing centers. The TCS is responsible for the operation of the testing center. A **Special Test Administrator (STA)** is a person selected by a CTD to administer FAA airmen knowledge tests in unique situations and remote or isolated areas. A test proctor is a properly trained and qualified person, appointed by a TCS, authorized to administer FAA airmen knowledge tests.

CTDs are selected by the FAA's Airmen Testing Standards Branch. Those selected may include companies, schools, universities, or other organizations that meet specific requirements. For example, they must clearly demonstrate competence in computer technology, centralized database management, national communications network operation and maintenance, national facilities management, software maintenance and support, and technical training and customer support. They must provide computer-assisted testing, test administration, and data transfer service on a national scale. This means they must maintain a minimum of 20 operational testing centers geographically dispersed throughout the United States. In addition, CTDs must offer operational hours that are convenient to the public. An acceptable plan for test security is also required.

TEST MATERIALS, REFERENCE MATERIALS, AND AIDS

You are allowed to use aids, reference materials, and test materials within specified guidelines, provided the actual test questions or answers are not revealed. All models of aviation-oriented computers, regardless of manufacturer, may be used, including hand-held computers designed expressly for aviation use, and also small electronic calculators that perform arithmetic functions. Simple programmable memories, which allow addition to, subtraction from, or retrieval of one number from the memory, are acceptable. Simple functions such as square root or percent keys are also acceptable.

In addition, you may use any reference materials provided with the test. You will find that these reference materials are the same as those in your Test Guide. They include a printed Computerized Testing Supplement with the legend data and the applicable figures. You also may use scales, straight-edges, protractors, plotters, navigation computers, log sheets, and, as already mentioned, electronic or mechanical calculators that are directly related to the test. Permanently inscribed manufacturer's instructions on the front and back of these aids, such as, formulas, conversions, regulations, signals, weather data, holding pattern diagrams, frequencies, weight and balance formulas, and ATC procedures, are permissible.

WHAT TO EXPECT ON A COMPUTER TEST

Computer testing centers are required to have an acceptable method for the "on-line" registration of test applicants during normal business hours. They must provide a dual method, for example, keyboard, touch screen, or mouse, for answering questions. Features that must be provided also include an introductory lesson to familiarize you with computer testing procedures, the ability to return to a test question previously answered (for the purpose of review or answer changes), and a suitable display of multiple-choice and other question types on the computer screen in one frame. Other required features include a display of the time remaining for the completion of the test, a "HELP" function which permits you to review test questions and optional responses, and provisions for your test score on an Airman Computer Test Report.

On computer tests, the selection of questions is done for you, and you will answer the questions that appear on the screen. You will be given a specific amount of time to complete the test, which is based on past experience with others who have taken the exam. If you are prepared, you should have plenty of time to complete the test. After you begin the test, the screen will show you the time remaining for completion. When taking the test, keep the following points in mind:

1. Answer each question in accordance with the latest regulations and procedures. If the regulation or procedure has recently changed, you will receive credit for the affected question. However, these questions will normally be deleted or updated on the FAA computerized exams.

2. Read each question carefully before looking at the possible answers. You should clearly understand the problem before attempting to solve it.

3. After formulating an answer, determine which of the alternatives most nearly corresponds with that answer. The answer chosen should completely resolve the problem.

4. From the answers given, it may appear that there is more than one possible answer; however, there is only one answer that is correct and complete. The other answers are either incomplete or are derived from popular misconceptions.

5. Make sure you select an answer for each question. Questions left unanswered will be counted as incorrect.

6. If a certain question is difficult for you, it is best to proceed to other questions. After you answer the less difficult questions, return to those which were unanswered. The computer-aided test format helps you identify unanswered questions, as well as those questions you wish to review.

7. When solving a calculator problem, select the answer nearest your solution. The problem has been checked with various types of calculators; therefore, if you have solved it correctly, your answer will be closer to the correct answer than the other choices.

8. Generally, the test results will be available almost immediately. Your score will be recorded on an Airman Computer Test Report form. [Figure 1]

```
1
2
3
4
5
6                    Federal Aviation Administration
7                     Airmen Computer Test Report
8
9  EXAM TITLE:  Private Pilot Airplane (PA)
10
11 NAME:  Jones David John
12
13 ID NUMBER:  123456789              TAKE 1
14
15 DATE:  08/14/—          SCORE: 82          GRADE: Pass
16
17
18
19
20 --------------------------------------------------------------
21
22
23 Knowledge area codes in which questions were answered incorrectly.
24 See Appendix 1. A code may represent more than one incorrect
25 response.
26
27 A20 B08 B13 H01 H04 H06 I21 I22 J03 J05 M52 N27
28
29
30
31 EXPIRATION DATE:  08/31/—
32
33
34
35                    DO NOT LOSE THIS REPORT
36
37 --------------------------------------------------------------
38 Authorized instructor's statement. (If applicable)
39
40 I have given Mr./Ms. _____  additional instruction in
41 each subject area shown to be deficient and consider the applicant competent to
42 pass the test.
43
44 Last _____ Initial _____ Cert. No. _____ Type _____
45 (Print Clearly)
46
47
48 Signature _____
49
50
51
52
53
54                                          CTD's Embossed Seal
```

FIGURE 1. This sample Airman Computer Test Report shows the applicants test results. Take 1 indicates this is the first time the applicant has taken this test. Knowledge area codes for incorrect answers are listed in the center portion of the report, and an additional instruction section is included in the last part.

The Airmen Computer Test Report includes subject matter knowledge codes for incorrect answers. To determine the knowledge area in which a particular question was incorrectly answered, compare the subject matter knowledge codes on this report to Appendix 1, Subject Matter Knowledge Codes.

Computer testing designees must provide a way for applicants, who challenge the validity of test questions, to enter comments into the computer. The test proctor should advise you, if you have complaints about test scores, or specific test questions, to write directly to the appropriate FAA office. In addition to comments, you will be asked to respond to a critique form which may vary at different computer testing centers. The TCS must provide a method for you to respond to critique questions projected on the computer screen. [Figure 2]

---

1. Did the test administration personnel give you an adequate briefing on testing procedures?

2. Was the "sign-on" accomplished efficiently?

3. Did you have any difficulty reading the computer presentation of test questions?

4. Was the test supplementary material (charts, graphs, tables, etc.) presented in a usable manner?

5. Did you have any difficulty using the "return to previous question for review" procedure?

6. Was the testing room noise level distracting?

7. Did you have adequate work space?

8. Did you have adequate lighting?

9. What is your overall evaluation of the computer testing experience?

   a. Unsatisfactory.

   b. Poor.

   c. Satisfactory.

   d. Highly satisfactory.

   e. Outstanding.

FIGURE 2. Critique forms used at different computer testing centers may vary. This sample form contains typical questions.

RETESTING AFTER FAILURE

The applicant shall surrender the previous test report to the test proctor prior to retesting. The original test report shall be destroyed by the test proctor after administering the retest. The latest test taken will reflect the official score.

As stated in 14 CFR section 61.49, an applicant may apply for retesting after receiving additional training and an endorsement from an authorized instructor who has determined the applicant has been found competent to pass the test.

WHERE TO TAKE THE FAA TEST

Almost all testing is now administered via computer at FAA-designated test centers. As indicated, these CTDs are located throughout the U.S. You can expect to pay a fee and the cost varies at different locations. The following is a listing of the approved computer testing designees at the time of publication of this Test Guide. You may want to check with your local FSDO for changes.

> Computer Assisted Testing Service (CATS)
> 1-800-947-4228
> Outside U.S. (650) 259-8550
>
> LaserGrade Computer Testing
> 1-800-211-2754
> Outside U.S. (360) 896-9111

DISCOVERING AVIATION

The beginnings of aviation, both as a craft and as your own pursuit, are discussed in this chapter. You will also read about the human factors that go into conducting every flight.

Each chapter and section in the *Private Pilot FAA Airmen Knowledge Study Guide* directly corresponds to the same chapter and section in Jeppesen's *Private Pilot Manual*, part of the Guided Flight Discovery Pilot Training System. The manual explores in depth each topic presented in this guide, and covers many areas not tested in the computer exam. This additional information is vital to your private pilot preparation, and we strongly encourage you to study the manual, in addition to this guide.

SECTION A
PILOT TRAINING

Throughout history, we have dreamed about achieving the freedom and power of flight. We have looked to the sky, marveled at the birds, and wondered what it must be like to escape the bonds of earth to join them.

THE HISTORY OF FLIGHT

Leonardo daVinci, one of history's greatest intellects, pondered the mysteries of flight as early as the 15th century, with fully developed drawings and schematics for making flight possible for humans. From these origins, we continued our quest for flight. The Mongolfier brothers designed the first lighter-than-air vehicle, a balloon that made its first flight in 1783. Otto Lillienthal answered with the first heavier-than-air craft: a glider, in the years between 1881 and 1896. Orville and Wilbur Wright achieved the first powered, sustained, and controlled airplane flights in history, in 1903 at Kitty Hawk.

Aviation firsts didn't end with that initial airplane. Amelia Earhart and Charles Lindbergh made Atlantic crossings within the next 30 years. With the impetus of World War II driving technology, jet flight and supersonic flight evolved quickly. And then, humans reached into space, when Neil Armstrong and Edwin Aldrin stepped onto the moon. With the space shuttles making routine flights into orbit, what lies next? The next hundred years should prove just as exciting as the first.

THE TRAINING PROCESS

Learning to fly, in the early days, was accomplished by trial and error. Although you may never encounter the same obstacles and hazards faced by the early aviators, becoming a pilot still presents a challenge which requires hard work and dedication. However, the time and energy which you invest in flying will yield countless rewards.

The Federal Aviation Administration oversees all regulatory aspects of flight, and they govern the process by which you will receive your private pilot certificate. You may start training at a fixed-base operator (FBO) at your local airport, or you may train through the military. No matter where you fly, though, you will pass through three phases of flight training: presolo, cross-country and test preparation, in addition to the ground training that supplements your time in the air. Along the way, you will acquire the flight hours necessary to meet the requirements for the certificate.

1-1   A01

With respect to the certification of airmen, which is a category of aircraft?

A — Gyroplane, rotorcraft, airship, free balloon.
B — Airplane, rotorcraft, glider, lighter-than-air.
C — Single-engine land and sea, multiengine land and sea.

1-2   A01

With respect to the certification of airmen, which is a class of aircraft?

A — Airplane, rotorcraft, glider, lighter-than-air.
B — Single-engine land and sea, multiengine land and sea.
C — Lighter-than-air, airship, hot air balloon, gas balloon.

1-3   A01

With respect to the certification of aircraft, which is a category of aircraft?

A — Normal, utility, acrobatic.
B — Airplane, rotorcraft, glider.
C — Landplane, seaplane.

1-4   A01

With respect to the certification of aircraft, which is a class of aircraft?

A — Normal, utility, acrobatic, limited.
B — Airplane, rotorcraft, glider, balloon.
C — Transport, restricted, provisional.

1-1. Answer B. GFDPPM 1-18 (FAR 1.1)

Airmen are certificated according to four categories of aircraft: airplane, rotorcraft, glider, and lighter-than-air. Answers (A) and (C) are wrong because they list classes of pilot certification and not categories.

1-2. Answer B. GFDPPM 1-18 (FAR 1.1)

Each category of aircraft is broken down into classes. The airplane category is divided into single-engine land and sea, and multi-engine land and sea. Answer (A) is wrong because it lists aircraft categories. Answer (C) is wrong because lighter-than-air is a category, not a class.

1-3. Answer A. GFDPPM 1-20 (FAR 1.1)

Normal, utility, and acrobatic are three of the categories under which aircraft are certified. Answer (B) lists aircraft classes, not categories. Answer (C) lists examples of airplane classes for pilot certification.

1-4. Answer B. GFDPPM 1-20 (FAR 1.1)

Aircraft are placed into groups having similar means of propulsion, flight, or landing. These classes include: airplane, rotorcraft, glider, balloon, and powered-lift. Answers (A) and (C) list aircraft categories, not classes.

SECTION B
AVIATION OPPORTUNITIES

One of the unique joys of aviation is that there is always a challenge to be met; a new adventure on which to embark; one more goal to be achieved. A private pilot certificate opens a door to a future of exciting opportunities and endless possibilities. There are no FAA test questions in this section.

NEW AVIATION EXPERIENCES

As soon as you are granted your private pilot certificate, new experiences await you; new scenery, new airports, and new responsibilities. You will be able to carry passengers for the first time, and you can fly cross-country to airports which you have not yet explored. As you gain flying experience and confidence, you may feel the need to expand your aviation horizons. The best way to sharpen your abilities, master new skills, and reenergize your enthusiasm for flight is to pursue additional training.

REFRESHER TRAINING

Refresher training maintains your proficiency as a pilot, and keeps you safe. You can stay current and develop your skills at the same time with some different types of flying. If you learned to fly close to sea level, mountain flying is an exciting challenge that tests all areas of your piloting abilities. Aerobatic flying shows you the limits of an airplane's envelope and puts you in control of a thrilling ride. Checkouts in new aircraft, such as tailwheel or high-performance airplanes, will add to your repertoire, and allow you to go places that you could not in the aircraft in which you trained.

ORGANIZATIONS

Organizations for pilots abound. Some cover a broad spectrum of pilots, such as the Aircraft Owners and Pilots Association (AOPA). Others target special interests within aviation. The Experimental Aircraft Association (EAA) involves those who are interested in homebuilt, classic and antique aircraft. The Ninety-Nines, International Organization of Women Pilots, provides networking, fellowship and financial aid for female pilots.

ADDITIONAL RATINGS AND CERTIFICATES

A proficient pilot is always learning, and you may decide in the future to pursue additional certificates and ratings. An instrument rating allows you to fly in clouds and low visibility by reference to instruments. A multi-engine rating puts you in command of larger aircraft with more than one engine. If you have ever wanted to land on water, getting a seaplane rating is a great experience. Fly an aircraft beyond the scope of airplanes: rotorcraft, glider and balloon ratings expand your view of aviation. Upgrade your certificate and level of expertise with a commercial certificate, which allows you to fly for hire. Teaching others to fly may be a next logical step, and you can do so with your flight instructor's certificate (CFI). In order to be an airline captain, you must acquire an airline transport pilot (ATP) license.

AVIATION CAREERS

Highly trained professional pilots use their skills in a variety of fields. Besides flying as an airline pilot, or teaching as a flight instructor, there are as many different jobs available in aviation as your imagination allows.

Air taxi and charter operations fly passengers or cargo during scheduled flights or provide on-call services. Aircraft sales representatives deliver aircraft from the factory to the dealer or from the dealer to the customer, as well as demonstrate aircraft. Land survey and photography services provide businesses and government agencies with information about commercial property, highways, mining operations, and drilling sites. In addition to providing a unique view of metropolitan areas and natural wonders, sightseeing services fly tourists over scenic areas which may be hard to reach by other means. Powerline and pipeline patrol flight operations consist of checking powerlines, towers, and pipelines for damage, as well as transporting repair crews. Air ambulance operations transport patients to health care facilities for specialized treatment. Helicopter pilots with trained paramedics on board carry critically ill or injured persons from accident scenes to hospitals.

SECTION C
INTRODUCTION TO HUMAN FACTORS

There is more to pilot training than acquiring technical knowledge and gaining proficiency in aircraft control. Understanding how your mind and body function when you fly is as important as knowing the operation of your airplane's systems and equipment. The goal of human factors training for pilots is to increase aviation safety by optimizing human performance and reducing human error. There are no FAA test questions in this section.

AERONAUTICAL DECISION MAKING
Approximately 75 percent of all aviation accidents are human factors related. The phrase *human factors related* more aptly describes these accidents than the term *pilot error*, since it usually is not a single decision made by the pilot, but a string of decisions, that leads to an accident.

CREW RESOURCE MANAGEMENT
The focus of crew resource management (CRM) programs is the effective use of all available resources; human resources, hardware, and information. Human resources include all groups routinely working with the cockpit crew (or pilot) who are involved in decisions which are required to operate a flight safely. These groups include, but are not limited to: dispatchers, cabin crewmembers, maintenance personnel, and air traffic controllers.

PILOT IN COMMAND RESPONSIBILITY
As pilot in command, you make the final decisions, and your choices determine the outcome of the flight. You are directly responsible for your own safety, as well as the safety of your passengers. Understanding your own personal limitations is an important part of being a responsible pilot in command.

COMMUNICATION
Effective communication requires that ideas are not only expressed but that they are conveyed in a clear and timely manner. Your ability to communicate professionally helps determine whether you are able to handle most aviation situations involving others in the system, especially during emergencies.

SITUATIONAL AWARENESS
Situational awareness is the accurate perception of the operational and environmental factors which affect the aircraft, pilot, and passengers during a specific period of time. Maintaining situational awareness requires an understanding of the significance of these factors and their impact on the flight. When you are situationally aware, you have an overview of the total operation and don't fixate on one factor.

AVIATION PHYSIOLOGY
Aviation physiology is the study of the performance and limitations of the body in the flight environment. Most healthy people do not experience any physical difficulties as a result of flying. However, there are some physiological factors which you should be aware of as you begin flight training.

PRESSURE EFFECTS
As the airplane climbs and descends, variations in atmospheric pressure effect many parts of your body. As outside air pressure changes, air trapped in the ears, teeth, sinus cavities, and gastrointestinal tract can cause pain and discomfort. Common associated ailments include ear and sinus block, toothaches, gastrointestinal pain, as well as the after-effects of scuba diving.

MOTION SICKNESS
Motion sickness is caused by the brain receiving conflicting messages about the state of the body. You may experience motion sickness during initial flights, but it generally goes away within the first 10 lessons. Anxiety and stress contribute to motion sickness. Symptoms of motion sickness include general discomfort, nausea, dizziness, paleness, sweating, and vomiting.

STRESS AND FATIGUE
We define stress as the body's response to physical and psychological demands placed upon it. Stress causes the release of chemical hormones (such as adrenaline) into the blood and the acceleration of the metabolism to provide

energy to the muscles. In addition, blood sugar, heart rate, respiration, blood pressure, and perspiration all increase. Stress can be caused by fatigue, and fatigue on its own can affect your ability to make timely and wise decisions.

DRUGS

Whether the drug is alcohol, an illicit drug, or an over-the-counter medication, it may affect your ability to safely act as pilot-in-command. Depressants, such as cold medication and alcohol, slow reaction times and decrease your sense of responsibility. Stimulants, like caffeine and appetite suppressants, put you on edge and may cause you to make rash decisions. Hallucinogens, such as some illegal drugs, may have after-effects that last for days or weeks. Consider carefully what the effects any drug you are taking will be on your piloting skill. If in doubt, consult an aviation medical examiner.

AIRPLANE SYSTEMS

SECTION A
AIRPLANES

Although airplanes are designed for a variety of purposes, the basic components of most airplanes are essentially the same. Once the practical aspects of building an airworthy craft are resolved, what ultimately becomes the final model is largely a matter of the original design objectives and aesthetics. In a sense then, airplane design is a combination of art and science.

The aircraft is the composite of many parts. The airframe consists of the fuselage, wings, empennage, trim devices and landing gear. The engine and propeller provide the motion by which the airplane develops lift, and flies. The pilot's operating handbook (POH) is so vital that it is considered to be part of the airplane as well.

2-1   B07
Where may an aircraft's operating limitations be found?

A — On the Airworthiness Certificate.
B — In the current, FAA-approved flight manual, approved manual material, markings, and placards, or any combination thereof.
C — In the aircraft airframe and engine logbooks.

2-1. Answer B. GFDPPM 2-10 (FAR 91.9)
Operating limits can be found in any of these sources. Answers (A) and (C) are incorrect because limitations are not found on the Airworthiness Certificate or in the logbooks.

SECTION B
THE POWERPLANT AND RELATED SYSTEMS

Airplanes require a means of thrust in order to achieve enough lift to overcome the effects of gravity. The modern aircraft powerplant still maintains several similarities with its predecessors, including the requirement for precise interaction of the engine, propeller, and other related systems.

ENGINES
In order to get the most performance out of your aircraft's engine, you need to know how the combustion process works, and what you can do to affect the efficiency of this operation.

MIXTURE
1. The purpose of adjusting the fuel/air mixture is to decrease fuel flow to compensate for decreased air density.
2. Takeoff at high-elevation airports may require leaning the engine during run-up for best power.
3. The mixture must be enriched prior to a descent.

CARBURETOR
4. The operating principle of float-type carburetors is based on the difference in air pressure between the venturi throat and the air inlet.
5. The conditions most favorable to icing include an outside temperature between 20 and 70 degrees F and high humidity.
6. In a normally aspirated engine with a fixed-pitch propeller, the first indication of carburetor ice is a loss of RPM.
7. Applying carburetor heat will: a. enrich the fuel/air mixture. b. cause a decrease in engine performance. c. cause a temporary decrease in RPM, followed by a gradual increase.
8. Float-type carburetors are more susceptible to icing than fuel-injected systems.

IGNITION
9. One purpose of a dual ignition system on aircraft is to provide for improved engine performance.

ABNORMAL COMBUSTION
10. If the grade of fuel used in an engine is lower than specified for the engine, it will most likely cause detonation.
11. Detonation occurs when the unburned charge in the cylinders explodes instead of burning normally.
12. If a pilot suspects detonation during climb-out, the initial corrective action would be to lower the nose slightly to increase airspeed.
13. The uncontrolled firing of the fuel/air charge in advance of normal spark ignition is known as pre-ignition.

FUEL SYSTEMS
14. On aircraft equipped with fuel pumps, the practice of running a fuel tank dry before switching tanks is unwise because the engine-driven or electric boost fuel pump may draw air into the fuel system and cause vapor lock.
15. Using fuel of a lower-than-specified grade may cause cylinder head and engine oil temperature gauges to exceed their normal operating ranges.
16. Fuel of the next higher octane can be substituted if the recommended octane is not available.
17. Filling the fuel tanks after the last flight of the day will prevent moisture condensation by eliminating air space in the tanks.

OIL SYSTEMS
18. For internal cooling, reciprocating aircraft engines rely on the circulation of lubricating oil.
19. An abnormally high oil temperature indication may be caused by the oil level being too low.

COOLING SYSTEMS
20. Excessively high engine temperatures will cause loss of power, excessive oil consumption, and possible permanent internal engine damage.
21. If the engine oil temperature and cylinder head temperature gauges have exceeded their normal operating range, the pilot may be operating with too much power and the mixture set too lean.
22. To aid engine cooling in a climb, the pilot can lower the nose, reduce the rate of climb and increase airspeed.
23. To cool an engine that is overheating, the pilot can enrich the fuel mixture.

PROPELLERS

The propellers found on single-engine aircraft can be divided, generally, into two basic types: fixed-pitch and constant-speed.

CONSTANT SPEED

24. The constant-speed propeller permits the pilot to select a blade angle for the most efficient performance.
25. Engine operation on an aircraft equipped with a constant-speed propeller is conducted with the throttle controlling power output, as registered on the manifold pressure gauge, and the propeller control regulating engine RPM.
26. When operating an engine equipped with a constant-speed propeller, the pilot must avoid high manifold pressure settings with low RPM.

2-2   H307
Excessively high engine temperatures will

A — cause damage to heat-conducting hoses and warping of the cylinder cooling fins.
B — cause loss of power, excessive oil consumption, and possible permanent internal engine damage.
C — not appreciably affect an aircraft engine.

2-3   H307
If the engine oil temperature and cylinder head temperature gauges have exceeded their normal operating range, the pilot may have been operating with

A — the mixture set too rich.
B — higher-than-normal oil pressure.
C — too much power and with the mixture set too lean.

2-4   H307
One purpose of the dual ignition system on an aircraft engine is to provide for

A — improved engine performance.
B — uniform heat distribution.
C — balanced cylinder head pressure.

2-5   H307
On aircraft equipped with fuel pumps, when is the auxiliary electric driven pump used?

A — In the event engine-driven fuel pump fails.
B — All the time to aid the engine-driven fuel pump.
C — Constantly except in starting the engine.

2-2. Answer B. GFDPPM 2-34 (PHB)
High temperature can cause detonation and a resulting loss of power, excessive oil consumption, and engine damage, including scoring of the cylinders and damage to pistons, rings, and valves. Answer (A) is not the best answer, since engine damage and power loss are more critical. Answer (C) is wrong because engine damage can be serious.

2-3. Answer C. GFDPPM 2-35 (PHB)
With high power settings and the mixture set too lean, overheating can result. This can be indicated by a high engine oil temperature and cylinder head temperature. Answer (A) is wrong because when the mixture is too rich, temperatures are usually lower than normal. Answer (B) is wrong because high oil pressure does not normally cause high temperatures. However, low oil levels can cause high oil temperatures.

2-4. Answer A. GFDPPM 2-24 (AFH)
Dual ignition systems fire two spark plugs, which improves combustion of the fuel/air mixture and results in slightly more power. Answer (B) is incorrect because the ignition system does not affect heat distribution. Answer (C) is wrong because the ignition system does not affect cylinder head pressure.

2-5. Answer A. GFDPPM 2-27 (PHB)
The auxiliary electric pump is a backup for an engine-driven pump. Although labeling, procedures for use, and control switches differ between manufacturers, these auxiliary pumps can cause operational problems if used inappropriately. In some systems, continuous use of both the auxiliary pump and the engine-driven pump can cause an excessively rich mixture. Besides the back-up function, auxiliary pumps are commonly used to provide fuel under pressure for engine starting.

2-6   H307
The operating principle of float-type carburetors is based on the

A — automatic metering of air at the venturi as the aircraft gains altitude.
B — difference in air pressure at the venturi throat and the air inlet.
C — increase in air velocity in the throat of a venturi causing an increase in air pressure.

2-7   H307
The basic purpose of adjusting the fuel/air mixture at altitude is to

A — decrease the amount of fuel in the mixture in order to compensate for increased air density.
B — decrease the fuel flow in order to compensate for decreased air density.
C — increase the amount of fuel in the mixture to compensate for the decrease in pressure and density of the air.

2-8   H307
During the run-up at a high-elevation airport, a pilot notes a slight engine roughness that is not affected by the magneto check but grows worse during the carburetor heat check. Under these circumstances, what would be the most logical initial action?

A — Check the results obtained with a leaner setting of the mixture.
B — Taxi back to the flight line for a maintenance check.
C — Reduce manifold pressure to control detonation.

2-9   H307
While cruising at 9,500 feet MSL, the fuel/air mixture is properly adjusted. What will occur if a descent to 4,500 feet MSL is made without readjusting the mixture?

A — The fuel/air mixture may become excessively lean.
B — There will be more fuel in the cylinders than is needed for normal combustion, and the excess fuel will absorb heat and cool the engine.
C — The excessively rich mixture will create higher cylinder head temperatures and may cause detonation.

2-6. Answer B. GFDPPM 2-18 (PHB)
The decreased pressure caused by air flowing rapidly through the venturi tube draws fuel from the float chamber. Answer (A) is wrong because air is not "metered" at the venturi. Answer (C) is not correct because the increased air velocity at the venturi throat causes a decrease in air pressure, not an increase.

2-7. Answer B. GFDPPM 2-19 (AFH)
If fuel flow is not decreased with altitude, the mixture becomes too rich with fuel. Therefore, the fuel mixture must be leaned to maintain the proper fuel/air ratio. Answer (A) is wrong because air density is decreased with altitude, not increased. Answer (C) is incorrect because increasing the fuel mixture would further enrich the fuel/air mixture.

2-8. Answer A. GFDPPM 2-19 (AFH)
In this case, engine roughness is probably caused by the mixture set too rich for the high altitude. When the carburetor heat is turned on, the warmer air entering the carburetor is less dense, and the mixture is further enriched. As a result, the engine roughness increases. The problem can usually be corrected by leaning the mixture. Answer (B) is wrong because the pilot should first try the runup with a leaner mixture. Answer (C) is not correct because detonation is the result of a mixture that is too lean.

2-9. Answer A. GFDPPM 2-19 (AFH)
With a decrease in altitude, air density increases. This means you will have to enrich the mixture as you descend, otherwise the fuel/air mixture can become excessively lean. Answers (B) and (C) are wrong because more air will enter the cylinders for the same amount of fuel, decreasing the fuel/air mixture, not increasing it.

2-10   H307
Which condition is most favorable to the development of carburetor icing?

A — Any temperature below freezing and a relative humidity of less than 50 percent.
B — Temperature between 32 and 50°F and low humidity.
C — Temperature between 20 and 70°F and high humidity.

2-10. Answer C. GFDPPM 2-20 (PHB)
Carburetor icing is most likely between 20° and 70°F in high humidity conditions. Answers (A) and (B) are wrong because carburetor icing is less likely with low humidity.

2-11   H307
The possibility of carburetor icing exists even when the ambient air temperature is as

A — high as 70°F and the relative humidity is high.
B — high as 95°F and there is visible moisture.
C — low as 0°F and the relative humidity is high.

2-11. Answer A. GFDPPM 2-20 (PHB)
(A) is correct because carburetor icing is most probable between 20°F and 70°F with high humidity or visible moisture. Answer (B) is incorrect, because icing usually does not occur at temperatures above 70°F. Answer (C) is incorrect because the possibility of carburetor icing decreases below 32°F, and usually does not occur below 20°F.

2-12   H307
If an aircraft is equipped with a fixed-pitch propeller and a float-type carburetor, the first indication of carburetor ice would most likely be

A — a drop in oil temperature and cylinder head temperature.
B — engine roughness.
C — loss of RPM.

2-12. Answer C. GFDPPM 2-21 (PHB)
The restricted airflow through the carburetor causes an enriched mixture and loss of RPM. Answer (A) is wrong because, while a drop in temperatures may result, they will not be the first indications of carburetor ice. Answer (B) is wrong because engine roughness may develop later, but will not be the first indication of carburetor ice.

2-13   H307
Applying carburetor heat will

A — result in more air going through the carburetor.
B — enrich the fuel/air mixture.
C — not affect the fuel/air mixture.

2-13. Answer B. GFDPPM 2-20, 21 (PHB)
When the carburetor heat is turned on, the warmer air entering the carburetor is less dense, and the mixture is enriched. Answer (A) is wrong because there is less air going through the carburetor. Answer (C) is not correct because the fuel/air mixture is enriched.

2-14   H307
What change occurs in the fuel/air mixture when carburetor heat is applied?

A — A decrease in RPM results from the lean mixture.
B — The fuel/air mixture becomes richer.
C — The fuel/air mixture becomes leaner.

2-14. Answer B. GFDPPM 2-20, 21 (PHB)
See explanation for Question 2-13. Answers (A) and (C) are wrong because the fuel/air mixture is not leaned.

2-15   H307
Generally speaking, the use of carburetor heat tends to

A — decrease engine performance.
B — increase engine performance.
C — have no effect on engine performance.

2-15. Answer A. GFDPPM 2-21 (PHB)
Since the warmer air entering the carburetor is less dense, the fuel/air mixture is enriched and power decreases. Answers (B) and (C) are wrong because performance decreases.

2-16   H307

The presence of carburetor ice in an aircraft equipped with a fixed-pitch propeller can be verified by applying carburetor heat and noting

A — an increase in RPM and then a gradual decrease in RPM.
B — a decrease in RPM and then a constant RPM indication.
C — a decrease in RPM and then a gradual increase in RPM.

2-17   H307

With regard to carburetor ice, float-type carburetor systems in comparison to fuel injection systems are generally considered to be

A — more susceptible to icing.
B — equally susceptible to icing.
C — susceptible to icing only when visible moisture is present.

2-18   H307

If the grade of fuel used in an aircraft engine is lower than specified for the engine, it will most likely cause

A — a mixture of fuel and air that is not uniform in all cylinders.
B — lower cylinder head temperatures.
C — detonation.

2-19   H307

Detonation occurs in a reciprocating aircraft engine when

A — the spark plugs are fouled or shorted out or the wiring is defective.
B — hot spots in the combustion chamber ignite the fuel/air mixture in advance of normal ignition.
C — the unburned charge in the cylinders explodes instead of burning normally.

2-20   H307

If a pilot suspects that the engine (with a fixed-pitch propeller) is detonating during climb-out after takeoff, the initial corrective action to take would be to

A — lean the mixture.
B — lower the nose slightly to increase airspeed.
C — apply carburetor heat.

2-16. Answer C. GFDPPM 2-21 (PHB)

When carburetor heat is first applied, the mixture is enriched, and RPM decreases. Then, as the ice melts, airflow into the carburetor increases, leaning the mixture, and RPM increases. Answer (A) is wrong because it is the opposite of what happens. Answer (B) is wrong because if the RPM decreases, then remains constant, it means there was no ice in the carburetor.

2-17. Answer A. GFDPPM 2-21 (PHB)

Because fuel injection systems do not have a venturi throat, they are not as susceptible to icing as float-type carburetors. Answer (B) is wrong because the venturi throat makes float-type carburetors more susceptible to icing. Icing is possible when the humidity is high, regardless of whether visible moisture is present or not (answer C).

2-18. Answer C. GFDPPM 2-26 (PHB)

The higher the grade of fuel, the more pressure it can withstand without detonating. Conversely, lower fuel grades are more prone to detonation. Answer (A) is wrong because the mixture should be the same in all cylinders, regardless of fuel grade. Answer (B) is not correct because when detonation occurs, cylinder head temperatures increase.

2-19. Answer C. GFDPPM 2-25 (PHB)

Detonation occurs when the fuel/air mixture suddenly explodes in the cylinders instead of burning smoothly. Answer (A) describes conditions which would cause an engine to run rough, but not cause detonation. Answer (B) describes pre-ignition.

2-20. Answer B. GFDPPM 2-26 (PHB)

Detonation can occur when the engine overheats. One action to help cool the engine is to increase airspeed, thus increasing the cooling airflow around the engine. Answer (A) is incorrect because detonation can result from a mixture that is too lean. Answer (C) is wrong because carburetor heat tends to increase engine temperature, making the problem worse.

2-21   H307

The uncontrolled firing of the fuel/air charge in advance of normal spark ignition is known as

A — combustion.
B — pre-ignition.
C — detonation.

2-22   H307

Which would most likely cause the cylinder head temperature and engine oil temperature gauges to exceed their normal operating ranges?

A — Using fuel that has a lower-than-specified fuel rating.
B — Using fuel that has a higher-than-specified fuel rating.
C — Operating with higher-than-normal oil pressure.

2-23   H307

What type fuel can be substituted for an aircraft if the recommended octane is not available?

A — The next higher octane aviation gas.
B — The next lower octane aviation gas.
C — Unleaded automotive gas of the same octane rating.

2-24   H307

Filling the fuel tanks after the last flight of the day is considered a good operating procedure because this will

A — force any existing water to the top of the tank away from the fuel lines to the engine.
B — prevent expansion of the fuel by eliminating airspace in the tanks.
C — prevent moisture condensation by eliminating airspace in the tanks.

2-25   H307

For internal cooling, reciprocating aircraft engines are especially dependent on

A — a properly functioning thermostat.
B — air flowing over the exhaust manifold.
C — the circulation of lubricating oil.

2-21. Answer B. GFDPPM 2-26 (PHB)
Pre-ignition occurs when the fuel/air mixture ignites too soon. Answer (A) is wrong because combustion is the normal burning of the mixture. Answer (C) is not right because detonation occurs when fuel explodes instead of burning smoothly.

2-22. Answer A. GFDPPM 2-30 (PHB)
Lower grade fuels will detonate under less pressure. Using a lower fuel rating than specified can cause excessive engine temperatures. Answer (B) is incorrect because using higher grade fuel does not normally cause excessive temperatures. A high oil pressure (answer C) may be an indication of a problem, but is not as likely to cause excessive temperatures as a lower-grade fuel.

2-23. Answer A. GFDPPM 2-30 (PHB)
If the manufacturer's recommendations are followed, the next higher grade of fuel may normally be used. Answer (B) is wrong because a lower grade of fuel can cause excessive engine temperatures. Answer (C) is incorrect because automotive gas is not normally recommended.

2-24. Answer C. GFDPPM 2-29 (PHB)
As the airplane cools overnight, water condenses in the tanks from vapor in the air and enters the fuel. Filling the tanks eliminates the air space and prevents condensation. Answer (A) is wrong because water is heavier than fuel and settles to the bottom of the tank. Answer (B) is wrong because fuel expands with increased temperatures. This is one reason vents are installed in fuel tanks.

2-25. Answer C. GFDPPM 2-32 (PHB)
Engine oil lubricates moving parts, reduces friction, and removes some of the heat from the cylinders. Answer (A) is wrong because reciprocating aircraft engines are not normally equipped with a thermostat. Outside air is important for engine cooling (answer B), but the air is primarily directed to the hottest parts of the engine, especially the cylinders.

2-26   H307

An abnormally high engine oil temperature indication may be caused by

A — the oil level being too low.
B — operating with a too high viscosity oil.
C — operating with an excessively rich mixture.

2-27   H307

What action can a pilot take to aid in cooling an engine that is overheating during a climb?

A — Reduce rate of climb and increase airspeed.
B — Reduce climb speed and increase RPM.
C — Increase climb speed and increase RPM.

2-28   H307

What is one procedure to aid in cooling an engine that is overheating?

A — Enrichen the fuel mixture.
B — Increase the RPM.
C — Reduce the airspeed.

2-29   H308

How is engine operation controlled on an engine equipped with a constant-speed propeller?

A — The throttle controls power output as registered on the manifold pressure gauge and the propeller control regulates engine RPM.
B — The throttle controls power output as registered on the manifold pressure gauge and the propeller control regulates a constant blade angle.
C — The throttle controls engine RPM as registered on the tachometer and the mixture control regulates the power output.

2-30   H308

What is an advantage of a constant-speed propeller?

A — Permits the pilot to select and maintain a desired cruising speed.
B — Permits the pilot to select the blade angle for the most efficient performance.
C — Provides a smoother operation with stable RPM and eliminates vibrations.

2-26. Answer A. GFDPPM 2-33 (PHB)

If the oil level is too low, it can cause high engine oil temperatures. Answer (B) is incorrect because, while it is important to use the proper oil type and weight, it is not as likely to cause abnormally high temperatures as a low oil level would. Answer (C) is not correct because a rich mixture tends to cool the engine slightly instead of causing high temperatures.

2-27. Answer A. GFDPPM 2-35 (PHB)

Reducing the rate of climb and increasing airspeed will increase the cooling airflow around the engine. Answers (B) and (C) are incorrect because increasing RPM increases temperature. Answer (B) is also incorrect because reducing the climb speed reduces the cooling airflow.

2-28. Answer A. GFDPPM 2-35 (PHB)

A richer fuel mixture burns at a slightly lower temperature and helps cool the engine. Answer (B) is not right because a higher RPM causes higher engine temperatures. Answer (C) is wrong because a lower airspeed reduces the cooling airflow around the engine.

2-29. Answer A. GFDPPM 2-38 (PHB)

The throttle controls the power output of the engine, which is indicated on the manifold pressure gauge. The propeller control changes the pitch of the propeller blades, thus controlling engine RPM, which is indicated on the tachometer. Answer (B) is wrong because the propeller control does not maintain a constant blade angle. Rather, it varies pitch to maintain a constant speed. Answer (C) is wrong because the throttle does not directly control engine RPM, and the mixture control is not used to regulate power.

2-30. Answer B. GFDPPM 2-38 (PHB)

By selecting the proper blade angle, the pilot can convert a high percentage of engine power into thrust over a wide range of RPM and airspeed combinations. This allows the most efficient performance to be gained from the engine. Answer (A) is not correct because a constant-speed propeller is not necessary for maintaining a desired airspeed. Answer (C) is wrong because a constant-speed propeller is not necessarily smoother than a fixed-pitch propeller, nor does it operate with less vibration.

2-31   H308

A precaution for the operation of an engine equipped with a constant-speed propeller is to

A — avoid high RPM settings with high manifold pressure.

B — avoid high manifold pressure settings with low RPM.

C — always use a rich mixture with high RPM settings.

2-31. Answer B. GFDPPM 2-39 (PHB)

For a given RPM setting, there is a maximum allowable manifold pressure. Generally, high manifold pressures with low RPM should be avoided to prevent internal stress within the engine. Answer (A) is incorrect because higher manifold pressures are allowable with higher RPM settings, within limits. Answer (C) is incorrect because the mixture should be leaned for optimum performance.

2-32   H308

What should be the first action after starting an aircraft engine?

A — Adjust for proper RPM and check for desired indications on the engine gauges.

B — Place the magneto or ignition switch momentarily in the OFF position to check for proper grounding.

C — Test each brake and the parking brake.

2-32. Answer A. GFDPPM 2-33 (PHB)

Immediately after starting an engine, set the proper RPM and check engine gauges for proper indications. Answers (B) and (C) are wrong because these items are not the first actions to be taken. Also, answer (B) may not be included in the airplane's checklist.

2-33   H308

Should it become necessary to handprop an airplane engine, it is extremely important that a competent pilot

A — call "contact" before touching the propeller.

B — be at the controls in the cockpit.

C — be in the cockpit and call out all commands.

2-33. Answer B. GFDPPM 2-39 (PHB)

When hand-propping an airplane, a competent pilot must be at the controls to prevent the airplane from moving and to set the engine controls properly. Answer (A) is not right because the person propping the engine does not have to be a pilot, nor do they have to call "contact." Answer (C) is wrong, since the pilot must be at the controls, not just in the cockpit, and the person hand-propping the engine is in charge of the starting procedure.

SECTION C
FLIGHT INSTRUMENTS

Of the instruments located in the airplane cockpit, the indicators which provide information regarding the airplane's attitude, direction, altitude, and speed are collectively referred to as the flight instruments. Traditionally, the flight instruments are sub-divided into categories according to their method of operation.

PITOT-STATIC INSTRUMENTS

The pitot-static system supplies ambient air pressure to operate the altimeter and vertical speed indicator (VSI), and both ambient and ram air to the airspeed indicator.

STANDARD TEMPERATURE AND PRESSURE

1. The standard temperature and pressure values for sea level are 15 degrees C and 29.92″ Hg.

PITOT SYSTEM

2. The pitot system provides impact pressure for the airspeed indicator.

V-SPEEDS

3. The red line on an airspeed indicator represents never-exceed speed, which is the maximum speed at which the airplane can be operated in smooth air.
4. The yellow arc indicates the caution range.
5. The green arc denotes the normal operating range, with the bottom of the arc representing the power-off stalling speed in a specified configuration, and the upper limit representing the maximum structural cruising speed.
6. The white arc identifies the normal flap operating range. The bottom of the white arc indicates the power-off stall speed in the landing configuration.
7. Maneuvering speed is an important airspeed limitation that is not marked on the airspeed indicator.
8. The indicated airspeed at which a given airplane stalls in a particular configuration will remain the same, regardless of altitude.

TYPES OF ALTITUDE

9. Altimeter setting is the value to which the barometric pressure scale of the altimeter is set so that the altimeter indicates true altitude at field elevation.
10. Variations in temperature affect the altimeter, as pressure levels are raised on warm days and the indicated altitude is lower than the true altitude.
11. True altitude is the vertical distance of the aircraft above sea level.
12. Absolute altitude is the vertical distance of the aircraft above the surface.
13. Pressure altitude is the altitude indicated when the barometric pressure scale is set to 29.92.
14. Density altitude is the pressure altitude corrected for nonstandard temperature.
15. Indicated altitude is the same as true altitude when at sea level under standard conditions.
16. Pressure altitude equals true altitude under standard conditions.
17. One inch of change of Hg in the altimeter causes 1000 feet of altitude change in the same direction.
18. The aircraft will be lower than indicated when flown into areas of colder than standard air temperature, or lower pressure.
19. An increase in ambient temperature will increase the density altitude at a given airport.
20. If the pitot tube becomes clogged, the airspeed indicator is affected; if the static vents are clogged, the altimeter, airspeed indicator, and vertical speed indicator are affected.

GYROSCOPIC INSTRUMENTS

Gyroscopic instruments include the turn coordinator, attitude indicator and heading indicator. They operate off of a gyro's tendency to remain rigid in space.

TURN COORDINATOR

21. A turn coordinator provides an indication of the aircraft's rate of movement about the yaw and roll axes.

ATTITUDE INDICATOR
22. To properly adjust the attitude indicator during level flight. align the miniature airplane to the horizon bar.
23. A pilot determines the direction of bank from the attitude indicator by the relationship of the miniature airplane to the deflected horizon bar.

HEADING INDICATOR
24. The heading indicator must be periodically realigned with the magnetic compass as the gyro precesses.

MAGNETIC COMPASS
The magnetic compass contains a bar magnet, which swings freely to align with the Earth's magnetic field.

DEVIATION
25. Deviation in a magnetic compass is caused by the magnetic fields in the aircraft distorting the lines of magnetic force.

TURNING AND ACCELERATION ERRORS
26. In the Northern Hemisphere, a magnetic compass will show a turn toward the west if a right turn is entered from a north heading, and a turn toward the east if a left turn is entered from a north heading. A turn toward the north is indicated if an aircraft is accelerated while on an east or west heading, a turn toward the south if an aircraft is decelerated while on a west heading, and correctly, if the aircraft is on a north or south heading.
27. The indications of a magnetic compass in flight are correct only when the aircraft is in straight and level, unaccelerated flight.

2-34   A02
Which V-speed represents maneuvering speed?

A — V_A.
B — V_{LO}.
C — V_{NE}.

2-34. Answer A. GFDPPM 2-53 (FAR 1.2)
V_A is defined as the design maneuvering speed. Answer (B) represents maximum landing gear operating speed. Answer (C) is the never exceed speed.

2-35   B08
If an altimeter setting is not available before flight, to which altitude should the pilot adjust the altimeter?

A — The elevation of the nearest airport corrected to mean sea level.
B — The elevation of the departure area.
C — Pressure altitude corrected for nonstandard temperature.

2-35. Answer B. GFDPPM 2-57 (FAR 91.121)
If unable to obtain a local altimeter setting, you should set the altimeter to the field elevation prior to departure.

2-36   B08
Prior to takeoff, the altimeter should be set to which altitude or altimeter setting?

A — The current local altimeter setting, if available, or the departure airport elevation.
B — The corrected density altitude of the departure airport.
C — The corrected pressure altitude for the departure airport.

2-36. Answer A. GFDPPM 2-57 (FAR 91.121)
See explanation for Question 2-35.

2-37   **H312**

If the pitot tube and outside static vents become clogged, which instruments would be affected?

A — The altimeter, airspeed indicator, and turn-and-slip indicator.

B — The altimeter, airspeed indicator, and vertical speed indicator.

C — The altimeter, attitude indicator, and turn-and-slip indicator.

2-38   **H312**

Which instrument will become inoperative if the pitot tube becomes clogged?

A — Altimeter.

B — Vertical speed.

C — Airspeed.

2-39   **H312**

Which instrument(s) will become inoperative if the static vents become clogged?

A — Airspeed only.

B — Altimeter only.

C — Airspeed, altimeter, and vertical speed.

2-40   **H312**

(Refer to figure 3.) Altimeter 1 indicates

A — 500 feet.

B — 1,500 feet.

C — 10,500 feet.

2-41   **H312**

(Refer to figure 3.) Altimeter 2 indicates

A — 1,500 feet.

B — 4,500 feet.

C — 14,500 feet.

2-42   **H312**

(Refer to figure 3.) Altimeter 3 indicates

A — 9,500 feet.

B — 10,950 feet.

C — 15,940 feet.

2-43   **H312**

(Refer to figure 3.) Which altimeter(s) indicate(s) more than 10,000 feet?

A — 1, 2, and 3.

B — 1 and 2 only.

C — 1 only.

2-37. Answer B. GFDPPM 2-61 (PHB)

The altimeter, the airspeed indicator, and the vertical speed indicator all use static air and would therefore be affected. Answers (A) and (C) are wrong because the turn-and-slip indicator and attitude indicator do not rely on static air.

2-38. Answer C. GFDPPM 2-61 (PHB)

The airspeed indicator operates by sensing ram air (impact pressure) in the pitot tube. Answers (A) and (B) are wrong because the altimeter and VSI use pressure readings from the static air ports.

2-39. Answer C. GFDPPM 2-61 (PHB)

See explanation for Question 2-37.

2-40. Answer C. GFDPPM 2-55 (PHB)

The small 10,000' pointer is just beyond the 1, indicating that the altitude is above 10,000 feet. The wide 1,000' pointer is between 0 and 1, which indicates less than 1,000 feet. Finally, the 100' pointer is on 5. The altimeter reading is 10,500 feet.

2-41. Answer C. GFDPPM 2-55 (PHB)

The 10,000' pointer is above 1, the 1,000' pointer is above 4, and the 100' pointer is on 5. This indicates an altitude of 14,500 feet.

2-42. Answer A. GFDPPM 2-55 (PHB)

The 10,000' pointer is near 1, the 1,000' pointer is above 9, and the 100' pointer is on 5. This indicates the altitude is 9,500 feet.

2-43. Answer B. GFDPPM 2-55 (PHB)

See explanations for Questions 2-40, 2-41, and 2-42. Altimeter 1 indicates 10,500 feet, altimeter 2 indicates 14,500 feet, and the indication on altimeter 3 is 9,500 feet.

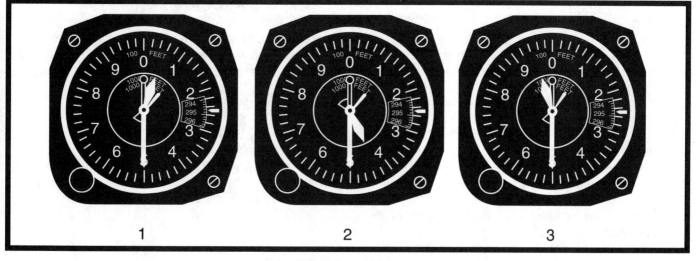

FIGURE 3.—Altimeter.

2-44   H312

Altimeter setting is the value to which the barometric pressure scale of the altimeter is set so the altimeter indicates

A — calibrated altitude at field elevation.
B — absolute altitude at field elevation.
C — true altitude at field elevation.

2-45   H312

How do variations in temperature affect the altimeter?

A — Pressure levels are raised on warm days and the indicated altitude is lower than true altitude.
B — Higher temperatures expand the pressure levels and the indicated altitude is higher than true altitude.
C — Lower temperatures lower the pressure levels and the indicated altitude is lower than true altitude.

2-46   H312

What is true altitude?

A — The vertical distance of the aircraft above sea level.
B — The vertical distance of the aircraft above the surface.
C — The height above the standard datum plane.

2-47   H312

What is absolute altitude?

A — The altitude read directly from the altimeter.
B — The vertical distance of the aircraft above the surface.
C — The height above the standard datum plane.

2-44. Answer C. GFDPPM 2-57 (AW)

When the current altimeter setting is set on the ground, the altimeter reads true altitude of the field, which is the actual height above mean sea level. Answer (A) is wrong because calibrated altitude is indicated altitude corrected for instrument error. Answer (B) is incorrect because absolute altitude is the actual height above the earth's surface, which would be zero at field elevation.

2-45. Answer A. GFDPPM 2-60 (PHB)

Because atmospheric pressure levels are raised on warm days, the aircraft will be at a higher altitude than indicated. In other words, the indicated altitude is lower than true altitude.

2-46. Answer A. GFDPPM 2-57 (PHB)

True altitude is the actual height (vertical distance) above mean sea level. Answer (B) describes absolute altitude. Answer (C) describes pressure altitude.

2-47. Answer B. GFDPPM 2-58 (PHB)

Absolute altitude is the height (vertical distance) above the surface. Answer (A) describes indicated altitude. Answer (C) describes pressure altitude.

2-48   H312

What is density altitude?

A — The height above the standard datum plane.
B — The pressure altitude corrected for nonstandard temperature.
C — The altitude read directly from the altimeter.

2-49   H312

What is pressure altitude?

A — The indicated altitude corrected for position and installation error.
B — The altitude indicated when the barometric pressure scale is set to 29.92.
C — The indicated altitude corrected for nonstandard temperature and pressure.

2-50   H312

Under what condition is indicted altitude the same as true altitude?

A — If the altimeter has no mechanical error.
B — When at sea level under standard conditions.
C — When at 18,000 feet MSL with the altimeter set at 29.92.

2-51   H312

If it is necessary to set the altimeter from 29.15 to 29.85, what change occurs?

A — 70-foot increase in indicated altitude.
B — 70-foot increase in density altitude.
C — 700-foot increase in indicated altitude.

2-52   H312

The pitot system provides impact pressure for which instrument?

A — Altimeter.
B — Vertical-speed indicator.
C — Airspeed indicator.

2-53   H312

As altitude increases, the indicated airspeed at which a given airplane stalls in a particular configuration will

A — decrease as the true airspeed decreases.
B — decrease as the true airspeed increases.
C — remain the same regardless of altitude.

2-48. Answer B. GFDPPM 2-56 (PHB)
Density altitude is found by applying a correction for nonstandard temperature to the pressure altitude. Answer (A) is pressure altitude and (C) is indicated altitude.

2-49. Answer B. GFDPPM 2-56 (PHB)
Pressure altitude is the height above the standard datum plane when 29.92 is set in the scale. Answer (A) does not describe any type of altitude. Answer (C) describes density altitude.

2-50. Answer B. GFDPPM 2-57 (AW)
In this situation, both indicated and true altitude would be zero. Answers (A) and (C) are wrong because indicated altitude must be corrected for nonstandard temperature and pressure.

2-51. Answer C. GFDPPM 2-59 (PHB)
A one inch change of Hg in the altimeter equals 1,000 feet of altitude change in the same direction. In this case, you increased the altimeter .7 of an inch (29.85 - 29.15 = .7), therefore, the indicated altitude increased 700 feet.

2-52. Answer C. GFDPPM 2-61 (PHB)
The airspeed indicator senses impact pressure to provide an airspeed reading. Answers (A) and (B) are wrong because these instruments utilize only static air.

2-53. Answer C. GFDPPM 2-55 (PHB)
Since airspeed indicators are calibrated to read true airspeed only under standard sea level conditions, the indicated airspeed does not reflect lower air density at higher altitudes. As a result, the indicated airspeed of a stall remains the same. Answers (A) and (B) are not correct because indicated airspeed does not change with an increase in altitude. Answer (A) is also incorrect because true airspeed increases with altitude.

2-54   H312
What does the red line on an airspeed indicator represent?

A — Maneuvering speed.
B — Turbulence or rough-air speed.
C — Never-exceed speed.

2-55   H312
(Refer to figure 4 on page 2-16.) What is the full flap operating range for the airplane?

A — 60 to 100 MPH.
B — 60 to 208 MPH.
C — 65 to 165 MPH.

2-56   H312
(Refer to figure 4 on page 2-16.) What is the caution range of the airplane?

A — 0 to 60 MPH.
B — 100 to 165 MPH.
C — 165 to 208 MPH.

2-57   H312
(Refer to figure 4 on page 2-16.) The maximum speed at which the airplane can be operated in smooth air is

A — 100 MPH.
B — 165 MPH.
C — 208 MPH.

2-58   H312
(Refer to figure 4 on page 2-16.) Which color identifies the never-exceed speed?

A — Lower limit of the yellow arc.
B — Upper limit of the white arc.
C — The red radial line.

2-59   H312
(Refer to figure 4 on page 2-16.) Which color identifies the power-off stalling speed in a specified configuration?

A — Upper limit of the green arc.
B — Upper limit of the white arc.
C — Lower limit of the green arc.

2-60   H312
(Refer to figure 4 on page 2-16.) What is the maximum flaps-extended speed?

A — 65 MPH.
B — 100 MPH.
C — 165 MPH.

2-54. Answer C. GFDPPM 2-53 (PHB)
The red line is the never-exceed speed. Answers (A) and (B) are incorrect because maneuvering, turbulent, or rough air speeds are not displayed on an airspeed indicator.

2-55. Answer A. GFDPPM 2-52 (PHB)
The white arc indicates the flap operating range, which, in this case, is 60 to 100. (MPH is implied from the answers.)

2-56. Answer C. GFDPPM 2-52 (PHB)
The yellow arc indicates the caution range. For this aircraft, the caution range is 165 to 208. (MPH is implied from the answers.)

2-57. Answer C. GFDPPM 2-52 (PHB)
In smooth air, an airplane can be operated in the yellow arc up to the red line, in this case, 208 MPH.

2-58. Answer C. GFDPPM 2-52 (PHB)
The red line is the never-exceed speed, the yellow arc is the caution range and the white arc is the flap operating range.

2-59. Answer C. GFDPPM 2-52 (PHB)
The lower limit of the green arc represents the power-off stall speed in a specified configuration (usually flaps up, gear retracted). Answer (A) is the maximum structural cruising speed. Answer (B) is the maximum speed with flaps extended.

2-60. Answer B. GFDPPM 2-52 (PHB)
This is represented by the upper limit of the white arc, which in this case is 100 MPH.

2-61   H312
(Refer to figure 4.) Which color identifies the normal flap operating range?

A — The lower limit of the white arc to the upper limit of the green arc.
B — The green arc.
C — The white arc.

2-61. Answer C. GFDPPM 2-52 (PHB)
The white arc indicates the normal flap operating range.

2-62   H312
(Refer to figure 4.) Which color identifies the power-off stalling speed with wing flaps and landing gear in the landing configuration?

A — Upper limit of the green arc.
B — Upper limit of the white arc.
C — Lower limit of the white arc.

2-62. Answer C. GFDPPM 2-52 (PHB)
Stall speed with flaps and gear down is represented by the lower limit of the white arc. The upper limit of the green arc (answer A) is the maximum structural cruising speed, while the upper limit of the white arc (answer B) is the maximum flaps-extended speed.

2-63   H312
(Refer to figure 4.) What is the maximum structural cruising speed?

A — 100 MPH.
B — 165 MPH.
C — 208 MPH.

2-63. Answer B. GFDPPM 2-52 (PHB)
This speed is indicated by the upper limit of the green arc, which in this case is 165 MPH.

2-64   H312
What is an important airspeed limitation that is not color coded on airspeed indicators?

A — Never-exceed speed.
B — Maximum structural cruising speed.
C — Maneuvering speed.

2-64. Answer C. GFDPPM 2-53 (PHB)
The maneuvering speed of an airplane is not shown on the airspeed indicator. It can be found in the airplane manual or on placards. Answer (A) is not correct because this is indicated by the red radial line. Answer (B) is incorrect because this is indicated by the upper limit of the green arc.

FIGURE 4.—Airspeed Indicator.

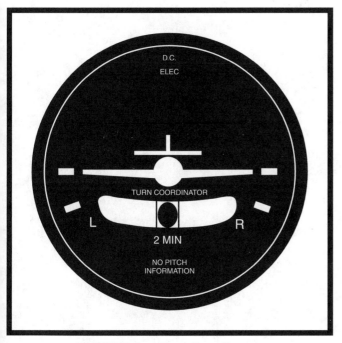

FIGURE 5.—Turn Coordinator.

2-65   H313
(Refer to figure 5.) A turn coordinator provides an indication of the

A — movement of the aircraft about the yaw and roll axes.
B — angle of bank up to but not exceeding 30°.
C — attitude of the aircraft with reference to the longitudinal axis.

2-65. Answer A. GFDPPM 2-66 (PHB)
The turn coordinator senses movement about the vertical axis (yaw) and the longitudinal axis (roll). Answers (B) and (C) are wrong because the miniature airplane indicates rate of turn, not angle of bank, which is the attitude of the aircraft in relation to the longitudinal axis.

2-66   H313
(Refer to figure 6 on page 2-18.) To receive accurate indications during flight from a heading indicator, the instrument must be

A — set prior to flight on a known heading.
B — calibrated on a compass rose at regular intervals.
C — periodically realigned with the magnetic compass as the gyro precesses.

2-66. Answer C. GFDPPM 2-70 (PHB)
To correct for precession, the pilot must realign the heading indicator with the magnetic compass at regular intervals. Answers (A) and (B) are wrong because they do not correct for precession in flight.

2-67   H313
(Refer to figure 7 on page 2-19.) The proper adjustment to make on the attitude indicator during level flight is to align the

A — horizon bar to the level-flight indication.
B — horizon bar to the miniature airplane.
C — miniature airplane to the horizon bar.

2-67. Answer C. GFDPPM 2-68 (PHB)
The miniature airplane is adjustable and should be set to match the level flight indication of the horizon bar. Answers (A) and (B) are incorrect because the horizon bar is not adjustable, it moves only when the aircraft changes pitch.

FIGURE 6.—Heading Indicator.

2-68   H313
(Refer to figure 7.) How should a pilot determine the direction of bank from an attitude indicator such as the one illustrated?

A — By the direction of deflection of the banking scale (A).
B — By the direction of deflection of the horizon bar (B).
C — By the relationship of the miniature airplane (C) to the deflected horizon bar (B).

2-69   H314
Deviation in a magnetic compass is caused by the

A — presence of flaws in the permanent magnets of the compass.
B — difference in the location between true north and magnetic north.
C — magnetic fields within the aircraft distorting the lines of magnetic force.

2-70   H314
In the Northern Hemisphere, a magnetic compass will normally indicate initially a turn toward the west if

A — a left turn is entered from a north heading.
B — a right turn is entered from a north heading.
C — an aircraft is accelerated while on a north heading.

2-68. Answer C. GFDPPM 2-66 (PHB)
As the airplane banks, the relationship between the miniature airplane and the horizon bar depict the direction of turn. Answer (A) is wrong because the bank scale does not deflect in the direction of bank. The combination of bank scale and pointer is used to determine bank angle only. Answer (B) is wrong because the horizon bar deflects opposite the miniature airplane; i.e., for a right turn, the horizon bar deflects to the left. (Note: Figure 7 is an example of an older style attitude indicator, not normally found in modern training airplanes.)

2-69. Answer C. GFDPPM 2-71 (PHB)
Metal and electronic components in the aircraft create magnetic fields which distort the lines of magnetic force. This causes deviation errors in the compass readings. Answer (A) is wrong because deviation is not caused by flaws in the magnets. Answer (B) is incorrect because the difference between true and magnetic north is called variation, not deviation.

2-70. Answer B. GFDPPM 2-74 (PHB)
When turning from a northerly heading, the compass initially indicates a turn in the opposite direction. When starting a right turn, toward the east, the compass begins to show a turn to the west. Answer (A) is wrong because a left turn, toward the west, would show an initial turn toward the east on the compass. Answer (C) is wrong because acceleration error does not occur when on a heading of north or south.

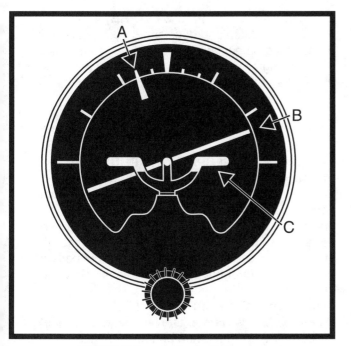

FIGURE 7.—Attitude Indicator.

2-71   H314
In the Northern Hemisphere, a magnetic compass will normally indicate initially a turn toward the east if

A — an aircraft is decelerated while on a south heading.
B — an aircraft is accelerated while on a north heading.
C — a left turn is entered from a north heading.

2-72   H314
In the Northern Hemisphere, a magnetic compass will normally indicate a turn toward the north if

A — a right turn is entered from an east heading.
B — a left turn is entered from a west heading.
C — an aircraft is accelerated while on an east or west heading.

2-73   H314
In the Northern Hemisphere, the magnetic compass will normally indicate a turn toward the south when

A — a left turn is entered from an east heading.
B — a right turn is entered from a west heading.
C — the aircraft is decelerated while on a west heading.

2-71. Answer C. GFDPPM 2-74 (PHB)
See explanation for Question 2-70. In this question, during a left turn toward the west, the magnetic compass would initially indicate a turn to the east.

2-72. Answer C. GFDPPM 2-73 (PHB)
Acceleration error is most pronounced on east/west headings. Using the acronym ANDS (Accelerate — North, Decelerate — South), acceleration will show a turn to the north, and deceleration will show a turn to the south. Answers (A) and (B) are wrong because turning errors are not evident when beginning turns from an east or west heading.

2-73. Answer C. GFDPPM 2-73 (PHB)
See explanation for Question 2-72.

2-74   H314
In the Northern Hemisphere, if an aircraft is accelerated or decelerated, the magnetic compass will normally indicate

A — a turn momentarily.
B — correctly when on a north or south heading.
C — a turn toward the south.

2-75   H314
During flight, when are the indications of a magnetic compass accurate?

A — Only in straight-and-level unaccelerated flight.
B — As long as the airspeed is constant.
C — During turns if the bank does not exceed 18°.

2-76   H312
If the outside air temperature (OAT) at a given altitude is warmer than standard, the density altitude is

A — equal to pressure altitude.
B — lower than pressure altitude.
C — higher than pressure altitude.

2-77   I21
What are the standard temperature and pressure values for sea level?

A — 15°C and 29.92″ Hg.
B — 59°C and 1013.2 millibars.
C — 59°F and 29.92 millibars.

2-78   I22
If a pilot changes the altimeter setting from 30.11 to 29.96, what is the approximate change in indication?

A — Altimeter will indicate .15″ Hg higher.
B — Altimeter will indicate 150 feet higher.
C — Altimeter will indicate 150 feet lower.

2-79   I22
Under which condition will pressure altitude be equal to true altitude?

A — When the atmospheric pressure is 29.92″ Hg.
B — When standard atmospheric conditions exist.
C — When indicated altitude is equal to the pressure altitude.

2-74. Answer B. GFDPPM 2-73 (PHB)
Since acceleration and deceleration errors are most pronounced on east/west headings, accelerating or decelerating on a north or south heading will not show much of an error on the magnetic compass.

2-75. Answer A. GFDPPM 2-74 (PHB)
Magnetic dip causes turning and acceleration/deceleration errors. For this reason, magnetic compass indications are accurate only in straight-and-level unaccelerated flight. Answer (B) is wrong because if the airspeed is constant in a turn, the compass will still show turning errors. Answer (C) is not right because errors will occur during turns regardless of bank angle.

2-76. Answer C. GFDPPM 2-56, 57 (PHB)
When the OAT is warmer than standard, the density altitude (DA) is higher than pressure altitude. Answer (A) would be correct only when the OAT is equal to standard. Answer (B) would be correct when the OAT is lower than standard.

2-77. Answer A. GFDPPM 2-51 (PHB)
The standard atmosphere is a temperature of 15°C (59°F) and 29.92″ Hg (1013.2 millibars).

2-78. Answer C. GFDPPM 2-59 (PHB)
Each .1″ change on the altimeter setting equates to about 100 feet. In this case, the change is .15 lower, or 150 feet.

2-79. Answer B. GFDPPM 2-57 (AW)
Pressure altitude equals true altitude when standard atmospheric conditions exist. When nonstandard conditions exist, true altitude will not equal pressure altitude. Answers (A) and (C) are wrong because they do not take into account temperatures that deviate from standard values.

2-80   I22

Under what condition is pressure altitude and density altitude the same value?

A — At sea level, when the temperature is 0°F.
B — When the altimeter has no installation error.
C — At standard temperature.

2-81   I22

If a flight is made from an area of low pressure into an area of high pressure without the altimeter setting being adjusted, the altimeter will indicate

A — the actual altitude above sea level.
B — higher than the actual altitude above sea level.
C — lower than the actual altitude above sea level.

2-82   I22

If a flight is made from an area of high pressure into an area of lower pressure without the altimeter setting being adjusted, the altimeter will indicate

A — lower than the actual altitude above sea level.
B — higher than the actual altitude above sea level.
C — the actual altitude above sea level.

2-83   I22

Under what condition will true altitude be lower than indicated altitude?

A — In colder than standard air temperature.
B — In warmer than standard air temperature.
C — When density altitude is higher than indicated altitude.

2-84   I22

Which condition would cause the altimeter to indicate a lower altitude than true altitude?

A — Air temperature lower than standard.
B — Atmospheric pressure lower than standard.
C — Air temperature warmer than standard.

2-85   I22

Which factor would tend to increase the density altitude at a given airport?

A — An increase in barometric pressure.
B — An increase in ambient temperature.
C — A decrease in relative humidity.

2-80. Answer C. GFDPPM 2-56 (PHB)
Since density altitude is pressure altitude corrected for nonstandard temperature, DA and PA are equal only at standard temperature. Answer (A) is wrong because at sea level, standard temperature is 59°F. Answer (B) is incorrect because pressure altitude and density altitude are not dependent on an altimeter which provides indicated altitude.

2-81. Answer C. GFDPPM 2-59 (AW)
The aircraft will be at a higher true (actual) altitude above sea level than is indicated. In other words, the altimeter will indicate lower than the actual altitude. Answer (A) is wrong because the only time the altimeter indicates actual (true) altitude is when standard atmospheric conditions exist, and the correct altimeter setting is used. Answer (B) is not correct because the altimeter will indicate a lower, not higher, altitude than actual.

2-82. Answer B. GFDPPM 2-59 (AW)
Remember, "from high to low, look out below." In other words, the aircraft will be at a lower true (actual) altitude than indicated, so the altimeter indicates higher than actual.

2-83. Answer A. GFDPPM 2-60 (AW)
When the air is colder than standard, the aircraft's actual (true) altitude will be lower than indicated. Answer (B) is wrong because in warmer than standard conditions, true altitude will be higher than indicated. Answer (C) is wrong because there is not a direct correlation between density altitude and indicated altitude.

2-84. Answer C. GFDPPM 2-60 (AW)
See explanation for Question 2-83. In this question, the air temperature is warmer than standard, so indicated altitude will be lower than actual (true) altitude.

2-85. Answer B. GFDPPM 2-56 (AW)
Since density altitude is pressure altitude corrected for temperature, it increases with increased temperature. Answer (A) is wrong because an increase in barometric pressure lowers the pressure altitude. Thus, density altitude would also decrease. Answer (C) is wrong because density altitude would increase with an increase in relative humidity.

AERODYNAMIC PRINCIPLES

SECTION A
FOUR FORCES OF FLIGHT

Understanding what makes an airplane fly begins with learning the four forces of flight.
1. The four forces that act on an aircraft in flight are lift, weight, thrust and drag.
2. The forces acting on an airplane are in equilibrium when the aircraft is in unaccelerated flight.
3. During straight-and-level flight, lift equals weight, and thrust equals drag.

CRITICAL ANGLE OF ATTACK
4. The angle between the chord line and the relative wind is the angle of attack.

FLAPS
5. One of the main functions of flaps during an approach is to increase the angle of descent without increasing the airspeed.
6. Flaps enable the pilot to make steeper approaches to a landing without increasing airspeed.

WEIGHT
7. The angle of attack at which an airplane wing stalls will remain the same regardless of gross weight.

GROUND EFFECT
8. Ground effect is the result of the interference of the surface of the Earth with the airflow patterns about an airplane.
9. As a result of ground effect, induced drag decreases, and any excess speed at the point of flare may cause considerable floating.
10. Ground effect may result in becoming airborne before reaching recommended takeoff speed.

3-1   **H300**
The four forces acting on an airplane in flight are

A — lift, weight, thrust, and drag.
B — lift, weight, gravity, and thrust.
C — lift, gravity, power, and friction.

3-1. Answer A. GFDPPM 3-2 (AFH)
In normal (nonacrobatic) flight conditions, lift is the upward force created by airflow over and under the wings. Weight, caused by the downward pull of gravity, opposes lift. Thrust is the forward force which propels the airplane, and drag is the retarding force opposing thrust. Answer (B) does not include drag, and, while gravity causes weight, it usually is not considered one of the four forces. Answer (C) is also wrong because, while power and friction affect thrust and drag, they are not aerodynamic forces.

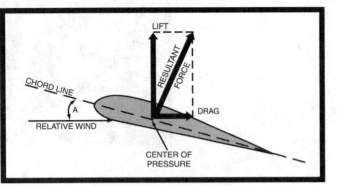

FIGURE 1.—Lift Vector.

3-2   H300
When are the four forces that act on an airplane in equilibrium?

A — During unaccelerated flight.
B — When the aircraft is accelerating.
C — When the aircraft is at rest on the ground.

3-3   H300
(Refer to figure 1.) The acute angle A is the angle of

A — incidence.
B — attack.
C — dihedral.

3-4   H300
The term "angle of attack" is defined as the angle

A — between the wing chord line and the relative wind.
B — between the airplane's climb angle and the horizon.
C — formed by the longitudinal axis of the airplane and the chord line of the wing.

3-5   H300
What is the relationship of lift, drag, thrust, and weight when the airplane is in straight-and-level flight?

A — Lift equals weight and thrust equals drag.
B — Lift, drag, and weight equal thrust.
C — Lift and weight equal thrust and drag.

3-2. Answer A. GFDPPM 3-3 (AFH)
In straight-and-level, unaccelerated flight, the four forces are in equilibrium. Lift equals weight, and thrust equals drag. Answer (B) would require thrust to be greater than drag in order for the aircraft to accelerate. Answer (C) is wrong because only weight is acting on the airplane. Lift, drag, and thrust are zero (assuming no wind).

3-3. Answer B. GFDPPM 3-5 (PHB)
The angle between the chord line and the relative wind is the angle of attack. Answer (A) cannot be correct because the angle of incidence is the angle between the wing chord line and the longitudinal axis of the airplane. Answer (C) is wrong because dihedral is the upward angle of the wings in relation to the lateral axis of the airplane.

3-4. Answer A. GFDPPM 3-4 (PHB)
The angle of attack is the angle between the chord line and the relative wind. Answer (B) does not describe any aerodynamic term. Answer (C) describes the angle of incidence.

3-5. Answer A. GFDPPM 3-3 (AFH)
Assuming the airplane is not accelerating, thrust equals drag, and lift equals weight. Answers (B) and (C) are wrong because all four forces do not have to be equal. Thrust must be equal to drag, and lift equal to weight.

3-6   H305

One of the main functions of flaps during approach and landing is to

A — decrease the angle of descent without increasing the airspeed.

B — permit a touchdown at a higher indicated airspeed.

C — increase the angle of descent without increasing the airspeed.

3-7   H305

What is one purpose of wing flaps?

A — To enable the pilot to make steeper approaches to a landing without increasing the airspeed.

B — To relieve the pilot of maintaining continuous pressure on the controls.

C — To decrease wing area to vary the lift.

3-8   H303

The angle of attack at which an airplane wing stalls will

A — increase if the CG is moved forward.

B — change with an increase in gross weight.

C — remain the same regardless of gross weight.

3-9   H317

What is ground effect?

A — The result of the interference of the surface of the Earth with the airflow patterns about an airplane.

B — The result of an alteration in airflow patterns increasing induced drag about the wings of an airplane.

C — The result of the disruption of the airflow patterns about the wings of an airplane to the point where the wings will no longer support the airplane in flight.

3-10   H317

Floating caused by the phenomenon of ground effect will be most realized during an approach to land when at

A — less than the length of the wingspan above the surface.

B — twice the length of the wingspan above the surface.

C — a higher-than-normal angle of attack.

3-6. Answer C. GFDPPM 3-12 (AFH)

Because flaps increase lift, induced drag is also increased, thus allowing a steeper angle of descent without increasing airspeed. Answer (A) is wrong because the angle of descent can be increased. Answer (B) is wrong since flaps increase lift, thereby allowing touchdown at a lower airspeed.

3-7. Answer A. GFDPPM 3-12 (AFH)

Flaps increase both lift and induced drag, allowing a steeper descent without increasing airspeed. Answer (B) is wrong because flaps simply increase the camber of the wing. Trim must still be applied to relieve control pressure. Answer (C) is not correct because most flaps change the wing area very little. Some flaps will increase wing area, but none will decrease it.

3-8. Answer C. GFDPPM 3-6 (FTP)

The critical angle of attack (angle of attack at which an airplane stalls) is determined by the lift coefficient of a particular wing configuration. An airplane will stall when the critical angle of attack is exceeded, regardless of weight or airspeed. Answers (A) and (B) are wrong because the center of gravity (CG) and weight do not affect the critical angle of attack.

3-9. Answer A. GFDPPM 3-18 (AFH)

When flying close to the ground, the airflow around an airplane is altered by interference with the surface of the earth. The resulting ground effect reduces the induced drag on the airplane. Answer (B) is wrong because the induced drag is reduced, not increased. Answer (C) is wrong because the upwash and downwash of airflow on the wing is reduced, and the airplane can fly at lower speeds.

3-10. Answer A. GFDPPM 3-18 (AFH)

Ground effect becomes noticeable when the height of the airplane above the ground is less than the length of the wingspan. Answer (B) is wrong because it states twice the length of the wingspan. Answer (C) is wrong because ground effect is not a result of angle of attack, and at a higher angle of attack, airspeed will be lower so that floating is decreased.

3-11   H317
What must a pilot be aware of as a result of ground effect?

A — Wingtip vortices increase creating wake turbulence problems for arriving and departing aircraft.
B — Induced drag decreases; therefore, any excess speed at the point of flare may cause considerable floating.
C — A full stall landing will require less up elevator deflection than would a full stall when done free of ground effect.

3-12   H317
Ground effect is most likely to result in which problem?

A — Settling to the surface abruptly during landing.
B — Becoming airborne before reaching recommended takeoff speed.
C — Inability to get airborne even though airspeed is sufficient for normal takeoff needs.

3-11. Answer B. GFDPPM 3-18 (AFH)
Since ground effect decreases induced drag, the airplane tends to float while excess speed bleeds off. Answer (A) is wrong because the reduction in induced drag causes wingtip vortices to decrease. Answer (C) is wrong because the wings produce more lift in ground effect than out of ground effect. Therefore, more up elevator deflection would be required.

3-12. Answer B. GFDPPM 3-18 (AFH)
The decreased induced drag while in ground effect allows the airplane to become airborne at a lower airspeed. This may fool you into thinking the airplane is capable of flying at the lower airspeed when you climb out of ground effect. Answer (A) is wrong because ground effect tends to cause an airplane to float during landing, not settle abruptly. Answer (C) is wrong because ground effect allows an airplane to become airborne at a lower than normal airspeed.

SECTION B
STABILITY

Although no airplane is completely stable, all airplanes must have desirable handling characteristics.
  1. An aircraft that is inherently stable will require less effort to control.

YAW
  2. The purpose of the rudder is to control yaw.

LONGITUDINAL STABILITY
Longitudinal stability in an airplane involves the pitching motion or tendency of the aircraft to move about its lateral axis.

LOCATION OF THE CG
  3. The location of the CG, with respect to the center of lift, determines the longitudinal stability of the airplane.
  4. An airplane loaded with the CG aft of the approved CG range will be difficult to recover from a stalled condition.
  5. Loading an aircraft to the most aft CG will cause the airplane to be less stable at all speeds.

HORIZONTAL STABILIZER
  6. When power is reduced, and the controls are not adjusted, an aircraft pitches nose down because the downwash on the elevators from the propeller slipstream is reduced and elevator effectiveness is reduced.

STALLS
The inherent stability of an airplane is particularly important as it relates to the aircraft's ability to avoid stalls and spins. Familiarization with the causes and effects of stalls is especially important during flight at slow airspeeds, such as during takeoff and landing, where the margin above the stall speed is small.

SPINS
  7. The aircraft must be placed in a stalled condition in order to spin.
  8. During a spin to the left, both wings are stalled.

3-13   H302
An airplane said to be inherently stable will

A — be difficult to stall.
B — require less effort to control.
C — not spin.

3-14   H302
What determines the longitudinal stability of an airplane?

A — The location of the CG with respect to the center of lift.
B — The effectiveness of the horizontal stabilizer, rudder, and rudder trim tab.
C — The relationship of thrust and lift to weight and drag.

3-13. Answer B. GFDPPM 3-23 (PHB)
An airplane that is inherently stable tends to return to its original attitude after it has been displaced, and is therefore easier to control. Answers (A) and (C) are wrong because stability does not prevent you from stalling or spinning an airplane.

3-14. Answer A. GFDPPM 3-26 (PHB)
The longitudinal stability of an airplane is determined primarily by the location of the center of gravity (CG) in relation to the center of lift. Answer (B) is wrong because the rudder and rudder trim tab affect the directional stability. Answer (C) is wrong because this relationship affects acceleration, but not longitudinal stability.

3-15   H302
What causes an airplane (except a T-tail) to pitch nose-down when power is reduced and controls are not adjusted?

A — The CG shifts forward when thrust and drag are reduced.
B — The downwash on the elevators from the propeller slipstream is reduced and elevator effectiveness is reduced.
C — When thrust is reduced to less than weight, lift is also reduced and the wings can no longer support the weight.

3-16   H302
What is the purpose of the rudder on an airplane?

A — To control yaw.
B — To control overbanking tendency.
C — To control roll.

3-17   H315
An airplane has been loaded in such a manner that the CG is located aft of the aft CG limit. One undesirable flight characteristic a pilot might experience with this airplane would be

A — a longer takeoff run.
B — difficulty in recovering from a stalled condition.
C — stalling at higher-than-normal airspeed.

3-18   H315
Loading an airplane to the most aft CG will cause the airplane to be

A — less stable at all speeds.
B — less stable at slow speeds, but more stable at high speeds.
C — less stable at high speeds, but more stable at low speeds.

3-19   H540
In what flight condition must an aircraft be placed in order to spin?

A — Partially stalled with one wing low
B — In a steep diving spiral
C — Stalled

3-15. Answer B. GFDPPM 3-30 (PHB)
At higher power settings, in airplanes other than T-tail designs, the propeller slipstream causes a greater downward force on the horizontal stabilizer. When power is reduced, this downward force on the tail is also reduced, and the nose pitches down. Answer (A) is wrong because CG is determined by how an airplane is built and loaded, and is not affected by changes in thrust and drag. Answer (C) is also wrong because most airplanes can fly with thrust less than the weight.

3-16. Answer A. GFDPPM 3-25 (PHB)
Since the rudder moves the airplane about its vertical axis, it is used to control yaw. Answers (B) and (C) are wrong because overbanking tendency and roll are controlled by ailerons.

3-17. Answer B. GFDPPM 3-28 (AFH)
With a CG aft of the rear CG limit, the airplane becomes tail heavy and unstable in pitch because the horizontal stabilizer is less effective. This condition makes it difficult, if not impossible, to recover from a stall or spin. Answer (A) is wrong because an aft CG tends to shorten the takeoff run, and it may cause the airplane to pitch up and lift off early at a lower than normal airspeed. Answer (C) is wrong because an airplane with an aft CG requires less downward force on the tail. The airplane can fly at a lower angle of attack and will stall at a lower airspeed.

3-18. Answer A. GFDPPM 3-28 (AFH)
In an airplane loaded to the aft CG limit, the horizontal stabilizer is less effective, causing the airplane to be less stable at all speeds. Answers (B) and (C) are wrong because an aft-loaded airplane is less stable at all speeds.

3-19. Answer C. GFDPPM 3-39 (AFH)
An airplane must be stalled before a spin can develop. Answer (A) is wrong because a spin occurs when both wings are in a stalled condition, with one wing more completely stalled than the other. Answer (B) is wrong because an airplane may be put into a steep diving spiral without being stalled.

3-20 H540

During a spin to the left, which wing(s) is/are stalled?

A — Both wings are stalled.
B — Neither wing is stalled.
C — Only the left wing is stalled.

3-20. Answer A. GFDPPM 3-39 (AFH)

In a spin, both wings are stalled. Answers (B) and (C) are wrong because both wings must be stalled for a spin to develop, although the outside wing may be less fully stalled than the inside wing.

SECTION C
AERODYNAMICS OF MANEUVERING FLIGHT

The extent to which an airplane can perform a variety of maneuvers is primarily a matter of design and a measure of its overall performance. Although aircraft design and performance may differ, the aerodynamic forces acting on any maneuvering aircraft are essentially the same. Understanding the aerodynamics of maneuvering flight can help you perform precise maneuvers while keeping your airplane within its design limitations.

TORQUE
1. Torque effect is greatest at low airspeeds, high power settings and high angles of attack.

P-FACTOR
2. P-factor is the result of the propeller blade descending on the right, and producing more thrust than the ascending blade on the left.
3. P-factor is most pronounced at high angles of attack.

LIFT/DRAG RATIO
4. Establishing the proper glide attitude and airspeed is critical to ensure the best possibility of reaching a suitable landing area.

HORIZONTAL COMPONENT OF LIFT
5. The horizontal component of lift is what makes an airplane turn.

LOAD FACTOR
Load factor is the ratio of the load supported by the airplane's wings to the actual weight of the aircraft and its contents.

IN TURNS
6. Turns increase the load factor on an airplane, as compared to straight-and-level flight.
7. The amount of excess load that can be imposed on an airplane depends on its speed.
8. At 60 degrees of bank, 2 G's are required to maintain level flight. To determine how much weight the airplane's wing structure must support, multiply the airplane's weight by the number of G's.

IN STALLS
9. During an approach to a stall, an increased load factor will cause the airplane to stall at a higher airspeed.

MANEUVERING SPEED
10. V_A is defined as maneuvering speed.

3-21   H300

In what flight condition is torque effect the greatest in a single-engine airplane?

A — Low airspeed, high power, high angle of attack.
B — Low airspeed, low power, low angle of attack.
C — High airspeed, high power, high angle of attack.

3-21. Answer A. GFDPPM 3-47 (PHB)
Torque effect is greatest at low airspeeds, high power settings, and high angles of attack. Answer (B) is wrong because these conditions produce the least amount of torque effect. Answer (C) is also wrong because it includes high airspeed.

3-22   H301
The left turning tendency of an airplane caused by P-factor is the result of the

A — clockwise rotation of the engine and the propeller turning the airplane counter-clockwise.
B — propeller blade descending on the right, producing more thrust than the ascending blade on the left.
C — gyroscopic forces applied to the rotating propeller blades acting 90° in advance of the point the force was applied.

3-23   H301
When does P-factor cause the airplane to yaw to the left?

A — When at low angles of attack.
B — When at high angles of attack.
C — When at high airspeeds.

3-24   H303
(Refer to figure 2 on page 3-10.) If an airplane weighs 2,300 pounds, what approximate weight would the airplane structure be required to support during a 60° banked turn while maintaining altitude?

A — 2,300 pounds.
B — 3,400 pounds.
C — 4,600 pounds.

3-25   H303
(Refer to figure 2 on page 3-10.) If an airplane weighs 3,300 pounds, what approximate weight would the airplane structure be required to support during a 30° banked turn while maintaining altitude?

A — 1,200 pounds.
B — 3,100 pounds.
C — 3,960 pounds.

3-26   H303
(Refer to figure 2 on page 3-10.) If an airplane weighs 4,500 pounds, what approximate weight would the airplane structure be required to support during a 45° banked turn while maintaining altitude?

A — 4,500 pounds.
B — 6,750 pounds.
C — 7,200 pounds.

3-22. Answer B. GFDPPM 3-49 (PHB)
P-factor, or asymmetric propeller loading, normally occurs at a high angle of attack. The descending propeller blade on the right side takes a larger "bite" of the air, and produces more thrust than the ascending blade on the left. The result is a left turning tendency of the airplane. Answer (A) describes torque reaction, not P-factor. Answer (C) describes gyroscopic precession, not P-factor.

3-23. Answer B. GFDPPM 3-49 (PHB)
P-factor is most pronounced at high angles of attack, which cause the descending propeller blade to produce more thrust. Answer (A) is wrong because at low angles of attack, thrust produced by the ascending and descending propeller blades is almost equalized. Answer (C) is wrong because at high airspeeds, the angle of attack is lower, thus reducing the P-factor.

3-24. Answer C. GFDPPM 3-60 (PHB)
At 60 degrees of bank, 2 G's are required to maintain level flight. This means that the airplane's wing structure must support twice the airplane's weight, or 2,300 × 2 = 4,600 pounds. Answer (A) reflects 1 G, or straight-and-level flight. Answer (B) is correct only if 1.48 G's (approximately 50° bank) are applied.

3-25. Answer C. GFDPPM 3-60 (PHB)
The load factor for 30 degrees of bank is 1.154, or about 1.2. The airplane weight (3,300) multiplied by the load factor (1.2) is 3,960 pounds which the wing structure must support. Answers (A) and (B) are both wrong because the weights are less than the airplane weight.

3-26. Answer B. GFDPPM 3-60 (PHB)
At 45 degrees of bank the load factor is 1.414, or approximately 1.5, the wing loading would be 4,500 × 1.5, or 6,750 pounds. Answer (A) reflects only 1 G, and is therefore incorrect. Answer (C) is wrong because 1.6 G's are required to produce a load of 7,200 pounds. Therefore, (B) is the closest correct answer.

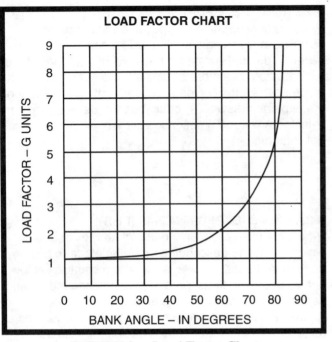

FIGURE 2.—Load Factor Chart

3-27   H303

The amount of excess load that can be imposed on the wing of an airplane depends upon the

A — position of the CG.
B — speed of the airplane.
C — abruptness at which the load is applied.

3-27. Answer B. GFDPPM 3-64 (PHB)

The amount of excess load that can be imposed on an airplane depends on its speed. If abrupt control movements or strong gusts are applied at low airspeeds, the airplane will stall before the load becomes excessive. At higher airspeeds, the increased airflow causes a greater lifting capacity. A sudden control input or gust at a high airspeed may result in an excessive load factor beyond safe limits. Answer (A) is wrong because position of the CG does not affect the load factor on the wings. Answer (C) is wrong because the amount of excess load depends on both the speed and total load. Although abruptness does affect the total load on the airplane, the determining factor is airspeed.

3-28   H303

Which basic flight maneuver increases the load factor on an airplane as compared to straight-and-level flight?

A — Climbs.
B — Turns.
C — Stalls.

3-28. Answer B. GFDPPM 3-60 (PHB)

In a level turn, lift must be increased to compensate for the loss of vertical lift as well as overcome centrifugal force. Since the wings must support not only the airplane's weight, but also the load imposed by centrifugal force, the load factor is greater than 1 G. Answer (A) is wrong because once established in a climb, there is no additional load factor imposed on the airplane. Answer (C) is wrong because when an airplane is in a stalled condition, it is producing insufficient lift, and the load factor decreases below 1 G.

3-29   **H534**
What force makes an airplane turn?

A — The horizontal component of lift.
B — The vertical component of lift.
C — Centrifugal force.

3-30   **H303**
During an approach to a stall, an increased load factor will cause the airplane to

A — stall at a higher airspeed.
B — have a tendency to spin.
C — be more difficult to control.

3-31   **H582**
The most important rule to remember in the event of a power failure after becoming airborne is to

A — immediately establish the proper gliding attitude and airspeed.
B — quickly check the fuel supply for possible fuel exhaustion.
C — determine the wind direction to plan for the forced landing.

3-29. Answer A. GFDPPM 3-56 (PHB)
In a turn, lift has both a vertical and a horizontal component. The horizontal component of lift, which is also referred to as centripetal force, opposes centrifugal force and causes the airplane to turn. Answer (B) is wrong because the vertical component of lift opposes weight. Answer (C) is wrong because centrifugal force acts outward from the turn and opposes the horizontal component of lift.

3-30. Answer A. GFDPPM 3-61 (PHB)
Stall speed increases in proportion to load factor. Added G-forces cause an airplane to stall at an airspeed higher than the normal 1 G airspeed. Answer (B) is wrong because load factor normally does not affect an airplane's tendency to spin. Answer (C) is wrong because load factor does not affect controllability. Rather, this is a function of the airplane's stability.

3-31. Answer A. GFDPPM 3-52 (AFH)
Establishing the proper glide attitude and airspeed is critical to ensure the best possibility of reaching a suitable landing area. It also tends to reduce the possibility of a stall/spin accident. Answer (B) is an important step in attempting an engine restart, but controlling the aircraft is the first action you should take. Answer (C) is another important step, but should be taken only after establishing the proper glide speed.

CHAPTER 4

THE FLIGHT ENVIRONMENT

SECTION A
SAFETY OF FLIGHT

Maintaining the safety of flight is your number one priority as a pilot. Some safety issues apply to every flight, such as collision avoidance and maintaining minimum safe altitudes. Other safety considerations only apply in certain situations; for example, taxiing in wind, flight over hazardous terrain, and effective exchange of flight controls with your instructor. As pilot in command, you need to consider the factors which can affect your flight and take the appropriate actions to ensure safety.

VISUAL SCANNING
1. The most effective method of scanning for other aircraft for collision avoidance during daylight hours is to use a series of short, regularly spaced eye movements to search each 10-degree section.
2. An aircraft on a collision course with your aircraft will show little relative movement.
3. Haze reduces visibility, making objects appear to be farther away than they really are.
4. When climbing or descending VFR along an airway, execute gentle banks left and right for continuous scanning of the airspace.
5. Prior to beginning each maneuver, make clearing turns to scan the entire area for other traffic.

RIGHT-OF-WAY
6. An aircraft in distress has right-of-way over all other aircraft.
7. When two aircraft are converging, the aircraft on the right has right-of-way.
8. The least maneuverable aircraft has the right-of-way: a glider has right-of-way over an airship, airplane or rotorcraft.
9. An aircraft that is towing or refueling another has the right-of-way over other engine-driven aircraft.
10. When aircraft are approaching head-on, each shall give way to the right.
11. When two or more aircraft are approaching the airport with the intention of landing, the one at the lower altitude has the right-of-way.

MINIMUM SAFE ALTITUDES
12. Except for conducting a normal takeoff or landing, the pilot must maintain enough altitude to allow for an emergency landing in the event of an engine failure, without creating an undue hazard to people or property on the surface.
13. Pilots must maintain at least 500 feet between their aircraft and any person, vessel, vehicle or structure on the surface.
14. If you aren't able to obtain a local altimeter setting before departing, set the altimeter to the local field elevation.

TAXIING IN WIND
15. When taxiing with a quartering tailwind, the aileron should be down on the side from which the wind is blowing.
16. When taxiing with a quartering headwind, the aileron should be up on the side from which the wind is blowing.
17. A quartering tailwind is the most critical wind condition to a tricycle-gear, high-wing airplane.

4-1   B08

Which aircraft has the right-of-way over all other air traffic?

A — A balloon.
B — An aircraft in distress.
C — An aircraft on final approach to land.

4-2   B08

What action is required when two aircraft of the same category converge, but not head-on?

A — The faster aircraft shall give way.
B — The aircraft on the left shall give way.
C — Each aircraft shall give way to the right.

4-3   B08

Which aircraft has the right-of-way over the other aircraft listed?

A — Glider.
B — Airship.
C — Aircraft refueling other aircraft.

4-4   B08

An airplane and an airship are converging. If the airship is left of the airplane's position, which aircraft has the right-of-way?

A — The airship.
B — The airplane.
C — Each pilot should alter course to the right.

4-5   B08

Which aircraft has the right-of-way over the other aircraft listed?

A — Airship.
B — Aircraft towing other aircraft.
C — Gyroplane.

4-6   B08

What action should the pilots of a glider and an airplane take if on a head-on collision course?

A — The airplane pilot should give way to the left.
B — The glider pilot should give way to the right.
C — Both pilots should give way to the right.

4-1. Answer B. GFDPPM 4-6 (FAR 91.113)
An aircraft in distress has the right-of-way over all other aircraft. Answers (A) and (C) are wrong because an aircraft in distress has right-of-way over all other air traffic.

4-2. Answer B. GFDPPM 4-6 (FAR 91.113)
The aircraft on the right has the right-of-way and the aircraft on the left shall give way.

4-3. Answer A. GFDPPM 4-7 (FAR 91.113)
In general, the least maneuverable aircraft normally has the right-of-way. A glider has the right-of-way over an airship, airplane, or rotorcraft. An aircraft that is towing or refueling another aircraft has the right-of-way over all other engine-driven aircraft (but not a glider).

4-4. Answer A. GFDPPM 4-7 (FAR 91.113)
See explanation for Question 4-3. Since an airship is less maneuverable than an airplane, the airship has the right-of-way.

4-5. Answer B. GFDPPM 4-7 (FAR 91.113)
An aircraft towing or refueling another aircraft has the right-of-way over all other engine-driven aircraft.

4-6. Answer C. GFDPPM 4-6 (FAR 91.113)
When any aircraft are approaching each other head-on, both pilots should alter their course to the right. For aircraft approaching head-on, the FARs do not make a distinction between aircraft categories.

4-7 B08

When two or more aircraft are approaching an airport for the purpose of landing, the right-of-way belongs to the aircraft

A — that has the other to its right.
B — that is the least maneuverable.
C — at the lower altitude, but it shall not take advantage of this rule to cut in front of or to overtake another.

4-8 B08

Except when necessary for takeoff or landing, what is the minimum safe altitude for a pilot to operate an aircraft anywhere?

A — An altitude allowing, if a power unit fails, an emergency landing without undue hazard to persons or property on the surface.
B — An altitude of 500 feet above the surface and no closer than 500 feet to any person, vessel, vehicle, or structure.
C — An altitude of 500 feet above the highest obstacle within a horizontal radius of 1,000 feet.

4-9 B08

Except when necessary for takeoff or landing, what is the minimum safe altitude required for a pilot to operate an aircraft over congested areas?

A — An altitude of 1,000 feet above any person, vessel, vehicle, or structure.
B — An altitude of 500 feet above the highest obstacle within a horizontal radius of 1,000 feet of the aircraft.
C — An altitude of 1,000 feet above the highest obstacle within a horizontal radius of 2,000 feet of the aircraft.

4-10 B08

Except when necessary for takeoff or landing, what is the minimum safe altitude required for a pilot to operate an aircraft over other than a congested area?

A — An altitude allowing, if a power unit fails, an emergency landing without undue hazard to persons or property on the surface.
B — An altitude of 500 feet AGL, except over open water or a sparsely populated area, which requires 500 feet from any person, vessel, vehicle, or structure.
C — An altitude of 500 feet above the highest obstacle within a horizontal radius of 1,000 feet.

4-7. Answer C. GFDPPM 4-8 (FAR 91.113)

When two or more aircraft are approaching an airport for landing, the one at the lower altitude has the right-of-way, but you should not use this rule to cut in front of another aircraft.

4-8. Answer A. GFDPPM 4-8 (FAR 91.119)

Except for a normal takeoff and landing, you must maintain enough altitude to allow an emergency landing in the event of an engine failure without undue hazard to people or property on the surface. Answer (B) is wrong because it combines minimum altitudes for operating over an uncongested area (500 feet above the surface), and a sparsely populated or open water area (500 feet from any person, vessel, vehicle, or structure). Answer (C) gives the wrong distances for operating over a congested area. It should be 1,000 feet above any obstacle within a horizontal radius of 2,000 feet.

4-9. Answer C. GFDPPM 4-8 (FAR 91.119)

See explanation for Question 4-8.

4-10. Answer B. GFDPPM 4-8 (FAR 91.119)

See explanation for Question 4-8.

4-11   B08
Except when necessary for takeoff or landing, an aircraft may not be operated closer than what distance from any person, vessel, vehicle, or structure?

A — 500 feet.
B — 700 feet.
C — 1,000 feet.

4-11. Answer A. GFDPPM 4-8 (FAR 91.119)
See explanation for Question 4-8. The words person, vessel, vehicle, or structure apply for operations over a sparsely populated or open water area, and the distance is 500 feet.

4-12   H516
When taxiing with strong quartering tailwinds, which aileron positions should be used?

A — Aileron down on the downwind side.
B — Ailerons neutral.
C — Aileron down on the side from which the wind is blowing.

4-12. Answer C. GFDPPM 4-9 (AFH)
With a quartering tailwind, the aileron should be down on the side from which the wind is blowing in order to prevent the wind from flowing under the wing and lifting it.

4-13   H516
Which aileron positions should a pilot generally use when taxiing in strong quartering headwinds?

A — Aileron up on the side from which the wind is blowing.
B — Aileron down on the side from which the wind is blowing.
C — Ailerons neutral.

4-13. Answer A. GFDPPM 4-9 (AFH)
To counteract the lifting tendency of a quartering headwind, the aileron should be up on the side from which the wind is blowing.

4-14   H516
Which wind condition would be most critical when taxiing a nosewheel equipped high-wing airplane?

A — Quartering tailwind.
B — Direct crosswind.
C — Quartering headwind.

4-14. Answer A. GFDPPM 4-11 (AFH)
A tricycle-gear, high-wing airplane is most susceptible to a quartering tailwind because a strong airflow beneath the wing and horizontal stabilizer can lift the airplane and tip or nose it over.

4-15   H516
(Refer to figure 9, area A.) How should the flight controls be held while taxiing a tricycle-gear equipped airplane into a left quartering headwind?

A — Left aileron up, elevator neutral.
B — Left aileron down, elevator neutral.
C — Left aileron up, elevator down.

4-15. Answer A. GFDPPM 4-11 (AFH)
While taxiing a tricycle-gear airplane in a quartering headwind, the aileron should be up on the side from which the wind is blowing, and the elevator neutral to prevent any lifting force on the tail. In this case, the wind is from the left, so the left aileron should be up.

4-16   H516
(Refer to figure 9, area B.) How should the flight controls be held while taxiing a tailwheel airplane into a right quartering headwind?

A — Right aileron up, elevator up.
B — Right aileron down, elevator neutral.
C — Right aileron up, elevator down.

4-16. Answer A. GFDPPM 4-11 (AFH)
In a tailwheel airplane, the aileron is held up on the upwind side, and the elevator is held up to prevent the tail from lifting. Since the tail of most tailwheel airplanes is lower than the nose while taxiing, a strong headwind blowing on a neutral or down elevator could cause the tail to rise.

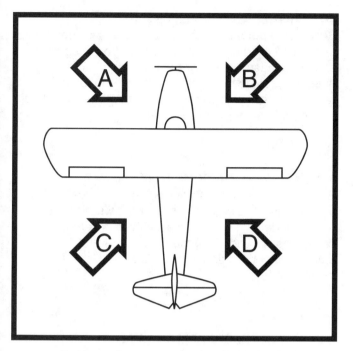

FIGURE 9.—Control Position for Taxi

4-17   H516
(Refer to figure 9, area C.) How should the flight controls be held while taxiing a tailwheel airplane with a left quartering tailwind?

A — Left aileron up, elevator neutral.
B — Left aileron down, elevator neutral.
C — Left aileron down, elevator down.

4-17. Answer C. GFDPPM 4-11 (AFH)
For a quartering tailwind, the controls are held the same for both tailwheel and tricycle-gear airplanes. Ailerons are down on the side from which the wind is blowing. The elevator is down to prevent the wind from lifting the tail.

4-18   H516
(Refer to figure 9, area C.) How should the flight controls be held while taxiing a tricycle-gear equipped airplane with a left quartering tailwind?

A — Left aileron up, elevator neutral.
B — Left aileron down, elevator down.
C — Left aileron up, elevator down.

4-18. Answer B. GFDPPM 4-11 (AFH)
See explanation for Questions 4-14 and 4-17.

4-19   H507
Prior to starting each maneuver, pilots should

A — check altitude, airspeed, and heading indications.
B — visually scan the entire area for collision avoidance.
C — announce their intentions on the nearest CTAF.

4-19. Answer B. GFDPPM 4-6 (AIM)
To ensure you can see other aircraft which may be blocked by blindspots, make clearing turns and scan the area. Answer (A) is wrong because, while it is important to maintain an instrument scan, it is critical to clear the area. Answer (C) is wrong because you should not practice maneuvers in the vicinity of an airport.

4-20   J14
What procedure is recommended when climbing or descending VFR on an airway?

A — Execute gentle banks, left and right for continuous visual scanning of the airspace.
B — Advise the nearest FSS of the altitude changes.
C — Fly away from the centerline of the airway before changing altitude.

4-21   J31
What effect does haze have on the ability to see traffic or terrain features during flight?

A — Haze causes the eyes to focus at infinity.
B — The eyes tend to overwork in haze and do not detect relative movement easily.
C — All traffic or terrain features appear to be farther away than their actual distance.

4-22   J31
The most effective method of scanning for other aircraft for collision avoidance during daylight hours is to use

A — regularly spaced concentration on the 3-, 9-, and 12-o'clock positions.
B — a series of short, regularly spaced eye movements to search each 10-degree sector.
C — peripheral vision by scanning small sectors and utilizing offcenter viewing.

4-23   J31
Which technique should a pilot use to scan for traffic to the right and left during straight-and-level flight?

A — Systematically focus on different segments of the sky for short intervals.
B — Concentrate on relative movement detected in the peripheral vision area.
C — Continuous sweeping of the windshield from right to left.

4-24   J31
How can you determine if another aircraft is on a collision course with your aircraft?

A — The other aircraft will always appear to get larger and closer at a rapid rate.
B — The nose of each aircraft is pointed at the same point in space.
C — There will be no apparent relative motion between your aircraft and the other aircraft.

4-20. Answer A. GFDPPM 4-5 (AIM)
Because of potential traffic on airways, it is important to scan. Making shallow turns allows you to compensate for blindspots. Answer (B) is wrong because FSS does not provide traffic control or advisories on airways. Answer (C) is wrong because ATC is expecting you to maintain the airway centerline.

4-21. Answer C. GFDPPM 4-4 (AIM)
Since haze reduces visibility, objects are closer than they appear. Answers (A) and (B) are wrong because without a definite visible object, which is sometimes the case in hazy conditions, the eyes tend to relax and focus on a point in space about 3 to 5 feet away, not infinity.

4-22. Answer B. GFDPPM 4-3 (AIM)
The eyes are able to focus clearly only on a small area, approximately 10°, so a series of short eye movements is most effective. Answer (A) is wrong because all sectors should be scanned. Answer (C) is not correct because peripheral vision and offcenter viewing are most effective at night, not during the day.

4-23. Answer A. GFDPPM 4-3 (AIM)
See explanation for Question 4-22.

4-24. Answer C. GFDPPM 4-3 (AIM)
A lack of relative movement can indicate that the two aircraft are moving toward one another on a collision course. Answer (A) is not correct because there are times when the other aircraft might not appear to get larger and closer until just before a collision. Answer (B) is wrong because even though the aircraft might be headed toward the same point, different aircraft speeds, might keep them from reaching the same point at the same time.

SECTION B
AIRPORTS

Each day, aircraft takeoff and land at private grass strips, busy international airports and every type of field in between. Whether most of your flying is out of your local airport or you frequently journey to new destinations, an airport will never be unfamiliar territory once you learn the basic procedures for operating in the terminal environment.

RUNWAY LAYOUT
1. Runway numbers correspond to the magnetic direction and are rounded to the nearest 10 degrees, with the last zero dropped out.

SEGMENTED CIRCLES
2. Traffic pattern indicators on the segmented circle show the final and base legs to various runways on the airport. The wind cone or sock in the center gives current wind direction.

RUNWAY MARKINGS
3. At many airports, the area before a displaced threshold may be used for taxi and takeoff.
4. Landings should be made after the displaced threshold.
5. A closed runway is marked with X's painted on its surface at each end.

AIRPORT LIGHTING

BEACON
6. When an airport's beacon is on during the daytime, it usually means that the weather is below basic VFR minimums (ceiling less than 1000 feet and/or visibility is less than 3 miles).
7. A military airport beacon alternates two quick flashes of white with one green flash.

VISUAL GLIDESLOPE INDICATORS
8. Pilots should fly at or above the glide path when approaching an airport with a VASI installed.
9. A slightly high indication on a precision approach path indicator shows three white lights and one red.
10. A below glideslope indication on a tri-color VASI is red.
11. An above glideslope indication on a tri-color VASI is amber.
12. Green is the indication on a tri-color VASI for being on the glide path.
13. A pulsating approach slope indicator provides a pulsating red light when below the glide path. Pulsating white is above glide path, and steady white is on the glide path.
14. On a two-bar VASI, red over white indicates you are on the glideslope. White over white is above the glideslope, and red over red is below the glideslope.

TAXIWAY LIGHTS
15. Taxiway edge lights are blue.

PILOT-CONTROLLED LIGHTING
16. At airports with a three-step pilot-controlled lighting system, seven clicks of the microphone will set the lights on high intensity. Five clicks turns the lights to medium, and three turns the lights to low.

4-25   B08
Each pilot of an aircraft approaching to land on a runway served by a visual approach slope indicator (VASI) shall

A — maintain a 3° glide to the runway.
B — maintain an altitude at or above the glide slope.
C — stay high until the runway can be reached in a power-off landing.

4-25. Answer B. GFDPPM 4-33 (FAR 91.129)
The VASI glide path provides safe obstruction clearance to the runway. Therefore, the pilot should fly at or above the glide path. Answer (A) is wrong because not all VASIs have a 3° glide path. Answer (C) is wrong because VASIs are intended to provide a glide path for a normal approach.

4-26   B08

When approaching to land on a runway served by a visual approach slope indicator (VASI), the pilot shall

A — maintain an altitude that captures the glide slope at least 2 miles downwind from the runway threshold.

B — maintain an altitude at or above the glide slope.

C — remain on the glide slope and land between the two-light bar.

4-26. Answer B. GFDPPM 4-33 (FAR 91.129)
See explanation for Question 4-25. Answer (A) is not a requirement for using a VASI. Answer (C) is also wrong because VASIs provide a glide path to the runway. There is no requirement to land between the light bars.

4-27   H568

Airport taxiway edge lights are identified at night by

A — white directional lights.

B — blue omnidirectional lights.

C — alternate red and green lights.

4-27. Answer B. GFDPPM 4-35 (AFH)
Taxiway edge lights are blue. Answer (A) is wrong because white lights are used for runway edges and centerlines. Answer (C) is wrong because alternating red and green lights are not used for taxiway lighting.

4-28   J03

A slightly high glide slope indication from a precision approach path indicator is

A — four white lights.

B — three white lights and one red light.

C — two white lights and two red lights.

4-28. Answer B. GFDPPM 4-34 (AIM)
A slightly high indication on a precision approach path indicator shows three white lights and one red light. Answer (A) is a high indication. Answer (C) is on the glide path.

4-29   J03

A below glide slope indication from a tri-color VASI is a

A — red light signal.

B — pink light signal.

C — green light signal.

4-29. Answer A. GFDPPM 4-33 (AIM)
A below glide slope indication on a tri-color is red. Answer (B) is wrong because the color pink is not used in a tri-color system. A green light (answer C) indicates you are on the glide path.

4-30   J03

An above glide slope indication from a tri-color VASI is

A — a white light signal.

B — a green light signal.

C — an amber light signal.

4-30. Answer C. GFDPPM 4-33 (AIM)
Amber is the color used for an above glide path indication. White (answer A) is not used in a tri-color VASI. Answer (B), green, is the indication for being on the glide path.

4-31   J03

An on glide slope indication from a tri-color VASI is

A — a white light signal.

B — a green light signal.

C — an amber light signal.

4-31. Answer B. GFDPPM 4-33 (AIM)
See explanation for Question 4-30.

4-32   J03

A below glide slope indication from a pulsating approach slope indicator is a

A — pulsating white light.

B — steady white light.

C — pulsating red light.

4-32. Answer C. GFDPPM 4-34 (AIM)
A pulsating approach slope indicator provides a pulsating red light when below glide slope. Answer (A), pulsating white, is above glide slope. Answer (B), steady white, is on glide slope.

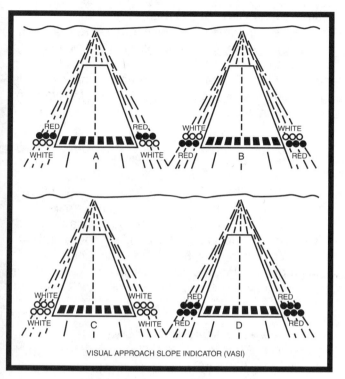

VISUAL APPROACH SLOPE INDICATOR (VASI)

FIGURE 48.—VASI Illustrations.

4-33   J03
(Refer to figure 48.) Illustration A indicates that the aircraft is

A — below the glide slope.
B — on the glide slope.
C — above the glide slope.

4-34   J03
(Refer to figure 48.) VASI lights as shown by illustration C indicate that the airplane is

A — off course to the left.
B — above the glide slope.
C — below the glide slope.

4-35   J03
(Refer to figure 48.) While on final approach to a runway equipped with a standard 2-bar VASI, the lights appear as shown by illustration D. This means that the aircraft is

A — above the glide slope.
B — below the glide slope.
C — on the glide slope.

4-33. Answer B. GFDPPM 4-33 (AIM)
A red over white indication is on glide slope.

4-34. Answer B. GFDPPM 4-33 (AIM)
A white over white indication is above glide slope.

4-35. Answer B. GFDPPM 4-33 (AIM)
A red over red indication is below the glide slope.

4-36   J03
To set the high intensity runway lights on medium intensity, the pilot should click the microphone seven times, then click it

A — one time.
B — three times.
C — five times.

4-37   J03
An airport's rotating beacon operated during daylight hours indicates

A — there are obstructions on the airport.
B — that weather at the airport located in Class D airspace is below basic VFR weather minimums.
C — the Air Traffic Control tower is not in operation.

4-38   J03
A military air station can be identified by a rotating beacon that emits

A — white and green alternating flashes.
B — two quick, white flashes between green flashes.
C — green, yellow, and white flashes.

4-39   J03
How can a military airport be identified at night?

A — Alternate white and green light flashes.
B — Dual peaked (two quick) white flashes between green flashes.
C — White flashing lights with steady green at the same location.

4-40   J05
(Refer to figure 49.) That portion of the runway identified by the letter A may be used for

A — landing.
B — taxiing and takeoff.
C — taxiing and landing.

4-41   J05
(Refer to figure 49.) According to the airport diagram, which statement is true?

A — Runway 30 is equipped at position E with emergency arresting gear to provide a means of stopping military aircraft.
B — Takeoffs may be started at position A on Runway 12, and the landing portion of this runway begins at position B.
C — The takeoff and landing portion of Runway 12 begins at position B.

4-36. Answer C. GFDPPM 4-36 (AIM)
At airports with three-step pilot-controlled runway lighting system, seven clicks turns all the lights on to the maximum intensity. Five clicks turns the lights to medium. One click, (answer A) does not change the light setting. Three clicks (answer B) turns the lights to the lowest intensity.

4-37. Answer B. GFDPPM 4-31 (AIM)
When the airport beacon is on during the daytime, it usually means that the ceiling is less than 1,000 feet and/or the visibility is less than three statute miles (below basic VFR minimums). The beacon is not used to indicate obstructions (answer A), nor does it indicate that the control tower is not in operation (answer C). Remember, though, the airport beacon may not always be turned on when the weather is below VFR minimums.

4-38. Answer B. GFDPPM 4-32 (AIM)
A military airport beacon has two quick flashes of white light between green flashes. Answer (A) indicates a civilian airport beacon. Answer (C) indicates a heliport.

4-39. Answer B. GFDPPM 4-32 (AIM)
See explanation for Question 4-38. Answer (C) does not describe any airport beacon.

4-40. Answer B. GFDPPM 4-24 (AIM)
At many airports, the area prior to a displaced threshold may be used for taxi and takeoff (and rollout after landing). Answers (A) and (C) are wrong because you may not land on this part of a runway.

4-41. Answer B. GFDPPM 4-24 (AIM)
See explanation for Question 4-40. Landings may be made after the displaced threshold at position "B." Answer (A) is not correct because area "E" is a blast-pad/stopway. Answer (C) is wrong because takeoffs may be started before the displaced threshold and landing rollouts may be completed in area "A."

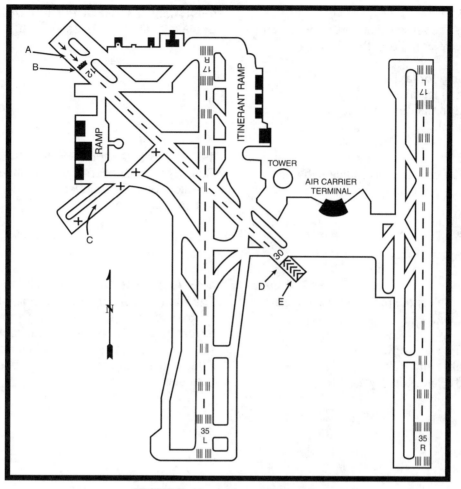

FIGURE 49.—Airport Diagram.

4-42   J05
(Refer to figure 49.) What is the difference between area A and area E on the airport depicted?

A — "A" may be used for taxi and takeoff; "E" may be used only as an overrun.
B — "A" may be used for all operations except heavy aircraft landings; "E" may be used only as an overrun.
C — "A" may be used only for taxiing; "E" may be used for all operations except landings.

4-42. Answer A. GFDPPM 4-24, 25 (AIM)
See explanation for Question 4-40. Area "E" is a blast-pad/stopway, and because of its pavement strength cannot support continuous operations, but may be used as an overrun. Answer (B) is wrong because area "A" cannot be used for any landings. Answer (C) is wrong because takeoffs and landing rollouts are allowed in area "A," and area "E" is unusable.

4-43   J05
(Refer to figure 49.) Area C on the airport depicted is classified as a

A — stabilized area.
B — multiple heliport.
C — closed runway.

4-43. Answer C. GFDPPM 4-25 (AIM)
A closed runway is marked by X's painted on its surface.

4-44   J05
(Refer to figure 50.) The arrows that appear on the end of the north/south runway indicate that the area

A — may be used only for taxiing.
B — is usable for taxiing, takeoff, and landing.
C — cannot be used for landing, but may be used for taxiing and takeoff.

4-45   J05
The numbers 9 and 27 on a runway indicate that the runway is oriented approximately

A — 009° and 027° true.
B — 090° and 270° true.
C — 090° and 270° magnetic.

4-46   J13
(Refer to figure 50.) Select the proper traffic pattern and runway for landing.

A — Left-hand traffic and Runway 18.
B — Right-hand traffic and Runway 18.
C — Left-hand traffic and Runway 22.

4-44. Answer C. GFDPPM 4-24 (AIM)
See explanation for Question 4-40.

4-45. Answer C. GFDPPM 4-17 (AIM)
Runway numbers correspond to the magnetic, not true, direction, and are rounded to the nearest 10°, with the last zero omitted.

4-46. Answer B. GFDPPM 4-17 (AIM)
The wind indicates a landing should be made to the south, and the segmented circle shows right-hand traffic for Runway 18. Answer (A) is wrong because the segmented circle indicates a right-hand pattern for Runway 18. Answer (C) is wrong because Runway 22 is closed.

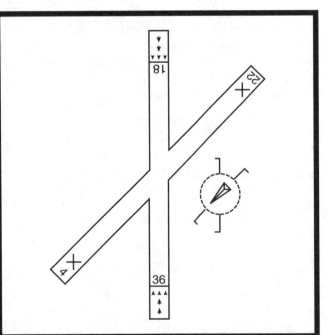

FIGURE 50.—Airport Diagram.

4-47   J13
(Refer to figure 50.) If the wind is as shown by the landing direction indicator, the pilot should land on

A — Runway 18 and expect a crosswind from the right.
B — Runway 22 directly into the wind.
C — Runway 36 and expect a crosswind from the right.

4-47. Answer A. GFDPPM 4-20 (AIM)
The wind is from the southwest, so a landing on Runway 18 would provide both a headwind component and a crosswind from the right. Answer (B) is wrong because Runway 22 is closed. Answer (C) is wrong because landing on Runway 36 would be made with a tailwind and a crosswind from the left.

4-48   J13
(Refer to figure 51.) The segmented circle indicates that the airport traffic is

A — left-hand for Runway 18 and right-hand for Runway 36.
B — right-hand for Runway 9 and left-hand for Runway 27.
C — left-hand for Runway 36 and right-hand for Runway 18.

4-48. Answer C. GFDPPM 4-21 (AIM)
The segmented circle indicates left-hand traffic for Runway 36, and right-hand traffic for Runway 18. Answer (A) is opposite this. Answer (B) is wrong because left-hand traffic is used for Runway 9 and right-hand traffic for Runway 27.

4-49   J13
(Refer to figure 51.) The traffic patterns indicated in the segmented circle have been arranged to avoid flights over an area to the

A — south of the airport.
B — north of the airport.
C — southeast of the airport.

4-49. Answer C. GFDPPM 4-21 (AIM)
Since the traffic pattern for the north-south runway is west of the field, and the pattern for the east-west runway is north of the field, there should be no flights southeast of the airport.

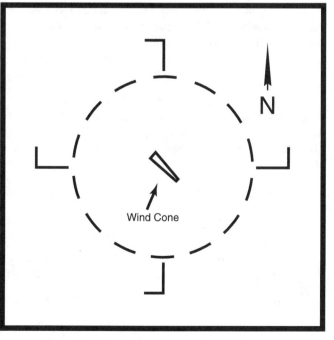

FIGURE 51.—Airport Landing Indicator.

4-50   J13
(Refer to figure 51 on page 4-13.) The segmented circle indicates that a landing on Runway 26 will be with a

A — right-quartering headwind.
B — left-quartering headwind.
C — right-quartering tailwind.

4-50. Answer A. GFDPPM 4-21 (AIM)
Since the wind cone shows wind from the northwest, a landing to the west will provide a right-quartering headwind.

4-51   J13
(Refer to figure 51 on page 4-13.) Which runway and traffic pattern should be used as indicated by the wind cone in the segmented circle?

A — Right-hand traffic on Runway 18.
B — Left-hand traffic on Runway 36.
C — Right-hand traffic on Runway 9.

4-51. Answer B. GFDPPM 4-21 (AIM)
With wind from the northwest, landing on Runway 36 would provide a quartering headwind. Answers (A) and (C) are poor choices because you would be landing with a tailwind.

4-52   J13
Who should not participate in the Land and Hold Short Operations (LAHSO) program?

A — Recreational pilots only.
B — Military pilots.
C — Student pilots.

4-52. Answer C. GFDPPM 4-30 (AIM 4-3-11)
Student pilots or pilots not familiar with LAHSO should not accept LAHSO clearances. Recreational and military pilots have no limitations, provided they are familiar with the LHASO program.

4-53   J13
Who has final authority to accept or decline any land and hold short (LAHSO) clearance?

A — Pilot-in-command.
B — Owner/operator.
C — Second-in-command.

4-53. Answer A. GFDPPM 4-30 (AIM 4-3-11)
The pilot in command (PIC) has the final authority to accept or decline any LHASO clearances. The PIC should decline a LAHSO clearance if he/she determines it will compromise safety.

4-54   J13
When should pilots decline a land and hold short (LAHSO) clearance?

A — When it will compromise safety.
B — Only when the tower operator concurs.
C — Pilots can not decline clearance.

4-54. Answer A. GFDPPM 4-30 (AIM 4-3-11)
The pilot in command (PIC) has the final authority to accept or decline any LHASO clearances. The PIC should decline a LAHSO clearance if he/she determines it will compromise safety.

4-55   J13
Where is the "Available Landing Distance" (ALD) data published for an airport that utilizes Land and Hold Short Operations (LAHSO) published?

A — Airport/Facility Directory (A/FD).
B — 14 CFR Part 91, General Operating and Flight Rules.
C — Aeronautical Information Manual (AIM).

4-55. Answer A. GFDPPM 4-30 (AIM 4-3-11)
ALD data is published in the special notices section of the Airport/Facility Directory (A/FD) and in the U.S. Terminal Procedures Publications.

4-56   J13
What is the minimum visibility for a pilot to receive a land and hold short (LAHSO) clearance?

A — 3 nautical miles
B — 3 statute miles.
C — 1 statute mile.

4-56. Answer B. (AIM 4-3-11)
Pilots should only receive a LAHSO clearance when there is a minimum ceiling of 1,000 feet and 3 statute miles visibility.

SECTION C
AERONAUTICAL CHARTS

Maps are essential in turning imaginary excursions into actual trips. Aeronautical charts are maps which provide a detailed portrayal of an area's topography and include aeronautical and navigational information. Before you learn about the specific features and symbology of aeronautical charts, you need to understand some basic concepts which apply to representations of the earth's surface on maps.

LATITUDE AND LONGITUDE
1. In the United States, latitude increases as you travel north, and longitude increases as you travel west. Each tick mark on the sectional chart represents one minute of latitude or longitude.

SECTIONAL CHARTS
2. A blue segmented circle on a sectional chart depicts Class D airspace.
3. Others- refer to figures

CHART SYMBOLS
4. (Refer to figures)

4-57   H340
(Refer to figure 21, area 3 on page 4-18.) Determine the approximate latitude and longitude of Currituck County Airport.

A — 36°24′N — 76°01′W.
B — 36°48′N — 76°01′W.
C — 47°26′N — 75°58′W.

4-57. Answer A. GFDPPM 4-41 (PHB)
This airport is located to the northeast of the number "3." Starting at the bottom of the chart at the 36° latitude, count upwards along the longitudinal line until you are opposite the airport. Each tick mark represents one minute of latitude, so the airport is located at 36°24′N. It also lies slightly more than one tick mark west of the 76° longitude line. In the United States (Western Hemisphere), longitude increases as you go west. Therefore, the airport is located at 36°24′N and 76°01′W.

4-58   H340
(Refer to figure 22, area 2 on page 4-19.) Which airport is located at approximately 47°39′30″N latitude and 100°53′00″W longitude?

A — Linrud.
B — Crooked Lake.
C — Johnson.

4-58. Answer B. GFDPPM 4-41 (PHB)
Note that the 48° latitude line crosses the top third of the chart. The latitude line along the bottom third is 30′ less, or 47°30′N. Count up 9-1/2 tick marks (minutes) for 47°39′30″N. Since the airport's longitude is less than 101°W, move to the right of the 101° line seven tick marks to arrive at 100°53′00″W. This intersection is at Crooked Lake Airport.

4-59   J11
(Refer to figure 22, area 2 on page 4-19.) The CTAF/MULTICOM frequency for Garrison Airport is

A — 123.0 MHz.
B — 122.8 MHz.
C — 122.9 MHz.

4-59. Answer C. GFDPPM 4-47 (AIM)
The frequency next to the CTAF symbol (the letter "C" in a dark circle) is the multicom frequency of 122.9.

4-60   J11
(Refer to figure 23, area 2 on page 4-20; and figure 32 on page 4-25.) At Coeur D'Alene, which frequency should be used as a Common Traffic Advisory Frequency (CTAF) to self-announce position and intentions?

A — 122.05 MHz.
B — 122.1/108.8 MHz.
C — 122.8 MHz.

4-61   J11
(Refer to figure 23, area 2 on page 4-20; and figure 32 on page 4-25.) At Coeur D'Alene, which frequency should be used as a Common Traffic Advisory Frequency (CTAF) to monitor airport traffic?

A — 122.05 MHz.
B — 122.8 MHz.
C — 135.075 MHz.

4-62   J11
(Refer to figure 23, area 2 on page 4-20; and figure 32 on page 4-25.) What is the correct UNICOM frequency to be used at Coeur D'Alene to request fuel?

A — 122.1/108.8 MHz.
B — 122.8 MHz.
C — 135.075 MHz.

4-63   J11
(Refer to figure 26, area 3 on page 4-23.) If Redbird Tower is not in operation, which frequency should be used as a Common Traffic Advisory Frequency (CTAF) to monitor airport traffic?

A — 120.3 MHz.
B — 122.95 MHz.
C — 126.35 MHz.

4-64   J11
(Refer to figure 27, area 4 on page 4-24.) The CTAF/UNICOM frequency at Jamestown Airport is

A — 122.0 MHz.
B — 123.0 MHz.
C — 123.6 MHz.

4-65   J11
(Refer to figure 27, area 6 on page 4-24.) What is the CTAF/UNICOM frequency at Barnes County Airport?

A — 122.0 MHz.
B — 122.8 MHz.
C — 123.6 MHz.

4-60. Answer C. GFDPPM 4-47 (AIM)
In this example, the airport data block located near Coeur D'Alene airport lists 122.8 as the CTAF frequency that should be used to self-announce your position and your intentions. In addition, the *Airport/Facility Directory* excerpt (figure 32) specifies 122.8 as both the CTAF and UNICOM frequency. The frequency 122.05 (answer A) is depicted on the VOR/DME box, and is used to communicate with Boise FSS. 108.8 (answer B) is the frequency used to tune and identify the Coeur D'Alene VOR/DME.

4-61. Answer B. GFDPPM 4-47 (AIM)
At non-towered airports, the CTAF frequency is used to self-announce position or intentions. Figure 32 lists the CTAF/Unicom Frequency as 122.8 MHz. The CTAF symbol in Figure 23 is beside the frequency of 122.8 MHz.

4-62. Answer B. GFDPPM 4-47 (AIM)
Use the Unicom/CTAF frequency of 122.8 to request fuel, transportation, or other airport information of a general nature.

4-63. Answer A. GFDPPM 4-47 (AIM)
Since the tower frequency, designated "CT - 120.3" is next to the CTAF symbol, the CTAF frequency is the tower frequency. UNICOM is 122.95 (answer B), and ATIS is 126.35 (answer C).

4-64. Answer B. GFDPPM 4-47 (AIM)
The CTAF symbol is next to the frequency 123.0. Answer (A) is wrong because 122.0 is the standard Enroute Fight Advisory Service (Flight Watch) frequency. Answer (C) is incorrect because 123.6 is an FSS frequency.

4-65. Answer B. GFDPPM 4-47 (AIM)
The CTAF symbol is next to the UNICOM frequency 122.8. 122.0 is the frequency for Flight Watch, and 123.6 is an FSS frequency used for airport advisory service.

LEGEND 1.—Sectional Aeronautical Chart

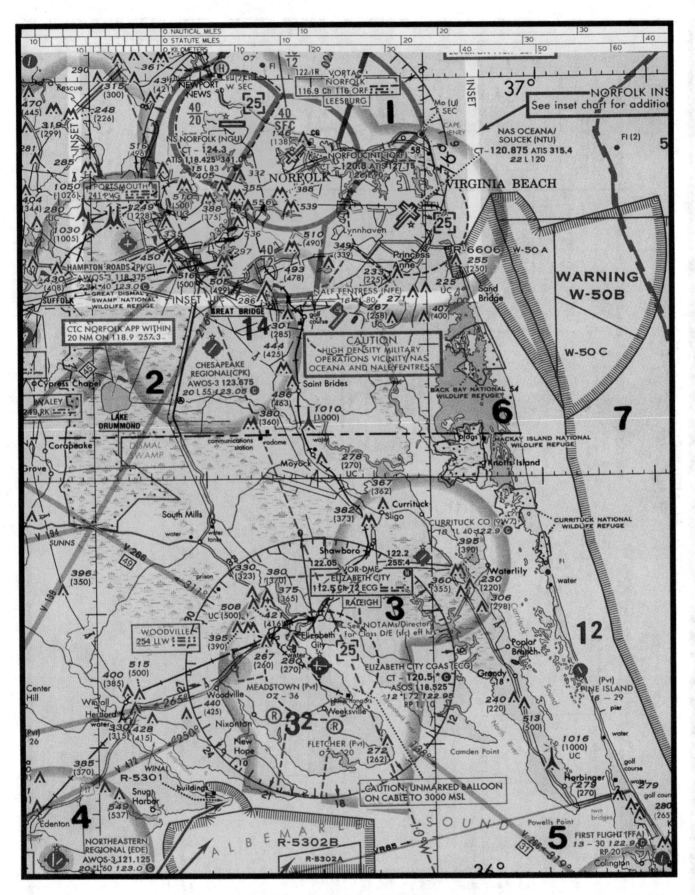

FIGURE 21.—Sectional Chart Excerpt.

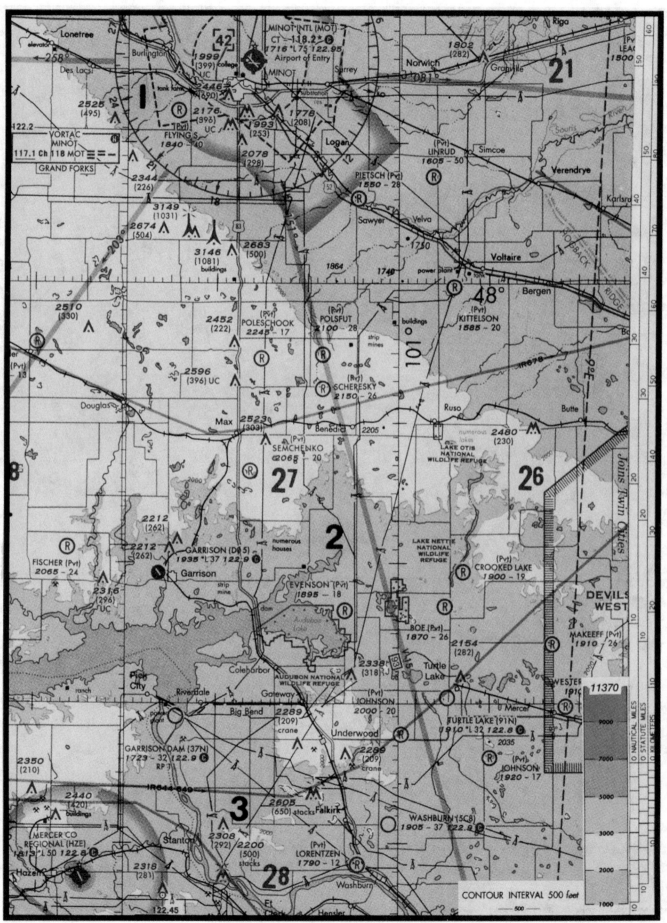

FIGURE 22.—Sectional Chart Excerpt.

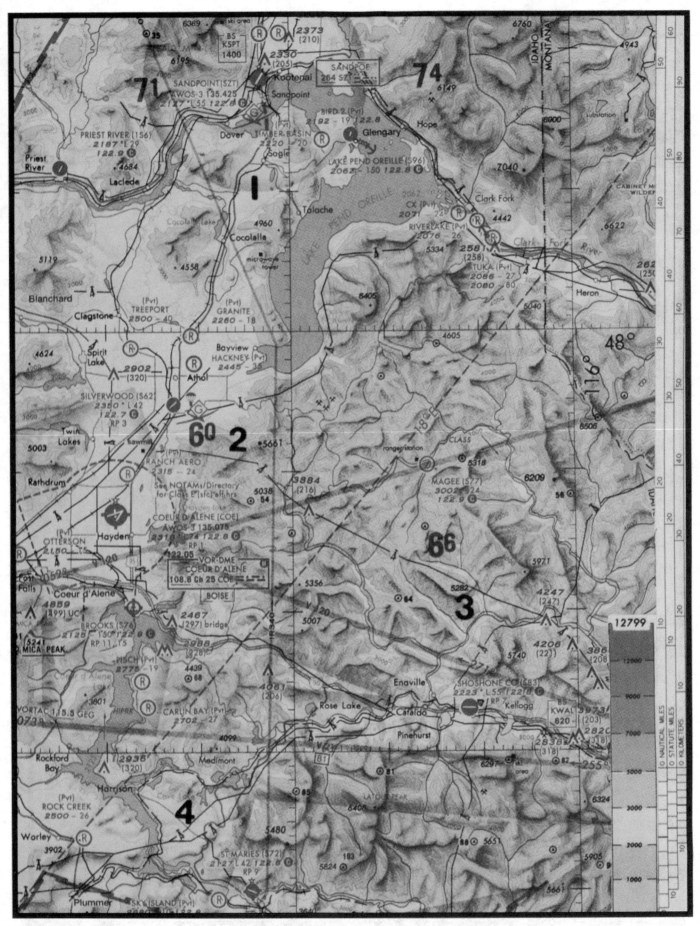

FIGURE 23.—Sectional Chart Excerpt.

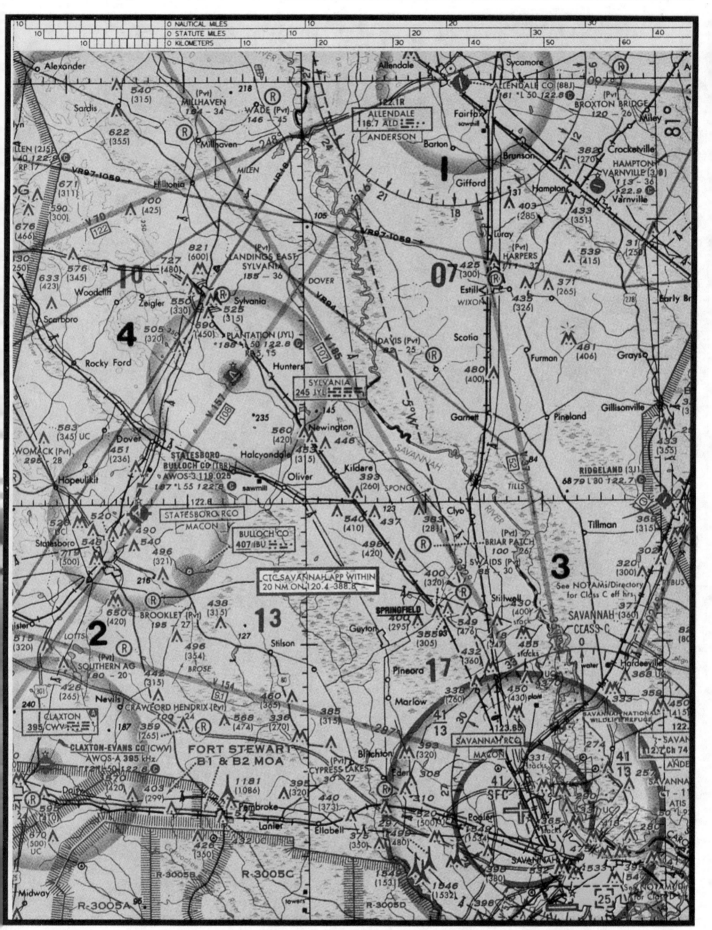

FIGURE 24.—Sectional Chart Excerpt.

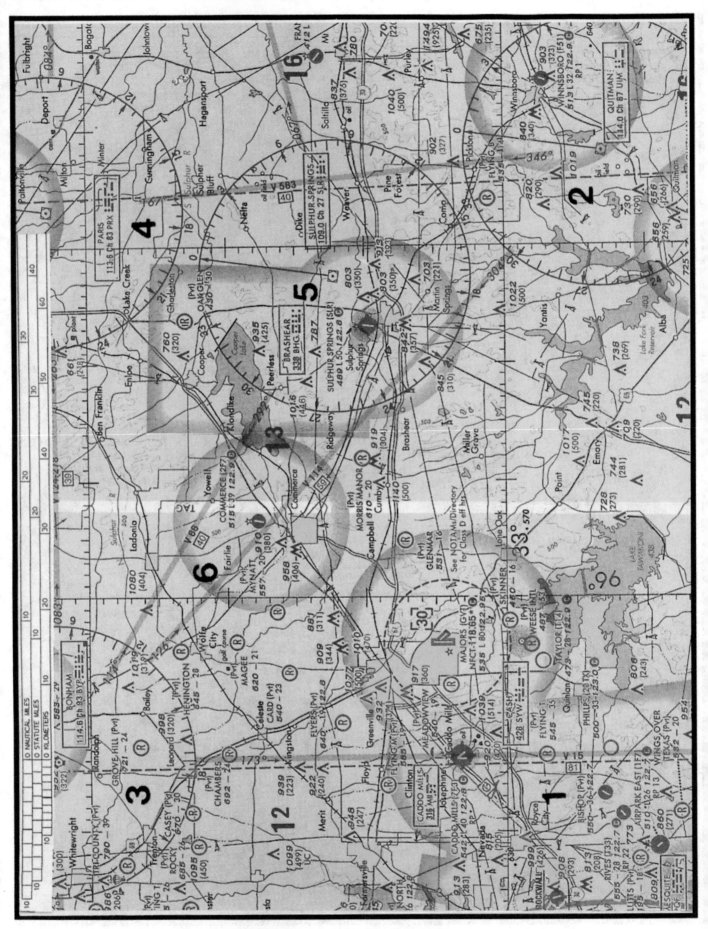

FIGURE 25.—Sectional Chart Excerpt.

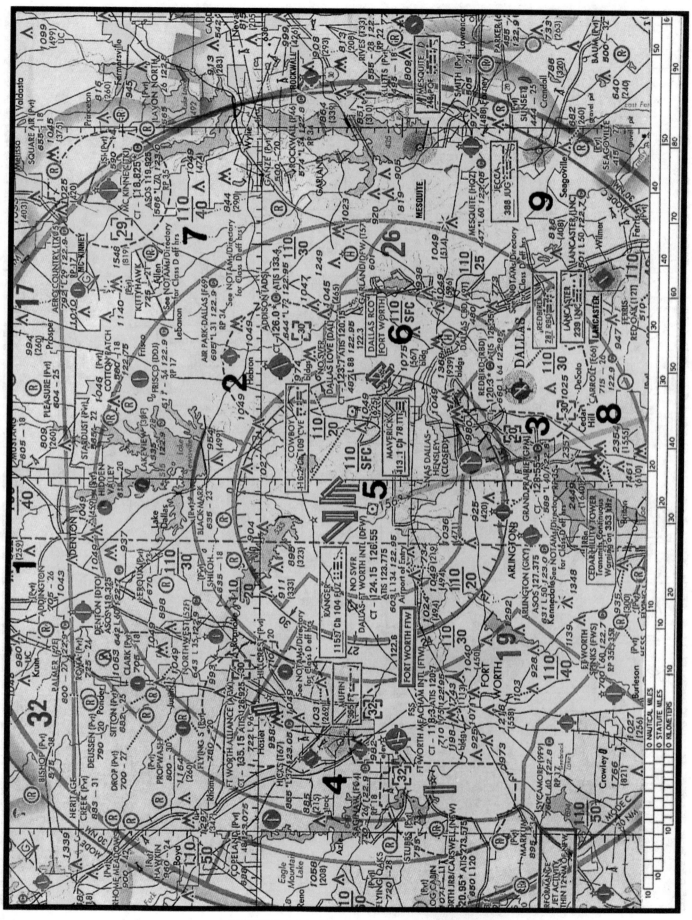

FIGURE 26.—Sectional Chart Excerpt.

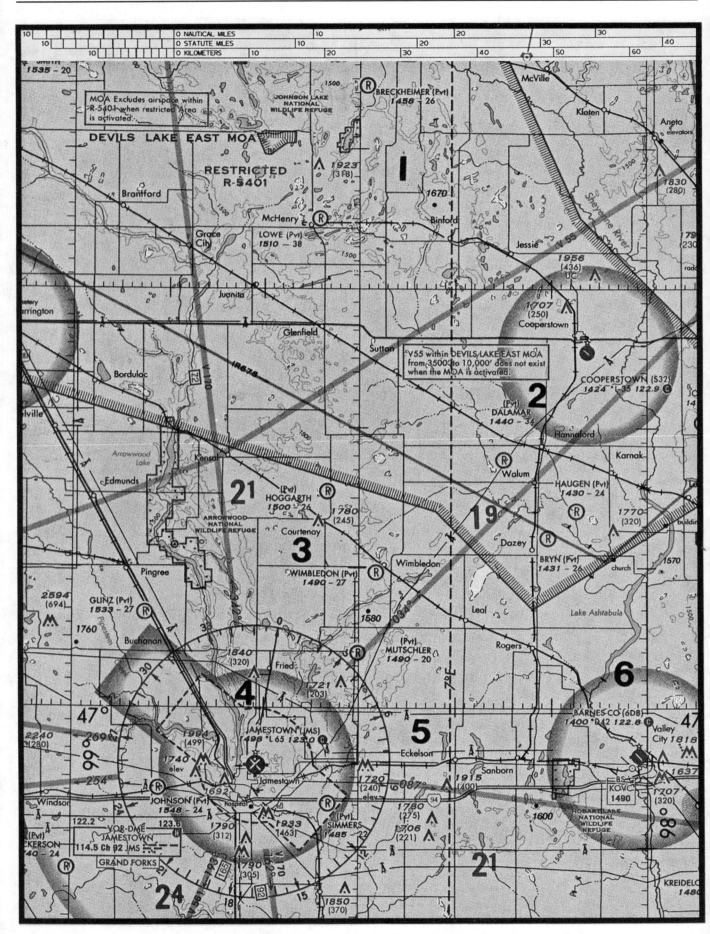

FIGURE 27.—Sectional Chart Excerpt.

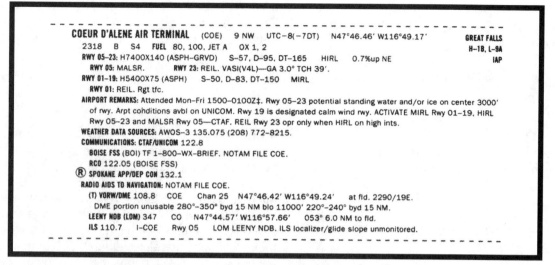

FIGURE 32.—Airport/Facility Directory Excerpt.

4-66   J28
(Refer to figure 27, area 3 on page 4-24.) When flying over Arrowwood National Wildlife Refuge, a pilot should fly no lower than

A — 2,000 feet AGL.
B — 2,500 feet AGL.
C — 3,000 feet AGL.

4-66. Answer A. GFDPPM 4-44 (AIM)
Pilots are requested to maintain a minimum of 2,000 feet above National Wildlife Refuges.

4-67   J37
(Refer to figure 22 on page 4-19.) On what frequency can a pilot receive Hazardous Inflight Weather Advisory Service (HIWAS) in the vicinity of area 1?

A — 117.1 MHz.
B — 118.0 MHz.
C — 122.0 MHz.

4-67. Answer A. GFDPPM 4-48 (Chart Legend)
The circled "H" in the corner of the Minot VORTAC indicates that weather information (HIWAS) is available over the VOR frequency, which is 117.1 (answer A). The TACAN channel is 118, but does not broadcast HIWAS. The frequency 118.0 MHz (answer B) is not listed. 122.0 (answer C) is the standard EFAS frequency.

4-68   J37
(Refer to figure 21, area 5 on page 4-18.) The CAUTION box denotes what hazard to aircraft?

A — Unmarked balloon on cable to 3,000 feet MSL.
B — Unmarked balloon on cable to 3,000 feet AGL.
C — Unmarked blimp hangers at 300 feet MSL.

4-68. Answer A. GFDPPM 4-51 (Chart Legend)
The CAUTION box indicates an unmarked balloon on a cable to 3,000 feet MSL. No other hazards to aircraft are included in the CAUTION box.

4-69   J37
(Refer to figure 21, area 2 on page 4-18.) The flag symbol at Lake Drummond represents a

A — compulsory reporting point for Norfolk Class C airspace.
B — compulsory reporting point for Hampton Roads Airport.
C — visual checkpoint used to identify position for initial callup to Norfolk Approach Control.

4-69. Answer C. GFDPPM 4-51 (Chart Legend)
The flag represents a visual checkpoint used to identify your position for approach control. Since the flag is 22 nautical miles southwest of Norfolk International Airport, it can be assumed that the checkpoint is used when contacting Norfolk Approach. The flag does not indicate a compulsory reporting point (answers A and B).

4-70   J37
(Refer to figure 21, area 2 on page 4-18.) The elevation of the Chesapeake Regional Airport is

A — 20 feet.
B — 360 feet.
C — 36 feet.

4-70. Answer A. GFDPPM 4-47 (Chart Legend)
The elevation is the first number listed on the last line of this airport description. In this case, it is 20 feet.

4-71   J37
(Refer to figure 22 on page 4-19.) The terrain elevation of the light tan area between Minot (area 1) and Audubon Lake (area 2) varies from

A — sea level to 2,000 feet MSL.
B — 2,000 feet to 2,500 feet MSL.
C — 2,000 feet to 2,700 feet MSL.

4-71. Answer B. GFDPPM 4-43 (Chart Legend)
The colored scale shows that the tan area represents terrain above 2,000 feet MSL. In addition, the legend states that the contour interval is 500 feet. Between Minot and Audubon Lake, there are no contour lines in the tan area, which indicates there is no terrain above 2,500 feet. A check of the airports in this area shows their elevations are all less than 2,500 feet. In addition, tower heights in MSL minus their AGL heights all yield base elevations less than 2,500 feet.

4-72   J37
(Refer to figure 22 on page 4-19.) Which public use airports depicted are indicated as having fuel?

A — Minot Intl. (area 1) and Garrison (area 2).
B — Minot Intl. (area 1) and Mercer County Regional Airport (area 3).
C — Mercer County Regional Airport (area 3) and Garrison (area 2).

4-72. Answer B. GFDPPM 4-46 (Chart Legend)
Tick marks around an airport symbol indicate fuel is available.

4-73   J37
(Refer to figure 24 on page 4-21.) The flag symbols at Statesboro Bullock County Airport, Claxton-Evans County Airport, and Ridgeland Airport are

A — airports with special traffic patterns.
B — outer boundaries of Savannah Class C airspace.
C — visual checkpoints to identify position for initial callup prior to entering Savannah Class C airspace.

4-73. Answer C. GFDPPM 4-47 (Chart Legend)
The flag symbols represent checkpoints used to identify the aircraft position for Approach Control. In this case, they are visual checkpoints used when contacting Savannah Approach Control.

4-74   J37
(Refer to figure 24, area 3 on page 4-21.) What is the height of the lighted obstacle approximately 6 nautical miles southwest of Savannah International?

A —1,500 feet MSL.
B —1,531 feet AGL.
C —1,549 feet MSL.

4-74. Answer C. GFDPPM 4-51 (Chart Legend)
About 6 nautical miles southwest of the center of Savannah International airport is a lighted obstacle with its elevation marked as 1,549 (1,534). The first number is height in MSL, and the number in parentheses is height AGL. Answer (B), although only three feet off, is not as good as Answer (C), which exactly agrees with the MSL altitude of the obstacle in question.

4-75   J37
(Refer to figure 24, area 3.) The top of the group obstruction approximately 11 nautical miles from the Savannah VORTAC on the 340° radial is

A — 400 feet AGL.
B — 455 feet AGL.
C — 432 feet AGL.

4-76   J37
(Refer to figure 25, area 1 on page 4-22.) What minimum altitude is necessary to vertically clear the obstacle on the northeast side of Airpark East Airport by 500 feet?

A — 1,010 feet MSL.
B — 1,273 feet MSL.
C — 1,283 feet MSL.

4-77   J37
(Refer to figure 25, area 2 on page 4-22.) What minimum altitude is necessary to vertically clear the obstacle on the southeast side of Winnsboro Airport by 500 feet?

A — 823 feet MSL.
B — 1,013 feet MSL.
C — 1,403 feet MSL.

4-78   J37
(Refer to figure 26, area 2 on page 4-23.) The control tower frequency for Addison Airport is

A — 122.95 MHz.
B — 126.0 MHz.
C — 133.4 MHz.

4-79   J37
(Refer to figure 26, area 8 on page 4-23.) What minimum altitude is required to fly over the Cedar Hill TV towers in the congested area south of NAS Dallas?

A — 2,555 feet MSL.
B — 3,349 feet MSL.
C — 3,449 feet MSL.

4-80   J37
(Refer to figure 26, area 5 on page 4-23.) The navigation facility at Dallas-Ft. Worth International (DFW) is a

A — VOR.
B — VORTAC.
C — VOR/DME.

4-75. Answer B. GFDPPM 4-51 (Chart Legend)
The callout below the group obstruction at the Savannah 340° radial for 11 n.m. is 455 feet MSL. If there was a callout in parentheses, it would indicate an AGL altitude.

4-76. Answer B. GFDPPM 4-51 (Chart Legend)
To clear the obstacle by 500 feet, you need to add 500 to the obstacle height of 773 feet MSL. The answer is 1,273 feet MSL. The airport elevation (510) plus 500 feet is 1,010 feet MSL (answer A). Answer (C), 1,283 feet MSL, can be derived by adding the airport elevation to the obstacle height.

4-77. Answer C. GFDPPM 4-51 (Chart Legend)
In this question, you need to add 500 feet to the obstacle height of 903 feet MSL. The answer is 1,403 feet MSL. Answer (A) can be found by adding 500 feet to 323 feet, which is the AGL height. However, this would place the aircraft below the top of the 903-foot obstacle. Answer (B) can be found by adding 500 feet to the airport elevation of 513 feet.

4-78. Answer B. GFDPPM 4-47 (Chart Legend)
The tower frequency at Addison Airport is 126.0 as indicated by the letters "CT." Answer (A) is wrong because 122.95 is the UNICOM frequency. 133.4 (answer C) is the ATIS frequency.

4-79. Answer C. GFDPPM 4-51 (14 CFR Part 91.119)
Since this is a congested area, add 1,000 feet to the highest obstacle. The elevation (height) of these towers is 2,449 feet MSL (1,640 feet AGL), so the minimum altitude would be 3,449 feet MSL.

4-80. Answer C. GFDPPM 4-48 (Chart Legend)
This symbol appears immediately south of the runways at DFW. According to Legend 1, which immediately precedes the sample sectional charts, a hexagon surrounded by a square is a VOR/DME symbol.

4-81   J28
Pilots flying over a national wildlife refuge are
requested to fly no lower than

A — 1,000 feet AGL.
B — 2,000 feet AGL.
C — 3,000 feet AGL.

4-81. Answer B. GFDPPM 4-44 (AIM)
Pilots should fly no lower than 2,000 feet AGL over a
national wildlife area.

SECTION D
AIRSPACE

To efficiently manage the large amount of air traffic that traverses the sky each day, the airspace above the United States is divided into several classes. In each airspace class, specific rules apply. For example, there are VFR weather minimums which you must maintain. In some areas, you need to communicate with ATC and comply with pilot certification and aircraft equipment requirements. In addition, the airspace over the United States includes special use and other airspace areas where certain restrictions apply or specific ATC services are provided.

CLASS G

1. VFR flight in Class G (uncontrolled) airspace requires 1 mile of visibility and clear of clouds.
2. Night VFR in Class G requires 3 miles visibility, and 500 feet below, 1000 feet above and 2000 feet horizontal distance from clouds.
3. (Refer to figures.)

CONTROLLED

4. Below 10,000 feet MSL in Class C, D and E airspace, the cloud clearances are 500 feet below, 1000 feet above and 2000 feet horizontal. Flight visibility is 3 statute miles. Above 10,000 feet MSL in Class C, D and E airspace, the cloud clearances are 1 mile horizontal and 1000 feet above and below. Flight visibility is 5 statute miles.
5. An operable 4096-code transponder with an encoding altimeter is required in Class A, Class C and within 30 n.m. of a primary Class B airport (within 10,000 feet of the surface).
6. Federal airways are considered Class E airspace; the same minimums apply. They extend four nautical miles on each side of the airway centerline. Altitudes normally include 1200 AGL up to 17,999 feet MSL.

CLASS D

7. VFR flight minimums in Class D airspace are 3 s.m. visibility and 1000 feet ceiling. Airspace becomes Class D only when there is an operating control tower.
8. Two-way radio communications are required for taking off and landing at an airport with an operating control tower.
9. When approaching Class D airspace, you must contact the primary airport's control tower. When departing a non-towered satellite airport, you must contact the primary airport's control tower as soon as practicable after takeoff.
10. The lateral dimensions of Class D airspace are based on the instrument procedures for which the controlled airspace is established.

CLASS C

11. Two-way communications must be established with approach control before entering Class C airspace.
12. Two way radio communications and an operable 4096 code transponder with an encoding altimeter are required for operating in Class C airspace.
13. The limits of Class C are normally 4000 feet AGL, with an outer circle radius of 10 n.m., and an outer area radius of 20 n.m.

CLASS B

14. A pilot must have either a private pilot certificate, or a student pilot certificate with a logbook endorsement from an appropriately rated instructor.
15. Two-way radio communication must be established, and a clearance granted, before the pilot enters Class B airspace.
16. Class B day VFR minimums are 3 miles visibility and clear of clouds.

CLASS A

17. The altimeter should be set to 29.92 at and above 18,000 feet MSL.
18. VFR flight is prohibited in Class A airspace.

SPECIAL VFR

19. A special VFR clearance allows the pilot to operate VFR within Class D airspace when the visibility is at least 1 mile and the aircraft can remain clear of clouds.
20. To operate under special VFR at night you must have a current instrument rating, and the airplane must be equipped for instrument flight.
21. Special VFR for fixed-wing aircraft is not authorized at airports with "No Special VFR" written over the airport identification name.

SPECIAL USE AIRSPACE

Special use airspace serves to confine certain flight activities and to place limitations on aircraft operations which are not part of these activities.

ALERT

22. All pilots flying within an alert area are equally responsible for collision avoidance.

MOAs

23. MOAs signify high density military training activities.
24. When operating VFR in an MOA, pilots should exercise extreme caution when military training is being conducted.

WARNING

25. Warning areas often contain hazards such as aerial gunnery and guided missiles.

RESTRICTED

26. Pilots may fly through a restricted area only with the controlling agency's authorization.

MILITARY TRAINING ROUTES

27. IR designates an IFR military training route, where aircraft may fly at speeds in excess of 250 knots.
28. When the route is a three digit number, the route contains one or more sections above 1500 feet AGL.

4-82   A60
The width of a Federal Airway from either side of the centerline is

A — 4 nautical miles.
B — 6 nautical miles.
C — 8 nautical miles.

4-82. Answer A. GFDPPM 4-60 (FAR 71.75)
Federal Airways include the airspace within four nautical miles each side of the airway centerline.

4-83   A60
Unless otherwise specified, Federal Airways include that Class E airspace extending upward from

A — 700 feet above the surface up to and including 17,999 feet MSL.
B — 1,200 feet above the surface up to and including 17,999 feet MSL.
C — the surface up to and including 18,000 feet MSL.

4-83. Answer B. GFDPPM 4-60 (AIM)
Federal Airways normally begin at 1,200 feet AGL and extend up to, but not including, 18,000 feet MSL. Answer (A) is not correct because 700 feet is the floor of Class E airspace associated with an airport for which an approved instrument approach procedure has been published. Answer (C) is wrong because airways do not normally begin at the surface, and do not include 18,000 feet MSL.

4-84   A60
Normal VFR operations in Class D airspace with an operating control tower require the ceiling and visibility to be at least

A — 1,000 feet and 1 mile.
B — 1,000 feet and 3 miles.
C — 2,500 feet and 3 miles.

4-85   B08
At what altitude shall the altimeter be set to 29.92, when climbing to cruising flight level?

A — 14,500 feet MSL.
B — 18,000 feet MSL.
C — 24,000 feet MSL.

4-86   B08
A blue segmented circle on a Sectional Chart depicts which class airspace?

A — Class B.
B — Class C.
C — Class D.

4-87   B08
Airspace at an airport with a part-time control tower is classified as Class D airspace only

A — when the weather minimums are below basic VFR.
B — when the associated control tower is in operation.
C — when the associated Flight Service Station is in operation.

4-88   B08
Unless otherwise authorized, two-way radio communications with Air Traffic Control are required for landings or takeoffs

A — at all tower controlled airports regardless of weather conditions.
B — at all tower controlled airports only when weather conditions are less than VFR.
C — at all tower controlled airports within Class D airspace only when weather conditions are less than VFR.

4-89   B08
Two-way radio communication must be established with the Air Traffic Control facility having jurisdiction over the area prior to entering which class airspace?

A — Class C.
B — Class E.
C — Class G.

4-84. Answer B. GFDPPM 4-82 (FAR 91.155)
In order to operate in Class D airspace, the VFR visibility minimum is three statute miles. In addition, the ceiling must be at least 1,000 feet. Answer (A) is incorrect because the visibility is less than that required. The 2,500 feet in answer (C) is the top of most Class D airspace areas.

4-85. Answer B. GFDPPM 4-71 (FAR 91.121)
To standardize altimeter settings in Class A airspace, all pilots are required to set their altimeters to 29.92 at and above 18,000 feet MSL.

4-86. Answer C. GFDPPM 4-79 (Chart Legend)
Class D airspace is designated on sectional charts by a blue segmented circle. Class B airspace is indicated by a solid blue line. Class C airspace is designated by a solid magenta line. Therefore, answers (A) and (B) are incorrect.

4-87. Answer B. GFDPPM 4-62 (AIM)
In order for airspace to be classified as Class D there must be an operating control tower. Answers (A) and (C) are incorrect because they do not address the part-time control tower.

4-88. Answer A. GFDPPM 4-63 (FAR 91.129)
When operating at an airport where a control tower is in operation, you must be in radio contact with ATC whether or not VFR conditions exist. Therefore, answers (B) and (C) are incorrect.

4-89. Answer A. GFDPPM 4-65 (FAR 91.130)
You must establish two-way communications prior to entering a Class C airspace area, and maintain it while operating within the Class C airspace. Answers (B) and (C) are wrong because two-way communications are not required in Class E or G airspace.

4-90   B08
What minimum radio equipment is required for operation within Class C airspace?

A — Two-way radio communications equipment and a 4096-code transponder.
B — Two-way radio communications equipment, a 4096-code transponder, and DME.
C — Two-way radio communications equipment, a 4096-code transponder, and an encoding altimeter.

4-91   B08
What minimum pilot certification is required for operation within Class B airspace?

A — Recreational Pilot Certificate.
B — Private Pilot Certificate or Student Pilot Certificate with appropriate logbook endorsements.
C — Private Pilot Certificate with an instrument rating.

4-92   B08
What minimum pilot certification is required for operation within Class B airspace?

A — Private Pilot Certificate or Student Pilot Certificate with appropriate logbook endorsements.
B — Commercial Pilot Certificate.
C — Private Pilot Certificate with an instrument rating.

4-93   B08
What minimum radio equipment is required for VFR operation within Class B airspace?

A — Two-way radio communications equipment and a 4096-code transponder.
B — Two-way radio communications equipment, a 4096-code transponder, and an encoding altimeter.
C — Two-way radio communications equipment, a 4096-code transponder, an encoding altimeter, and a VOR or TACAN receiver.

4-94   B08
An operable 4096-code transponder and Mode C encoding altimeter are required in

A — Class B airspace and within 30 miles of the Class B primary airport.
B — Class D airspace.
C — Class E airspace below 10,000 feet MSL.

4-90. Answer C. GFDPPM 4-65 (FAR 91.130, 91.215)
To operate in a Class C airspace area, you are required to have both a two-way radio and a 4096-code transponder with encoding altimeter. Answer (A) does not include the requirement for an encoding altimeter and DME is not a requirement for Class C airspace (answer B).

4-91. Answer B. GFDPPM 4-65 (FAR 91.131)
To operate in a Class B airspace area, a pilot must hold a private pilot certificate. However, within certain Class B airspace areas, student pilot operations may be conducted after receiving specific training and a logbook endorsement from an authorized flight instructor.

4-92. Answer A. GFDPPM 4-65 (FAR 91.131)
To operate in a Class B airspace area, a pilot must hold a private pilot certificate. However, within certain Class B airspace areas, student pilot operations may be conducted after receiving specific training and a logbook endorsement from an authorized flight instructor.

4-93. Answer B. GFDPPM 4-65 (FAR 91.131)
VFR operations within Class B airspace areas require a two-way radio and a 4096-code transponder with an encoding altimeter. Answer (A) does not include the requirement for an encoding altimeter, and VOR or TACAN receivers are only required for instrument flight (answer C).

4-94. Answer A. GFDPPM 4-65 (FAR 91.131)
A 4096-code transponder with an encoding altimeter is required for operations within a Class B airspace area. It is not required in Class D airspace or Class E airspace below 10,000 feet MSL (answers B and C).

4-95   B08
In which type of airspace are VFR flights prohibited?

A — Class A.
B — Class B.
C — Class C.

4-95. Answer A. GFDPPM 4-71 (FAR 91.135)
Only IFR operations are allowed in Class A airspace. VFR flights are allowed in Class B and C airspace if authorized by ATC.

4-96   B09
During operations within controlled airspace at altitudes of less than 1,200 feet AGL, the minimum horizontal distance from clouds requirement for VFR flight is

A — 1,000 feet.
B — 1,500 feet.
C — 2,000 feet.

4-96. Answer C. GFDPPM 4-82 (FAR 91.155)
In controlled airspace, other than Class B, below 10,000 feet, it does not matter whether you are above or below 1,200 feet AGL. The VFR cloud clearance is 2,000 feet horizontal.

4-97   B09
What minimum visibility and clearance from clouds are required for VFR operations in Class G airspace at 700 feet AGL or below during daylight hours?

A — 1 mile visibility and clear of clouds.
B — 1 mile visibility, 500 feet below, 1,000 feet above, and 2,000 feet horizontal clearance from clouds.
C — 3 miles visibility and clear of clouds.

4-97. Answer A. GFDPPM 4-82 (FAR 91.155)
For VFR flight in uncontrolled airspace below 1,200 feet during daytime, you are only required to have 1 mile visibility and remain clear of clouds. Answer (B) applies between 1,200 feet AGL and 10,000 feet MSL during daytime in uncontrolled airspace. Answer (C) does not apply to any airspace.

4-98   B09
What minimum flight visibility is required for VFR flight operations on an airway below 10,000 feet MSL?

A — 1 mile.
B — 3 miles.
C — 4 miles.

4-98. Answer B. GFDPPM 4-82 (FAR 91.155)
Since an airway is Class E airspace, the minimum visibility below 10,000 feet MSL is 3 statute miles.

4-99   B09
The minimum distance from clouds required for VFR operations on an airway below 10,000 feet MSL is

A — remain clear of clouds.
B — 500 feet below, 1,000 feet above, and 2,000 feet horizontally.
C — 500 feet above, 1,000 feet below, and 2,000 feet horizontally.

4-99. Answer B. GFDPPM 4-82 (FAR 91.155)
The VFR cloud clearances for Class E airspace apply. Below 10,000 feet MSL, you must remain 500 feet below, 1,000 feet above, and 2,000 feet horizontally.

4-100   B09
During operations within controlled airspace at altitudes of more than 1,200 feet AGL, but less than 10,000 feet MSL, the minimum distance above clouds requirement for VFR flight is

A — 500 feet.
B — 1,000 feet.
C — 1,500 feet.

4-100. Answer B. GFDPPM 4-82 (FAR 91.155)
Below 10,000 feet MSL in Class C and D airspace, the cloud clearances are 500 feet below, 1,000 feet above, and 2,000 feet horizontal. In Class B airspace, however, the cloud clearance is just "clear of clouds." "Clear of clouds" is not offered in answers (A) or (C). Therefore, answer (B) has to be the correct choice.

4-101   B09

VFR flight in controlled airspace above 1,200 feet AGL and below 10,000 feet MSL requires a minimum visibility and vertical cloud clearance of

A — 3 miles, and 500 feet below or 1,000 feet above the clouds in controlled airspace.
B — 5 miles, and 1,000 feet below or 1,000 feet above the clouds at all altitudes.
C — 5 miles, and 1,000 feet below or 1,000 feet above the clouds only in Class A airspace.

4-102   B09

During operations outside controlled airspace at altitudes of more than 1,200 feet AGL, but less than 10,000 feet MSL, the minimum flight visibility for VFR flight at night is

A — 1 mile.
B — 3 miles.
C — 5 miles.

4-103   B09

Outside controlled airspace, the minimum flight visibility requirement for VFR flight above 1,200 feet AGL and below 10,000 feet MSL during daylight hours is

A — 1 mile.
B — 3 miles.
C — 5 miles.

4-104   B09

During operations outside controlled airspace at altitudes of more than 1,200 feet AGL, but less than 10,000 feet MSL, the minimum distance below clouds requirement for VFR flight at night is

A — 500 feet.
B — 1,000 feet.
C — 1,500 feet.

4-105   B09

The minimum flight visibility required for VFR flights above 10,000 feet MSL and more than 1,200 feet AGL in controlled airspace is

A — 1 mile.
B — 3 miles.
C — 5 miles.

4-101. Answer A. GFDPPM 4-82 (FAR 91.155)
See explanation for Question 4-100. The visibility and cloud clearances listed in answers (B) and (C) apply only above 1,200 feet AGL and at or above 10,000 feet MSL.

4-102. Answer B. GFDPPM 4-82 (FAR 91.155)
In Class G airspace at these altitudes, night VFR operations require 3 miles visibility. Answer (A) is wrong, as 1 mile is the minimum required for daytime at these altitudes. Answer (C) is wrong, since 5 miles is required above 1,200 AGL and at or above 10,000 feet MSL for both day and night.

4-103. Answer A. GFDPPM 4-82 (FAR 91.155)
See explanation for Question 4-102. In uncontrolled airspace below 10,000 feet MSL and above 1,200 feet AGL, required daytime visibility is 1 mile.

4-104. Answer A. GFDPPM 4-82 (FAR 91.155)
At night, in uncontrolled airspace below 10,000 feet MSL (both above and below 1,200 feet AGL), the VFR cloud clearance is 500 feet below. Answer (B), 1,000 feet, is the clearance above clouds at these altitudes. Answer (C), 1,500 feet, is inappropriate.

4-105. Answer C. GFDPPM 4-82 (FAR 91.155)
At or above 10,000 feet MSL and above 1,200 feet AGL, the required visibility is 5 statute miles, whether in controlled or uncontrolled airspace.

4-106   B09

For VFR flight operations above 10,000 feet MSL and more than 1,200 feet AGL, the minimum horizontal distance from clouds required is

A — 1,000 feet.
B — 2,000 feet.
C — 1 mile.

4-106. Answer C. GFDPPM 4-82 (FAR 91.155)
Whether in controlled or uncontrolled airspace at these altitudes, the minimum VFR horizontal distance from clouds is 1 statute mile.

4-107   B09

During operations at altitudes of more than 1,200 feet AGL and at or above 10,000 feet MSL, the minimum distance above clouds requirement for VFR flight is

A — 500 feet.
B — 1,000 feet.
C — 1,500 feet.

4-107. Answer B. GFDPPM 4-82 (FAR 91.155)
For VFR flights at these altitudes, whether in controlled airspace or not, you are required to remain 1,000 feet above clouds. The only exception is for daytime operations below 1,200 feet AGL in uncontrolled airspace. In this case it is clear of clouds.

4-108   B09

No person may take off or land an aircraft under basic VFR at an airport that lies within Class D airspace unless the

A — flight visibility at that airport is at least 1 mile.
B — ground visibility at that airport is at least 1 mile.
C — ground visibility at that airport is at least 3 miles.

4--108. Answer C. GFDPPM 4-63 (FAR 91.155)
To take off or land under VFR in a Class D airspace area, the ceiling must be at least 1,000 feet and the ground visibility must be at least 3 statute miles. Flight visibility may be used if ground visibility is not available. Answers (A) and (B) are wrong since they reflect 1 statute mile visibility which only applies under special VFR.

4-109   B09

The basic VFR weather minimums for operating an aircraft within Class D airspace are

A — 500-foot ceiling and 1 mile visibility.
B — 1,000-foot ceiling and 3 miles visibility.
C — clear of clouds and 2 miles visibility.

4-109. Answer B. GFDPPM 4-82 (FAR 91.155)
See explanation for Question 4-108. Answers (A) and (C) do not reflect normal or special VFR weather minimums.

4-110   B09

A special VFR clearance authorizes the pilot of an aircraft to operate VFR while within Class D airspace when the visibility is

A — less than 1 mile and the ceiling is less than 1,000 feet.
B — at least 1 mile and the aircraft can remain clear of clouds.
C — at least 3 miles and the aircraft can remain clear of clouds.

4-110. Answer B. GFDPPM 4-71 (FAR 91.157)
When authorized by ATC, special VFR allows you to operate with one statute mile visibility as long as you can remain clear of clouds.

4-111   B09

What is the minimum weather condition required for airplanes operating under special VFR in Class D airspace?

A — 1 mile flight visibility.
B — 1 mile flight visibility and 1,000-foot ceiling.
C — 3 miles flight visibility and 1,000-foot ceiling.

4-111. Answer A. GFDPPM 4-71 (FAR 91.157)
See explanation for Question 4-110.

4-112   B09
What are the minimum requirements for airplane operations under special VFR in Class D airspace at night?

A — The airplane must be under radar surveillance at all times while in Class D airspace.
B — The airplane must be equipped for IFR with an altitude reporting transponder.
C — The pilot must be instrument rated, and the airplane must be IFR equipped.

4-112 Answer C. GFDPPM 4-72 (FAR 91.157)
For special VFR at night, you must have a current instrument rating, and the airplane must be equipped for IFR operations. Answer (A) is wrong because radar is not a requirement for Class D airspace. Answer (B) is incorrect because a transponder is not required in Class D airspace.

4-113   B09
No person may operate an airplane within Class D airspace at night under special VFR unless the

A — flight can be conducted 500 feet below the clouds.
B — airplane is equipped for instrument flight.
C — flight visibility is at least 3 miles.

4-113. Answer B. GFDPPM 4-72 (FAR 91.157)
See explanation for Question 4-112. Answers (A) and (C) are wrong because minimums for special VFR at night are the same as for day (1 statute mile visibility and clear of clouds).

4-114   B11
An operable 4096-code transponder with an encoding altimeter is required in which airspace?

A — Class A, Class B (and within 30 miles of the Class B primary airport), and Class C.
B — Class D and Class E (below 10,000 feet MSL).
C — Class D and Class G (below 10,000 feet MSL).

4-114. Answer A. GFDPPM 4-59 (FAR 91.215)
A transponder with an encoding transponder is required in Class A, Class B, and Class C airspace. It is not required in the areas listed in answers (B) and (C).

4-115   B11
With certain exceptions, all aircraft within 30 miles of a Class B primary airport from the surface upward to 10,000 feet MSL must be equipped with

A — an operable VOR or TACAN receiver and an ADF receiver.
B — instruments and equipment required for IFR operations.
C — an operable transponder having either Mode S or 4096-code capability with Mode C automatic altitude reporting capability.

4-115. Answer C. GFDPPM 4-59 (FAR 91.215)
An appropriate transponder capable of providing altitude encoding is required to be in use when within 30 miles of a Class B primary airport. Answer (A) is incorrect because a VOR or TACAN receiver (ADF is not applicable) is only required for IFR operations within Class B airspace. Answer (B) is incorrect because IFR instruments and equipment are not required for Class B airspace operations.

4-116   J08
(Refer to figure 26, area 4 on page 4-23.) The floor of Class B airspace overlying Hicks Airport (T67) north-northwest of Fort Worth Meacham Field is

A — at the surface.
B — 3,200 feet MSL.
C — 4,000 feet MSL.

4-116. Answer C. GFDPPM 4-67 (Chart Legend)
The altitudes of this portion of the Class B airspace are indicated by "110" over "40." This means the Class B airspace extends from a floor of 4,000 feet MSL up to 11,000 feet MSL. Answer (A) is wrong because the Class B airspace does not begin at the surface in this area. Answer (B) is incorrect because 3,200 feet MSL is the ceiling of the Class D airspace associated with Fort Worth Meacham.

4-117 J08
(Refer to figure 26, area 2 on page 4-23.) The floor of Class B airspace at Addison Airport is

A — at the surface.
B — 3,000 feet MSL.
C — 3,100 feet MSL.

4-118 J09
(Refer to figure 21 area 4 on page 4-18.) What hazards to aircraft may exist in restricted areas such as R-5302B?

A — Military training activities that necessitate acrobatic or abrupt flight maneuvers.
B — Unusual, often invisible, hazards such as aerial gunnery or guided missiles.
C — High volume of pilot training or an unusual type of aerial activity.

4-119 J09
(Refer to figure 27, area 2 on page 4-24.) What hazards to aircraft may exist in areas such as Devils Lake East MOA?

A — Military training activities that necessitate acrobatic or abrupt flight maneuvers.
B — High volume of pilot training or an unusual type of aerial activity.
C — Unusual, often invisible, hazards to aircraft such as artillery firing, aerial gunnery, or guided missiles.

4-120 J10
(Refer to figure 22, area 3 on page 4-19.) What type military flight operations should a pilot expect along IR 644?

A — VFR training flights above 1,500 feet AGL at speeds less than 250 knots.
B — IFR training flights above 1,500 feet AGL at speeds in excess of 250 knots.
C — Instrument training flights below 1,500 feet AGL at speeds in excess of 150 knots.

4-117. Answer B. GFDPPM 4-67 (Chart Legend)
The altitudes of this portion of the Class B airspace are indicated by "110" over "30." This means the Class B airspace extends from a floor of 3,000 feet MSL up to 11,000 feet MSL.

4-118. Answer B. GFDPPM 4-74 (AIM)
Restricted areas have invisible hazards to aircraft, such as artillery firing, aerial gunnery, or guided missiles. Answer (A) describes activities in a MOA.

4-119. Answer A. GFDPPM 4-74 (AIM)
Most training activities in a MOA involve acrobatic or abrupt flight maneuvers.

4-120. Answer B. GFDPPM 4-77 (AIM)
IR routes are designed to be flown by military aircraft at speeds often in excess of 250 kts. An IR Route with three letters in the designator (IR 644) indicates one or more segments are above 1,500 feet AGL.

4-121   J37
(Refer to figure 23, area 1 on page 4-20.) The visibility and cloud clearance requirements to operate VFR during daylight hours over Sandpoint Airport at 1,200 feet AGL are

A — 1 mile and 1,000 feet above, 500 feet below, and 2,000 feet horizontally from each cloud.
B — 1 mile and clear of clouds.
C — 3 miles and 1,000 feet above, 500 feet below, and 2,000 feet horizontally from each cloud.

4-122   J37
(Refer to figure 27, area 2 on page 4-24.) The visibility and cloud clearance requirements to operate VFR during daylight hours over the town of Cooperstown between 1,200 feet AGL and 10,000 feet MSL are

A.   3 miles and 1,000 feet above, 500 feet below, and 2,000 feet horizontally from clouds.
B.   1 mile and clear of clouds.
C.   1 mile and 1,000 feet above, 500 feet below, and 2,000 feet horizontally from clouds.

4-123   J37
(Refer to figure 27, area 1 on page 4-24.) Identify the airspace over Lowe Airport.

A — Class G airspace - surface up to but not including 18,000 feet MSL.
B — Class G airspace - surface up to but not including 1,200 feet AGL, Class E airspace - 1,200 feet AGL up to but not including 18,000 feet MSL.
C — Class G airspace - surface up to but not including 700 feet MSL, Class E airspace - 700 feet to 14,500 feet MSL.

4-124   J37
(Refer to figure 27, area 6 on page 4-24.) The airspace overlying and within 5 miles of Barnes County Airport is

A — Class D airspace from the surface to the floor of the overlying Class E airspace.
B — Class E airspace from the surface to 1,200 feet MSL.
C — Class G airspace from the surface to 700 feet AGL.

4-121. Answer C. GFDPPM 4-58 (FAR 91.155)
The airspace is Class E above 700 feet AGL. The day VFR minimums are 3 miles visibility and 1,000 feet above, 500 feet below, and 2,000 feet horizontally from all clouds.

4-122. Answer A. GFDPPM 4-58,82 (FAR 91.155)
Cooperstown is within the Class E airspace of the Cooperstown Airport. The floor of this airspace is 700 feet AGL. Visibility of 3 miles and 1,000 feet above, 500 feet below, and 2,000 feet horizontally from clouds is required to operate VFR in controlled airspace below 10,000 feet MSL.

4-123. Answer B. GFDPPM 4-74 (Chart Legend)
The lower left corner of the sectional reflects a small amount of the Class E designation line that surrounds this portion of the chart including Lowe Airport. The soft side of the blue line is facing the direction of Lowe Airport, which means that class E extends from 1200 ft AGL to 18,000 MSL.

4-124. Answer C. GFDPPM 4-61 (Chart Legend)
The magenta color indicates Class E airspace. If there were magenta segmented lines around the airport, the Class E airspace would begin at the surface. Magenta shading indicates the airspace starts at 700 feet AGL. Below 700 feet the airspace is uncontrolled or Class G. Class D airspace is indicated by segmented blue lines.

4-125   J37
(Refer to figure 26, area 7 on page 4-23.) The airspace overlying Mc Kinney (TKI) is controlled from the surface to

A — 2,900 feet MSL.
B — 2,500 feet AGL.
C — 700 feet MSL.

4-125. Answer A. GFDPPM 4-61 (Chart Legend)
The controlled airspace this question is referring to is Class D airspace. The top of Class D airspace (MSL) is shown within the square dashed box.

4-126   J37
(Refer to figure 26, area 4 on page 4-23.) The airspace directly overlying Fort Worth Meacham is

A — Class B airspace to 10,000 feet MSL.
B — Class C airspace to 5,000 feet MSL.
C — Class D airspace to 3,200 feet MSL.

4-126. Answer C. GFDPPM 4-63 (Chart Legend)
The blue segmented circle indicates Fort Worth Meacham is located in Class D airspace. The ⌐32⌐ indicates the ceiling of the Class D airspace is 3,200 feet MSL.

4-127   J37
(Refer to figure 24, area 3 on page 4-21.) What is the floor of the Savannah Class C airspace at the shelf area (outer circle)?

A — 1,300 feet AGL.
B — 1,300 feet MSL.
C — 1,700 feet MSL.

4-127 Answer B. GFDPPM 4-64 (AIM)
The floor of the outer circle of Class C airspace is normally APPROXIMATELY 1,200 feet AGL. At Savannah, the 1,200 feet AGL has been rounded up to 1,300 feet MSL (airport elevation is 51 feet) The exact limits in MSL are depicted on the chart ("41/13"). Answer A is not correct because the height is MSL not AGL. Answer (C) is not right because the 1^7 indicates the maximum elevation within the quadrangle is 1,700 feet MSL and has nothing to do with controlled airspace.

4-128   J37
(Refer to figure 21, area 1 on page 4-18.) What minimum radio equipment is required to land and take off at Norfolk International?

A — Mode C transponder and omnireceiver.
B — Mode C transponder and two-way radio.
C — Mode C transponder, omnireceiver, and DME.

4-128. Answer B. GFDPPM 4-59, 65 (FAR 91.130)
The area depicted is Class C airspace. Aircraft operating in Class C airspace must be equipped with a Mode C transponder and pilots are required to maintain two-way radio communications. Answers (A) and (C) are wrong because no navigation equipment is specified for operating in Class C airspace.

4-129   J37
(Refer to figure 26 on page 4-23.) At which airports is fixed-wing Special VFR not authorized?

A — Fort Worth Meacham and Fort Worth Spinks.
B — Dallas/Fort Worth International and Dallas Love Field.
C — Addison and Redbird.

4-129. Answer B. GFDPPM 4-72 (Chart Legend)
The "NO SVFR" over the airport identification name indicates that fixed-wing special VFR is not authorized. The airports listed in answers (A) and (C) permit special VFR.

4-130   J37
(Refer to figure 23, area 3 on page 4-20.) The vertical limits of that portion of Class E airspace designated as a Federal Airway over Magee Airport are

A — 1,200 feet AGL to 17,999 feet MSL.
B — 7,500 feet MSL to 17,999 feet MSL.
C — 700 feet MSL to 12,500 feet MSL.

4-130. Answer A. GFDPPM 4-60 (Chart Legend)
Class E airspace includes Federal, or Victor, airways which usually extend to 4 nautical miles on each side of the airway centerline and, unless otherwise indicated, extends from 1,200 feet AGL up to, but not including, 18,000 feet MSL.

4-131   J08
The vertical limit of Class C airspace above the primary airport is normally

A — 1,200 feet AGL.
B — 3,000 feet AGL.
C — 4,000 feet AGL.

4-131. Answer C. GFDPPM 4-64 (AIM)
The vertical limit of Class C airspace is 4,000 feet above the primary airport. This is the same for both the inner and outer circles. Answer (A) is wrong because this is the floor of the outer circle (5 n.m to 10 n.m. radius). Answer (B) is wrong because the vertical limit is 4,000 feet AGL, not 3,000 feet.

4-132   J08
The normal radius of the outer area of Class C airspace is

A — 5 nautical miles.
B — 15 nautical miles.
C — 20 nautical miles.

4-132 Answer C. GFDPPM 4-64 (AIM)
The outer area of Class C airspace normally extends 20 nautical miles from the primary airport. Answer (A) is the dimension of the inner circle, while answer (B) is not used to define any portion of Class C airspace. The outer circle has a radius of 10 nautical miles.

4-133   J08
Under what condition may an aircraft operate from a satellite airport within Class C airspace?

A — The pilot must file a flight plan prior to departure.
B — The pilot must monitor ATC until clear of the Class C airspace.
C — The pilot must contact ATC as soon as practicable after takeoff.

4-133. Answer C. GFDPPM 4-65 (FAR 91.130)
A pilot must establish two-way communications with ATC as soon as practical after takeoff. Answer (A) is not a requirement for operating in Class C airspace. Answer (B) is not entirely correct, as it does not state that two-way communications must be established.

4-134   J09
Under what condition, if any, may pilots fly through a restricted area?

A — When flying on airways with an ATC clearance.
B — With the controlling agency's authorization.
C — Regulations do not allow this.

4-134. Answer B. GFDPPM 4-75 (FAR 91.133)
The controlling agency may grant permission to fly through a restricted area. Answer (A) is wrong because airways do not usually transit a restricted area. Answer (C) is wrong because the FARs do allow pilots to fly through restricted areas if they have authorization from the controlling agency.

4-135   J09
What action should a pilot take when operating under VFR in a Military Operations Area (MOA)?

A — Obtain a clearance from the controlling agency prior to entering the MOA.
B — Operate only on the airways that transverse the MOA.
C — Exercise extreme caution when military activity is being conducted.

4-135. Answer C. GFDPPM 4-74 (AIM)
Due to the possibility of military training activities, pilots operating in a MOA should use extra caution and be alert for other aircraft. Answer (A) is wrong because a clearance is not required. Answer (B) is wrong because VFR pilots are not restricted to airways in a MOA.

4-136   J09
Responsibility for collision avoidance in an alert area rests with

A — the controlling agency.
B — all pilots.
C — Air Traffic Control.

4-137   J10
The lateral dimensions of Class D airspace are based on

A — the number of airports that lie within the Class D airspace.
B — five statute miles from the geographical center of the primary airport.
C — the instrument procedures for which the controlled airspace is established.

4-138   J10
A non-tower satellite airport, within the same Class D airspace as that designated for the primary airport, requires radio communications be established and maintained with the

A — satellite airport's UNICOM.
B — associated Flight Service Station.
C — primary airport's control tower.

4-139   J11
Which initial action should a pilot take prior to entering Class C airspace?

A — Contact approach control on the appropriate frequency.
B — Contact the tower and request permission to enter.
C — Contact the FSS for traffic advisories.

4-140   J14
What ATC facility should the pilot contact to receive a special VFR departure clearance in Class D airspace?

A — Automated Flight Service Station.
B — Air Traffic Control Tower.
C — Air Route Traffic Control Center.

4-136. Answer B. GFDPPM 4-73 (AIM)
All pilots flying in an alert area, whether participating in activities or transitioning the area, are equally responsible for collision avoidance. Answers (A) and (C) are wrong, because even when operating under Air Traffic Control, pilots are not relieved of their responsibility for collision avoidance.

4-137. Answer C. GFDPPM 4-63 (AIM)
The actual lateral dimensions of Class D airspace varies with each location, but, in general, Class D airspace is based on the instrument procedures for the airports in that area. Answer (A) is wrong because, to the maximum extent practical and consistent with safety, satellite airports have been excluded from Class D airspace. Answer (B) is the dimension of the old "airport traffic area" designation, which is no longer valid.

4-138. Answer C. GFDPPM 4-63 (FAR 91.129)
When approaching Class D airspace, you must contact the primary airport's control tower before entering the airspace. When departing a nontowered satellite airport, contact the controlling tower as soon as practical after takeoff. Answers (A) and (B) are wrong because the regulation specifically states you must contact the ATC facility providing air traffic services. UNICOM and the Flight Service Station, in this context, do not fit the definition of an ATC facility providing these services.

4-139. Answer A. GFDPPM 4-65 (AIM)
Prior to entering Class C airspace, you need to establish contact with approach control. Answer (B) is wrong because the tower sequences traffic for landing, but is not the facility to contact before entering Class C airspace. Answer (C) is not correct because flight service provides traffic advisories in an airport advisory area.

4-140. Answer B. GFDPPM 4-71 (FAR 91.157)
The control tower is the ATC facility which issues a special VFR clearance.

CHAPTER 5

COMMUNICATION AND FLIGHT INFORMATION

SECTION A
RADAR AND ATC SERVICES

The advance of computer technology has greatly expanded the capabilities of air traffic control, providing you with an extra "crewmember" whenever you fly. This section reviews the various radar and air traffic control facilities in use. Topics include equipment, such as transponders, radar and VHF communication radios, and services available to pilots operating under visual flight rules (VFR).

TRANSPONDER OPERATIONS
1. No person may use an ATC transponder unless it has been tested and inspected within at least the preceding 24 calendar months.
2. Pilots should avoid making inadvertent selection of the following transponder codes: 7500, 7600, 7700.
3. Unless otherwise authorized, pilots operating under VFR should squawk 1200 on the transponder.
4. Pilots should select 1200 on the transponder, once advised that radar service is terminated, upon leaving Class B, C or D airspace.

VFR RADAR SERVICES
5. Traffic information is given with respect to the clock, with the aircraft in the center of the clock face, and the clock face on a horizontal plane. The pilot's 12 o'clock is directly ahead, 6 o'clock is directly behind, with 3 o'clock to the right and 9 o'clock to the left.
6. To use VHF/DH facilities for assistance in locating an aircraft's position, the aircraft must have a VHF transmitter and receiver.

TERMINAL VFR RADAR SERVICES
7. Basic radar service for VFR aircraft provides traffic advisories and limited vectoring on a workload permitting basis.
8. You should notify ground control, on initial contact, when requesting Stage II Terminal Radar Advisory Service during ground operations. Note: The terminology is changing to Basic, TRSA, Class C and Class B.
9. Stage III in the terminal radar program provides sequencing and separation for participating VFR aircraft.

AUTOMATIC TERMINAL INFORMATION SERVICE (ATIS)
10. Automatic Terminal Information Service (ATIS) is the continuous broadcast of recorded information concerning noncontrol data in selected high-activity terminal areas.

FLIGHT SERVICE STATIONS (FSS)
11. The callsign for a flight service station is its name, followed by the word "radio." The aircraft's full callsign should be given, using the phonetic alphabet.

5-1   B13
No person may use an ATC transponder unless it has been tested and inspected within at least the preceding

A — 6 calendar months.
B — 12 calendar months.
C — 24 calendar months.

5-1. Answer C. GFDPPM 5-4 (FAR 91.413)
The transponder must have been tested and inspected within the preceding 24 calendar months.

5-2   J01
To use VHF/DF facilities for assistance in locating an aircraft's position, the aircraft must have a

A — VHF transmitter and receiver.
B — 4096-code transponder.
C — VOR receiver and DME.

5-3   J11
Automatic Terminal Information Service (ATIS) is the continuous broadcast of recorded information concerning

A — pilots of radar-identified aircraft whose aircraft is in dangerous proximity to terrain or to an obstruction.
B — nonessential information to reduce frequency congestion.
C — noncontrol information in selected high-activity terminal areas.

5-4   J11
An ATC radar facility issues the following advisory to a pilot flying on a heading of 090°:
"TRAFFIC 3 O'CLOCK, 2 MILES, WEST-BOUND..."
Where should the pilot look for this traffic?

A — East.
B — South.
C — West.

5-5   J11
An ATC radar facility issues the following advisory to a pilot flying on a heading of 360°:
"TRAFFIC 10 O'CLOCK, 2 MILES, SOUTH-BOUND..."
Where should the pilot look for this traffic?

A — Northwest.
B — Northeast.
C — Southwest.

5-6   J11
An ATC radar facility issues the following advisory to a pilot during a local flight:
"TRAFFIC 2 O'CLOCK, 5 MILES, NORTH-BOUND..."
Where should the pilot look for this traffic?

A — Between directly ahead and 90° to the left.
B — Between directly behind and 90° to the right.
C — Between directly ahead and 90° to the right.

5-2. Answer A. GFDPPM 5-14 (AIM)
VHF/DF facilities use a directional antenna and a VHF radio receiver. The equipment displays the direction of the aircraft each time it transmits on its VHF radio. Answer (B) is wrong because a transponder code will show up on a radar screen, but not on a VHF/DF facility. Answer (C) is wrong because a VOR and DME will indicate an aircraft's position relative to a ground station, but is not part of the direction finder facilities on the ground.

5-3. Answer C. GFDPPM 5-12 (AIM)
ATIS is broadcast at certain busy airports, and provides noncontrol weather and runway information.

5-4. Answer B. GFDPPM 5-8 (AIM)
Since the pilot is heading east, the 3 o'clock position is to the right, which is south.

5-5. Answer A. GFDPPM 5-8 (AIM)
Since the pilot's 12 o'clock position is north, the 10 o'clock position is northwest.

5-6. Answer C. GFDPPM 5-8 (AIM)
Since the pilot's 12 o'clock is directly ahead, and 3 o'clock is 90° to the right, 2 o'clock is approximately 60° right.

5-7   J11
An ATC radar facility issues the following advisory to a pilot flying north in a calm wind: "TRAFFIC 9 O'CLOCK, 2 MILES, SOUTH-BOUND..."
Where should the pilot look for this traffic?

A — South.
B — North.
C — West.

5-7. Answer C. GFDPPM 5-8 (AIM)
The pilot's 12 o'clock is north, so 9 o'clock is left, or west.

5-8   J11
Basic radar service in the terminal radar program is best described as

A — mandatory radar service provided by the Automated Radar Terminal System (ARTS) program.
B — safety alerts, traffic advisories, and limited vectoring to VFR aircraft.
C — wind-shear warning at participating airports.

5-8. Answer B. GFDPPM 5-10 (AIM)
Basic radar service for VFR aircraft provides safety alerts, traffic advisories, and limited vectoring on a workload-permitting basis. Unlike Class B and Class C service, basic service is not mandatory for VFR aircraft. Wind shear warning is NOT part of the basic radar service. Note: The terminology for radar service has changed to Basic, TRSA, Class C, and Class B.

5-9   J11
From whom should a departing VFR aircraft request radar traffic information during ground operations?

A — Clearance delivery.
B — Ground control, on initial contact.
C — Tower, just before takeoff.

5-9. Answer B. GFDPPM 5-10 (AIM)
You should request radar traffic information by notifying ground control on initial contact with your request and proposed direction of flight. Clearance delivery is incorrect because normally, it only provides IFR clearances, and it may not be available at all airports. Requesting the service from the tower, just before takeoff, could delay either the departure or availability of the service. Note: The terminology for radar service has changed to Basic, TRSA, Class C, and Class B.

5-10   J11
TRSA Service in the terminal radar program provides

A — sequencing and separation for participating VFR aircraft.
B — IFR separation (1,000 feet vertical and 3 miles lateral) between all aircraft.
C — warning to pilots when their aircraft are in unsafe proximity to terrain, obstructions, or other aircraft.

5-10. Answer A. GFDPPM 5-10 (AIM)
TRSA service provides separation between all participating VFR aircraft and all IFR aircraft operating in the TRSA. Pilot participation is urged but not mandatory.

5-11   J11
When making routine transponder code changes, pilots should avoid inadvertent selection of which codes?

A — 0700, 1700, 7000.
B — 1200, 1500, 7000.
C — 7500, 7600, 7700.

5-11. Answer C. GFDPPM 5-5 (AIM)
You should avoid inadvertent selection of transponder codes which may set off false alarms at radar facilities. These codes are: 7500 for hijacking, 7600 for radio communications failure, and 7700 for emergencies.

5-12   J11
When operating under VFR below 18,000 feet MSL, unless otherwise authorized, what transponder code should be selected?

A — 1200.
B — 7600.
C — 7700.

5-12. Answer A. GFDPPM 5-5 (AIM)
The transponder code for VFR aircraft is 1200. Aircraft operating above 18,000 feet MSL are in Class A airspace and must have an IFR clearance. Answer (B) is wrong because 7600 is the code for radio failure. Answer (C) is wrong because 7700 is the code for emergencies.

5-13   J11
Unless otherwise authorized, if flying a transponder equipped aircraft, a recreational pilot should squawk which VFR code?

A — 1200.
B — 7600.
C — 7700.

5-13. Answer A. GFDPPM 5-5 (AIM)
See explanation for Question 5-12.

5-14   J11
If Air Traffic Control advises that radar service is terminated when the pilot is departing Class C airspace, the transponder should be set to code

A — 0000.
B — 1200.
C — 4096.

5-14. Answer B. GFDPPM 5-5 (AIM)
Since you would then be operating under VFR, the transponder should be set to 1200. Answer (A) is not a designated VFR transponder code. Answer (C) is the number of discrete codes which are available on a four digit transponder with each digit starting at 0 and ending at 7.

5-15   J34
(Refer to figure 53 on page 5-5.) Which type radar service is provided to VFR aircraft at Lincoln Municipal?

A — Sequencing to the primary Class C airport and standard separation.
B — Sequencing to the primary Class C airport and conflict resolution so that radar targets do not touch, or 1,000 feet vertical separation.
C — Sequencing to the primary Class C airport, traffic advisories, conflict resolution, and safety alerts.

5-15. Answer C. GFDPPM 5-11 (AIM)
The VFR services provided within a Class C airspace area (formerly ARSA) include: sequencing all arriving aircraft to the primary Class C airport; providing traffic advisories and conflict resolutions between IFR and VFR aircraft so that radar targets do not touch, or 500 feet vertical separation, and between VFR aircraft, traffic advisories and safety alerts.

NEBRASKA

LINCOLN MUNI (LNK) 4 NW UTC-6(-5DT) N40°51.05' W96°45.55' OMAHA
1218 B S4 FUEL 100LL. JET A TPA—2218(1000) ARFF Index B H-1E, 3F, 4F, L-11B
RWY 17R-35L: H12901X200 (ASPH-CONC-GRVD) S-100. D-200. DT-400 HIRL IAP
  RWY 17R: MALSR. VASI(V4L)—GA 3.0° TCH 55'. Rgt tfc. 0.4% down.
  RWY 35L: MALSR. VASI(V4L)—GA 3.0° TCH 55'.
RWY 14-32: H8620X150 (ASPH-CONC-GRVD) S-80. D-170. DT-280 MIRL
  RWY 14: REIL. VASI(V4L)—GA 3.0° TCH 48'.
  RWY 32: VASI(V4L)—GA 3.0° TCH 53'. Thld dsplcd 431'. Pole. 0.3% up.
RWY 17L-35R: H5400X100 (ASPH-CONC-AFSC) S-49. D-60 HIRL 0.8% up N
  RWY 17L: PAPI(P4L)—GA 3.0° TCH 33'. RWY 35R: PAPI(P4L)—GA 3.0° TCH 40'. Pole. Rgt tfc.
AIRPORT REMARKS: Attended continuously. Birds in vicinity of arpt. Twy D clsd between taxiways S and H indef. For
  MALSR Rwy 17R and Rwy 35L ctc twr. When twr clsd MALSR Rwy 17R and Rwy 35L preset on med ints, and REIL
  Rwy 14 left on when wind favor. NOTE: See Land and Hold Short Operations Section.
WEATHER DATA SOURCES: ASOS (402) 474-9214. LLWAS
COMMUNICATIONS: CTAF 118.5 ATIS 118.05 UNICOM 122.95
  COLUMBUS FSS (OLU) TF 1-800-WX-BRIEF. NOTAM FILE LNK.
  RCO 122.65 (COLUMBUS FSS)
  (R) APP/DEP CON 124.0 (170°-349°) 124.8 (350°-169°) (1130-0630Z‡)
  (R) MINNEAPOLIS CENTER APP/DEP CON 128.75 (0630-1130Z‡)
  TOWER 118.5 125.7 (1130-0630Z‡) GND CON 121.9 CLNC DEL 120.7
AIRSPACE: CLASS C svc 1130-0630Z‡ ctc APP CON other times CLASS E.
RADIO AIDS TO NAVIGATION: NOTAM FILE LNK. VHF/DF ctc FSS.
  (H) VORTACW 116.1 LNK Chan 108 N40°55.43' W96°44.52' 181° 4.5 NM to fld. 1370/9E
  POTTS NDB (MHW/LOM) 385 LN N40°44.83' W96°45.75' 355° 6.2 NM to fld. Unmonitored when twr clsd.
  ILS 111.1 I-OCZ Rwy 17R. MM and OM unmonitored.
  ILS 109.9 I-LNK Rwy 35L LOM POTTS NDB. MM unmonitored. LOM unmonitored when twr clsd.
COMM/NAVAID REMARKS: Emerg frequency 121.5 not available at tower.

LOUP CITY MUNI (NE03) 1 NW UTC-6(-5DT) N41°17.42' W98°59.44' OMAHA
2070 B FUEL 100LL L-11B
RWY 15-33: H3200X50 (ASPH) S-8 LIRL
  RWY 33: Trees.
RWY 04-22: 2100X100 (TURF)
  RWY 04: Tree. RWY 22: Road.
AIRPORT REMARKS: Unattended. For svc call 308-745-0328/1244/0664.
COMMUNICATIONS: CTAF 122.9
  COLUMBUS FSS (OLU) TF 1-800-WX-BRIEF. NOTAM FILE OLU.
RADIO AIDS TO NAVIGATION: NOTAM FILE OLU.
  WOLBACH (H) VORTAC 114.8 OBH Chan 95 N41°22.54' W98°21.22' 253° 29.3 NM to fld. 2010/7E.

MARTIN FLD (See SO SIOUX CITY)

MC COOK MUNI (MCK) 2 E UTC-6(-5DT) N40°12.36' W100°35.51' OMAHA
2579 B S4 FUEL 100LL. JET A ARFF Index Ltd. H-2D, L-11A
RWY 12-30: H5999X100 (CONC) S-30. D-38 MIRL 0.6% up NW IAP
  RWY 12: MALS. VASI(V4L)—GA 3.0° TCH 33'. Tree. RWY 30: REIL. VASI(V4L)—GA 3.0° TCH 42'.
RWY 03-21: H3999X75 (CONC) S-30. D-38 MIRL
  RWY 03: VASI(V2L)—GA 3.0° TCH 26'. Rgt tfc. RWY 21: VASI(V2L)—GA 3.0° TCH 26'.
RWY 17-35: 1350X200 (TURF)
AIRPORT REMARKS: Attended daylight hours. Parachute Jumping. Deer on and in vicinity of arpt. Numerous
  waterfowl/migratory birds invof arpt. Arpt closed to air carrier operations with more than 30 passengers except
  24 hour PPR, call arpt manager 308-345-2022. Avoid McCook State (abandoned) arpt 7 miles NW on the MCK
  VOR/DME 313° radial at 8.3 DME. ACTIVATE VASI Rwys 12 and 30 and MALS Rwy 12—CTAF.
COMMUNICATIONS: CTAF/UNICOM 122.8
  COLUMBUS FSS (OLU) TF 1-800-WX-BRIEF. NOTAM FILE MCK.
  RCO 122.6 (COLUMBUS FSS)
  DENVER CENTER APP/DEP CON 132.7
AIRSPACE: CLASS E svc effective 1100-0500Z‡ except holidays other times CLASS G.
RADIO AIDS TO NAVIGATION: NOTAM FILE MCK.
  (H) VORW/DME 115.3 MCK Chan 100 N40°12.23' W100°35.65' at fld. 2570/8E.

MILLARD (See OMAHA)

MILLER FLD (See VALENTINE)

FIGURE 53.—Airport/Facility Directory Excerpt.

SECTION B
RADIO PROCEDURES

Pilots use a special language, so that communication between aircraft and ground facilities is smooth and concise. This section covers VHF radio characteristics, common terms and proper phraseology. Coordinated Universal Time (UTC), radio procedures and ground radio facilities are also included.

USING NUMBERS ON THE RADIO

1. Altitudes should be stated as individual numbers, with the words "hundreds" and "thousands" included as appropriate. At altitudes of 10,000 feet and above, each digit of the thousands is pronounced, i.e. "One zero thousand."

COORDINATED UNIVERSAL TIME (UTC)

2. (figure of time conversion table required) To convert the local departure or arrival time to UTC, add the hours of difference from the number on the time conversion table. For example, converting MST to UTC involves adding 7 hours to MST.

5-16   B08
A steady green light signal directed from the control tower to an aircraft in flight is a signal that the pilot

A — is cleared to land.
B — should give way to other aircraft and continue circling.
C — should return for landing.

5-16. Answer A. GFDPPM 5-31 (FAR 91.125)
A steady green light while in flight means you are cleared to land. A steady red light would be used for answer (B). A flashing green light would be used for answer (C).

5-17   B08
Which light signal from the control tower clears a pilot to taxi?

A — Flashing green.
B — Steady green.
C — Flashing white.

5-17. Answer A. GFDPPM 5-31 (FAR 91.125)
While on the ground, a flashing green light means cleared to taxi. A steady green light (answer B) means cleared for takeoff. A flashing white light (answer C) means return to the aircraft's starting point on the airport.

5-18   B08
If the control tower uses a light signal to direct a pilot to give way to other aircraft and continue circling, the light will be

A — flashing red.
B — steady red.
C — alternating red and green.

5-18. Answer B. GFDPPM 5-31 (FAR 91.125)
While in flight, a steady red light means give way and continue circling. A flashing red light (answer A) means that the airport is unsafe; do not land. An alternating red and green light (answer C) means to exercise extreme caution.

5-19   B08
A flashing white light signal from the control tower to a taxiing aircraft is an indication to

A — taxi at a faster speed.
B — taxi only on taxiways and not cross runways.
C — return to the starting point on the airport.

5-19. Answer C. GFDPPM 5-31 (FAR 91.125)
A flashing white light while operating on the ground means return to the starting point on the airport.

5-20   B08
An alternating red and green light signal directed from the control tower to an aircraft in flight is a signal to

A — hold position.
B — exercise extreme caution.
C — not land; the airport is unsafe.

5-21   B08
While on final approach for landing, an alternating green and red light followed by a flashing red light is received from the control tower. Under these circumstances, the pilot should

A — discontinue the approach, fly the same traffic pattern and approach again, and land.
B — exercise extreme caution and abandon the approach, realizing the airport is unsafe for landing.
C — abandon the approach, circle the airport to the right, and expect a flashing white light when the airport is safe for landing.

5-22   H340
(Refer to figure 28 on page 5-8.) An aircraft departs an airport in the eastern daylight time zone at 0945 EDT for a 2-hour flight to an airport located in the central daylight time zone. The landing should be at what coordinated universal time?

A — 1345Z.
B — 1445Z.
C — 1545Z.

5-23   H340
(Refer to figure 28 on page 5-8) An aircraft departs an airport in the central standard time zone at 0930 CST for a 2-hour flight to an airport located in the mountain standard time zone. The landing should be at what time?

A — 0930 MST.
B — 1030 MST.
C — 1130 MST.

5-24   H340
(Refer to figure 28 on page 5-8.) An aircraft departs an airport in the central standard time zone at 0845 CST for a 2-hour flight to an airport located in the mountain standard time zone. The landing should be at what coordinated universal time?

A — 1345Z.
B — 1445Z.
C — 1645Z.

5-20. Answer B. GFDPPM 5-31 (FAR 91.125)
An alternating red and green signal means the same whether you are in flight or on the ground — exercise extreme caution.

5-21. Answer B. GFDPPM 5-31 (FAR 91.125)
An alternating red and green signal means exercise extreme caution. This is followed by a flashing red signal, which, in flight, means that the airport is unsafe.

5-22. Answer C. GFDPPM 5-23 (AIM)
To convert the local departure time to UTC, add 4 hours (0945 + 4:00 = 1345). Two hours later is 1545Z.

5-23. Answer B. GFDPPM 5-23 (AIM)
Add 2 hours to the 0930 departure time to find the arrival time of 1130 CST. Since Mountain time is 1 hour earlier than Central, subtract 1 hour, for a landing time of 1030 MST.

5-24. Answer C. GFDPPM 5-23 (AIM)
Departure time (0845) plus 2 hours is 1045 CST. Convert CST to UTC by adding 6 hours, for a landing time of 1645Z.

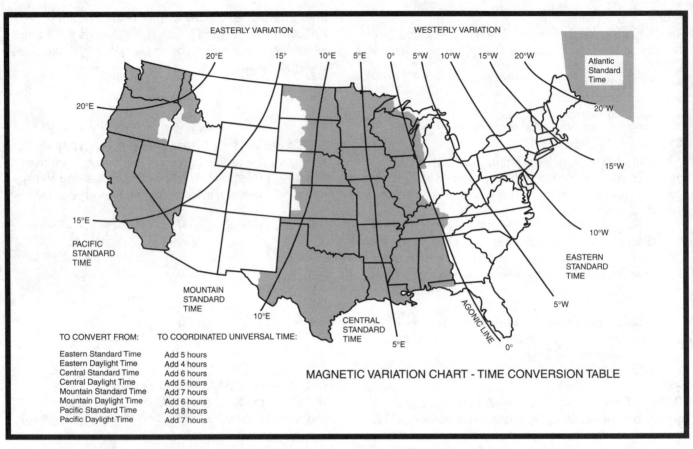

FIGURE 28.—Time Conversion Table.

5-25   H340
(Refer to figure 28.) An aircraft departs an airport in the mountain standard time zone at 1615 MST for a 2-hour 15-minute flight to an airport located in the Pacific standard time zone. The estimated time of arrival at the destination airport should be

A — 1630 PST.
B — 1730 PST.
C — 1830 PST.

5-26   H340
(Refer to figure 28.) An aircraft departs an airport in the Pacific standard time zone at 1030 PST for a 4-hour flight to an airport located in the central standard time zone. The landing should be at what coordinated universal time?

A — 2030Z.
B — 2130Z.
C — 2230Z.

5-25. Answer B. GFDPPM 5-23 (AIM)
Add 2:15 to 1615 MST to find the arrival time of 1830 MST. Since Pacific time is one hour earlier than MST, the arrival time is 1730 PST.

5-26. Answer C. GFDPPM 5-23 (AIM)
Add 4 hours to 1030 PST to find the arrival time of 1430 PST. To convert PST to UTC, add 8 hours. The landing time is 2230Z.

5-27   H340
(Refer to figure 28.) An aircraft departs an airport in the mountain standard time zone at 1515 MST for a 2-hour 30-minute flight to an airport located in the Pacific standard time zone. What is the estimated time of arrival at the destination airport?

A — 1645 PST.
B — 1745 PST.
C — 1845 PST.

5-27. Answer A. GFDPPM 5-23 (AIM)
Add 2:30 to 1515 MST to find the arrival time of 1745 MST. Convert MST to PST by subtracting 1 hour. The answer is 1645 PST.

5-28   J11
(Refer to figure 21, area 3 on page 4-18.) What is the recommended communications procedure for a landing at Currituck County Airport?

A — Transmit intentions on 122.9 MHz when 10 miles out and give position reports in the traffic pattern.
B — Contact Elizabeth City FSS for airport advisory service.
C — Contact New Bern FSS for area traffic information.

5-28. Answer A. GFDPPM 5-25 (AIM)
The CTAF symbol is next to the frequency of 122.9. The normal procedure is to transmit intentions when 10 miles out and give position reports in the pattern. An FSS (answers B and C) provides airport advisory service only when located at airports without a tower. The flight service stations at Elizabeth City and New Bern do not provide airport advisory service for Currituck County.

5-29   J11
(Refer to figure 27, area 2 on page 4-24.) What is the recommended communication procedure when inbound to land at Cooperstown Airport?

A — Broadcast intentions when 10 miles out on the CTAF/MULTICOM frequency, 122.9 MHz.
B — Contact UNICOM when 10 miles out on 122.8 MHz.
C — Circle the airport in a left turn prior to entering traffic.

5-29. Answer A. GFDPPM 5-25 (AIM)
The CTAF/MULTICOM frequency, 122.9, is depicted next to the CTAF symbol. Pilots should broadcast intentions on this frequency when 10 miles from the field. When a separate CTAF is listed, the UNICOM frequency (answer B) is used only for fuel and other requests, not traffic pattern calls. Answer (C) is wrong because when radios are available, you should make the standard calls prior to entering the traffic pattern.

5-30   J12
When flying HAWK N666CB, the proper phraseology for initial contact with McAlester AFSS is

A — "MC ALESTER RADIO, HAWK SIX SIX SIX CHARLIE BRAVO, RECEIVING ARDMORE VORTAC, OVER."
B — "MC ALESTER STATION, HAWK SIX SIX SIX CEE BEE, RECEIVING ARDMORE VORTAC, OVER."
C — "MC ALESTER FLIGHT SERVICE STATION, HAWK NOVEMBER SIX CHARLIE BRAVO, RECEIVING ARDMORE VORTAC, OVER."

5-30. Answer A. GFDPPM 5-21 (AIM)
The callsign for a flight service station is its name, followed by the word "radio." The aircraft's full callsign should be given, using the phonetic alphabet. Answer (B) is wrong because the phonetic alphabet is not used (i.e., "CHARLIE BRAVO" versus "CEE BEE"). Answer (C) is wrong because the correct callsign is McAlester Radio, not McAlester Flight Service Station.

5-31   J12
The correct method of stating 4,500 feet MSL to ATC is

A — "FOUR THOUSAND FIVE HUNDRED."
B — "FOUR POINT FIVE."
C — "FORTY-FIVE HUNDRED FEET MSL."

5-31. Answer A. GFDPPM 5-22 (AIM)
Altitudes should be stated as individual numbers with the word hundreds or thousands added as appropriate. In this case, 4,500 feet should be read as "FOUR THOUSAND FIVE HUNDRED."

5-32   J12

The correct method of stating 10,500 feet MSL to ATC is

A — "TEN THOUSAND, FIVE HUNDRED FEET."
B — "TEN POINT FIVE."
C — "ONE ZERO THOUSAND, FIVE HUNDRED."

5-33   J10

Prior to entering an Airport Advisory Area, a pilot should

A — monitor ATIS for weather and traffic advisories.
B — contact approach control for vectors to the traffic pattern.
C — contact the local FSS for airport and traffic advisories.

5-34   J12

If the aircraft's radio fails, what is the recommended procedure when landing at a controlled airport?

A — Observe the traffic flow, enter the pattern, and look for a light signal from the tower.
B — Enter a crosswind leg and rock the wings.
C — Flash the landing lights and cycle the landing gear while circling the airport.

5-35   J13

After landing at a tower-controlled airport, when should the pilot contact ground control?

A — When advised by the tower to do so.
B — Prior to turning off the runway.
C — After reaching a taxiway that leads directly to the parking area.

5-36   J13

If instructed by ground control to taxi to Runway 9, the pilot may proceed

A — via taxiways and across runways to, but not onto, Runway 9.
B — to the next intersecting runway where further clearance is required.
C — via taxiways and across runways to Runway 9, where an immediate takeoff may be made.

5-32. Answer C. GFDPPM 5-22 (AIM)
See explanation for Question 5-31. In addition, for altitudes at and above 10,000 feet MSL, each digit of the thousands is pronounced, so that 10,500 becomes "ONE ZERO THOUSAND FIVE HUNDRED."

5-33. Answer C. GFDPPM 5-24 (AIM)
A local nonautomated FSS provides airport and traffic advisories for an Airport Advisory Area. Answer (A) is wrong because an ATIS may not be available, and does not give traffic advisories. Answer (B) is wrong because, whether or not you receive assistance from approach control, you should contact the local FSS for airport and traffic advisories.

5-34. Answer A. GFDPPM 5-31 (AIM)
To avoid conflicts and cause the least disruption in the traffic flow, determine the landing direction, and enter the pattern. Watch the tower for a light signal and acknowledge by rocking the wings. At night, acknowledge by flashing the landing or navigation lights. Answer (B) is wrong because this does not state that you have observed the traffic flow. In addition, a crosswind entry is not normal, and rocking the wings is done to acknowledge tower light signals. Answer (C) is wrong because flashing the lights is an acknowledgment of the tower light signals. Also, cycling the gear is not a signal, and you should stay outside or above the pattern instead of circling the airport when determining traffic flow.

5-35. Answer A. GFDPPM 5-28 (AIM)
The tower will normally instruct you to exit the runway and contact ground control. Answer (B) is wrong because you should exit the runway first. Answer (C) is wrong because the taxiway used to exit the runway may not lead directly to a parking area, and you must still receive a clearance from ground control to taxi.

5-36. Answer A. GFDPPM 5-27 (AIM)
A clearance to taxi to a runway allows the pilot to proceed to that runway and cross any intersecting runways. Answer (B) is wrong because you do not have to hold at an intersecting runway and await clearance. Answer (C) is wrong because you have neither been cleared to taxi onto the runway or cleared for takeoff.

5-37   **J22**

When activated, an emergency locator transmitter (ELT) transmits on

A — 118.0 and 118.8 MHz.
B — 121.5 and 243.0 MHz.
C — 123.0 and 119.0 MHz.

5-38   **J22**

When must the battery in an emergency locator transmitter (ELT) be replaced (or recharged if the battery is rechargeable)?

A — After one-half the battery's useful life.
B — During each annual and 100-hour inspection.
C — Every 24 calendar months.

5-39   **J22**

When may an emergency locator transmitter (ELT) be tested?

A — Anytime.
B — At 15 and 45 minutes past the hour.
C — During the first 5 minutes after the hour.

5-40   **J22**

Which procedure is recommended to ensure that the emergency locator transmitter (ELT) has not been activated?

A — Turn off the aircraft ELT after landing.
B — Ask the airport tower if they are receiving an ELT signal.
C — Monitor 121.5 before engine shutdown.

5-41   **J33**

An ATC clearance provides

A — priority over all other traffic.
B — adequate separation from all traffic.
C — authorization to proceed under specified traffic conditions in controlled airspace.

5-37. Answer B. GFDPPM 5-33 (AIM)
The frequencies used for ELTs are the emergency frequencies of 121.5 MHz (VHF) and 243.0 MHz (UHF).

5-38. Answer A. GFDPPM 5-34 (FAR 91.207)
The ELT battery must be replaced or recharged after one-half the battery's useful life.

5-39. Answer C. GFDPPM 5-34 (AIM)
To prevent false alerts, ELT testing should be conducted only during the first 5 minutes after any hour.

5-40. Answer C. GFDPPM 5-34 (AIM)
By monitoring 121.5, you will be able to hear the ELT signal if it has been activated.

5-41. Answer C. GFDPPM 5-26 (AIM)
A clearance is authorization from ATC to operate under specific conditions in controlled airspace. It does not give a pilot priority over all other traffic (answer A), as other aircraft may also have an ATC clearance. While the purpose of a clearance is to provide separation from known traffic, it does not guarantee separation from unknown or nonparticipating aircraft (answer B).

5-42   J34
(Refer to figure 53 on page 5-5.) When approaching
Lincoln Municipal from the west at noon for the pur-
pose of landing, initial communications should be with

A — Lincoln Approach Control on 124.0 MHz.
B — Minneapolis Center on 128.75 MHz.
C — Lincoln Tower on 118.5 MHz.

5-43   J34
(Refer to figure 53 on page 5-5.) What is the recommended communications procedure for landing at
Lincoln Municipal during the hours when the tower is
not in operation?

A — Monitor airport traffic and announce your position and intentions on 118.5 MHz.
B — Contact UNICOM on 122.95 MHz for traffic
advisories.
C — Monitor ATIS for airport conditions, then
announce your position on 122.95 MHz.

5-42. Answer A. GFDPPM 5-26 (A/FD)
The communications section of the *Airport/Facility
Directory* indicates that the airport is in Class C airspace (formerly ARSA), and that you should contact
approach control. When west of the airport (170° –
349°), the frequency to use is 124.0. To confirm that
Lincoln Approach Control is operational at noon, check
the hours of operation. These are listed as 1200 —
0600Z, which is 0600 — 2400 local standard time.
Minneapolis Center (answer B) would be contacted
between 0600 and 1200 Z, which is midnight to 6 A.M.
local standard time. Contact should be made with
approach control, where available, prior to contacting
the tower (answer C).

5-43. Answer A. GFDPPM 5-23 (A/FD)
The CTAF frequency is listed as 118.5, and is used
when the tower is not in operation. Standard procedures are to monitor airport traffic and announce your
position on CTAF. UNICOM (answers B and C) is not
used for airport advisories when a CTAF is listed. It is a
good idea to listen to ATIS, but it might not be updated
after the tower closes.

SECTION C
SOURCES OF FLIGHT INFORMATION

Several aviation publications exist to aid you in planning a flight. These materials include the *Aeronautical Information Manual, Airport/Facility Directory, Federal Aviation Regulations, advisory circulars, Jeppesen Pilot Resource Services*, and *Notices to Airmen*.

AIRPORT/FACILITY DIRECTORY
1. The letters VHF/DF appearing in the *Airport/Facility Directory* for a certain airport indicate that the FSS has equipment with which to determine your direction from the station.
2. Information regarding parachute jumping is listed in the *Airport/Facility Directory*.

ADVISORY CIRCULARS
3. FAA advisory circulars may be ordered directly from the Government Printing Office.
4. Particular FAA advisory circulars that relate to certain subject matters are identified by codes. Those pertaining to Airmen are issued under subject number 60. Those relating to Airspace are listed under subject number 70. Those which involve ATC and General Operations are listed under subject number 90.

5-44   J34
(Refer to figure 23, area 2 and legend 1 on pages 4-20 and 4-17.) For information about the parachute jumping and glider operations at Silverwood Airport, refer to

A — notes on the border of the chart.
B — the Airport/Facility Directory.
C — the Notices to Airmen (NOTAM) publication.

5-45   M52
FAA advisory circulars (some free, others at cost) are available to all pilots and are obtained by

A — distribution from the nearest FAA district office.
B — ordering those desired from the Government Printing Office.
C — subscribing to the Federal Register.

5-46   J34
(Refer to figure 53 on page 5-5.) Where is Loup City Municipal located with relation to the city?

A — Northeast approximately 3 miles.
B — Northwest approximately 1 mile.
C — East approximately 10 miles.

5-47   J34
(Refer to figure 53 on page 5-5.) Traffic patterns in effect at Lincoln Municipal are

A — to the right on Runway 17L and Runway 35L; to the left on Runway 17R and Runway 35R.
B — to the left on Runway 17L and Runway 35L; to the right on Runway 17R and Runway 35R.
C — to the right on Runways 14 — 32.

5-44. Answer B. GFDPPM 5-39 (Chart Legend)
The *Airport/Facility Directory* lists information on parachute jumping areas. This information is not found on the border of the chart (answer A) or in the NOTAM publication (answer C).

5-45. Answer B. GFDPPM 5-46 (PHB)
Advisory circulars may be ordered directly from the Government Printing Office. FAA district offices (answer A) do not stock advisory circulars for sale to the public. The Federal Register (answer C) contains notices of proposed rulemaking and final rules, but does not contain advisory circulars.

5-46. Answer B. GFDPPM 5-38 (A/FD)
The first line of the A/FD includes the distance and direction from the associated city. The entry 1 NW indicates that the airport is 1 mile northwest of the city. The entry (NE03) is the location identifier, not a direction and distance (answer A). The last line of the A/FD entry contains the entry 2010/10E, which is the site elevation of the VORTAC, followed by the magnetic variation, not direction and distance (answer C).

5-47. Answer B. GFDPPM 5-38 (A/FD)
Remarks following the runway data for each runway include nonstandard traffic patterns. Left-hand patterns are used if not otherwise stated. Right-hand traffic is noted for Runway 17R and Runway 35R. Left traffic is used for Runways 17L, 35L, 14, and 32.

5-48   J34

The letters VHF/DF appearing in the Airport/Facility Directory for a certain airport indicate that

A — this airport is designated as an airport of entry.
B — the Flight Service Station has equipment with which to determine your direction from the station.
C — this airport has a direct-line phone to the Flight Service Station.

5-49   M52

FAA advisory circulars containing subject matter specifically related to Airmen are issued under which subject number?

A — 60.
B — 70.
C — 90.

5-50   M52

FAA advisory circulars containing subject matter specifically related to Airspace are issued under which subject number?

A — 60.
B — 70.
C — 90.

5-51   M52

FAA advisory circulars containing subject matter specifically related to Air Traffic Control and General Operations are issued under which subject number?

A — 60.
B — 70.
C — 90.

5-48. Answer B. GFDPPM 5-38 (A/FD)
Some Flight Service Stations have direction finding equipment. This capability is noted in the A/FD listing for the FSS airport under Radio Aids to Navigation. An airport of entry (answer A) is designated by the letters AOE. Flight service phone numbers (answer C) are listed in the A/FD, usually with an 800 number.

5-49. Answer A. GFDPPM 5-45 (AC 00-2)
Advisory circulars relating to Airmen are issued under subject number 60. Airspace is covered under number 70 (answer B), and 90 covers Air Traffic Control and General Operating Rules (answer C).

5-50. Answer B. GFDPPM 5-45 (AC 00-2)
See explanation for Question 5-49.

5-51. Answer C. GFDPPM 5-45 (AC 00-2)
See explanation for Question 5-49.

METEOROLOGY FOR PILOTS

SECTION A
BASIC WEATHER THEORY

Weather touches every aspect of flight. As pilots we are inextricably linked to the weather. In this section, we'll look at the basic framework of weather theory and its significance to flight operations. Subject areas include the atmosphere, circulation/pressure, temperature and moisture. In addition to the *Private Pilot Manual*, you may wish to consult Jeppesen's *Aviation Weather*.

ATMOSPHERIC CIRCULATION
Atmospheric circulation refers to the movement of air relative to the earth's surface.

TEMPERATURE
1. Every physical process of weather is accompanied by, or is the result of, a heat exchange.

ATMOSPHERIC PRESSURE
2. Unequal heating of the Earth's surface causes variations in altimeter settings between weather reporting points.

FRICTIONAL FORCE
3. Below 2000 feet AGL, friction with the Earth's surface deflects the wind, making the winds at the surface generally different from the winds aloft.

LOCAL WIND PATTERNS
4. Convective circulation patterns associated with sea breezes are caused by cool, dense air moving inland from over the water.

6-1 **I21**
What causes variations in altimeter settings between weather reporting points?

A — Unequal heating of the Earth's surface.
B — Variation of terrain elevation.
C — Coriolis force.

6-1. Answer A. GFDPPM 6-7 (AW)
Temperature changes cause variations in air pressure and density. Because the earth's surface is heated unevenly, altimeter settings will be different between weather stations. Answer (B) is wrong because altimeter settings are referenced to a standard datum, and elevation alone is not the cause of variations. Answer (C) is incorrect because Coriolis force deflects the circulation of air masses, but does not directly cause variations in altimeter settings.

6-2 **I23**
The wind at 5,000 feet AGL is southwesterly while the surface wind is southerly. This difference in direction is primarily due to

A — stronger pressure gradient at higher altitudes.
B — friction between the wind and the surface.
C — stronger Coriolis force at the surface.

6-2. Answer B. GFDPPM 6-9 (AW)
Above 2,000 feet AGL, wind flows along isobars. Below that altitude, friction with the earth's surface deflects the wind. Answer (A) is wrong because the pressure gradient is not always stronger at higher altitudes. Answer (C) is wrong because winds are generally calmer at lower altitudes. As a result, Coriolis force is not as effective as friction near the surface.

6-3   I35

Convective circulation patterns associated with sea breezes are caused by

A — warm, dense air moving inland from over the water.

B — water absorbing and radiating heat faster than the land.

C — cool, dense air moving inland from over the water.

6-3. Answer C. GFDPPM 6-11 (AW)

During the day, land surfaces become warmer than the adjacent water surfaces. This warms the air above the land causing the air to rise. The rising air is replaced by the inland flow of cooler, denser air located over the water. As the warm air flows over the water it cools and descends. This starts the cycle all over again. During the night, the process is reversed as the land cools off faster than the water. Answer (A) is wrong because cool, not warm, air moves inland. Answer (B) is incorrect because sea breezes are a result of the land, not the water, absorbing and radiating heat faster.

SECTION B
WEATHER PATTERNS

Weather patterns clue you into trends that directly affect your flying. Grasping the movement of weather patterns will aid you greatly during all of your flights. This section covers atmospheric stability, cloud types, air masses, and fronts.

ATMOSPHERIC STABILITY
1. Stability of the air can be measured by its actual lapse rate.
2. A characteristic of stable air is the presence of stratiform clouds.
3. When moist, stable air flows upslope, you can expect the formation of stratus type clouds.
4. Characteristics of unstable air include turbulence and good surface visibility.

TEMPERATURE INVERSIONS
5. A temperature inversion most often denotes an increase in temperature as altitude is increased.
6. The most frequent type of ground or surface-based temperature inversion is that which is produced by terrestrial radiation on a clear, relatively still night.
7. The weather conditions that can be expected beneath a low-level temperature inversion layer when the relative humidity is high are smooth air, poor visibility, fog, haze or low clouds.
8. A temperature inversion is associated with a stable layer of air.

MOISTURE
9. The processes by which moisture is added to unsaturated air are evaporation and sublimation.

DEWPOINT
10. The dewpoint is the temperature to which the air must be cooled in order to become saturated.
11. The amount of water vapor which air can hold depends on the air temperature.

FROST
12. If the temperature of the collecting surface is at or below the dewpoint of the adjacent air, and the dewpoint is below freezing, frost will form.
13. Frost on the wings affects takeoff performance by disrupting the smooth flow of air over the airfoil, adversely affecting its lifting capacity. Frost may prevent the airplane from becoming airborne at normal takeoff speed. Frost is considered a hazard to flight for this reason.

CLOUDS
14. Cloud bases can be estimated by using a lapse rate of 4.5 degrees per 1000 feet and the temperature/dewpoint spread. Divide the temperature/dewpoint spread by the lapse rate to find the height of the cloud bases above the surface, in thousands of feet.
15. Clouds, fog or dew will always form when water vapor condenses.

TYPES
16. Clouds are divided into four families according to their height range. These are low clouds, middle clouds, high clouds, and clouds with vertical development.

NIMBUS
17. The suffix "nimbus," used in naming clouds, denotes a rain cloud.

STRATUS
18. Stratus clouds form when moist, stable air flows upslope.

FOG
19. If the temperature/dewpoint spread is small and decreasing, and the temperature is above freezing, fog or low clouds are likely to develop.

20. Radiation fog forms as warm, moist air lies over flatland areas on clear, calm nights.
21. Advection fog forms when a warm air mass moves inland from the coast in winter.
22. Advection fog and upslope fog depend upon wind in order to exist.
23. Low-level turbulence can occur, and icing can become hazardous in steam fog.

CLOUDS WITH VERTICAL DEVELOPMENT
24. Clouds with extensive vertical development and associated turbulence can be expected when an unstable air-mass is forced upward.

PRECIPITATION
Precipitation can range from light rain that is easy to fly through, to freezing rain that poses a serious hazard to all types of aircraft, even those with de-ice and anti-ice equipment.

TYPES
25. The presence of ice pellets at the surface is evidence that there is a temperature inversion with freezing rain at a higher altitude.

AIRMASSES
Airmasses are large-scale parcels of air that have a set of characteristics (i.e. moist, unstable) that distinguishes them from one another.

CLASSIFICATIONS
27. Characteristics of a moist, unstable airmass are cumuliform clouds and showery precipitation.
28. A stable airmass generally contains smooth air.

FRONTS
29. The boundary between two different airmasses is referred to as a front.

FRONTAL DISCONTINUITIES
30. One of the most easily recognizable discontinuities across a front is a change in temperature.
31. One weather phenomenon which will always occur when flying across a front is a change in the wind direction.

FRONTAL WEATHER
32. Steady precipitation preceding a front is an indication of stratiform clouds with little or no turbulence.

6-4   H300
How will frost on the wings of an airplane affect take-off performance?

A — Frost will disrupt the smooth flow of air over the wing, adversely affecting its lifting capability.
B — Frost will change the camber of the wing, increasing its lifting capability.
C — Frost will cause the airplane to become airborne with a higher angle of attack, decreasing the stall speed.

6-4. Answer A. GFDPPM 6-20 (PHB)
Frost disrupts the smooth airflow over the wing and can cause early separation of the airflow, resulting in a loss of lift. Frost does not significantly change the camber (answer B), but it can disrupt the airflow and decrease the lift. The decreased lift caused by frost can cause the stall speed to increase, not decrease (answer C).

6-5   I21
Every physical process of weather is accompanied by, or is the result of, a

A — movement of air.
B — pressure differential.
C — heat exchange.

6-5. Answer C. GFDPPM 6-19 (AW)
Every physical process of weather such as heating, cooling, evaporation, and condensation, is caused by, or is the result of, a heat exchange. Answers (A) and (B) are wrong because air movement and pressure differential are not always involved in the physical processes of weather.

6-6 **I21**

A temperature inversion would most likely result in which weather condition?

A — Clouds with extensive vertical development above an inversion aloft.
B — Good visibility in the lower levels of the atmosphere and poor visibility above an inversion aloft.
C — An increase in temperature as altitude is increased.

6-7 **I21**

The most frequent type of ground or surface-based temperature inversion is that which is produced by

A — terrestrial radiation on a clear, relatively still night.
B — warm air being lifted rapidly aloft in the vicinity of mountainous terrain.
C — the movement of colder air under warm air, or the movement of warm air over cold air.

6-8 **I21**

Which weather conditions should be expected beneath a low-level temperature inversion layer when the relative humidity is high?

A — Smooth air, poor visibility, fog, haze, or low clouds.
B — Light wind shear, poor visibility, haze, and light rain.
C — Turbulent air, poor visibility, fog, low stratus type clouds, and shower precipitation.

6-9 **I24**

What is meant by the term "dewpoint"?

A — The temperature at which condensation and evaporation are equal.
B — The temperature at which dew will always form.
C — The temperature to which air must be cooled to become saturated.

6-10 **I24**

The amount of water vapor which air can hold depends on the

A — dewpoint.
B — air temperature.
C — stability of the air.

6-6. Answer C. GFDPPM 6-17 (AW)
Normally, temperature decreases with altitude. During an inversion, cooler air is trapped beneath a warmer layer of air. Therefore, temperature increases with altitude. Answer (A) is wrong since inversions occur in stable air, and vertical development of clouds requires unstable air. Answer (B) is incorrect because weather and pollutants are trapped beneath inversions, and visibility near the surface is usually poor.

6-7. Answer A. GFDPPM 6-18 (AW)
An inversion commonly forms on clear, cool nights when the ground radiates heat and cools faster than the overlying air. Answers (B) and (C) are not examples of surface-based temperature inversions. Answer (B) describes orographic lifting of air over rising terrain and answer (C) describes a cold front inversion.

6-8. Answer A. GFDPPM 6-17 (AW)
Low-level temperature inversions normally occur in stable, smooth air, with poor visibility due to trapped pollutants which are commonly referred to as condensation nuclei. In addition, high humidity tends to cause formation of fog and low clouds. Answers (B) and (C) are not entirely correct, because wind shear, turbulence, and showery precipitation are uncharacteristic conditions in the stable air below the inversion layer.

6-9. Answer C. GFDPPM 6-20 (AW)
When air is cooled to its dewpoint, it can hold no more moisture, and is said to be saturated. Answer (A) is incorrect because dewpoint is not a measure of condensation or evaporation. Answer (B) is wrong because the formation of dew requires the surface temperature of objects to cool below the dewpoint of the surrounding air.

6-10. Answer B. GFDPPM 6-19 (AW)
The amount of moisture in the air primarily depends on the temperature. For example, warm air can hold more moisture than cool air. The dewpoint (answer A) is the temperature at which the air reaches saturation (see explanation for Question 6-9). Answer (C) is wrong because stability of the air does not directly affect the moisture content.

6-11　　　I24
Clouds, fog, or dew will always form when

A — water vapor condenses.
B — water vapor is present.
C — relative humidity reaches 100 percent.

6-12　　　I24
What are the processes by which moisture is added to unsaturated air?

A — Evaporation and sublimation.
B — Heating and condensation.
C — Supersaturation and evaporation.

6-13　　　I24
Which conditions result in the formation of frost?

A — The temperature of the collecting surface is at or below freezing when small droplets of moisture fall on the surface.
B — The temperature of the collecting surface is at or below the dewpoint of the adjacent air and the dewpoint is below freezing.
C — The temperature of the surrounding air is at or below freezing when small drops of moisture fall on the collecting surface.

6-14　　　I24
The presence of ice pellets at the surface is evidence that there

A — are thunderstorms in the area.
B — has been cold frontal passage.
C — is a temperature inversion with freezing rain at a higher altitude.

6-15　　　I25
What measurement can be used to determine the stability of the atmosphere?

A — Atmospheric pressure.
B — Actual lapse rate.
C — Surface temperature.

6-11. Answer A. GFDPPM 6-22 (AW)
Condensation occurs when water vapor changes to liquid form. Examples are when water vapor changes to clouds, fog, or dew. Answer (B) is incorrect, because the water vapor, which is present in the air, must be cooled to a temperature at or near the dewpoint before it condenses to its liquid form. Relative humidity (answer C) is a measure of how much water the air can hold. At 100% relative humidity, the air is saturated, but the water vapor may not always condense to form clouds, fog, or dew.

6-12. Answer A. GFDPPM 6-19 (AW)
Evaporation occurs when liquid water changes to water vapor. Sublimation is the changing of ice directly to water vapor. Both processes add moisture to the air. Answer (B) is wrong because condensation removes water vapor from the air by changing it to liquid form. Answer (C) is wrong because super-saturation can occur only in air that is already saturated after it has been cooled from a higher temperature to a temperature below the point at which saturation occurs.

6-13. Answer B. GFDPPM 6-20 (AW)
When the dewpoint of the surrounding air is below freezing, and the collecting surface is at or below the dewpoint, water vapor sublimates directly into ice crystals or frost instead of condensing into dew. Answer (A) describes conditions resulting in frozen dew or raindrops, which form hard, clear ice, not frost. Answer (C) is incorrect because the collecting surface must be below the dewpoint, and the dewpoint must be below freezing.

6-14. Answer C. GFDPPM 6-27 (AW)
Due to a temperature inversion, a warm layer of air is aloft and keeps the rain in liquid form. As the rain falls through colder air, it begins to freeze, finally turning into ice pellets. Ice pellets always indicate freezing rain at a higher altitude. Ice pellets can form under various conditions, and do not necessarily indicate thunderstorms (answer A). Answer (B) is wrong because ice pellets may be formed in either a warm front or a cold front.

6-15. Answer B. GFDPPM 6-17 (AW)
The stability of air refers to its resistance to displacement upward or downward; it is determined by the actual lapse rate. Lapse rate generally refers to the decrease in temperature with an increase in altitude. A high lapse rate tends to indicate unstable air, and a low lapse rate is an indicator of stability in the atmosphere. Answers (A) and (C) are wrong because air pressure and surface temperature do not directly affect stability.

6-16   I25
What would decrease the stability of an air mass?

A — Warming from below.
B — Cooling from below.
C — Decrease in water vapor.

6-17   I25
What is a characteristic of stable air?

A — Stratiform clouds.
B — Unlimited visibility.
C — Cumulus clouds.

6-18   I25
Moist, stable air flowing upslope can be expected to

A — produce stratus type clouds.
B — cause showers and thunderstorms.
C — develop convective turbulence.

6-19   I25
If an unstable air mass is forced upward, what type clouds can be expected?

A — Stratus clouds with little vertical development.
B — Stratus clouds with considerable associated turbulence.
C — Clouds with considerable vertical development and associated turbulence.

6-20   I25
What feature is associated with a temperature inversion?

A — A stable layer of air.
B — An unstable layer of air.
C — Chinook winds on mountain slopes.

6-21   I25
What is the approximate base of the cumulus clouds if the surface air temperature at 1,000 feet MSL is 70°F and the dewpoint is 48°F?

A — 4,000 feet MSL.
B — 5,000 feet MSL.
C — 6,000 feet MSL.

6-16. Answer A. GFDPPM 6-16 (AW)
Stability is altered by a change in the lapse rate of an air mass. Warming from below or cooling from above will increase the lapse rate and make the air less stable. Cooling from below (answer B) and a decrease in water vapor (answer C) both cause the air to become more dense and tend to increase stability.

6-17. Answer A. GFDPPM 6-23 (AW)
There is very little vertical development of clouds in stable air, and stratiform clouds and poor visibility are typical. Cumulus clouds and good visibility are indicators of unstable air.

6-18. Answer A. GFDPPM 6-23 (AW)
Stratus clouds are produced in stable air. When moist air flows upslope it cools to its saturation point, and clouds are formed. Showers and thunderstorms (answer B) and convective turbulence (answer C) are indicative of unstable air.

6-19. Answer C. GFDPPM 6-25 (AW)
Clouds with extensive vertical development are formed when unstable air is lifted. These cumulus type clouds are associated with moderate to severe turbulence. Stratus clouds (answers A and B) are a characteristic of smooth, stable air.

6-20. Answer A. GFDPPM 6-17 (AW)
Temperature inversions occur in stable air. Inversions cannot form in unstable air (answer B). As Chinook winds (answer C) descend, the temperature rises. This is the opposite of an inversion (cooler air under a warmer layer). In the U.S., the typical example of Chinook winds is the downslope, easterly flow from the Rocky Mountains.

6-21. Answer C. GFDPPM 6-20 (AW)
Cloud bases can be estimated by using a lapse rate of 4.5°F per 1,000 feet and the temperature/dewpoint spread (70 – 48 = 22). Divide 22 by 4.5 to find the approximate cloud base in thousands of feet. In this case, the cloud bases will be 4,889 (22 ÷ 4.5 × 1,000) feet above the surface, or rounded to 5,000 feet. Since the surface is 1,000 feet MSL, the cloud base should be approximately 6,000 feet MSL.

6-22   I25

At approximately what altitude above the surface would the pilot expect the base of cumuliform clouds if the surface air temperature is 82°F and the dewpoint is 38°F?

A — 9,000 feet AGL.
B — 10,000 feet AGL.
C — 11,000 feet AGL.

6-23   I25

What are characteristics of a moist, unstable air mass?

A — Cumuliform clouds and showery precipitation.
B — Poor visibility and smooth air.
C — Stratiform clouds and showery precipitation.

6-24   I25

What are characteristics of unstable air?

A — Turbulence and good surface visibility.
B — Turbulence and poor surface visibility.
C — Nimbostratus clouds and good surface visibility.

6-25   I25

A stable air mass is most likely to have which characteristic?

A — Showery precipitation.
B — Turbulent air.
C — Smooth air.

6-26   I26

The suffix "nimbus," used in naming clouds, means

A — a cloud with extensive vertical development.
B — a rain cloud.
C — a middle cloud containing ice pellets.

6-27   I26

Clouds are divided into four families according to their

A — outward shape.
B — height range.
C — composition.

6-22. Answer B. GFDPPM 6-20 (AW)

See explanation for Question 6-22. The temperature/dewpoint spread is 44 (82 – 38). Divide 44 by the lapse rate of 4.5°F per 1,000 feet to find cloud bases at 9,778 feet AGL, rounded to 10,000 feet AGL.

6-23. Answer A. GFDPPM 6-29 (AW)

Cumuliform clouds are indicative of unstable air. These clouds normally produce showery, not continuous, precipitation. Poor visibility, smooth air (answer B), and stratiform clouds (answer C) are characteristic of stable air.

6-24. Answer A. GFDPPM 6-29 (AW)

The lifting motion of unstable air produces turbulence. Clouds and pollutants are not trapped as they are in stable layers of air, and good visibility is typical with unstable air. Poor surface visibility (answer B) and nimbostratus clouds (answer C) are typical of stable air masses.

6-25. Answer C. GFDPPM 6-29 (AW)

Stable air resists the lifting motion that is associated with turbulence, and is typically smooth. Showery precipitation (answer A) and turbulent air (answer B) are characteristics of unstable air.

6-26. Answer B. GFDPPM 6-22 (AW)

The word "nimbus" is the Latin word for rainstorm or cloud, and is used today to designate rain clouds, such as cumulonimbus or nimbostratus. Answer (A) describes a cumuliform cloud which commonly is called a towering cumulus. Answer (C) is wrong because nimbus means a rain cloud, not a middle cloud, or a cloud with ice pellets.

6-27. Answer B. GFDPPM 6-22 (AW)

Clouds are also grouped by families according to their altitudes (height range). The four families are low, middle, high, and clouds with extensive vertical development. Outward shape (answer A) and composition (answer C) are used to determine specific cloud types, such as cumulus, nimbostratus, and cirrus. These are not characteristics of the family classification.

6-28   I27

The boundary between two different air masses is referred to as a

A — frontolysis.
B — frontogenesis.
C — front.

6-29   I27

One of the most easily recognized discontinuities across a front is

A — a change in temperature.
B — an increase in cloud coverage.
C — an increase in relative humidity.

6-30   I27

One weather phenomenon which will always occur when flying across a front is a change in the

A — wind direction.
B — type of precipitation.
C — stability of the air mass.

6-31   I27

Steady precipitation preceding a front is an indication of

A — stratiform clouds with moderate turbulence.
B — cumuliform clouds with little or no turbulence.
C — stratiform clouds with little or no turbulence.

6-32   I31

What situation is most conducive to the formation of radiation fog?

A — Warm, moist air over low, flatland areas on clear, calm nights.
B — Moist, tropical air moving over cold, offshore water.
C — The movement of cold air over much warmer water.

6-33   I31

If the temperature/dewpoint spread is small and decreasing, and the temperature is 62°F, what type weather is most likely to develop?

A — Freezing precipitation.
B — Thunderstorms.
C — Fog or low clouds.

6-28. Answer C. GFDPPM 6-30 (AW)

The boundary area where two air masses of different properties meet is called a front. Frontolysis (answer A) is incorrect because it means the dissipation of a weather front. Frontogenesis (answer B) means the initial formation of a front.

6-29. Answer A. GFDPPM 6-31 (AW)

Since a front is the boundary between air masses of differing temperatures, one of the easiest ways to recognize frontal passage is the change in temperature. Cloud coverage (answer B) may increase or decrease, depending on the type of front. A change in relative humidity (answer C) also depends on the type of front.

6-30. Answer A. GFDPPM 6-31 (AW)

A shift in wind direction always occurs across a front. A change in the type of precipitation (answer B) sometimes, but not always, accompanies frontal passage. The same is true of stability (answer C); it does not always change.

6-31. Answer C. GFDPPM 6-23, 32 (AW)

Steady precipitation, stratiform clouds, and little or no turbulence are all typical of stable air. Stratiform clouds and steady precipitation are not usually associated with moderate turbulence (answer A). Cumuliform clouds are found in unstable air and are accompanied by turbulence and showery precipitation (answer B).

6-32. Answer A. GFDPPM 6-23 (AW)

On clear, calm nights in flat areas, radiation fog forms when moist air cools to its dewpoint. Ground fog is a form of radiation fog. Fog that forms when warm, moist air moves over a cooler surface (answer B) is called advection fog. Cold, dry air moving over warmer water (answer C) causes the formation of steam fog.

6-33. Answer C. GFDPPM 6-22 (AW)

When the temperature/dewpoint spread decreases to zero, the likely result is the condensation of water vapor into visible moisture, such as fog or low clouds. Answer (A) is incorrect, since 62°F is well above freezing, and the water will be in liquid form, not freezing precipitation. Answer (B) is wrong because thunderstorms are associated with unstable air rather than temperature/dewpoint spread.

6-34   I31

In which situation is advection fog most likely to form?

A — A warm, moist air mass on the windward side of mountains.
B — An air mass moving inland from the coast in winter.
C — A light breeze blowing colder air out to sea.

6-35   I31

What types of fog depend upon wind in order to exist?

A — Radiation fog and ice fog.
B — Steam fog and ground fog.
C — Advection fog and upslope fog.

6-36   I33

Low-level turbulence can occur and icing can become hazardous in which type of fog?

A — Rain-induced fog.
B — Upslope fog.
C — Steam fog.

6-34. Answer B. GFDPPM 6-23 (AW)

See explanation for Question 6-32. When warmer air moves inland, advection fog is likely to form. Warm, moist air being lifted up a mountain slope (answer A) would form upslope fog. Colder air moving over the sea (answer C) would tend to form steam fog.

6-35. Answer C. GFDPPM 6-23 (AW)

See explanations for Questions 6-32 and 6-34. Answer (C) is the only correct choice since steam fog also requires the movement of air. Both ice fog and radiation fog (answer A), also known as ground fog (answer B), form in calm air.

6-36. Answer C. GFDPPM 6-23 (AW)

Steam fog is formed by cold, dry air moving over warmer water. As the water particles evaporate and rise, they often freeze and fall back into the water. Icing and low-level turbulence can result. Normally, turbulence and icing are not common with rain-induced fog (answer A) or upslope fog (answer B).

SECTION C
WEATHER HAZARDS

As a pilot, you can combine knowledge of the weather with respect for what it can do to avoid flying in the most hazardous conditions. This section covers such hazards as thunderstorms, turbulence, icing and restrictions to visibility, addressing cause, as well as hazardous effects.

THUNDERSTORMS
1. Cumulonimbus clouds have the greatest turbulence.
2. The conditions necessary for the formation of cumulonimbus clouds are a lifting action and unstable, moist air.
3. Thunderstorms are formed when high humidity, lifting force and unstable conditions combine.

TYPES
4. Thunderstorms which generally produce the most intense hazard to aircraft are squall line thunderstorms.
5. A non-frontal, narrow band of active thunderstorms that often develops ahead of a cold front is known as a squall line.

LIFE CYCLE
6. The cumulus stage of a thunderstorm is associated with a continuous updraft.
7. The mature stage of a thunderstorm begins with precipitation beginning to fall.
8. Thunderstorms reach their greatest intensity during the mature stage.
9. The dissipating stage is characterized predominantly by downdrafts.

HAZARDS
10. If there is thunderstorm activity in the vicinity of an airport at which you plan to land, you can expect to encounter wind-shear turbulence during the landing approach.
11. Lightning is always associated with thunderstorms.

TURBULENCE
12. Upon encountering severe turbulence, the pilot should attempt to maintain a level flight attitude.
13. Towering cumulus clouds indicate convective turbulence.

WAKE TURBULENCE
14. Wingtip vortices are created only when an aircraft is developing lift.
15. The greatest vortex strength occurs when the generating aircraft is heavy, clean and slow.
16. Wingtip vortices created by a large aircraft tend to sink below the aircraft that is generating the turbulence.
17. When taking off or landing at an airport where heavy aircraft are operating, one should be particularly alert to the hazards of wingtip vortices because this turbulence tends to sink into the flight path of the aircraft operating below the aircraft generating the turbulence.
18. The wind condition that requires maximum caution when avoiding wake turbulence on landing is a light, quartering tailwind.

MOUNTAIN WAVE TURBULENCE
19. An almond or lens-shaped cloud which appears stationary, but which may contain winds of up to 50 knots or more, is referred to as a lenticular cloud.
20. Crests of standing mountain waves may be marked by stationary, lens-shaped clouds known as standing lenticular clouds.
21. Possible mountain wave turbulence could be anticipated when winds of 40 knots or greater blow across a mountain ridge, when the air is stable.

WIND SHEAR
22. Wind shear can occur at all altitudes, in all directions.
23. Hazardous wind shear may be expected in areas of low-level temperature inversion, frontal zones and clear air turbulence.

24. A pilot can expect a wind shear zone in a temperature inversion whenever the wind speed at 2000 to 4000 feet above the surface is at least 25 knots.

ICING
25. Visible moisture is necessary for the formation of in-flight structural icing.
26. Areas of freezing rain create the environment in which structural icing is most likely to have the highest accumulation rate.

6-37   I26
An almond or lens-shaped cloud which appears stationary, but which may contain winds of 50 knots or more, is referred to as

A — an inactive frontal cloud.
B — a funnel cloud.
C — a lenticular cloud.

6-38   I26
Crests of standing mountain waves may be marked by stationary, lens-shaped clouds known as

A — mammatocumulus clouds.
B — standing lenticular clouds.
C — roll clouds.

6-39   I26
What clouds have the greatest turbulence?

A — Towering cumulus.
B — Cumulonimbus.
C — Nimbostratus.

6-40   I26
What cloud types would indicate convective turbulence?

A — Cirrus clouds.
B — Nimbostratus clouds.
C — Towering cumulus clouds.

6-41   I28
Possible mountain wave turbulence could be anticipated when winds of 40 knots or greater blow

A — across a mountain ridge, and the air is stable.
B — down a mountain valley, and the air is unstable.
C — parallel to a mountain peak, and the air is stable.

6-37. Answer C. GFDPPM 6-50 (AW)
Lenticular clouds are the lens-shaped clouds that form at the crests of mountain waves. An inactive frontal cloud (answer A) is obviously an incorrect choice. Frontal clouds with 50-knot winds would not be stationary. A funnel cloud (answer B) is associated with a tornado, and is neither lens-shaped or stationary.

6-38. Answer B. GFDPPM 6-50 (AW)
See explanation for Question 6-37. Mammatocumulus clouds (answer A) are typically associated with thunderstorms, not mountain waves. Roll clouds (answer C) are commonly found on the leading edge of thunderstorms, not mountain waves.

6-39. Answer B. GFDPPM 6-42 (AW)
Cumulonimbus clouds, which form thunderstorms and tornadoes, produce the most severe turbulence. Towering cumulus clouds (answer A) will have some turbulence, but not nearly as severe as a thunderstorm. Nimbostratus (answer C), a type of stratus cloud, usually has little or no turbulence.

6-40. Answer C. GFDPPM 6-45 (AW)
Towering cumulus clouds are formed by convective currents, caused by rising heated air. These rising air currents cause convective turbulence. Cirrus clouds (answer A) are found at high altitude and are not formed by convection. Nimbostratus clouds (answer B) usually have little or no turbulence.

6-41. Answer A. GFDPPM 6-50 (AW)
Mountain waves are formed when strong winds (40 knots or greater) flow across a barrier, such as a mountain ridge. When the air is stable, the flow is laminar, or layered, and creates a series of waves. Unstable air that is forced upward tends to continue rising, often creating thunderstorms. Wind flowing down a valley (answer B) will not form mountain waves. Wind blowing parallel to a mountain peak (answer C) may create some turbulence, but a single peak would not normally cause a mountain wave.

6-42   I28

Where does wind shear occur?

A — Only at higher altitudes.
B — Only at lower altitudes.
C — At all altitudes, in all directions.

6-43   I28

When may hazardous wind shear be expected?

A — When stable air crosses a mountain barrier where it tends to flow in layers forming lenticular clouds.
B — In areas of low-level temperature inversion, frontal zones, and clear air turbulence.
C — Following frontal passage when stratocumulus clouds form indicating mechanical mixing.

6-44   I28

A pilot can expect a wind shear zone in a temperature inversion whenever the windspeed at 2,000 to 4,000 feet above the surface is at least

A — 10 knots.
B — 15 knots.
C — 25 knots.

6-45   I28

One in-flight condition necessary for structural icing to form is

A — small temperature/dewpoint spread.
B — stratiform clouds.
C — visible moisture.

6-46   I29

In which environment is aircraft structural ice most likely to have the highest accumulation rate?

A — Cumulus clouds with below freezing temperatures.
B — Freezing drizzle.
C — Freezing rain.

6-42. Answer C. GFDPPM 6-51 (AW)
Wind shear can occur at middle and high altitudes near thunderstorms or the jet stream, and near the ground in the vicinity of thunderstorms or temperature inversions. The shear can be either vertical or horizontal. Answers (A) and (B) are wrong because wind shear can occur at any altitude.

6-43. Answer B. GFDPPM 6-50, 51 (AW)
Wind shear can be found above a temperature inversion when the surface air is cold and calm, and the warmer layer above it is moving at 25 knots or more. Since frontal zones are identified by a shift in the wind, wind shear can be expected. Clear air turbulence can be associated with either vertical or horizontal wind shear. Answer (A) describes a mountain wave, and wind shear may or may not be present. Some turbulence is common with stratocumulus clouds (answer C), but hazardous wind shear is not typical.

6-44. Answer C. GFDPPM 6-51 (AW)
A temperature inversion with light surface winds may form near the surface on a clear night. You can expect a shear zone in the inversion if the winds at 2,000 to 4,000 feet are 25 knots or more. Answers (A) and (B) are incorrect because of insufficient wind speed 2,000 to 4,000 feet above the surface.

6-45. Answer C. GFDPPM 6-53 (AW)
Structural icing requires two conditions to form: (1) visible moisture, such as rain or cloud droplets, and (2) temperature of the aircraft surface must be at or below freezing. A small temperature/dewpoint spread (answer A) may be present without visible moisture. Stratiform clouds (answer B) are not the only cloud types in which icing can occur.

6-46. Answer C. GFDPPM 6-53 (AW)
The rate of structural ice accumulation is usually the highest in freezing rain below a frontal surface. As the rain falls through air with temperatures below freezing it becomes supercooled. The supercooled drops freeze on impact with the large water droplets, and heavy rain accelerates the build up. Cumulus clouds (answer A) have varying sizes of water drops, and may not always cause a rapid buildup of ice. Freezing drizzle (answer B) has smaller droplets and icing will build up more slowly than larger drops.

6-47   I29

Why is frost considered hazardous to flight?

A — Frost changes the basic aerodynamic shape of the airfoils, thereby decreasing lift.
B — Frost slows the airflow over the airfoils, thereby increasing control effectiveness.
C — Frost spoils the smooth flow of air over the wings, thereby decreasing lifting capability.

6-48   I29

How does frost affect the lifting surfaces of an airplane on takeoff?

A — Frost may prevent the airplane from becoming airborne at normal takeoff speed.
B — Frost will change the camber of the wing, increasing lift during takeoff.
C — Frost may cause the airplane to become airborne with a lower angle of attack at a lower indicated airspeed.

6-49   I30

The conditions necessary for the formation of cumulonimbus clouds are a lifting action and

A — unstable air containing an excess of condensation nuclei.
B — unstable, moist air.
C — either stable or unstable air.

6-50   I30

What feature is normally associated with the cumulus stage of a thunderstorm?

A — Roll cloud.
B — Continuous updraft.
C — Frequent lightning.

6-51   I30

Which weather phenomenon signals the beginning of the mature stage of a thunderstorm?

A — The appearance of an anvil top.
B — Precipitation beginning to fall.
C — Maximum growth rate of the clouds.

6-47. Answer C. GFDPPM 6-20 (AW)

See explanation for Question 6-4. Frost does not significantly change the shape of the airfoil (answer A), but will cause early separation of the airflow. The airflow over the airfoil is not slowed (answer B), and control effectiveness is not increased.

6-48. Answer A. GFDPPM 6-20 (AW)

See explanations for Questions 6-4 and 6-47. By disrupting the airflow over the wings, frost can prevent an airplane from becoming airborne at the normal takeoff speed. Frost does not change the camber of a wing (answer B). The disrupted airflow would prevent the airplane from becoming airborne at a lower airspeed (answer C). Ground effect, not frost, is what causes an airplane to become airborne at a lower-than-normal angle of attack and airspeed.

6-49. Answer B. GFDPPM 6-38, 42 (AW)

Three conditions are normally required for the formation of cumulonimbus clouds. These are lifting action, instability, and moisture. An excess of condensation nuclei (answer A) would aid in the formation of water droplets, but moisture must also be present. Stable air (answer C) resists any upward (or downward) displacement and, therefore, inhibits the formation of cumulonimbus clouds.

6-50. Answer B. GFDPPM 6-40 (AW)

In the early, or cumulus, stage of a thunderstorm, continuous updrafts cause the cloud to build upwards. A roll cloud (answer A) forms at the leading edge of a mature thunderstorm. Frequent lightning (answer C) is seldom found in the cumulus stage, but is typical of the mature stage.

6-51. Answer B. GFDPPM 6-41 (AW)

The mature stage of a thunderstorm begins when the rain drops grow too large to be supported by the updrafts, and precipitation begins to fall. An anvil top (answer A) appears as a thunderstorm reaches the dissipating stage, not the mature stage. Maximum growth rate of the clouds (answer C) occurs during the cumulus stage, not the mature stage.

6-52   I30
What conditions are necessary for the formation of thunderstorms?

A — High humidity, lifting force, and unstable conditions.
B — High humidity, high temperature, and cumulus clouds.
C — Lifting force, moist air, and extensive cloud cover.

6-53   I30
During the life cycle of a thunderstorm, which stage is characterized predominately by downdrafts?

A — Cumulus.
B — Dissipating.
C — Mature.

6-54   I30
Thunderstorms reach their greatest intensity during the

A — mature stage.
B — downdraft stage.
C — cumulus stage.

6-55   I30
Thunderstorms which generally produce the most intense hazard to aircraft are

A — squall line thunderstorms.
B — steady-state thunderstorms.
C — warm front thunderstorms.

6-56   I30
A nonfrontal, narrow band of active thunderstorms that often develop ahead of a cold front is known as a

A — prefrontal system.
B — squall line.
C — dryline.

6-57   I30
If there is thunderstorm activity in the vicinity of an airport at which you plan to land, which hazardous atmospheric phenomenon might be expected on the landing approach?

A — Precipitation static.
B — Wind-shear turbulence.
C — Steady rain.

6-52. Answer A. GFDPPM 6-38 (AW)
See explanation for Question 6-49. As moist, unstable air is lifted, it builds cumulonimbus clouds, which form thunderstorms. Unless unstable conditions are present, thunderstorms will not form, so answers (B) and (C) are incorrect.

6-53. Answer B. GFDPPM 6-41 (AW)
As a thunderstorm dissipates, updrafts weaken and downdrafts become predominate. Also see explanations for Questions 6-50 and 6-51.

6-54. Answer A. GFDPPM 6-41 (AW)
Thunderstorms are most violent during the mature stage, with strong updrafts and downdrafts, severe turbulence, lightning, heavy rain, hail, strong surface winds, and gust fronts. Neither the dissipating stage, with its downdrafts (answer B), or the cumulus stage (answer C) and its updrafts, are as intense as the mature stage.

6-55. Answer A. GFDPPM 6-39 (AW)
Squall lines often contain severe steady-state thunderstorms and present the most hazardous conditions to aircraft. Steady-state thunderstorms (answer B) by themselves are hazardous, but squall line thunderstorms are the most severe. Warm front thunderstorms (answer C) are generally not as severe as squall line thunderstorms.

6-56. Answer B. GFDPPM 6-39 (AW)
Squall lines are a narrow band of thunderstorms that often develop ahead of a cold front. A prefrontal system (answer A) or dry line (answer C) are not terms used to describe this narrow band of thunderstorms.

6-57. Answer B. GFDPPM 6-50 (AW)
In the vicinity of thunderstorms, hazardous wind-shear turbulence should always be expected. Precipitation static (answer A), known as "St. Elmo's fire," is not hazardous. Steady rain (answer C) is not normally found with thunderstorms, and is not hazardous unless it is freezing.

6-58   I30
Upon encountering severe turbulence, which flight condition should the pilot attempt to maintain?

A — Constant altitude and airspeed.
B — Constant angle of attack.
C — Level flight attitude.

6-59   I36
Which weather phenomenon is always associated with a thunderstorm?

A — Lightning.
B — Heavy rain.
C — Hail.

6-60   J27
Wingtip vortices are created only when an aircraft is

A — operating at high airspeeds.
B — heavily loaded.
C — developing lift.

6-61   J27
The greatest vortex strength occurs when the generating aircraft is

A — light, dirty, and fast.
B — heavy, dirty, and fast.
C — heavy, clean, and slow.

6-62   J27
Wingtip vortices created by large aircraft tend to

A — sink below the aircraft generating turbulence.
B — rise into the traffic pattern.
C — rise into the takeoff or landing path of a crossing runway.

6-63   J27
When taking off or landing at an airport where heavy aircraft are operating, one should be particularly alert to the hazards of wingtip vortices because this turbulence tends to

A — rise from a crossing runway into the takeoff or landing path.
B — rise into the traffic pattern area surrounding the airport.
C — sink into the flightpath of aircraft operating below the aircraft generating the turbulence.

6-58. Answer C. GFDPPM 6-44 (AW)
If entering severe turbulence, the best procedure is to slow to a speed not faster than maneuvering airspeed and maintain a constant level flight attitude. Variations in airspeed and altitude should be expected and tolerated. Constant altitude and airspeed (answer A) or constant angle of attack (answer B) will be practically impossible to maintain.

6-59. Answer A. GFDPPM 6-43 (AW)
Since thunder is caused by lightning, the name thunderstorm implies that lightning is always associated with a thunderstorms. Heavy rain (answer B) or hail (answer C) may not always be present, depending on the severity of the storm.

6-60. Answer C. GFDPPM 6-47 (PHB)
Anytime an aircraft is developing lift, air flows over the wingtip to form wingtip vortices. High speed (answer A) would tend to decrease wingtip vortices, and the heavier an aircraft (answer B), the stronger the vortices, but they are created at any weight.

6-61. Answer C. GFDPPM 6-47 (PHB)
Heavy aircraft, in a clean configuration, flying at low airspeeds with high angles of attack, generate the strongest vortices. A "dirty" configuration, or gear and flaps down (answers A and B), reduces the vortex strength.

6-62. Answer A. GFDPPM 6-47 (PHB)
Wingtip vortices tend to sink below the flight path of the aircraft which generated them. Vortices are not known to rise (answers B and C).

6-63. Answer C. GFDPPM 6-47 (PHB)
See explanation for Question 6-62.

6-64   J27

The wind condition that requires maximum caution when avoiding wake turbulence on landing is a

A — light, quartering headwind.
B — light, quartering tailwind.
C — strong headwind.

6-64. Answer B. GFDPPM 6-47 (PHB)

A light, quartering tailwind is the most hazardous because it can move the upwind vortex over the runway and forward into the landing zone. A light, quartering headwind (answer A) would move the upwind vortex over the runway, but would also move it back away from the landing zone. A strong headwind (answer C) would help dissipate wake turbulence, and is not as hazardous as a light, quartering tailwind.

6-65   J27

When landing behind a large aircraft, the pilot should avoid wake turbulence by staying

A — above the large aircraft's final approach path and landing beyond the large aircraft's touchdown point.
B — below the large aircraft's final approach path and landing before the large aircraft's touchdown point.
C — above the large aircraft's final approach path and landing before the large aircraft's touchdown point.

6-65. Answer A. GFDPPM 6-47 (PHB)

Since wake turbulence tends to sink, a following aircraft should stay above the large aircraft's flight path and land beyond its touchdown point. Staying below the large aircraft's final approach path (answer B) or landing before its touchdown point (answers B and C) would place the aircraft in the path of the wake turbulence.

6-66   J27

When departing behind a heavy aircraft, the pilot should avoid wake turbulence by maneuvering the aircraft

A — below and downwind from the heavy aircraft.
B — above and upwind from the heavy aircraft.
C — below and upwind from the heavy aircraft.

6-66. Answer B. GFDPPM 6-47 (PHB)

Because wake turbulence tends to sink and drift downwind, an aircraft should stay above and upwind of the preceding aircraft. Maneuvering below and downwind (answer A) would put the aircraft into the wake turbulence. Depending on the circumstances, below and upwind (answer C) may not keep the aircraft clear.

INTERPRETING WEATHER DATA

SECTION A
THE FORECASTING PROCESS

Pilots depend on reliable weather predictions. These are generated through a complex process involving both observers and intricate computer programs. Covered in this section are forecasting methods and the accuracy and limitations of those methods. Although no FAA questions on the knowledge exam pertain to this section, this information is critical to your general knowledge as a safe pilot.

SECTION B
PRINTED REPORTS AND FORECASTS

By learning to interpret printed weather reports and forecasts, you will add much to your ability to picture the weather patterns that affect your flying.

PRINTED WEATHER REPORTS
Printed weather reports give information that reflects actual conditions.

METARS
1. Winds on an aviation routine weather report are referenced to true north.
2. Peak gusts on an aviation routine weather report are denoted by a number following a "G" after the wind direction and base speed.
3. Cloud heights or visibility into an obscuration are reported with three digits in hundreds of feet. Visibility is reported in statute miles and is indicated by the abbreviation "SM."
4. For aviation purposes, ceiling is defined as the height above the Earth's surface of the lowest broken or overcast layer or vertical visibility into an obscuration.
5. The definition of VFR is a visibility of at least 3 miles and a ceiling of at least 1000 feet.
6. The remarks section of a METAR is used to report weather considered significant to aircraft operations. The contraction "RMK" precedes the remarks.

PIREPS
7. In a PIREP, identified by the letters "UA," sky condition is designated by the letters "SK," followed by the base and top of each cloud layer.
8. The wind direction and velocity in a PIREP are shown as "WV" and the direction and speed, with the last digit of the wind direction dropped.
9. The ceiling is the lowest layer reported as broken, overcast, or obscured.
10. Turbulence is reported in a PIREP as "TB" followed by an intensity designation, such as "SVR," "MDT," or "LGT." The altitude of the turbulence layer is also reported.
11. Icing is reported in a PIREP after the letters "IC." This is followed by the intensity of the icing, and the altitude of the layers in which it was encountered.

PRINTED WEATHER FORECASTS
Printed weather forecasts are a useful tool in planning ahead for a flight and predicting potential weather at your destination.

TAFs

12. TAFs are usually valid for a 24-hour period and are scheduled four times a day (0000Z, 0600Z, 1200Z and 1800Z). The six-digit issuance date/time group is followed by the valid date/time group.
13. In a TAF, the abbreviation "SHRA" stands for rain showers.
14. A gradual change in the weather is prefaced by the abbreviation "BECMG" and the Zulu time during which the weather is forecast to change- i.e. "BECMG 1012" would mean that the weather change is expected to happen between 1000Z and 1200Z. The time frame is followed by the change expected, such as "3 SM" would mean the visibility is forecast to change to 3 statute miles.
15. When rapid changes in the forecast are expected (usually within one hour), the code "FM" is used. When the abbreviation "VRB" appears before the wind speed, the wind is expected to be variable at that speed.
16. A change group is used when a significant, lasting change to the weather conditions is forecast during the valid time.
17. Wind blocks read as follows: wind direction comes first, followed by speed, and then any gust factor expected. Ceilings are given by the amount of coverage, followed by the cloud base height, in hundreds of feet.
18. The code "NSW" means that no significant weather change is forecast to occur.
19 Cumulonimbus clouds are the only cloud type included in the TAFs.

AVIATION AREA FORECASTS (FAs)

20. Area forecasts cover the expected general weather conditions over several states. They are useful in determining the forecast weather at airports without a dedicated terminal forecast.
21. The outlook for a specific period of time is marked by the abbreviation "OTLK" followed by the date and Zulu time. For example, the block "042300-050500" stands for the period between 2300Z on the 4th day of the month, to 0500Z on the 5th day of the month.
22. To determine the freezing level and the areas of probable icing aloft, the pilot should refer to the area forecast.
23. The section of the area forecast titled "SIG CLDS AND WX" contains a summary of cloudiness and weather significant to flight operations broken down by states or other geographical areas. Obstructions to vision, such as IFR conditions and fog, are included in this section.
24. The HAZARDS section lists hazards to aviation, such as turbulence and icing, for selected areas.

WINDS AND TEMPERATURES ALOFT FORECASTS (FDs)

25. The first two digits represent the wind direction in relation to true north. The next two digits are the speed. Temperatures follow the wind block. Note that temperatures are assumed negative above 24,000 feet.
26. Winds of 100 to 199 knots have 50 added to the direction. For example, when there is a wind direction above 360, subtract 50 to get a reasonable wind direction, and add 100 to the listed wind speed.
27. When the term "light and variable" is used in reference to a winds aloft forecast, the coded group and wind speed is 9900 and less than 5 knots.

SEVERE WEATHER REPORTS AND FORECASTS
Severe weather reports and forecasts alert pilots to hazardous flight conditions, both potential and actual.

AIRMETS

28. AIRMETs are issued as a warning of weather conditions particularly hazardous to small, single-engine aircraft.

SIGMETS

29. SIGMETs are issued as a warning of weather conditions hazardous to all aircraft.
30. A SIGMET would contain information on severe icing, since it is a hazard to all aircraft.

CONVECTIVE SIGMETS

31. Tornadoes, embedded thunderstorms, and hail 3/4 inch or greater in diameter are all weather phenomenon contained within a convective SIGMET.
32. When a current convective SIGMET forecasts thunderstorms, those indicated are obscured by massive cloud layers.

7-1   I55
(Refer to figure 12.) Which of the reporting stations have VFR weather?

A — All.
B — KINK, KBOI, and KJFK.
C — KINK, KBOI, and KLAX.

7-2   I55
For aviation purposes, ceiling is defined as the height above the Earth's surface of the

A — lowest reported obscuration and the highest layer of clouds reported as overcast.
B — lowest broken or overcast layer or vertical visibility into an obscuration.
C — lowest layer of clouds reported as scattered, broken, or thin.

7-3   I55
(Refer to figure 12.) The wind direction and velocity at KJFK is from

A — 180° true at 4 knots.
B — 180° magnetic at 4 knots.
C — 040° true at 18 knots.

7-4   I55
(Refer to figure 12.) What are the wind conditions at Wink, Texas (KINK)?

A — Calm.
B — 110° at 12 knots, gusts 18 knots.
C — 111° at 2 knots, gusts 18 knots.

7-1. Answer C. GFDPPM 7-13, 15 (AWS)
To answer this question you must know that the definition of VFR is a visibility of at least 3 statute miles and ceiling of at least 1,000 feet. KINK has 15 miles visibility with clear skies, KBOI has 30 miles visibility with a scattered layer at 15,000 feet, and KLAX has 6 miles visibility, with scattered layers at 700 feet and 25,000 feet. Remember, a scattered layer does not consititute a ceiling. Answers (A) and (B) are wrong because neither KMDW or KJFK are VFR. KDMW has 1-1/2 miles visibility with a 700 feet overcast, and KJFK has 1/2 mile in fog, and 500 feet overcast.

7-2. Answer B. GFDPPM 7-15 (AWS)
According to *Aviation Weather Services*, AC 00-45D, a ceiling is defined as the lowest broken or overcast layer, or vertical visibility into an obscuration. The highest layer of clouds reported as overcast (answer A), and scattered or thin clouds (answer C) do not fit the criteria.

7-3. Answer A. GFDPPM 7-11, 12 (AWS)
The wind at KJFK is shown as 18004KT. This means the wind is from 180 degrees at 04 knots. Winds on an aviation routine weather report are referenced to true north. Answer (B) is wrong because the winds are reported as true, not magnetic. Answer (C) is wrong because the direction (180°) is listed first, and velocity (4 knots) follows.

7-4. Answer B. GFDPPM 7-11, 12 (AWS)
The winds at KINK are shown as 11012G18KT. The direction is 110 degrees, and the velocity is 12 knots, with peak gusts of 18 knots. Answer (A) is wrong because calm winds are shown as 00000KT. Answer (C) is wrong because the first three digits, rounded to the nearest 10 degrees, represent the direction. The velocity, which follows is shown in two digits (three digits when it is greater than 99 knots).

METAR KINK 121845Z 11012G18KT 15SM SKC 25/17 A3000.

METAR KBOI 121854Z 13004KT 30SM SCT150 17/6 A3015.

METAR KLAX 121852Z 25004KT 6SM BR SCT007 SCT250 16/15 A2991.

SPECI KMDW 121856Z 32005KT 1 1/2SM RA OVC007 17/16 A2980 RMK RAB35.

SPECI KJFK 121853Z 18004KT 1/2SM FG R04/2200 OVC005 20/18 A3006

FIGURE 12.—Aviation Routine Weather Reports(METAR).

7-5   I55

(Refer to figure 12 on page 7-3.) The remarks section for KMDW has RAB35 listed. This entry means

A — blowing mist has reduced the visibility to 1-1/2 SM.
B — rain began at 1835Z.
C — the barometer has risen .35″ Hg.

7-6   I55

(Refer to figure 12 on page 7-3.) What are the current conditions depicted for Chicago Midway Airport (KMDW)?

A — Sky 700 feet overcast, visibility 1-1/2SM, rain.
B — Sky 7000 feet overcast, visibility 1-1/2SM, heavy rain.
C — Sky 700 feet overcast, visibility 11, occasionally 2SM, with rain.

7-7   I56

(Refer to figure 14.) The base and tops of the overcast layer reported by a pilot are

A — 1,800 feet MSL and 5,500 feet MSL.
B — 5,500 feet AGL and 7,200 feet MSL.
C — 7,200 feet MSL and 8,900 feet MSL.

7-8   I56

(Refer to figure 14.) The wind and temperature at 12,000 feet MSL as reported by a pilot are

A — 080° at 21 knots and -7 °C.
B — 090° at 21 MPH and -9 °F.
C — 090° at 21 knots and -9 °C.

7-5. Answer B. GFDPPM 7-16 (AWS)

The remarks section of a METAR is used to report weather considered significant to aircraft operations. According to AC 00-45D, the contraction "RMK" precedes remarks. Included are the beginning and ending times of certain weather phenomena. In this case, "RA" is the abbreviation for rain and "B35" indicates the rain began at thirty-five minutes past the hour, or 1835Z. Therefore, answer (B) is correct. Answer (A) is wrong because blowing, "BL" is not a descriptor that can be used to modify mist, "BR." Answer (C) is wrong because a rising barometer is not indicated.

7-6. Answer A. GFDPPM 7-13, 14, 16 (AWS)

Cloud heights or the vertical visibility into an obscuration are reported with three digits in hundreds of feet. Visibility is reported in statute miles and is indicated by the abbreviation "SM." In this case, the METAR from KMDW indicates Midway has visibility of 1-1/2 miles and the sky is overcast at 700 feet. The "RA" indicates precipitation in the form of rain. Answer (B) is wrong because heavy rain is not indicated and the overcast is not at 7,000 feet. Answer (C) is wrong because the visibility is 1-1/2 statute miles, not 11, occasionally 2.

7-7. Answer C. GFDPPM 7-17 (AWS)

In the PIREP, which is identified by the letters, UA, sky cover is designated by the letters, SK, followed by the base and top of each cloud layer. The overcast layer is shown as OVC 072-TOP 089, which means the base is 7,200 feet and the tops are 8,900 feet. Altitudes are MSL unless otherwise noted. Answer (A) is wrong because it describes the broken (not overcast) layer. Answer (B) is wrong because it describes the type of turbulence, moderate (MDT), and altitudes at which it was encountered.

7-8. Answer A. GFDPPM 7-17 (AWS)

The ambient temperature and wind velocity appear in the part of the pilot report that says "/TA M7/WV 08021/". All temperatures aloft are given in degrees Celsius, and the "M" indicates temperatures below zero. Wind speed is reported in knots.

UA/OV KOKC-KTUL/TM 1800/FL120/TP BE90//SK BKN018-TOP055/OVC072-TOP089/CLR ABV/TA M7/WV 08021/TB LGT 055-072/IC LGT-MOD RIME 072-089

FIGURE 14.—Pilot Weather Reports.

7-9 I56

(Refer to figure 14.) If the terrain elevation is 1,295 feet MSL, what is the height above ground level of the base of the ceiling?

A — 505 feet AGL.
B — 1,295 feet AGL.
C — 6,586 feet AGL.

7-9. Answer A. GFDPPM 7-17 (AWS)
The ceiling is the lowest cloud layer reported as broken, overcast, or obscured. In this case, the lowest layer is 1,800 feet broken (MSL). Subtract the ground elevation to find the AGL height (1,800 – 1,295 = 505 feet AGL). Answer (B) is wrong because this is the terrain elevation in feet MSL, not the base of the clouds. Answer (C) is obviously incorrect. According to the PIREP in Figure 14, the broken ceiling is only 1,800 feet MSL, well below the answer choice figure of 6,586 feet AGL.

7-10 I56

(Refer to figure 14.) The intensity of the turbulence reported at a specific altitude is

A — moderate from 5,500 feet to 7,200 feet.
B — moderate at 5,500 feet and at 7,200 feet.
C — light from 5,500 feet to 7,200 feet.

7-10. Answer C. GFDPPM 7-17 (AWS))
Turbulence is reported as "/TB LGT 055-072/". This means the turbulence is light between 5,500 and 7,200 feet MSL.

7-11 I56

(Refer to figure 14.) The intensity and type of icing reported by a pilot is

A — light to moderate rime.
B — light to moderate.
C — light to moderate clear.

7-11. Answer A. GFDPPM 7-17 (AWS))
Icing intensity and type is shown in this pilot report (PIREP) as "/IC LGT-MDT RIME/" or light to moderate rime.

7-12 I57

From which primary source should information be obtained regarding expected weather at the estimated time of arrival if your destination has no Terminal Forecast?

A — Low-Level Prognostic Chart.
B — Weather Depiction Chart.
C — Area Forecast.

7-12. Answer C. GFDPPM 7-20 (AWS)
The area forecast (FA) is useful to help determine expected weather at airports which do not have terminal forecasts. The low-level prognostic chart (answer A) is more useful for flight planning several hours before a flight; however, it generally does not provide enough detail for an accurate estimate of destination weather. The weather depiction chart (answer B) shows general weather conditions and is also useful for flight planning purposes, but it does not show forecast conditions.

7-13 I57

(Refer to figure 15 on page 7-6.) What is the valid period for the TAF for KMEM?

A — 1200Z to 1200Z.
B — 1200Z to 1800Z.
C — 1800Z to 1800Z.

7-13. Answer C. GFDPPM 7-18, 19 (AWS)
TAFs are usually valid for a twenty-four hour period and are scheduled four times a day (0000Z, 0600Z, 1200Z, and 1800Z). The six-digit issuance date/time group is followed by the valid date/time group. Therefore, "121720Z 121818" indicates the KMEM TAF was issued on the 12th at 1720 Zulu. This report is valid from 1800 Zulu on the 12th until 1800 Zulu on the 13th. Answer (A) lists an incorrect 24-hour valid period and answer (B) contains a valid period of less than 24 hours.

```
TAF

KMEM   121720Z 121818 20012KT 5SM HZ BKN030 PROB40 2022 1SM TSRA OVC008CB
       FM2200 33015G20KT P6SM BKN015 OVC025 PROB40 2202 3SM SHRA
       FM0200 35012KT OVC008 PROB40 0205 2SM -RASN BECMG 0608 02008KT BKN012
        BECMG 1012 00000KT 3SM BR SKC TEMPO 1214 1/2SM FG
       FM1600 VRB06KT P6SM SKC=

KOKC   051130Z 051212 14008KT 5SM BR BKN030 TEMPO 1316 1 1/2SM BR
       FM1600 18010KT P6SM SKC BECMG 2224 20013G20KT 4SM SHRA OVC020
        PROB40 0006 2SM TSRA OVC008CB BECMG 0608 21015KT P6SM SCT040=
```

FIGURE 15.—Terminal Aerodrome Forecasts (TAF).

7-14   I57
(Refer to figure 15.) In the TAF for KMEM, what does "SHRA" stand for?

A — Rain showers.
B — A shift in wind direction is expected.
C — A significant change in precipitation is possible.

7-14. Answer A. GFDPPM 7-13, 14, 18 (AWS)
This group of the TAF, "PROB40 2202 3SM SHRA," indicates there is a forty percent probability, between 2200 Zulu and 0200 Zulu, the visibility will be 3 statute miles with showery precipitation or rain showers. The next entry, "FM0200 35012KT OVC008" indicates, from 0200 Zulu, the wind is expected to be from 350° at 12 knots, but this is not abbreviated by the code "SHRA." Therefore, answer (B) is wrong. A significant change in precipitation most likely would be included in the becoming (BECMG) group. In any event, answer (C) is wrong since it is not abbreviated by the code "SHRA."

7-15   I57
(Refer to figure 15.) Between 1000Z and 1200Z the visibility at KMEM is forecast to be

A — 1/2 statute mile.
B — 3 statute miles.
C — 6 statute miles.

7-15. Answer B. GFDPPM 7-19 (AWS)
During a specified time period when changes in the weather conditions are forecast, a change group is appended to the forecast. In this case, "BECMG 1012" indicates a change in the weather will occur between 1000Z and 1200Z. The "3SM" indicates the visibility should become 3 statute miles. Answer (A) is wrong because 1/2 mile visibility is forecast between 1200 and 1400 Zulu. Answer (C) is wrong because P6SM, which actually means greater than six statute miles, is forecast after 1600Z.

7-16   I57
(Refer to figure 15 on page 7-6.) What is the forecast wind for KMEM from 1600Z until the end of the forecast?

A — Variable in direction at 6 knots.
B — No significant wind.
C — Variable in direction at 4 knots.

7-16. Answer A. GFDPPM 7-19 (AWS)
This part of the forecast reads, "FM1600 VRB06KT P6SM SKC= ". From 1600Z until the end of forecast the wind is variable in direction at 6 knots, with visibility greater than 6 miles.

7-17   I57
(Refer to figure 15 on page 7-6.) In the TAF from KOKC, the "FM (FROM) Group" is forecast for the hours from 1600Z to 2200Z with the wind from

A — 180° at 10 knots, becoming 200° at 13 knots.
B — 160° at 10 knots.
C — 180° at 10 knots.

7-17. Answer C. GFDPPM 7-19 (AWS)
Rapid changes in the forecast are indicated by the code "FM" followed by the time the change should occur. 18010KT indicates wind from 180 degrees at 10 knots. "BECMG 2224" means that the next change will be happening gradually from 2200 to 2400Z.

7-18   I57
(Refer to figure 15 on page 7-6.) In the TAF from KOKC the clear sky becomes

A — overcast at 2,000 feet during the forecast period between 2200Z and 2400Z.
B — overcast at 200 feet with a 40% probability of becoming overcast at 600 feet during the forecast period between 2200Z and 2400Z.
C — overcast at 200 feet with the probability of becoming overcast at 400 feet during the forecast period between 2200Z and 2400Z.

7-18. Answer A. GFDPPM 7-19 (AWS)
When a gradual change in the forecast weather is expected, the becoming (BECMG) change group is used, followed by the beginning and ending times. The TAF from KOKC, "BECMG 2224 20013G20KT 4SM SHRA OVC020" means between 2200Z and 2400Z the weather will gradually change to winds from 200° at 13 knots gusting to 20 knots, 4 miles visibility in rain showers, and overcast skies at 2,000 feet. Answers (B) and (C) are wrong because the overcast is expected to become 2,000 feet not 200 feet.

7-19   I57
(Refer to figure 15 on page 7-6.) During the time period from 0600Z to 0800Z, what visibility is forecast for KOKC?

A — Greater than 6 statute miles.
B — Not forecasted.
C — Possibly 6 statute miles.

7-19. Answer A. GFDPPM 7-19 (AWS)
This section reads, "BECMG 0608 21015KT P6SM SCT040= ". This means that between 0600-0800Z, the wind will become 210° at 15 knots, visibility is forecast to be greater than (not possibly) 6 statute miles, and clouds will become scattered at 4,000 feet.

7-20   I57
(Refer to figure 15 on page 7-6.) The only cloud type forecast in TAF reports is

A — Nimbostratus.
B — Cumulonimbus.
C — Scattered cumulus.

7-20. Answer B. GFDPPM 7-20 (AWS)
According to AC 00-45E, cumulonimbus clouds are the only cloud type included in TAFs. If cumulonimbus clouds are expected at the airport, the contraction "CB" is appended to the height of the cloud layer to indicate the base of the cumulonimbus cloud.

7-21   I57
To best determine general forecast weather conditions over several states, the pilot should refer to

A.   Satellite Maps.
B.   Aviation Area Forecasts.
C.   Weather Depiction Charts.

7-22   I57
(Refer to figure 16 on page 7-9.) What is the outlook for the southern half of Indiana after 0700Z?

A — VFR
B — Scattered clouds at 3,000 feet AGL.
C — Scattered clouds at 10,000 feet.

7-23   I57
To determine the freezing level and areas of probable icing aloft, the pilot should refer to the

A — Inflight Aviation Weather Advisories.
B — Area Forecast.
C — Weather Depiction Chart.

7-24   I57
The section of the Area Forecast entitled "VFR CLDS/ WX" contains a general description of

A — forecast sky cover, cloud tops, visibility, and obstructions to vision along specific routes.
B — cloudiness and weather significant to flight operations broken down by states or other geographical areas.
C — clouds and weather which cover an area greater than 3,000 square miles and is significant to VFR flight operations.

7-25   I57
(Refer to figure 16 on page 7-9.) What sky condition and visibility are forecast for upper Michigan in the eastern portions after 2300Z?

A — Ceiling 100 feet overcast and 3 to 5 statute miles visibility.
B — Ceiling 1,000 feet overcast and 3 to 5 nautical miles visibility.
C — Ceiling 1,000 feet overcast and 3 to 5 statute miles visibility.

7-21. Answer B. GFDPPM 7-20 (AWS)
An Aviation Area Forecast (FA) covers the expected general weather conditions over several states. The FA also provides information on general weather conditions at airports that are not covered by other weather reports of forecasts.

7-22. Answer A. GFDPPM 7-21, 22 (AWS)
The last section is the VFR Clouds and Weather Section of the Chicago FA that includes southern Indiana. The outlook period is on the 25th of the month from 0800 to 1400, and for southern Indiana (at the very bottom) the outlook is for VFR. The definition of VFR is no ceiling, or a ceiling greater than 3,000 feet and visibility greater than 5 miles.

7-23. Answer A. GFDPPM 7-22 (AWS)
Freezing level and icing aloft are contained in inflight weather advisories which include SIGMETs, convective SIGMETs, AIRMETs, alert service weather watch bulletins (AWWs), center weather advisories (CWAs), and urgent PIREPs. These advisories are broadcast via Enroute Flight Advisory Service (EFAS) and Hazardous In-flight Weather Advisory Service (HIWAS).

7-24. Answer C. GFDPPM 7-21 (AWS)
"VFR Clouds and Weather" includes visibility and cloud cover by state or other well-known geographic areas. Specific forecast sections give a general description of clouds and weather which cover an area greater than 3,000 square miles and that are significant to VFR flight operations. Answer (A) is incorrect because each section of an Area Forecast covers specific areas, not routes. Answer (B) is incorrect because it does not specify "VFR" flight operations.

7-25. Answer C. GFDPPM 7-21 (AWS)
In VFR clouds and weather section in the UPR MI LS (upper Michigan, Lake Superior) and ERN PTNS (eastern portions) the ceiling and visibility, after 23Z, are listed as CLG OVC 010 VIS 3-5 SM (Ceiling 1,000 overcast, 3-5 statute miles visibility).

```
BOSC FA 241845
SYNOPSIS AND VFR CLDS/WX
SYNOPSIS VALID UNTIL 251300
CLDS/WX VALID UNTIL 250700...OTLK VALID 250700-251300
ME NH VT MA RI CT NY LO NJ PA OH LE WV MD DC DE VA AND CSTL WTRS

.
SEE AIRMET SIERRA FOR IFR CONDS AND MTN OBSCN.
TS IMPLY SEV OR GTR TURB SEV ICE LLWS AND IFR CONDS.
NON MSL HGTS DENOTED BY AGL OR CIG.

.
SYNOPSIS...19Z CDFNT ALG A 160NE ACK-ENE LN...CONTG AS A QSTNRY
FNT ALG AN END-50SW MSS LN. BY 13Z...CDFNT ALG A 140ESE ACK-HTO
LN...CONTG AS A QSTNRY FNT ALG A HTO-SYR-YYZ LN. TROF ACRS CNTRL
PA INTO NRN VA.  ...REYNOLDS...

.
OH LE
NRN HLF OH LE...SCT-BKN025 OVC045. CLDS LYRD 150. SCT SHRA. WDLY
    SCT TSRA. CB TOPS FL350. 23-01Z OVC020-030. VIS 3SM BR. OCNL -
    RA. OTLK...IFR CIG BR FG.
SWRN QTR OH...BKN050-060 TOPS 100. OTLK...MVFR BR.
SERN QTR OH...SCT-BKN040 BKN070 TOPS 120. WDLY SCT -TSRA. 00Z
    SCT-BKN030 OVC050. WDLY SCT -TSRA. CB TOPS FL350. OTLK...VFR
    SHRA.

.
CHIC FA 241945
SYNOPSIS AND VFR CLDS/WX
SYNOPSIS VALID UNTIL 251400
CLDS/WX VALID UNTIL 250800...OTLK VALID 250800-251400
ND SD NE KS MN IA MO WI LM LS MI LH IL IN KY

.
SEE AIRMET SIERRA FOR IFR CONDS AND MTN OBSCN.
TS IMPLY SEV OR GTR TURB SEV ICE LLWS AND IFR CONDS.
NON MSL HGTS DENOTED BY AGL OR CIG.

.
SYNOPSIS...LOW PRES AREA 20Z CNTRD OVR SERN WI FCST MOV NEWD INTO
LH BY 12Z AND WKN. LOW PRES FCST DEEPEN OVR ERN CO DURG PD AND
MOV NR WRN KS BORDER BY 14Z. DVLPG CDFNT WL MOV EWD INTO S CNTRL
NE-CNTRL KS BY 14Z.  ..SMITH..

.
UPR MI LS
WRN PTNS...AGL SCT030 SCT-BKN050. TOPS 080. 02-05Z BECMG CIG
    OVC010 VIS 3-5SM BR. OTLK...IFR CIG BR.
ERN PTNS...CIG BKN020 OVC040. OCNL VIS 3-5SM -RA BR. TOPS FL200.
    23Z CIG OVC010 VIS 3-5SM -RA BR. OTLK...IFR CIG BR.

.
LWR MI LM LH
CNTRL/NRN PTNS...CIG OVC010 VIS 3-5SM -RA BR. TOPS FL200.
    OTLK...IFR CIG BR.

.
SRN THIRD...CIG OVC015-025. SCT -SHRA. TOPS 150. 00-02Z BECMG CIG
    OVC010 VIS 3-5SM BR. TOPS 060. OTLK...IFR CIG BR.

.
IN
NRN HALF...CIG BKN035 BKN080. TOPS FL200. SCT -SHRA. 00Z CIG
    BKN-SCT040  BKN-SCT080. TOPS 120. 06Z AGL SCT-BKN030. TOPS 080.
    OCNL VIS 3-5SM BR. OTLK...MVFR CIG BR.
SRN HALF...AGL SCT050 SCT-BKN100. TOPS 120. 07Z AGL SCT 030
    SCT100. OTLK...VFR.
```

FIGURE 16.—Area Forecast.

7-26   I57

(Refer to figure 16 on page 7-9.) The Chicago FA forecast section is valid until the twenty-fifth at

A — 1945Z.
B — 0800Z.
C — 1400Z.

7-27   I57

(Refer to figure 16 on page 7-9.) What sky condition and type obstructions to vision are forecast for upper Michigan in the western portions from 0200Z until 0500Z?

A — Ceiling becoming 1,000 feet overcast with visibility 3 to 5 statute miles in mist.
B — Ceiling becoming 100 feet overcast with visibility 3 to 5 statue miles in mist.
C — Ceiling becoming 1,000 feet overcast with visibility 3 to 5 nautical miles in mist.

7-28   I57

What is indicated when a current CONVECTIVE SIGMET forecasts thunderstorms?

A — Moderate thunderstorms covering 30 percent of the area.
B — Moderate or severe turbulence.
C — Thunderstorms obscured by massive cloud layers.

7-29   I57

What information is contained in a CONVECTIVE SIGMET?

A — Tornadoes, embedded thunderstorms, and hail 3/4 inch or greater in diameter.
B — Severe icing, severe turbulence, or widespread dust storms lowering visibility to less than 3 miles.
C — Surface winds greater than 40 knots or thunderstorms equal to or greater than video integrator processor (VIP) level 4.

7-26. Answer B. GFDPPM 7-21 (AWS)

In the first line, "CHI" indicates the area for which the FA is valid. The "C" following CHI indicates VFR clouds and weather while the FA indicates what type of forecast message it is. The "241945" indicates the date and time the FA was issued. The next line "SYNOPSIS AND VFR CLDS/WX" states what information is contained in this forecast message. "CLDS/WX VALID UNTIL 250800" means that the forecast section of the FA is valid until the 25th at 0800Z, while the outlook portion is valid from the 25th at 0800Z until the 25th at 1400Z. ND SD NE KS MN IA MO WI LM LS MI LH IL IN KY describes the area for which this FA forecast is valid.

3493. Answer A. GFDPPM 7-21,22 (AWS)

Upper Michigan and Lake Superior, western portion is abbreviated UPR MI LS, WRN PTNS. From 02-05Z, the ceiling is becoming 1,000 overcast (OVC 010) and visibility 3-5 statute miles (3-5 SM) with mist (BR).

7-28. Answer C. GFDPPM 7-27 (AIM)

None of these answers is entirely correct, but by process of elimination, answer (C) is the best choice. One of the criteria for issuing a Convective SIGMET is embedded thunderstorms. A Convective SIGMET is issued when level 4 thunderstorms (very strong, not moderate) cover 40 percent (not 30 percent) of an area (answer A). Severe or greater turbulence is implied, not moderate or severe (answer B).

7-29. Answer A. GFDPPM 7-27 (AIM)

Convective SIGMETs are issued for any of the following phenomena: tornadoes, lines of thunderstorms, embedded thunderstorms, areas of level 4 thunderstorms covering 40 percent of the area, and hail of 3/4 inch or greater in diameter. Severe icing and severe turbulence (answer B) are implied but not specified in the advisory. Convective SIGMETs are not issued for surface winds over 40 knots (answer C); however, if the surface winds are 50 knots, or greater, a Convective SIGMET may be issued.

7-30   I57

SIGMET's are issued as a warning of weather conditions hazardous to which aircraft?

A — Small aircraft only.
B — Large aircraft only.
C — All aircraft.

7-31   I57

Which in-flight advisory would contain information on severe icing not associated with thunderstorms?

A — Convective SIGMET.
B — AIRMET.
C — SIGMET.

7-32   I57

AIRMET's are advisories of significant weather phenomena but of lower intensities than Sigmets and are intended for dissemination to

A — only IFR pilots.
B — all pilots.
C — only VFR pilots.

7-33   I57

(Refer to figure 17.) What wind is forecast for STL at 9,000 feet?

A — 230° true at 32 knots.
B — 230° magnetic at 25 knots.
C — 230° true at 25 knots.

7-30. Answer C. GFDPPM 7-26 (AWS)

SIGMETs are issued for weather potentially hazardous to all aircraft. An AIRMET advises of weather which is of operational interest to all aircraft, but may be hazardous to aircraft with limited capabilities, such as light single-engine airplanes.

7-31. Answer C. GFDPPM 7-26 (AWS)

A SIGMET advises of weather potentially hazardous to all aircraft, which would include severe icing. A Convective SIGMET is an advisory of especially hazardous thunderstorm activity. Answer (A) is incorrect because the question asks about severe icing not associated with thunderstorm activity. Answer (B) is incorrect because AIRMETs cover moderate, not severe, icing.

7-32. Answer B. GFDPPM 7-25 (AWS)

An AIRMET advises of weather that is of operational interest to all aircraft, but may be hazardous to aircraft with limited capabilities, such as light single-engine airplanes.

7-33. Answer A. GFDPPM 7-23 (AWS)

In the Winds and Temperatures Aloft Forecast (FD), directions are relative to TRUE NORTH and rounded to the nearest 10 degrees. The wind information is given as 2332+02. The first two digits represent the wind direction in relation to true north, 230°. The next two digits are the speed, which in this case is 32 knots. The temperature is +2°C.

```
FD WBC 151745
DATA BASED ON 151200Z
VALID 1600Z FOR USE 1800-0300Z. TEMPS NEG ABV 24000
```

FT	3000	6000	9000	12000	18000	24000	30000	34000	39000
ALS			2420	2635-08	2535-18	2444-30	245945	246755	246862
AMA		2714	2725+00	2625-04	2531-15	2542-27	265842	256352	256762
DEN			2321-04	2532-08	2434-19	2441-31	235347	236056	236262
HLC		1707-01	2113-03	2219-07	2330-17	2435-30	244145	244854	245561
MKC	0507	2006+03	2215-01	2322-06	2338-17	2348-29	236143	237252	238160
STL	2113	2325+07	2332+02	2339-04	2356-16	2373-27	239440	730649	731960

FIGURE 17.—Winds and Temperatures Aloft Forecast.

7-34   I57

What values are used for Winds Aloft Forecasts?

A — Magnetic direction and knots.
B — Magnetic direction and miles per hour.
C — True direction and knots.

7-35   I57

When the term "light and variable" is used in reference to a Winds Aloft Forecast, the coded group and wind-speed is

A — 0000 and less than 7 knots.
B — 9900 and less than 5 knots.
C — 9999 and less than 10 knots.

7-34. Answer C. GFDPPM 7-23 (AWS)

The best rule of thumb is to remember that all forecast winds are given in true direction, and speed is always in knots.

7-35. Answer B. GFDPPM 7-24 (AWS)

The direction is shown as 99, which means the direction is variable. When the second two digits are listed as 00, the speed is less than 5 knots.

SECTION C
GRAPHIC WEATHER PRODUCTS

Graphic weather products help you grasp the overall weather picture by giving you maps of actual and forecast patterns.

GRAPHIC REPORTS
Graphic weather reports use information gathered from ground observations, weather radar, satellites, and other sources to give you a pictorial view of large-scale weather patterns and trends.

SURFACE ANALYSIS CHART
1. A stationary front is depicted with rounded warm front symbols on one side and triangular cold front symbols on the opposite side.

WEATHER DEPICTION CHART
2. (Refer to figure 18) The shaded area is an area of IFR weather. The symbol with two horizontal lines (=) indicates fog.
3. An outlined area enclosed by contour lines without shading indicates marginal VFR weather. The station models on the weather depiction chart give the percentage of cloud coverage. The ceiling is shown below the model in hundreds of feet AGL.

RADAR SUMMARY CHART
4. Radar weather reports are of special interest to pilots because they indicate the location of precipitation along with type, intensity and trend.
5. (Refer to figure 19) The movement pennant points in the direction of the return's movement. Each barb on the pennant indicates 10 knots, with half barbs being 5 knots.
6. The symbol "RW+" denotes a rain shower (RW) with an increasing intensity or new echo (+).
7. The top of the precipitation is shown in hundreds of feet MSL.
8. The dashed line encloses a severe weather watch area.

GRAPHIC FORECASTS
Graphic forecasts take reported conditions and trends and extrapolate future weather from them, displaying these predictions pictorially.

SIGNIFICANT WEATHER PROGNOSTIC CHART
9. The significant weather prognostic charts are best used by a pilot for determining areas to avoid, due to freezing levels and turbulence.
10. (Refer to figure 20) A hat-shaped symbol in the upper left-hand panel indicates moderate turbulence. The figure 180 means the turbulence is from the surface up to 18,000 feet.
11. (Refer to figure 20) An outlined area shows showery precipitation ahead of a cold front. The symbols indicate thunderstorms and rain showers.
12. The movement and direction of an area of high or low pressure is indicated by an arrow, with the speed listed in knots. The underlined two-digit number below the pressure symbol represents the sea level pressure in millibars.
13. A dashed line represents the freezing level. Numbers on the edge of the chart show the altitude of the freezing level in hundreds of feet MSL.

7-36   I58
(Refer to figure 18 on page 7-15.) What is the status of the front that extends from Nebraska through the upper peninsula of Michigan?

A — Cold.
B — Warm
C — Stationary.

7-37   I58
(Refer to figure 18 on page 7-15.) The IFR weather in northern Texas is due to

A. low ceilings.
B. dust devils.
C. intermittent rain.

7-38   I59
(Refer to figure 18 on page 7-15.) Of what value is the Weather Depiction Chart to the pilot?

A — For determining general weather conditions on which to base flight planning.
B — For a forecast of cloud coverage, visibilities, and frontal activity.
C — For determining frontal trends and air mass characteristics.

7-39   I59
(Refer to figure 18 on page 7-15.) The marginal weather in central Kentucky is due to low

A — visibility.
B — ceiling and visibility.
C — ceiling.

7-40   I59
(Refer to figure 18 on page 7-15.) What weather phenomenon is causing IFR conditions in central Oklahoma?

A — Low visibility only.
B — Heavy rain showers.
C — Low ceilings and visibility.

7-36. Answer A. GFDPPM 7-31(AWS)
This front is depicted with triangular symbols on the south side of the front. This symbology indicates a cold front. A warm front has rounded symbols on one side of the frontal line, while a stationary front has triangular symbols on one side and rounded symbols on the other.

7-37. Answer A. GFDPPM 7-33 (AWS)
The shaded area in northern Texas is an area of IFR weather. This shaded area indicates a ceiling of less than 1,000 feet AGL and/or visibility of less than 3 s.m. Since the visibility in northern Texas is indicated as 3 s.m. (near the double dash fog symbol), the IFR weather is caused by low ceilings.

7-38. Answer A. GFDPPM 7-33 (AWS)
The weather depiction chart shows a "birds eye" view of general weather conditions over a wide area, and is useful for flight planning purposes by showing areas of adverse weather. It depicts actual weather conditions, and is not a forecast (answer B). Although it does show locations of fronts, it does not indicate trends or high and low pressure areas (answer C).

7-39. Answer C. GFDPPM 7-32, 33 (AWS)
An area enclosed by non-shaded contour lines indicates marginal VFR weather conditions. This means the visibility is three to five miles and/or the ceiling is 1,000 to 3,000 feet. The station in central Kentucky is reporting 3,000-foot overcast, with no visibility indication (meaning 6 or more miles visibility).

7-40. Answer C. GFDPPM 7-32,33 (AWS)
The shaded area indicates IFR. In this case, the filled station model in central Oklahoma indicates overcast sky and the "3" below the model indicates 300 foot ceiling. The "2-1/2" to the left of the model indicates IFR visibility of 2-1/2 statute miles. The bracket to the right of the model indicates an automatic weather observation.

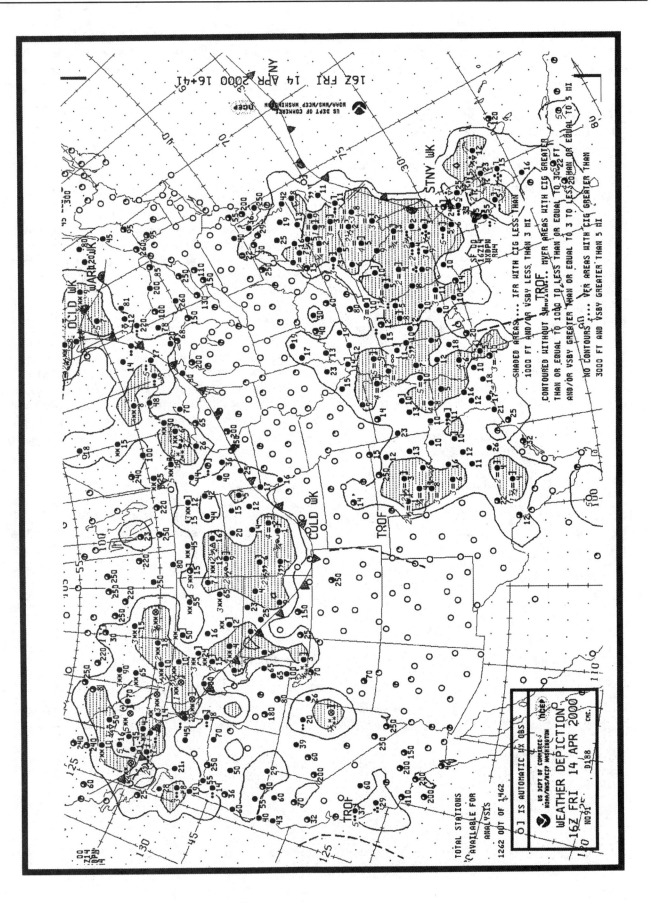

FIGURE 18.—Weather Depiction Chart.

7-41   I59
(Refer to figure 18 on page 7-15.) According to the Weather Depiction Chart, the weather for a flight from southern Michigan to north Indiana is ceilings

A — 1,000 to 3,000 feet and/or visibility 3 to 5 miles.
B — less than 1,000 feet and/or visibility less than 3 miles.
C — greater than 3,000 feet and visibility greater than 5 miles.

7-41. Answer C. GFDPPM 7-32,33 (AWS)
There are no shaded or contoured areas along this route. This indicates VFR areas with a ceiling greater than 3,000 feet and a visibility greater than 5 miles.

7-42   I60
Radar weather reports are of special interest to pilots because they indicate

A — location of precipitation along with type, intensity, and cell movement of precipitation.
B — location of precipitation along with type, intensity, and trend.
C — large areas of low ceilings and fog.

7-42. Answer A. GFDPPM 7-33 (AWS)
Radar weather reports show areas of precipitation; type, such as rain showers; intensity, such as light or heavy; and azimuth of movement. Intensity trend is no longer coded on the Radar Weather Report.

7-43   I60
What information is provided by the Radar Summary Chart that is not shown on other weather charts?

A — Lines and cells of hazardous thunderstorms.
B — Ceilings and precipitation between reporting stations.
C — Types of clouds between reporting stations.

7-43. Answer A. GFDPPM 7-33, 35 (AWS)
Individual thunderstorm cells as well as lines of thunderstorms are depicted on radar summary charts. Since the radar returns are reflected off precipitation, not clouds, they do not show ceilings (answer B) or types of clouds (answer C).

7-44   I60
(Refer to figure 19, area B on page 7-17.) What is the top for precipitation of the radar return?

A — 24,000 feet AGL.
B — 2,400 feet MSL.
C — 24,000 feet MSL.

7-44. Answer C. GFDPPM 7-34 (AWS)
240 indicates the highest precipitation top in the area in hundreds of feet above mean sea level, which in this case is 24,000 feet MSL.

7-45   Reserved

7-45. Reserved

7-46   I60
(Refer to figure 19, area D on page 7-17.) What is the direction and speed of movement of the cell?

A — North at 17 knots.
B — South at 17 knots.
C — North at 17 MPH.

7-46. Answer A. GFDPPM 7-34 (AWS)
Cell movement is indicated by an arrow pointing north and a number (17) indicating speed in knots.

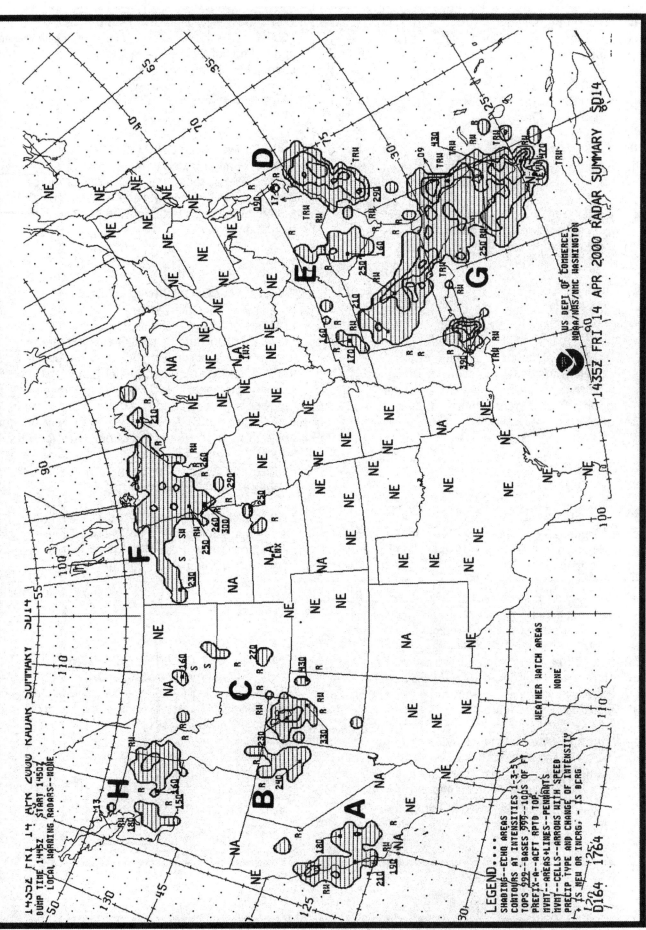

FIGURE 19.—Radar Summary Chart.

7-47   I60
(Refer to figure 19, area E on page 7-17.) The top of the precipitation of the cell is

A — 16,000 feet MSL.
B — 25,000 feet MSL.
C — 16,000 feet AGL.

7-48   I60
What does the heavy dashed line that forms a large rectangular box on a radar summary chart refer to?

A — Severe weather watch area.
B — Areas of hail 1/4 inch in diameter.
C — Areas of heavy rain.

7-49   I64
(Refer to figure 20 on page 7-19.) How are Significant Weather Prognostic Charts best used by a pilot?

A — For overall planning at all altitudes.
B — For determining areas to avoid (freezing levels and turbulence).
C — For analyzing current frontal activity and cloud coverage.

7-50   I64
(Refer to figure 20 on page 7-19.) Interpret the weather symbol depicted in Utah on the 12-hour Significant Weather Prognostic Chart.

A — Moderate turbulence, surface to 18,000 feet.
B — Base of clear air turbulence, 18,000 feet.
C — Thunderstorm tops at 18,000 feet.

7-51   I64
(Refer to figure 20 on page 7-19.) What weather is forecast for the Florida area just ahead of the stationary front during the first 12 hours?

A — Ceiling 1,000 to 3,000 feet and/or visibility 3 to 5 miles with intermittent precipitation.
B — Ceiling 1,000 to 3,000 feet and/or visibility 3 to 5 miles with continuous precipitation.
C — Ceiling less than 1,000 feet and/or visibility less than 3 miles with continuous precipitation.

7-47. Answer A. GFDPPM 7-34 (AWS)
160 indicates the highest precipitation top in the area in hundreds of feet above mean sea level, which in this case is 16,000 feet MSL.

7-48. Answer A. GFDPPM 7-34 (AWS)
Severe weather watch areas are outlined by heavy dashed lines, usually in the form of a large rectangular box. The watch number, if any, is also printed at the bottom of the chart together with the issuance time and expiration time.

7-49. Answer B. GFDPPM 7-37 (AWS)
In addition to outlining areas of instrument flight rule (IFR) and marginal visual flight rule (MVFR) weather, these charts include freezing levels and areas of turbulence. Since the significant weather panels are valid from the surface up to 24,000 feet, they are intended for planning flights below this altitude, not all altitudes (answer A). These charts do not depict current frontal activity (answer C) because they are forecasts, not observations. The lower two panels are 12- and 24-hour surface progs and the upper two panels are 12- and 24-hour progs for the surface up to 400 millibars, or approximately 24,000 feet.

7-50. Answer A. GFDPPM 7-38,39 (AWS)
On the upper left panel, the symbol indicates moderate turbulence. The notation 240/ means the turbulence is from the surface up to 24,000 feet.

7-51. Answer B. GFDPPM 7-37,38 (AWS)
The upper left panel indicates a ceiling 1,000-3,000 feet and/or a visibility of 3-5 miles. This is marginal VFR (MVFR). The dot symbols in the lower left panel indicates continuous rain.

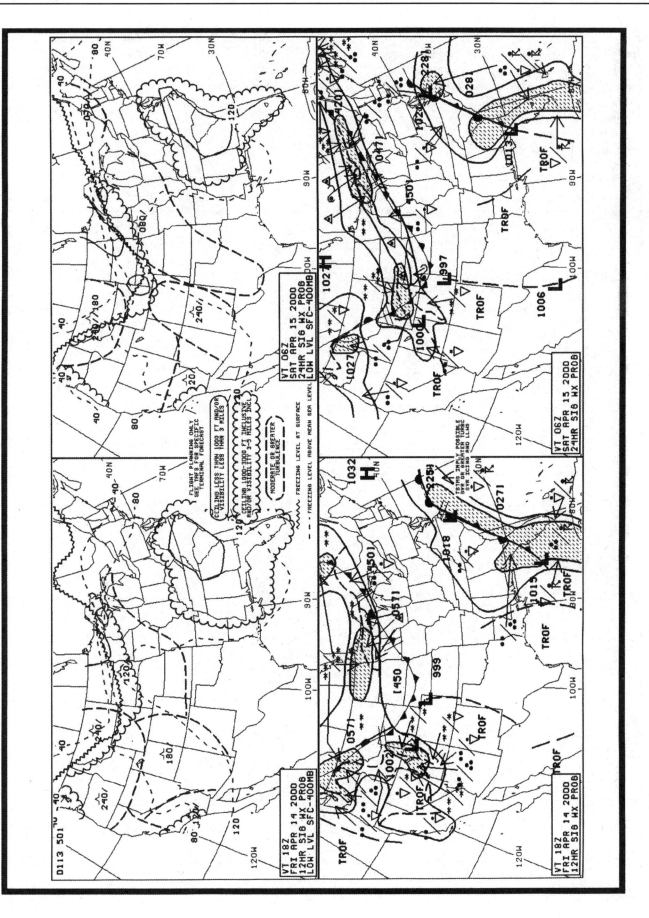

FIGURE 20.—Significant Weather Prognostic Chart.

7-52   I64
(Refer to figure 20 on page 7-19.) The enclosed shaded area associated with the low pressure system over northern Utah is forecast to have

A — continuous snow.
B — intermittent snow.
C — continuous snow showers.

7-53   I64
(Refer to figure 20 on page 7-19.) At what altitude is the freezing level over the middle of Florida on the 12-hour Significant Weather Prognostic Chart?

A — 4,000 feet.
B — 12,000 feet.
C — 8,000 feet.

7-52. Answer A. GFDPPM 7-37,38 (AWS)
The area is shaded, indicating continuous precipitation. Two snow symbols also indicate continuous snow (not snow showers).

7-53. Answer B. GFDPPM 7-37,38 (AWS)
The upper right panel contains a dashed line marked with the number 120, which crosses central Florida. This represents the location of the 12,000-foot freezing level.

SECTION D
SOURCES OF WEATHER INFORMATION

The sources of weather information are as varied as the weather itself. You can divide the information into those products used during preflight and those you would access during your flight for updates. In this section, we look at three types of briefings, and various supplement sources. Many are automated outlets, such as the pilot's automatic telephone weather answering service (PATWAS).

PREFLIGHT WEATHER SOURCES
There are a number of ways of receiving preflight weather information, including television and on-line sources. The Flight Service Station remains a primary source.

FLIGHT SERVICE STATIONS (FSS)
1. When telephoning a weather briefing facility for preflight weather information, pilots should state the aircraft identification or the pilot's name. The pilot should also state the intended route, destination, type of aircraft and whether or not they intend to fly VFR only.
2. To get a complete weather briefing for the planned flight, the pilot should request a standard briefing.
3. The pilot should request an abbreviated briefing to supplement mass-disseminated data, or to update a previous briefing.
4. An outlook briefing is the weather briefing provided when the information requested is six or more hours in advance of the proposed departure time. A pilot requesting information for the following morning should ask for an outlook briefing.

IN-FLIGHT WEATHER SOURCES
Often, you will need to receive updated information during a flight. In-flight weather services include the En Route Flight Advisory Service (EFAS) and the Transcribed Weather Broadcast (TWEB).

EN ROUTE FLIGHT ADVISORY SERVICE (EFAS)
5. The pilot should expect actual weather information and thunderstorm activity along the route from an EFAS.
6. EFAS can be contacted by calling Flight Watch on 122.0.

TRANSCRIBED WEATHER BROADCAST (TWEB)
7. To obtain a continuous transcribed weather briefing, including winds aloft and route forecasts for a cross-country flight, pilots should monitor a TWEB on an ADF radio receiver or VOR receiver, using appropriate NDB or VOR frequencies.

7-54   I54
Individual forecasts for specific routes of flight can be obtained from which weather source?

A — Transcribed Weather Broadcasts (TWEB's).
B — Terminal Forecasts.
C — Area Forecasts.

7-55   I54
Transcribed Weather Broadcasts (TWEB's) may be monitored by tuning the appropriate radio receiver to certain

A — airport advisory frequencies.
B — VOR and NDB frequencies.
C — ATIS frequencies.

7-54. Answer A. GFDPPM 7-49 (AWS)
The information in a transcribed weather broadcast (TWEB) varies, but generally it contains route-oriented data. Terminal and area forecasts (answers B and C) contain terminal forecasts and forecasts for large geographical areas respectively, not route-oriented information.

7-55. Answer B. GFDPPM 7-49 (AWS)
TWEB's are broadcast over certain VOR and NDB frequencies. Airport advisory frequencies (answer A) are used by an FSS at uncontrolled airports to provide general airport information to pilots. Automatic terminal information service (ATIS) frequencies (answer C) are used to broadcast recorded airport information.

7-56   I54

When telephoning a weather briefing facility for pre-flight weather information, pilots should state

A — the aircraft identification or the pilot's name.
B — true airspeed.
C — fuel on board.

7-57   I54

To get a complete weather briefing for the planned flight, the pilot should request

A — a general briefing.
B — an abbreviated briefing.
C — a standard briefing.

7-58   I54

Which type weather briefing should a pilot request, when departing within the hour, if no preliminary weather information has been received?

A — Outlook briefing.
B — Abbreviated briefing.
C — Standard briefing.

7-59   I54

Which type of weather briefing should a pilot request to supplement mass disseminated data?

A — An outlook briefing.
B — A supplemental briefing.
C — An abbreviated briefing.

7-60   I54

To update a previous weather briefing, a pilot should request

A — an abbreviated briefing.
B — a standard briefing.
C — an outlook briefing.

7-61   I54

A weather briefing that is provided when the information requested is 6 or more hours in advance of the proposed departure time is

A — an outlook briefing.
B — a forecast briefing.
C — a prognostic briefing.

7-56. Answer A. GFDPPM 7-44 (AWS)
Pilots should give their name or the aircraft number, as well as other specific information, to the weather briefer. True airspeed (answer B) or fuel on board (answer C) are not required. These are items that are included on a flight plan.

7-57. Answer C. GFDPPM 7-45 (AIM)
A standard briefing is the most compete type of weather briefing. Since the three types of briefings are standard, abbreviated, and outlook, the term "general briefing" (answer A) is not used. An abbreviated briefing (answer B) may be obtained when the pilot has used other sources of weather data for a preliminary briefing, and needs to update that information.

7-58. Answer C. GFDPPM 7-45 (AIM)
See explanation for Question 7-57. An outlook briefing (answer A) is used for long-range planning, six or more hours ahead of time. Answer (B), the abbreviated briefing, is intended primarily for updating previous briefing information.

7-59. Answer C. GFDPPM 7-46 (AIM)
See explanation for Questions 7-57 and 7-58. The term "supplemental briefing" (answer B) is not used.

7-60. Answer A. GFDPPM 7-46 (AIM)
See explanation for Questions 7-57 and 7-58.

7-61. Answer A. GFDPPM 7-46 (AIM)
See explanation for Question 7-58. The terms "forecast briefing" (answer B) and "prognostic briefing" (answer C) are not official names for weather briefings provided by an FSS on the National Weather Service.

7-62   I54
When requesting weather information for the following morning, a pilot should request

A — an outlook briefing.
B — a standard briefing.
C — an abbreviated briefing.

7-63   I57
To obtain a continuous transcribed weather briefing, including winds aloft and route forecasts for a cross-country flight, a pilot should monitor a

A — VHF radio receiver tuned to an Automatic Terminal Information Service (ATIS) frequency.
B — Transcribed Weather Broadcast (TWEB) on an NDB or a VOR facility.
C — regularly scheduled weather broadcast on a VOR frequency.

7-64   H320
What should pilots state initially when telephoning a weather briefing facility for preflight weather information?

A — Tell the number of occupants on board.
B — State their total flight time.
C — Identify themselves as pilots.

7-65   H320
What should pilots state initially when telephoning a weather briefing facility for preflight weather information?

A — The intended route of flight and destination.
B — The intended route of flight radio frequencies.
C — The address of the pilot in command.

7-62. Answer A. GFDPPM 7-46 (AIM)
Assuming this would be 6 or more hours away, the pilot would request an outlook briefing (see explanation for Questions 7-57 and 7-58).

7-63. Answer B. GFDPPM 7-49 (AIM)
Transcribed Weather Broadcasts, or TWEBs, can be monitored on many NDB and/or VOR stations. ATIS broadcasts are local airport information only. Scheduled VOR weather broadcasts may also be local only. The answers to this question can be somewhat misleading, since a TWEB can be broadcast over either an NDB (ADF) or a VOR. However, some VORs broadcast only local information and do not include route forecasts. In general, most TWEBs include route information, so answer (B) appears to be the most correct choice.

7-64. Answer C. GFDPPM 7-44 (AWS)
You should identify yourself as a pilot or student pilot and include concise facts about your flight.

1. Type of flight VFR or IFR
2. Aircraft identification or pilot's name
3. Aircraft type
4. Departure point
5. Route of flight
6. Destination
7. Altitude
8. Estimated time of departure
9. Estimated time enroute or estimated time of arrival

Briefers do not need to know how many hours the pilot has flown. They also do not need to know the number of occupants on board the aircraft; this information will be on the flight plan.

7-65. Answer A. GFDPPM 7-44 (AWS)
The briefer is able to tailor the briefing and supply pertinent information if the route and destination are known, however, the briefer does not need to know the radio frequencies. The address of the pilot in command is not essential during initial contact with the weather briefing facility.

7-66   H320

When telephoning a weather briefing facility for pre-flight weather information, pilots should state

A — the full name and address of the formation commander.
B — that they possess a current pilot certificate.
C — whether they intend to fly VFR only.

7-66. Answer C. GFDPPM 7-44 (AWS)
It is important that the briefer knows whether a pilot intends to fly VFR or IFR, so that the information can help the pilot make a go/no-go decision. The pilot's full name and address (answer A) are not necessary for the briefer (whether a formation or single airplane). Since a pilot should not be flying without a current pilot certificate (answer B), there is no need to state the obvious.

7-67   J25

How should contact be established with an En Route Flight Advisory Service (EFAS) station, and what service would be expected?

A — Call EFAS on 122.2 for routine weather, current reports on hazardous weather, and altimeter settings.
B — Call flight assistance on 122.5 for advisory service pertaining to severe weather.
C — Call Flight Watch on 122.0 for information regarding actual weather and thunderstorm activity along proposed route.

7-67. Answer C. GFDPPM 7-48 (AWS)
Below FL180, EFAS is contacted on 122.0. Actual weather and thunderstorm activity along the pilot's route is provided. The frequency is not 122.2 (answer A) or 122.5 (answer B).

7-68   J25

What service should a pilot normally expect from an En Route Flight Advisory Service (EFAS) station?

A — Actual weather information and thunderstorm activity along the route.
B — Preferential routing and radar vectoring to circumnavigate severe weather.
C — Severe weather information, changes to flight plans, and receipt of routine position reports.

7-68. Answer A. GFDPPM 7-47, 48 (AWS)
See explanation for Question 7-67. EFAS provides weather information only, not routing or radar vectoring (answer B). It is not intended for updates to flight plans, or position reports (answer C).

7-69   J25

Below FL180, en route weather advisories should be obtained from an FSS on

A — 122.0 MHz.
B — 122.1 MHz.
C — 123.6 MHz.

7-69. Answer A. GFDPPM 7-48 (AIM)
See explanation for Question 7-67.

CHAPTER 8

AIRPLANE PERFORMANCE

SECTION A
PREDICTING PERFORMANCE

Performance describes the effectiveness of an aircraft in doing the jobs for which it was designed. In this section, we'll look at performance speeds, factors affecting performance, and the pilot's operating handbook (POH). Included are typical examples of performance charts and tables.

FACTORS AFFECTING PERFORMANCE
Many outside factors can affect the way your aircraft performs in various situations.

DENSITY ALTITUDE
1. If the outside air temperature at a given altitude is warmer than standard, the density altitude is higher than pressure altitude.
2. High temperature, high relative humidity, and high density altitude all reduce aircraft takeoff and climb performance.
3. (Refer to figure 8 on page 8-22) In order to find the density altitude for given conditions, first find the pressure altitude, using the pressure altitude conversion factor scale and interpolating for the current pressure. Then, find the temperature on the OAT scale at the bottom of the graph and follow its line vertically to where it intersects the pressure altitude line. From this point, follow the horizontal density altitude line to the left scale to find an approximate density altitude.
4. Density altitude and pressure altitude are the same value at standard temperature.

TAKEOFF AND LANDING PERFORMANCE
5. (Refer to figure 37) To find the headwind and crosswind components, first determine the difference between the runway heading and the wind direction. Then, find the intersection of the degrees line and the wind velocity arc.
6. (Refer to figure 37) To find a velocity at an aircraft's maximum crosswind component, begin with the crosswind component at the bottom of the chart. Follow the line up to where it intersects the degree line representing the angle of crosswind. Then, read the wind velocity.
7. (Refer to figure 38) To determine the total distance required to land, start at the bottom left side of the chart. Find the OAT and follow the line up to the corresponding pressure altitude. Move right to the reference line and parallel the diagonal guide line downward to intersect the weight line. Move straight across to the next reference line, and parallel the diagonal headwind guide line down to intersect the wind component line. Move straight across to the next reference line and parallel the diagonal obstacle height guide line up to the obstacle given. The landing distance is read on the right side.
8. (Refer to figure 39) To determine the landing distance, find the table that corresponds to the temperature and pressure altitudes that most closely resemble the given conditions. If you need to take into account an obstacle, select that distance. Be sure to check additional factors listed at the bottom of the chart, including headwind, nonstandard temperature and surface conditions.
9. (Refer to figure 41) To determine takeoff distance, start at the bottom left of the chart, and find the temperature and pressure altitude. Move straight across to the reference line, and follow the guide line down to the given weight. Move across to the next reference line, and follow the headwind guide line down to the given value. Follow the line straight across to the next reference line, and move down to the stated obstacle height. Move parallel to the guide line and read the distance from the right side of the chart. If there is no wind or obstacle, move straight across the corresponding section to the next reference line.

CLIMB PERFORMANCE

10. V_X is the best angle of climb, and it provides the greatest gain in altitude over the shortest distance during climb after takeoff.
11. V_Y is the best rate of climb, and it provides the greatest gain in altitude over a given period of time.
12. An aircraft's operating limitations are found in several places, including the current, FAA-approved flight manual, approved manual material, markings, placards, or any combination thereof.

CRUISE PERFORMANCE

13. (Refer to figure 36) To determine the TAS in given conditions, use the left-hand portion of the table, under the appropriate temperature heading. Interpolate between the given pressure altitudes, if necessary, to find the TAS.
14. (Refer to figure 36) To determine the expected fuel consumption, first go to the table under the appropriate temperature heading. Go down to the given pressure altitude and read across to find the fuel flow and TAS. Find the time enroute by dividing the distance by the TAS. Multiply the time by the fuel flow.
15. (Refer to figure 36) To determine the manifold pressure setting, go to the appropriate temperature heading, and go down to the pressure altitude. Read the MP from the table, noting all RPM values are the same.

8-1   A02
Which would provide the greatest gain in altitude in the shortest distance during climb after takeoff?

A — V_Y.
B — V_A.
C — V_X.

8-1. Answer C. GFDPPM 8-16 (AFH)
V_X is the best angle of climb. This gives you the greatest gain in altitude for horizontal distance traveled. Answer (A) is wrong because V_Y is the best rate of climb. This provides you the greatest gain in altitude over a period of time. Answer (B) is wrong because V_A is maneuvering airspeed.

8-2   A02
After takeoff, which airspeed would the pilot use to gain the most altitude in a given period of time?

A — V_Y.
B — V_X.
C — V_A.

8-2. Answer A. GFDPPM 8-16 (AFH)
See explanation for Question 8-1.

8-3   H308
What effect does high density altitude, as compared to low density altitude, have on propeller efficiency and why?

A — Efficiency is increased due to less friction on the propeller blades.
B — Efficiency is reduced because the propeller exerts less force at high density altitudes than at low density altitudes.
C — Efficiency is reduced due to the increased force of the propeller in the thinner air.

8-3. Answer B. GFDPPM 8-19 (PHB)
Because the air is less dense, there is less airflow through the propeller, and the force and efficiency are reduced. Answers (A) and (C) are wrong because the propeller force and efficiency are reduced, not increased.

8-4   H317
Which combination of atmospheric conditions will reduce aircraft takeoff and climb performance.

A — Low temperature, low relative humidity, and low density altitude.
B — High temperature, low relative humidity, and low density altitude.
C — High temperature, high relative humidity, and high density altitude.

8-4. Answer C. GFDPPM 8-10 (PHB)
High temperatures increase density altitude with a resulting decrease in aircraft performance. In addition, high humidity reduces engine performance.

8-5   H317

What effect does high density altitude have on aircraft performance?

A — It increases engine performance.
B — It reduces climb performance.
C — It increases takeoff performance.

8-6   H317

What effect, if any, does high humidity have on aircraft performance?

A — It increases performance.
B — It decreases performance.
C — It has no effect on performance.

8-7   H317

(Refer to figure 36.) Approximately what true airspeed should a pilot expect with 65 percent maximum continuous power at 9,500 feet with a temperature of 36°F below standard?

A — 178 MPH.
B — 181 MPH.
C — 183 MPH.

8-5. Answer B. GFDPPM 8-19 (PHB)
A high density altitude decreases engine performance with a resulting reduction in climb performance.

8-6. Answer B. GFDPPM 8-8 (PHB)
High humidity reduces engine performance by slightly increasing the density altitude of air entering the engine and retarding smooth burning of the fuel.

8-7. Answer C. GFDPPM 8-22 (PHB)
Use the left-hand portion of the table, under ISA −36°F. Interpolate between the TAS values for 8,000 feet (181 MPH) and 10,000 feet (184 MPH). The closest answer is 183 MPH.

CRUISE POWER SETTINGS

65% MAXIMUM CONTINUOUS POWER (OR FULL THROTTLE)
2800 POUNDS

PRESS ALT.									ISA −20 °C (−36 °F)									STANDARD DAY (ISA)									ISA +20 °C (+36 °F)	
	IOAT		ENGINE SPEED	MAN. PRESS	FUEL FLOW PER ENGINE		TAS		IOAT		ENGINE SPEED	MAN. PRESS	FUEL FLOW PER ENGINE		TAS		IOAT		ENGINE SPEED	MAN. PRESS	FUEL FLOW PER ENGINE		TAS	
FEET	°F	°C	RPM	IN HG	PSI	GPH	KTS	MPH	°F	°C	RPM	IN HG	PSI	GPH	KTS	MPH	°F	°C	RPM	IN HG	PSI	GPH	KTS	MPH
SL	27	-3	2450	20.7	6.6	11.5	147	169	63	17	2450	21.2	6.6	11.5	150	173	99	37	2450	21.8	6.6	11.5	153	176
2000	19	-7	2450	20.4	6.6	11.5	149	171	55	13	2450	21.0	6.6	11.5	153	176	91	33	2450	21.5	6.6	11.5	156	180
4000	12	-11	2450	20.1	6.6	11.5	152	175	48	9	2450	20.7	6.6	11.5	156	180	84	29	2450	21.3	6.6	11.5	159	183
6000	5	-15	2450	19.8	6.6	11.5	155	178	41	5	2450	20.4	6.6	11.5	158	182	79	26	2450	21.0	6.6	11.5	161	185
8000	-2	-19	2450	19.5	6.6	11.5	157	181	36	2	2450	20.2	6.6	11.5	161	185	72	22	2450	20.8	6.6	11.5	164	189
10000	-8	-22	2450	19.2	6.6	11.5	160	184	28	-2	2450	19.9	6.6	11.5	163	188	64	18	2450	20.3	6.5	11.4	166	191
12000	-15	-26	2450	18.8	6.4	11.3	162	186	21	-6	2450	18.8	6.1	10.9	163	188	57	14	2450	18.8	5.9	10.6	163	188
14000	-22	-30	2450	17.4	5.8	10.5	159	183	14	-10	2450	17.4	5.6	10.1	160	184	50	10	2450	17.4	5.4	9.8	160	184
16000	-29	-34	2450	16.1	5.3	9.7	156	180	7	-14	2450	16.1	5.1	9.4	156	180	43	6	2450	16.1	4.9	9.1	155	178

NOTES: 1. Full throttle manifold pressure settings are approximate.
          2. Shaded area represents operation with full throttle.

FIGURE 36.—Airplane Power Setting Table.

8-8   H317
(Refer to figure 36 on page 8-3.) What is the expected fuel consumption for a 1,000-nautical mile flight under the following conditions?
Pressure altitude.................................8,000 ft
Temperature ....22°C
Manifold pressure ....20.8″ Hg
Wind ....Calm

A — 60.2 gallons.
B — 70.1 gallons.
C — 73.2 gallons.

8-8. Answer B. GFDPPM 8-22 (PHB)
The temperature of 22°C is found on the right-hand portion of the table (ISA + 20°C) at 8,000 feet. Read across to find a fuel flow of 11.5 GPH, and TAS of 164 KTS (use knots because the distance is in nautical miles). Now, find the time enroute by dividing 1,000 n.m. by 164 KTS. (Normally you would use ground-speed, but with a calm wind, TAS equals ground-speed.) The time enroute is approximately 6:06 hrs. Then multiply the time by fuel flow. The total fuel consumption is 70.1 gallons.

8-9   H317
(Refer to figure 36 on page 8-3) What fuel flow should a pilot expect at 11,000 feet on a standard day with 65 percent maximum continuous power?

A — 10.6 gallons per hour.
B — 11.2 gallons per hour.
C — 11.8 gallons per hour.

8-9. Answer B. GFDPPM 8-22 (PHB)
Use the center portion of the table for a standard day. You will need to interpolate to find the fuel flow for 11,000 feet which is halfway between 12,000 and 10,000 feet. The answer is 11.2 (11.5 − 10.9 = .6 ÷ 2 = .3 + 10.9 = 11.2).

8-10   H317
(Refer to figure 36 on page 8-3.) Determine the approximate manifold pressure setting with 2,450 RPM to achieve 65 percent maximum continuous power at 6,500 feet with a temperature of 36°F higher than standard.

A — 19.8″ Hg.
B — 20.8″ Hg.
C — 21.0″ Hg.

8-10. Answer C. GFDPPM 8-22 (PHB)
The RPM is the same for all altitudes. Therefore, to determine what manifold pressure (MP) is required to achieve 65% maximum continuous power, enter the table under ISA + 36°F. The MP for 6,000 feet is 21.0″, and for 8,000 feet it is 20.8″. The interpolated MP for 6,500 feet is 20.95″. The closest answer is 21.0″ Hg.

8-11   H317
(Refer to figure 37 on page 8-5.) What is the headwind component for a landing on Runway 18 if the tower reports the wind as 220° at 30 knots?

A — 19 knots.
B — 23 knots.
C — 26 knots.

8-11. Answer B. GFDPPM 8-12 (PHB)
First, compute the difference between the runway (180°) and the wind (220°). The result is an angle of 40 degrees. Find the intersection of the 40 degree line and the 30 knot wind velocity arc, then read across to the left side to find the headwind component of 23 knots.

8-12   H317
(Refer to figure 37 on page 8-5.) Determine the maximum wind velocity for a 45° crosswind if the maximum crosswind component for the airplane is 25 knots.

A — 25 knots.
B — 29 knots.
C — 35 knots.

8-12. Answer C. GFDPPM 8-12 (PHB)
Start with the crosswind component of 25 knots at the bottom of the chart, and follow the line straight up to where it intersects the 45 degree angle line. This intersection is midway between the 30 and 40 knot wind velocity lines, or 35 knots.

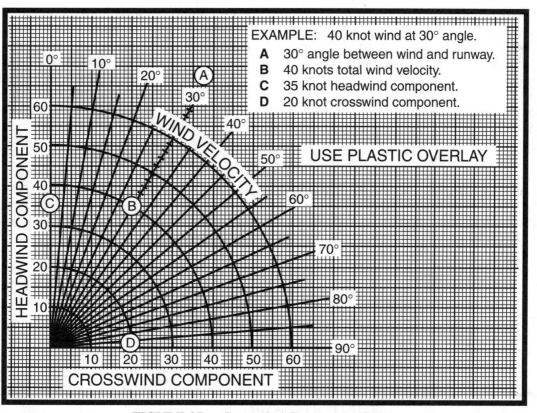

FIGURE 37.—Crosswind Component Graph.

8-13   H317
(Refer to figure 37.) What is the maximum wind velocity for a 30° crosswind if the maximum crosswind component for the airplane is 12 knots?

A — 16 knots.
B — 20 knots.
C — 24 knots.

8-14   H317
(Refer to figure 37.) With a reported wind of north at 20 knots, which runway (6, 29, or 32) is acceptable for use for an airplane with a 13-knot maximum crosswind component?

A — Runway 6.
B — Runway 29.
C — Runway 32.

8-13. Answer C. GFDPPM 8-12 (PHB)
Start with the crosswind component of 12 knots at the bottom of the chart, and follow the line straight up to where it intersects the 30 degree angle line. This intersection is approximately 24 knots on the wind velocity scale.

8-14. Answer C. GFDPPM 8-12 (PHB)
At first glance, Runway 32 is most closely aligned with north (360°). To verify, find the crosswind component for each runway. Runway 32 is 40 degrees from the wind, and since the windspeed is 20 knots, the crosswind component is slightly less than 13 knots, so Runway 32 is acceptable. Runway 6 is 60 degrees from the wind, and the crosswind component is about 17.5 knots. Runway 29 is 70 degrees from the wind, and the crosswind component is about 19 knots. Both Runways 6 and 29 exceed the 13 knot maximum crosswind component.

8-15   H317
(Refer to figure 37 on page 8-5.) With a reported wind of south at 20 knots, which runway (10, 14, or 24) is appropriate for an airplane with a 13-knot maximum crosswind component?

A — Runway 10.
B — Runway 14.
C — Runway 24.

8-16   H317
(Refer to figure 37 on page 8-5.) What is the crosswind component for a landing on Runway 18 if the tower reports the wind as 220° at 30 knots?

A — 19 knots.
B — 23 knots.
C — 30 knots.

8-15. Answer B. GFDPPM 8-12 (PHB)
The same process is used as in Question 8-14. Runway 14 is most closely aligned with the wind and would have the least crosswind. The crosswind angle and component for each runway is: Runway 14, 40 degrees, 12.5 knots; Runway 10, 80 degrees, 19.7 knots; Runway 24, 60 degrees, 17.5 knots. Runway 14 is the only appropriate runway because the crosswind component is less than 13 knots.

8-16. Answer A. GFDPPM 8-12 (PHB)
The crosswind angle is 40 degrees (220° – 180° = 40°). Find the intersection of 40 degrees and 30 knots. Then read down to find the crosswind component of about 19 knots.

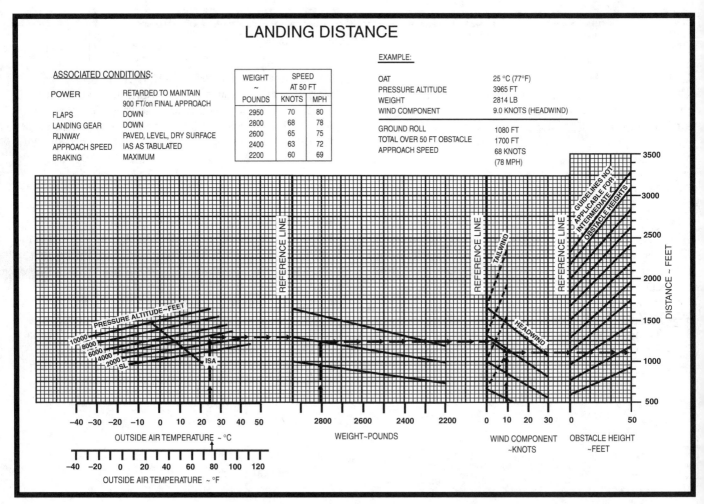

FIGURE 38.—Airplane Landing Distance Graph.

8-17   H317
(Refer to figure 38 on page 8-6.) Determine the approximate total distance required to land over a 50-foot obstacle.
OAT ....90°F
Pressure altitude................................4,000 ft
Weight ....2,800 lb
Headwind component...........................10 kts

A — 1,525 feet.
B — 1,950 feet.
C — 1,775 feet.

8-18   H317
(Refer to figure 39.) Determine the approximate landing ground roll distance.
Pressure altitude..............................Sea level
Headwind...4 kts
Temperature ....Std

A — 356 feet.
B — 401 feet.
C — 490 feet.

8-19   H317
(Refer to figure 39.) Determine the total distance required to land over a 50-foot obstacle.
Pressure altitude...............................7,500 ft
Headwind..8 kts
Temperature...32°F
Runway..................................Hard surface

A — 1,506 feet.
B — 1,004 feet.
C — 1,205 feet.

8-17. Answer C. GFDPPM 8-15 (PHB)
Start at the lower left at 90°F (32°C), and move up to where it intersects the 4,000-foot pressure altitude line. Go right to the weight reference line and then down and to the right to 2,800 lbs. Go straight right to the wind component reference line, down and to the right to the 10 knot headwind line, and straight right to the obstacle height reference line. Move up and to the right through the obstacle height and read the landing distance over a 50-foot obstacle on the right-hand scale. It is approximately 1,775 feet.

8-18. Answer B. GFDPPM 8-14, 15 (PHB)
Use the table listed under sea level and 59°F, which is the standard temperature. Since you need to find the landing ground roll distance, do not include obstacle clearance. The ground roll is given as 445, but according to Note 1, you need to correct for headwind by decreasing the distance 10% for each 4 knots of headwind. In this case, subtract 10% of 445 (44.5) from 445. The closest answer is 401 feet.

8-19. Answer B. GFDPPM 8-14, 15 (PHB)
According to the table, the landing distance over a 50-foot obstacle is 1,255 feet at 7,500 feet and 32°F. Note 1 says to decrease this distance by 10% for each 4 knots of headwind, so with 8 knots headwind, subtract 20 percent. 1,255 x .80 = 1,004 feet.

—————— LANDING DISTANCE ——————   FLAPS LOWERED TO 40 ° - POWER OFF
HARD SURFACE RUNWAY - ZERO WIND

GROSS WEIGHT LB	APPROACH SPEED IAS, MPH	AT SEA LEVEL & 59 °F		AT 2500 FT & 50 °F		AT 5000 FT & 41 °F		AT 7500 FT & 32 °F	
		GROUND ROLL	TOTAL TO CLEAR 50 FT OBS	GROUND ROLL	TOTAL TO CLEAR 50 FT OBS	GROUND ROLL	TOTAL TO CLEAR 50 FT OBS	GROUND ROLL	TOTAL TO CLEAR 50 FT OBS
1600	60	445	1075	470	1135	495	1195	520	1255

NOTES: 1. Decrease the distances shown by 10% for each 4 knots of headwind.
2. Increase the distance by 10% for each 60 °F temperature increase above standard.
3. For operation on a dry, grass runway, increase distances (both "ground roll" and "total to clear 50 ft obstacle") by 20% of the "total to clear 50 ft obstacle" figure.

FIGURE 39.—Airplane Landing Distance Table.

8-20   H317

(Refer to figure 39 on page 8-7.) Determine the total distance required to land over a 50-foot obstacle.

Pressure altitude...5,000 ft
Headwind..8 kts
Temperature...41°F
Runway...Hard surface

A — 837 feet.
B — 956 feet.
C — 1,076 feet.

8-21   H317

(Refer to figure 39 on page 8-7.) Determine the approximate landing ground roll distance.

Pressure altitude...5,000 ft
Headwind..Calm
Temperature...101°F

A — 495 feet.
B — 545 feet.
C — 445 feet.

8-22   H317

(Refer to figure 39 on page 8-7.) Determine the total distance required to land over a 50-foot obstacle.

Pressure altitude...3,750 ft
Headwind...12 kts
Temperature ....Std

A — 794 feet.
B — 836 feet.
C — 816 feet.

8-23   H317

(Refer to figure 39 on page 8-7.) Determine the approximate landing ground roll distance.

Pressure altitude...1,250 ft
Headwind..8 kts
Temperature ....Std

A — 275 feet.
B — 366 feet.
C — 470 feet.

8-20. Answer B. GFDPPM 8-14, 15 (PHB)

Use the table at 5,000 feet and 41°F. The distance to land over a 50 ft obstacle is 1,195. According to Note 1, decrease the distance by 20% (239′) for the 8 knot headwind: (1,195 – 239 = 956 total landing distance).

8-21. Answer B. GFDPPM 8-14, 15 (PHB)

At 5,000 feet and 41°F (ISA Standard Temperature), the ground roll distance is 495 feet. According to Note 2, this distance is increased 10% for each 60°F above standard.

8-22. Answer C. GFDPPM 8-14, 15 (PHB)

1. At 2,500 feet and Standard ISA temperature, the landing distance over a 50-foot obstacle with zero wind is 1,135 feet. At 5,000 feet this distance is 1,195 feet. At 3,750 feet assume the landing distance is half way between 1,135 and 1,195 feet. (1,135 + 1,195) feet ÷ 2 = 1,165 feet.

2. Note 1 says to decrease the distance 10% for each 4 knots of headwind. The headwind is 12 knots. 12 knots x 10% decrease/4 knots = 30% decrease. 1,165 feet x (100% - 30%) = 816 feet.

8-23. Answer B. GFDPPM 8-14, 15 (PHB)

This problem requires that you interpolate between the ground roll distances at sea level and 2,500 feet PA. Since 1,250 feet is midway between the two values, the ground roll would be 457.5 (470 – 445 = 25 ÷ 2 = 13.5 + 445 = 457.5). To correct for headwind, subtract 20% of the distance (10% for each 4 kts). 20% of 457.5 is 91.5. The landing distance is 457.5 – 91.5 or 366 feet.

8-24 **H317**

(Refer to figure 41.) Determine the total distance required for takeoff to clear a 50-foot obstacle.

OAT...Std
Pressure altitude..4,000 ft
Takeoff weight ....2,800 lb
Headwind component...Calm

A — 1,500 feet.
B — 1,750 feet.
C — 2,000 feet.

8-24. Answer B. GFDPPM 8-6, 7 (PHB)

Since temperature is standard, start at the intersection of the ISA and 4,000 foot pressure altitude line. Move right to the reference line and follow the guide line diagonally downward to the 2,800 pound line. Since winds are calm, move straight across to the obstacle height reference line. Follow the guide line upward to the 50 foot line, which is on the right-hand border. The takeoff distance is approximately 1,700 feet.

8-25 **H317**

(Refer to figure 41.) Determine the total distance required for takeoff to clear a 50-foot obstacle.

OAT...Std
Pressure altitude......................................Sea level
Takeoff weight ....2,700 lb
Headwind component...Calm

A — 1,000 feet.
B — 1,400 feet.
C — 1,700 feet.

8-25. Answer B. GFDPPM 8-6, 7 (PHB)

Since temperature is standard, start at the intersection of the ISA line and sea level (S.L.). Move right to the reference line and follow the guide line diagonally downward to the 2,700 pound line. Move straight across to the obstacle height reference line, since winds are calm. Follow the guide line upward to the 50 foot line. The takeoff distance is about 1,400 feet.

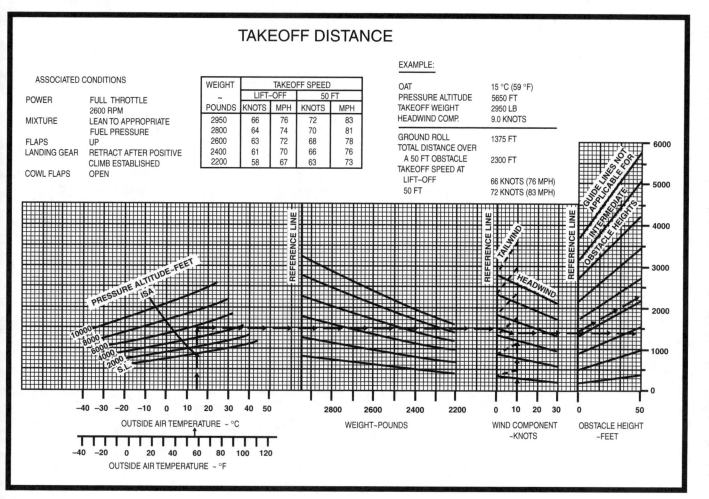

FIGURE 41.—Airplane Takeoff Distance Graph.

8-26   H317
(Refer to figure 41 on page 8-9.) Determine the
approximate ground roll distance required for takeoff.
OAT ....100°F
Pressure altitude................................2,000 ft
Takeoff weight ....2,750 lb
Headwind component.........................Calm

A — 1,150 feet.
B — 1,300 feet.
C — 1,800 feet.

8-27   H317
(Refer to figure 41 on page 8-9.) Determine the
approximate ground roll distance required for takeoff.
OAT ....90°F
Pressure altitude................................2,000 ft
Takeoff weight ....2,500 lb
Headwind component.........................20 kts

A — 650 feet
B — 850 feet
C — 1,000 feet

8-26. Answer A. GFDPPM 8-6, 7 (PHB)
Start at 100°F, move up to the 2,000 foot pressure altitude line, then right to the reference line. Follow the
guide line down to 2,750 pounds. Since winds are
calm, and there is no obstacle, move straight across
to the right-hand border. The ground roll is about
1,150 feet.

8-27. Answer A. GFDPPM 8-6, 7 (PHB)
Start at 90°F, move up to the 2,000 foot pressure altitude line, then right to the reference line. Follow the
guide line down to 2,500 pounds. Move across to the
next reference line, and follow the headwind guide line
down to 20 knots. Since there is no obstacle, move
straight across to the right-hand border. The ground
roll is about 650 feet.

SECTION B
WEIGHT AND BALANCE

Pilots need to keep weight within specified limits and to balance the load on board the aircraft carefully in order to maintain control of the airplane. This section covers weight and balance charts and tables, how to determine weight and balance, and how to apply the weight shift formula.

WEIGHT AND BALANCE TERMS
1. Included in the empty weight of an aircraft are the unusable fuel and undrainable oil.
2. The standard weight of gasoline is six pounds per gallon. To determine the amount of fuel to drain, if necessary, divide the excess weight by six.

PRINCIPLES OF WEIGHT AND BALANCE
3. The CG is the total moment divided by the total weight. Datum is a vertical plane in the aircraft from which weight and balance distances are measured. Arm is the distance from datum of a particular station, or place in the aircraft. To calculate aircraft moment, multiply the weight at a station by the arm. Positive CG values are aft of datum, negative CG values are ahead of datum.

DETERMINING TOTAL WEIGHT AND CENTER OF GRAVITY
There are several formulas which will aid you in calculating your aircraft's center of gravity and total weight, and the change in CG with a shift in weight.

TABLE METHOD
4. The best way to determine aircraft weight and balance is to construct a table which lists the stations of the aircraft, the weight at each station, and the arm of each station. From here, you can find the moment at each station, and add up the total weight and moments. The CG is the total moment divided by the total weight.
5. (Refer to figures 33 and 34) To find the arm at each station, look for the station, i.e. usable fuel, on the table and read the arm listed at the top. Many charts calculate moments for a specific weight range, so that you can simply read these off the table as well.
6. (Refer to figure 35) Other charts provide arm and moment information graphically. To read the moment from the chart, find the line that corresponds to the station, and follow it to the given weight at the station. Move down to the bottom of the graph to find the moment.

WEIGHT SHIFT FORMULA
7. Use the weight shift formula to determine how far the center of gravity shifts when weight is added to or removed from the aircraft:

$$\frac{\text{Weight Moved}}{\text{Weight of Airplane}} = \frac{\text{Distance CG Moves}}{\text{Distance Between Arms}}$$

8. Some weight shift questions will require you to construct a table of weights and moments first.

8-28   H316

Which items are included in the empty weight of an aircraft?

A — Unusable fuel and undrainable oil.
B — Only the airframe, powerplant, and optional equipment.
C — Full fuel tanks and engine oil to capacity.

8-28. Answer A. GFDPPM 8-32 (PHB)

The empty weight of an aircraft includes unusable fuel. The term basic empty weight includes full engine oil. On older airplanes, the term licensed empty weight includes only undrainable oil. Therefore, answer (A) is the best choice. Answer (B) is wrong because empty weight also includes full operating fluids and unusable fuel. Answer (C) is wrong because empty weight does not include full fuel tanks.

8-29   H316

An aircraft is loaded 110 pounds over maximum certificated gross weight. If fuel (gasoline) is drained to bring the aircraft weight within limits, how much fuel should be drained?

A — 15.7 gallons.
B — 16.2 gallons.
C — 18.4 gallons.

8-30   H316

GIVEN:

	WEIGHT (LB)	ARM (IN)	MOMENT (LB-IN)
Empty weight	1,495.0	101.4	151,593.0
Pilot and pass	380.0	64.0	—
Fuel (30 gal usable no reserve)	—	96.0	—

The CG is located how far aft of datum?

A — CG 92.44.
B — CG 94.01.
C — CG 119.8.

8-31   H316

(Refer to figures 33 and 34 on pages 8-13 and 8-14.)
What is the maximum amount of baggage that can be carried when the airplane is loaded as follows?
Front seat occupants..387 lb
Rear seat occupants..293 lb
Fuel..35 gal

A — 45 pounds.
B — 63 pounds.
C — 220 pounds.

8-29. Answer C. GFDPPM 8-33 (PHB)

This problem requires converting the weight of fuel to gallons. Since the standard weight of gasoline is 6 pounds per gallon, divide 110 pounds by 6, to find an answer of 18.33, or 18.4 gallons.

8-30. Answer B. GFDPPM 8-36 (PHB)

First, fill in the table by entering the fuel weight (30 gal. × 6 lb/gal = 180 lbs). Then, multiply each weight by the arm to find the moment.

	WEIGHT (LB)	ARM (IN)	MOMENT (LB-IN)
Empty weight	1,495.0	101.4	151,593.0
Pilot & pass	380.0	64.0	24,320.0
Fuel 30 gals	180.0	96.0	17,280.0
Totals	2,055.0		193,193.0

$$CG = \frac{193,193}{2,055} = 94.01$$

The CG is the total moment divided by the total weight.

8-31. Answer A. GFDPPM 8-39 (PHB)

Add up all the weights and you will find the airplane is 45 lbs. underweight. When adding the 45 lbs. of baggage, be sure to verify that the resulting center of gravity (CG) is within limits.

USEFUL LOAD WEIGHTS AND MOMENTS

OCCUPANTS

FRONT SEATS ARM 85		REAR SEATS ARM 121	
Weight	Moment/100	Weight	Moment/100
120	102	120	145
130	110	130	157
140	119	140	169
150	128	150	182
160	136	160	194
170	144	170	206
180	153	180	218
190	162	190	230
200	170	200	242

BAGGAGE OR 5TH SEAT OCCUPANT ARM 140

Weight	Moment/100
10	14
20	28
30	42
40	56
50	70
60	84
70	98
80	112
90	126
100	140
110	154
120	168
130	182
140	196
150	210
160	224
170	238
180	252
190	266
200	280
210	294
220	308
230	322
240	336
250	350
260	364
270	378

USABLE FUEL

MAIN WING TANKS ARM 75

Gallons	Weight	Moment/100
5	30	22
10	60	45
15	90	68
20	120	90
25	150	112
30	180	135
35	210	158
40	240	180
44	264	198

AUXILIARY WING TANKS ARM 94

Gallons	Weight	Moment/100
5	30	28
10	60	56
15	90	85
19	114	107

*OIL

Quarts	Weight	Moment/100
10	19	5

*Included in basic Empty Weight

Empty Weight ~ 2015

MOM / 100 ~ 1554

MOMENT LIMITS vs WEIGHT

Moment limits are based on the following weight and center of gravity limit data (landing gear down).

WEIGHT CONDITION	FORWARD CG LIMIT	AFT CG LIMIT
2950 lb (takeoff or landing)	82.1	84.7
2525 lb	77.5	85.7
2475 lb or less	77.0	85.7

FIGURE 33.—Airplane Weight and Balance Tables

MOMENT LIMITS vs WEIGHT (Continued)

Weight	Minimum Moment 100	Maximum Moment 100	Weight	Minimum Moment 100	Maximum Moment 100
2100	1617	1800	2600	2037	2224
2110	1625	1808	2610	2048	2232
2120	1632	1817	2620	2058	2247
2130	1640	1825	2630	2069	2255
2140	1648	1834	2640	2080	2263
2150	1656	1843	2650	2090	2271
2160	1663	1851	2660	2101	2279
2170	1671	1860	2670	2112	2287
2180	1679	1868	2680	2123	2295
2190	1686	1877	2690	2133	
2200	1694	1885	2700	2144	2303
2210	1702	1894	2710	2155	2311
2220	1709	1903	2720	2166	2319
2230	1717	1911	2730	2177	2326
2240	1725	1920	2740	2188	2334
2250	1733	1928	2750	2199	2342
2260	1740	1937	2760	2210	2350
2270	1748	1945	2770	2221	2358
2280	1756	1954	2780	2232	2366
2290	1763	1963	2790	2243	2374
2300	1771	1971			
2310	1779	1980	2800	2254	2381
2320	1786	1988	2810	2265	2389
2330	1794	1997	2820	2276	2397
2340	1802	2005	2830	2287	2405
2350	1810	2014	2840	2298	2413
2360	1817	2023	2850	2309	2421
2370	1825	2031	2860	2320	2428
2380	1833	2040	2870	2332	2436
2390	1840	2048	2880	2343	2444
			2890	2354	2452
2400	1848	2057	2900	2365	2460
2410	1856	2065	2910	2377	2468
2420	1863	2074	2920	2388	2475
2430	1871	2083	2930	2399	2483
2440	1879	2091	2940	2411	2491
2450	1887	2100	2950	2422	2499
2460	1894	2108			
2470	1902	2117			
2480	1911	2125			
2490	1921	2134			
2500	1932	2143			
2510	1942	2151			
2520	1953	2160			
2530	1963	2168			
2540	1974	2176			
2550	1984	2184			
2560	1995	2192			
2570	2005	2200			
2580	2016	2208			
2590	2026	2216			

FIGURE 34.—Airplane Weight and Balance Tables

8-32   H316
(Refer to figures 33 and 34 on pages 8-13 and 8-14.)
Determine if the airplane weight and balance is within
limits.

Front seat occupants	415 lb
Rear seat occupants	110 lb
Fuel, main tanks	44 gal
Fuel, aux. tanks	19 gal
Baggage	32 lb

A — 19 pounds overweight, CG within limits.
B — 19 pounds overweight, CG out of limits forward.
C — Weight within limits, CG out of limits.

8-33   H316
(Refer to figure 35 on page 8-16.) What is the maximum amount of baggage that may be loaded aboard
the airplane for the CG to remain within the moment
envelope?

	WEIGHT (LB)	MOM/1000
Empty weight	1,350	51.5
Pilot and front passenger	250	—
Rear passengers	400	—
Baggage	—	—
Fuel, 30 gal	—	—
Oil, 8 qt	—	–0.2

A — 105 pounds.
B — 110 pounds.
C — 120 pounds.

8-32. Answer C. GFDPPM 8-36, 39 (PHB)
First, construct a weight and moment table.

	WEIGHT (lbs)	ARM (in)	MOMENT (lb-in/100)
Empty weight	2,015		1,554.0
Front seat	415	85	352.8
Rear seat	110	121	133.1
Fuel 44 gal	264	75	198.0
Aux 19 gal	114	94	107.2
Baggage	32	140	44.8
Totals	2,950		2,389.9

The total weight is at the maximum limit. Divide total
moments by total weight to find the CG of 81.0, which
is outside the limits.

$$CG = \frac{2,389 \times 100}{2,950} = 81.0$$

8-33. Answer A. GFDPPM 8-40 (PHB)
Refer to Figure 35 to convert oil and fuel to pounds.
Add up the known weights, for a total of 2,195 pounds.
Subtract 2,195 pounds from 2,300 max weight to find
the maximum possible baggage weight of 105 pounds.
While it appears that choice A is the only correct
answer, it is a good idea to check the CG limits. Use
the LOADING GRAPH and find the moment for each
weight.

	WEIGHT (lbs)	MOMENT (lb-in/1000)
Empty wt.	1,350	51.5
Front seat	250	9.4
Rear seat	400	29.3
Fuel 30 gal	180	8.7
Oil 8 qts	15	–0.2
Subtotal	2,195	98.7
Baggage	105	10.0
Totals	2,300	108.7

Total the moments and locate the maximum weight on
the CENTER OF GRAVITY MOMENT ENVELOPE
graph. The intersection of the loaded weight and
moment is at the upper right-hand corner of the normal
category envelope, and is just barely within limits.

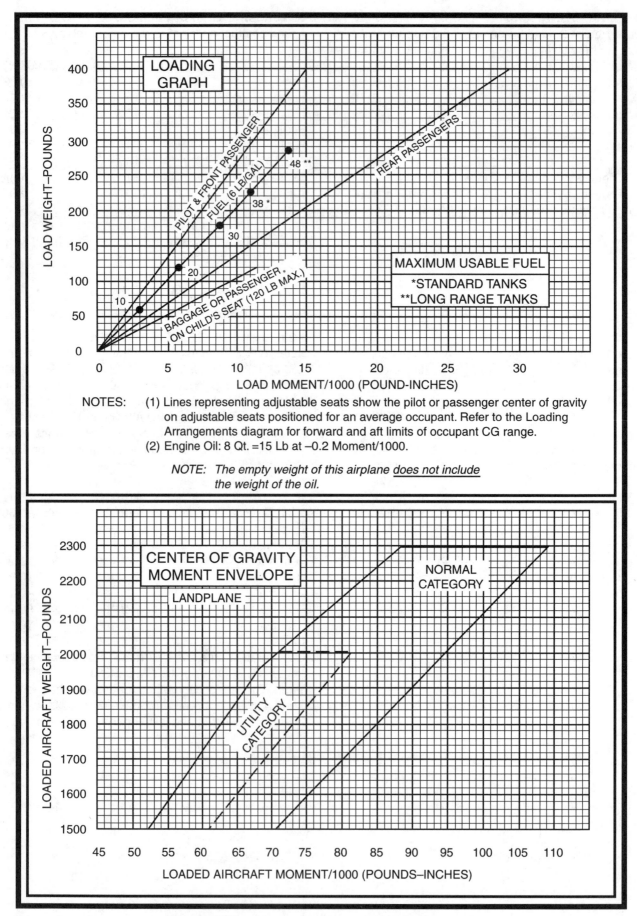

NOTES: (1) Lines representing adjustable seats show the pilot or passenger center of gravity
              on adjustable seats positioned for an average occupant. Refer to the Loading
              Arrangements diagram for forward and aft limits of occupant CG range.
          (2) Engine Oil: 8 Qt. =15 Lb at –0.2 Moment/1000.

          *NOTE: The empty weight of this airplane does not include
                  the weight of the oil.*

FIGURE 35.—Airplane Weight and Balance Graphs.

8-34   H316

(Refer to figure 35 on page 8-16.) Calculate the moment of the airplane and determine which category is applicable.

	WEIGHT (LB)	MOM/1000
Empty weight	1,350	51.5
Pilot and front pass	310	—
Rear passengers	96	—
Fuel, 38 gal	—	—
Oil, 8 qt	—	-0.2

A — 79.2, utility category.
B — 80.8, utility category.
C — 81.2, normal category

8-35   H316

(Refer to figure 35 on page 8-16.) What is the maximum amount of fuel that may be aboard the airplane on takeoff if loaded as follows?

	WEIGHT (LB)	MOM/1000
Empty weight	1,350	51.5
Pilot and front passenger	340	—
Rear passengers	310	—
Baggage	45	—
Oil, 8 qt	—	—

A — 24 gallons.
B — 32 gallons.
C — 40 gallons.

•

8-36   H316

(Refer to figure 35 on page 8-16.) Determine the moment with the following data:

	WEIGHT (LB)	MOM/1000
Empty weight	1,350	51.5
Pilot and front passenger	340	—
Fuel (std. tanks)	Capacity	—
Oil, 8 qt	—	—

A — 69.9 pound-inches.
B — 74.9 pound-inches.
C — 77.6 pound-inches.

8-34. Answer B. GFDPPM 8-40 (PHB)

Complete the table of weights and moments, using the LOADING GRAPH

	WEIGHT (lbs.)	MOMENT (lb-in/1000)
Empty wt.	1,350	51.5
Front seat	310	11.6
Rear seat	96	7.0
Fuel 38 gal	228	11.0
Oil 8 qts	15	-0.2
Totals	1,999	80.9

The total moment is 80.9. Use the CENTER OF GRAVITY MOMENT ENVELOPE graph to find the total weight and total moment. The intersection falls within the upper right-hand corner of the utility category envelope.

8-35. Answer C. GFDPPM 8-40 (PHB)

Complete the table of weights and moments, using the LOADING GRAPH.

	WEIGHT (lbs)	MOMENT (lb-in/1000)
Empty wt	1,350	51.5
Front seat	340	12.7
Rear seat	310	22.6
Baggage	45	4.3
Oil 8 qts	15	-.2
Subtotal	2060	90.9
Fuel 40 gal	240	11.5
Totals	2300	102.4

The total weight without fuel is 2,060 pounds. This is 240 pounds below the maximum of 2,300 pounds. Dividing by 6 lb/gal, the maximum fuel load is 40 gallons. It is a good idea to check the moments as well. The total moment of 102.4 is within the CG envelope, so 40 gallons is acceptable.

8-36. Answer B. GFDPPM 8-40 (PHB)

Use the LOADING GRAPH to determine the moments. Add these to find the total moment of 74.9.

	WEIGHT (lbs.)	MOMENT (lb-in/1000)
Empty wt.	1,350	51.5
Front seat	340	12.6
Fuel 38 gal.	228	11.0
Oil 8 qts.	15	-0.2
Totals	1,933	74.9

8-37   H316
(Refer to figure 35 on page 8-16.) Determine the aircraft loaded moment and the aircraft category.

	WEIGHT (LB)	MOM/1000
Empty weight	1,350	51.5
Pilot and front pass	380	—
Fuel, 48 gal	288	—
Oil, 8 qt	—	—

A — 78.2, normal category.
B — 79.2, normal category.
C — 80.4, utility category.

8-37. Answer B. GFDPPM 8-40 (PHB)
Use the LOADING GRAPH to determine the moments

	WEIGHT (lbs)	MOMENT (lb-in/1000)
Empty wt	1,350	51.5
Front seat	380	14.2
Fuel 48 gal	288	13.7
Oil 8 qts	15	−0.2
Totals	2,033	79.2

The total weight is 2,033 pounds, and the total moment
is 79.2. Use the CENTER OF GRAVITY MOMENT
ENVELOPE graph with the total weight and total
moment. The intersection falls within the normal category, and outside the utility category.

8-38   H316
(Refer to figures 33 and 34 on pages 8-13 and 8-14.)
Upon landing, the front passenger (180 pounds)
departs the airplane. A rear passenger (204 pounds)
moves to the front passenger position. What effect
does this have on the CG if the airplane weighed 2,690
pounds and the MOM/100 was 2,260 just prior to the
passenger transfer?

A — The CG moves forward approximately 3 inches.
B — The weight changes, but the CG is not affected.
C — The CG moves forward approximately 0.1 inch.

8-38. Answer A. GFDPPM 8-36, 41 (PHB)
Use the weight shift formula to determine how far the
CG shifts.

$$\frac{Weight\ Moved}{Weight\ of\ Airplane} = \frac{Distance\ CG\ Moves}{Dist.\ Btwn.\ Arms}$$

The front passenger that departs reduces the total
weight of the aircraft by 180 pounds (2,690 − 180 =
2,510.) The weight that is moved is the rear passenger
(204 pounds). The arms for the front and rear passenger seats are found in Figure 33, and the difference is
121 − 85 = 36.

$$\frac{204}{2,510} = \frac{Distance\ CG\ Moves}{36}$$

$$Distance\ CG\ Moves = \frac{204 \times 36}{2,510} = 2.93$$

The change in CG is approximately 2.93, which is closest to answer (A).

8-39   H316
(Refer to figures 33 and 34 on pages 8-13 and 8-14.)
Which action can adjust the airplane's weight to
maximum gross weight and the CG within limits for
takeoff?
Front seat occupants..425 lb
Rear seat occupants...300 lb
Fuel, main tanks ....44 gal

A — Drain 12 gallons of fuel.
B — Drain 9 gallons of fuel.
C — Transfer 12 gallons of fuel from the main tanks to
the auxiliary tanks.

8-40   H316
(Refer to figures 33 and 34 on pages 8-13 and 8-14.)
What effect does a 35-gallon fuel burn (main tanks)
have on the weight and balance if the airplane weighed
2,890 pounds and the MOM/100 was 2,452 at takeoff.

A — Weight is reduced by 210 pounds and the CG is
aft of limits.
B — Weight is reduced by 210 pounds and the CG is
unaffected.
C — Weight is reduced to 2,680 pounds and the CG
moves forward.

8-39. Answer B. GFDPPM 8-39 (PHB)
Complete the weight and moment table as shown
below.

	WEIGHT (lbs)	ARM (in)	MOMENT (lb-in/100)
Empty wt	2,015		1,554.0
Front seat	425	85	361.3
Rear seat	300	121	363.0
Fuel 44 gal	264	75	198.0
Total	3,004		2,476.3
Max wt.	−2,950		
	54		

The total weight of 3,004 is 54 pounds over maximum
weight. If we drain 54 pounds of fuel to attain the maximum weight, this is equal to 9 gallons (54 pounds ÷ 6
= 9 gallons). Now adjust the moments by entering a
new fuel moment for the 35 gallons that remain, and
find a total moment of 2,436.

	WEIGHT (lbs)	ARM (in)	MOMENT (lb-in/100)
Empty wt.	2,015		1,554.0
Front seat	425	85	361.3
Rear seat	300	121	363.0
Fuel 35 gal.	210	75	157.5
Total	2,950		2,435.8

Using the table in Figure 34, you'll find the total weight
and total moment are within the limits.

8-40. Answer A. GFDPPM 8-39 (PHB)
Use the chart in Figure 33 to find the weight and
moment for 35 gallons of fuel (main tanks), and subtract
these values from the total weight and moment. The
result is the total weight and moment after the fuel burn.

	WEIGHT (lbs)	MOMENT (lb-in/100)
Total	2,890	2,452
Fuel 35 gal	−210	−158
Adjusted	2,680	2,294

Refer to the chart in Figure 34 for the weight of
2,680. The moment of 2,294 exceeds the maximum
(aft) CG limit.

8-41   H316

(Refer to figures 33 and 34 on pages 8-13 and 8-14.)
With the airplane loaded as follows, what action can be
taken to balance the airplane?

Front seat occupants ....411 lb
Rear seat occupants ....100 lb
Main wing tanks ....44 gal

A — Fill the auxiliary wing tanks.
B — Add a 100-pound weight to the baggage compartment.
C — Transfer 10 gallons of fuel from the main tanks to
the auxiliary tanks.

8-41. Answer B. GFDPPM 8-36, 39, 41 (PHB)

Construct the table as shown below, find the subtotal
weight and moment, and use the chart in Figure 34.
The subtotal moment (2,222.4) at the original weight is
less than the minimum (forward) limit.

	WEIGHT (lbs)	ARM (in)	MOMENT (lb-in/100)
Empty wt	2,015		1,554.0
Front seat	411	85	349.4
Rear seat	100	121	121.0
Fuel 44 gal	264	75	198.0
Subtotal	2,790		2,222.4
Baggage	100		140.0
Total	2,890		2,362.4

Since the baggage compartment is in an aft location,
adding weight to this part of the airplane will shift the
CG aft. Add the baggage weight and moment to the
subtotals to find adjusted totals. Check the chart in
Figure 34 to ensure that the moment is within limits.
Answer (A) is wrong because if the auxiliary wing tanks
are filled and the total weight and moment are adjusted,
the moment will be less than the minimum. To check
answer (C), find the original CG using the subtotals:

$$CG = \frac{Total\ Moments}{Total\ Weight} = \frac{2222.4}{2,790} = 79.7$$

Then use the weight shift formula:

$$\frac{Weight\ Moved}{Weight\ of\ Airplane} = \frac{Distance\ CG\ Moves}{Dist.\ Btwn.\ Arms}$$

The weight of fuel is 10 gal × 6 lb/gal = 60 lbs. The distance between arms is 94 − 75 = 19. Since the fuel is
transferred from an arm of 75 to an arm of 94, the CG
moves aft 0.4 inches.

$$Distance\ CG\ Moves = \frac{60 \times 19}{2,790} = 0.4$$

The new CG is 80.1 (79.7 + 0.4). Then, find the new
moment on the chart in Figure 34. The new moment is
less than the minimum.

SECTION C
FLIGHT COMPUTERS

Flight computers help the pilot manage a variety of calculations. Whether flight computers are mechanical or electronic, they are essential for flight planning. This section looks at the basic principles of flight computers, as well as covering detailed procedures for problem solving.

MECHANICAL FLIGHT COMPUTERS

1. In some questions, you will need to calculate the groundspeed and then the estimated time of arrival. a. Determine the groundspeed of the aircraft: measure the distance between the departure point and the destination. Determine the elapsed time. Divide the distance by the time to derive the groundspeed. b. Determine the estimated time of arrival (ETA) at the destination by adding the elapsed time to the departure time.

2. Some questions require you to calculate groundspeed and then complete a time-speed-distance problem. a. Measure the distance between the departure point and the destination. b. Determine the true course (TC). c. Determine the groundspeed, using your flight computer: Enter the wind direction and speed. Enter the TC. Enter the true airspeed (TAS) and find the groundspeed. d. Determine the time en route- distance divided by time equals speed. e. Add departure and climb-out time (if any is given). You may need to round to arrive at one of the answer selections.

8-42　　H317
(Refer to figure 8 on page 8-22.) What is the effect of a temperature increase from 25 to 50°F on the density altitude if the pressure altitude remains at 5,000 feet?

A — 1,200-foot increase.
B — 1,400-foot increase.
C — 1,650-foot increase.

8-43　　H317
(Refer to figure 8 on page 8-22.) Determine the pressure altitude with an indicated altitude of 1,380 feet MSL with an altimeter setting of 28.22 at standard temperature.

A — 3,010 feet MSL.
B — 2,991 feet MSL.
C — 2,913 feet MSL.

8-44　　H317
(Refer to figure 8 on page 8-22.) Determine the density altitude for these conditions:
Altimeter setting...29.25
Runway temperature ....+81°F
Airport elevation....................................5,250 ft MSL

A — 4,600 feet MSL.
B — 5,877 feet MSL.
C — 8,500 feet MSL.

8-42. Answer C. GFDPPM 8-9 and 8-56 (PHB)
Follow the line above 25°F up to where it intersects 5,000 feet pressure altitude, and read 3,850 feet density altitude on the left scale. Do the same with 50°F, up to 5,000 feet, and then left to read 5,500 feet. The difference is an increase of 1,650 feet.

8-43. Answer B. GFDPPM 8-9 and 8-56 (PHB)
Using the table on the right side of the chart, interpolate between 28.2 and 28.3 to get a conversion factor of 1,611 (a value 20% of the way between 1,630 and 1,533). Add this to the indicated altitude of 1,380 for a pressure altitude of 2,991 feet. Answer (A) is what you get if you use 28.2 without interpolating. Answer (C) is what you get if you use 28.3 without interpolating.

8-44. Answer C. GFDPPM 8-9 and 8-56 (PHB)
First find the pressure altitude by using the pressure altitude conversion factor scale and interpolate for 29.25. The conversion factor is 626 (673 − 579 = 94 ÷ 2 = 47 + 579 = 626). This is added to 5,250 feet to find a pressure altitude of 5,876 feet. Now, find 81°F on the OAT scale at the bottom of the graph and follow its line vertically to where it intersects with the 5,876-foot pressure altitude line. From this point, follow the horizontal density altitude line to the left scale to find an approximate density altitude of 8,500 feet.

DENSITY ALTITUDE CHART

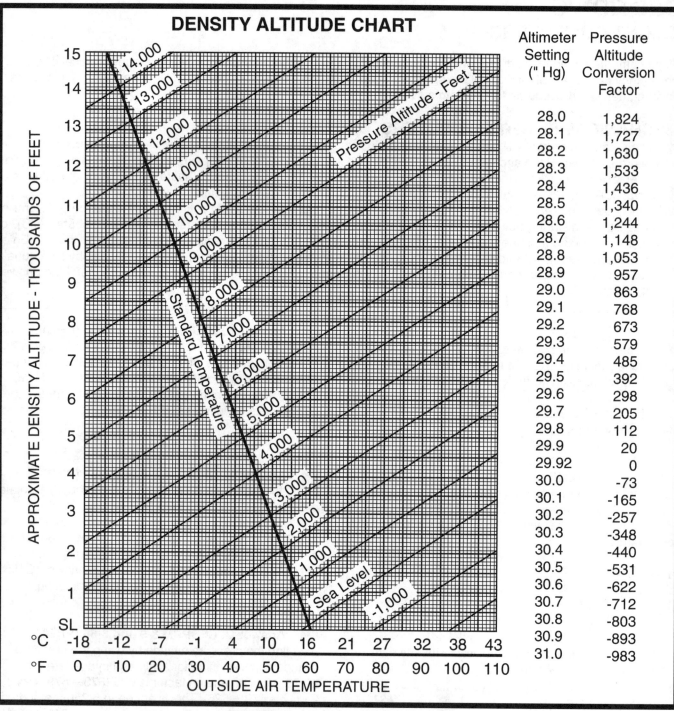

Altimeter Setting (" Hg)	Pressure Altitude Conversion Factor
28.0	1,824
28.1	1,727
28.2	1,630
28.3	1,533
28.4	1,436
28.5	1,340
28.6	1,244
28.7	1,148
28.8	1,053
28.9	957
29.0	863
29.1	768
29.2	673
29.3	579
29.4	485
29.5	392
29.6	298
29.7	205
29.8	112
29.9	20
29.92	0
30.0	-73
30.1	-165
30.2	-257
30.3	-348
30.4	-440
30.5	-531
30.6	-622
30.7	-712
30.8	-803
30.9	-893
31.0	-983

FIGURE 8.—Density Altitude Chart.

8-45   H317
(Refer to figure 8.) Determine the pressure altitude at an airport that is 3,563 feet MSL with an altimeter setting of 29.96.

A — 3,527 feet MSL.
B — 3,556 feet MSL.
C — 3,639 feet MSL.

8-45. Answer A. GFDPPM 8-9 and 8-56 (PHB)
Find the conversion factors for 30.00 and 29.92, and interpolate to find the factor for 29.96 (−73 − 0 = −73 ÷ 2 = −36.5). Subtract 36.5 from the elevation of 3,563 feet, to find a pressure altitude of 3,526.5 feet. This is rounded to 3,527 feet.

8-46 **H317**
(Refer to figure 8 on page 8-22.) What is the effect of a temperature increase from 30 to 50°F on the density altitude if the pressure altitude remains at 3,000 feet MSL?

A — 900-foot increase.
B — 1,100-foot decrease.
C — 1,300-foot increase.

8-47 **H317**
(Refer to figure 8 on page 8-22.) Determine the pressure altitude at an airport that is 1,386 feet MSL with an altimeter setting of 29.97.

A — 1,341 feet MSL.
B — 1,451 feet MSL.
C — 1,562 feet MSL.

8-48 **H317**
(Refer to figure 8 on page 8-22.) What is the effect of a temperature decrease and a pressure altitude increase on the density altitude from 90°F and 1,250 feet pressure altitude to 55°F and 1,750 feet pressure altitude?

A — 1,700-foot increase.
B — 1,300-foot decrease.
C — 1,700-foot decrease.

8-49 **H342**
(Refer to figure 21 on page 4-18.) En route to First Flight Airport (area 5), your flight passes over Hampton Roads Airport (area 2) at 1456 and then over Chesapeake Municipal at 1501. At what time should your flight arrive at First Flight?

A — 1516.
B — 1521.
C — 1526.

8-46. Answer C. GFDPPM 8-9 and 8-56 (PHB)
First you must find the density altitude (DA) for 30°F. It is 1,600 feet. At 50°F, the DA is 2,900 feet, for an increase of 1,300 feet. Keep in mind that an increase in temperature will increase density altitude.

8-47. Answer A. GFDPPM 8-9 and 8-56 (PHB)
First you must interpolate to find the conversion factor for 29.97 (−73 − 0 = −73 ÷ 8 increments = −9 × 5 increments = −45). Subtract 45 from 1,386 to find the pressure altitude of 1,341 feet.

8-48. Answer C. GFDPPM 8-9 and 8-56 (PHB)
1. Enter the graph at 90°F on the bottom scale. Draw a line straight up to meet the upsloping 1,250 ft. pressure altitude line (visualize this line or draw it in between the 1,000 and 2,000 ft. lines), then go left to 3,600 feet on the density altitude scale.
2. Repeat for 55°F and 1,750 ft. pressure altitude to get a density altitude of 1,900 feet.
3. The difference is (1,900 - 3,600) feet = -1,700 feet.

8-49. Answer C. GFDPPM 8-54 (PHB)
This question requires you to calculate groundspeed and then estimated time of arrival.

1. Determine the actual groundspeed (GS) of the aircraft.
   a. Measure the distance between Hampton Roads Airport and Chesapeake Municipal (CPK) using your plotter (10 n.m.).
   b. Determine the elapsed time (15:01 − 14:56 = 5 min.).
   c. Determine the GS (10 n.m. in 5 min. = 2 n.m./min. X 60 min. = 120 n.m. per hour groundspeed).
2. Determine the estimated time of arrival (ETA) at First Flight Airport.
   a. Measure the distance between Chesapeake Municipal and First Flight Airport (50 n.m.).
   b. Determine the time enroute between the two points (50 n.m. at 120 knots = approximately 25 minutes).
   c. If the aircraft was over Chesapeake Municipal at 15:01, the ETA at First Flight Airport is approx. 15:26. (15:01 + 25 min. = 15:26).

8-50   H346
(Refer to figure 22 on page 4-19.) What is the estimated time en route from Mercer County Regional Airport (area 3) to Minot International (area 1)? The wind is from 330° at 25 knots and the true airspeed is 100 knots. Add 3-1/2 minutes for departure and climb-out.

A — 44 minutes.
B — 48 minutes.
C — 52 minutes.

8-51   H346
(Refer to figure 23 on page 4-20.) What is the estimated time en route from Sandpoint Airport (area 1) to St. Maries Airport (area 4)? The wind is from 215° at 25 knots, and the true airspeed is 125 knots.

A — 38 minutes.
B — 34 minutes.
C — 30 minutes.

8-52   H346
(Refer to figure 23 on page 4-20.) Determine the estimated time en route for a flight from Priest River Airport (area 1) to Shoshone County Airport (area 3). The wind is from 030 at 12 knots and the true airspeed is 95 knots. Add 2 minutes for climb-out.

A — 27 minutes.
B — 29 minutes.
C — 31 minutes.

8-50. Answer B. GFDPPM 8-54 (PHB)
This question requires you to calculate groundspeed and then complete a time-speed-distance problem.

1. Measure the distance between Mercer County Regional Airport and Minot International (59 n.m.).
2. Determine the True Course (TC) (012°).
3. Determine the groundspeed using your flight computer.
    a. Enter the wind direction and speed (330° True at 25 kts.)
    b. Enter the TC (012°)
    c. Enter the True Air Speed (TAS) (100 kts.)
    d. GS = 80 kts.
4. Determine the time enroute using your flight computer (59 n.m. at 80 n.m./hr. = 44 min. 15 sec.)
5. Add departure and climb-out time (3 min. 30 sec. + 44 min. 15 sec. = 47 min. 45 sec.) This is rounded to 48 minutes.

8-51. Answer B. GFDPPM 8-54 (PHB)
This question requires you to calculate groundspeed and then complete a time-speed-distance problem.

1. Measure the distance from Sandpoint Airport to St. Maries Airport (approximately 58 n.m.).
2. Determine the true course (TC = 181°).
3. Determine groundspeed using the flight computer.
    a. Enter the wind direction and speed (215° True at 25 kts.).
    b. Enter the TC (181°).
    c. Enter the True Airspeed (125 kts.).
    d. GS=103 kts.
4. Determine the time enroute using the flight computer (58 n.m. at 103 n.m./hr. = 34 min.).

8-52. Answer C. GFDPPM 8-54 (PHB)
This question requires you to calculate groundspeed and then complete a time-speed-distance problem.

1. Measure the distance from Priest River Airport to Shoshone County Airport (48 n.m.).
2. Determine the true course (TC = 143°).
3. Determine groundspeed using the flight computer.
    a. Enter the wind direction and speed (030° True at 12 kts.).
    b. Enter the TC (143°).
    c. Enter the True Airspeed (95 kts.).
    d. GS=99 kts.
4. Determine the time enroute using the flight computer (48 n.m. at 99 n.m./hr. = 29 min.).
5. Add 2 min. for departure and climb-out (2 min. + 29 min. = 31 min.).

8-53   H346
(Refer to figure 23 on page 4-20.) What is the estimated time en route for a flight from St. Maries Airport (area 4) to Priest River airport (area 1)? The wind is from 300° at 14 knots and the true airspeed is 90 knots. Add 3 minutes for climb-out.

A — 38 minutes.
B — 43 minutes.
C — 48 minutes.

8-54   H346
(Refer to figure 24 on page 4-21.) What is the estimated time en route for a flight from Allendale County Airport (area 1) to Claxton-Evans County Airport (area 2)? The wind is from 100° at 18 knots and the true airspeed is 115 knots. Add 2 minutes for climb-out.

A.   33 minutes.
B.   27 minutes.
C.   30 minutes.

8-53. Answer B. GFDPPM 8-54 (PHB)
This question requires you to calculate groundspeed and then complete a time-speed-distance problem.

1. Measure the distance from St. Maries Airport to Priest River Airport (53 n.m.).
2. Determine the True Course (345°).
3. Determine groundspeed using your flight computer.
   a. Enter the wind direction and speed (300° at 14 kts.).
   b. Enter the True Course (345°).
   c. Enter the TAS (90 kts.).
   d. GS = 80 kts.
4. Determine the time enroute using your flight computer (53 n.m. at 80 n.m./hr. = 39 min. 45 sec.).
5. Add 3 min. for departure and climb-out (3 min. + 39 min. 45 sec. = 42 min. 45 sec.). This is rounded to 43 minutes.

8-54. Answer C. GFDPPM 8-54 (PHB)
This question requires you to calculate groundspeed and then complete a time-speed-distance problem.

1. Measure the distance from Allendale County to Claxton-Evans County Airport (57 n.m.).
2. Determine the true course (TC = 212°).
3. Determine groundspeed using the flight computer.
   a. Enter the wind direction and speed (100° True at 18 kts.).
   b. Enter the TC (212°).
   c. Enter the True Airspeed (115 kts.).
   d. GS = 121 kts.
4. Determine the time enroute using the flight computer (57 n.m. at 121 n.m./hr. = 28 min. 15 sec.).
5. Add 2 min. for departure and climb-out (2 min + 28 min. 15 sec. = 30 min. 15 sec.). This is rounded to 30 minutes.

8-55   H346
(Refer to figure 24 on page 4-21.) What is the estimated time en route for a flight from Claxton-Evans County Airport (area 2) to Hampton Varnville Airport (area 1)? The wind is from 290° at 18 knots and the true airspeed is 85 knots. Add 2 minutes for climb-out.

A — 35 minutes.
B — 39 minutes.
C — 44 minutes.

8-56   H342
(Refer to figure 24 on page 4-21.) While en route on Victor 185, a flight crosses the 248° radial of Allendale VOR at 0953 and then crosses the 216° radial of Allendale VOR at 1000. What is the estimated time of arrival at Savannah VORTAC?

A — 1023.
B — 1036.
C — 1028.

8-55. Answer B. GFDPPM 8-54 (PHB)
This question requires you to calculate groundspeed and then complete a Time-Speed-Distance problem.

1. Measure the distance from Claxton-Evans County Airport to Hampton Varnville Airport (57 n.m.).
2. Determine the True Course (045°).
3. Determine the groundspeed using your flight computer.
   a. Enter the wind direction and speed (290° at 18 kts.).
   b. Enter the True Course (045°).
   c. Enter the TAS (85 kts.).
   d. GS = 91 kts.
4. Determine the time enroute using your flight computer (57 n.m. at 91 n.m./hr. = 37 min. 30 sec.).
5. Add 2 minutes for departure and climb-out (2 min. + 37 min. 30 sec. = 39 min. 30 sec.) The closest answer is 39 minutes.

8-56. Answer C. GFDPPM 8-54 (PHB)
This question requires you to calculate groundspeed and then estimated time of arrival.

1. Determine actual groundspeed of the aircraft.
   a. Measure the distance along Victor 185 where it crosses the 248° radial and the 216° radial of Allendale VOR (10 n.m.).
   b. Determine the elapsed time. (10:00 - 09:53 = 7 min.).
   c. Determine the groundspeed (10 n.m. in 7 min. = 86 knots).
2. Determine the Estimated Time of Arrival (ETA) over the Savannah VORTAC.
   a. Measure the Distance along Victor 185 from the 216° radial of Allendale VORTAC to the Savannah VORTAC (40 n.m.).
   b. Determine time enroute (GS is 86 kts.) (40 n.m. at 86 n.m./hr. = 28 min.)
   c. Determine estimated time of arrival (10:00 + 28 mins. = 10:28).

8-57 **H346**

(Refer to figure 26 on page 4-23.) What is the estimated time en route for a flight from Denton Muni (area 1) to Addison (area 2)? The wind is from 200° at 20 knots, the true airspeed is 110 knots, and the magnetic variation is 7° east.

A — 13 minutes.
B — 16 minutes.
C — 19 minutes.

8-58 **H346**

(Refer to figure 26 on page 4-23.) Estimate the time enroute from Addison (area 2) to Redbird (area 3). The wind is from 300° at 15 knots, the true airspeed is 120 knots, and the magnetic variation is 7° east.

A — 8 minutes.
B — 11 minutes.
C — 14 minutes.

8-57. Answer A. GFDPPM 8-54 (PHB)

This question requires you to calculate groundspeed, then complete a time-speed-distance problem.

1. Measure the distance from Denton Muni to Addison Airport (23 n.m.).
2. Determine True Course (128°).
3. Determine the groundspeed using your flight computer.
   a. Enter the wind direction and speed (200° at 20 kts.).
   b. Enter the True Course (128°).
   c. Enter the TAS (110 kts.).
   d. GS = 102 kts.
4. Determine time enroute (23 n.m. at 102 n.m./hr = 13 min. 30 sec.). The closest answer is 13 minutes.

8-58. Answer A. GFDPPM 8-54 (PHB)

This question requires you to calculate groundspeed, then complete a time-speed-distance problem.

1. Measure the distance from Addison Airport to Redbird Airport (17 n.m.).
2. Determine the True Course (186°).
3. Determine the groundspeed using your flight computer.
   a. Enter the wind direction and speed (300° at 15 kts.).
   b. Enter the TC (186°).
   c. Enter the TAS (120 kts.).
   d. GS = 125 kts.
4. Determine time enroute (17 n.m. at 125 n.m./hr. = 8 min. 8 sec.). The closest answer is 8 minutes.

CHAPTER 9

NAVIGATION

SECTION A
PILOTAGE AND DEAD RECKONING

Pilotage and dead reckoning allow pilots to navigate over unfamiliar terrain. The two systems are used to cross-check each other, and together they let pilots to create a course and stay on that course. This section covers pilotage, which is navigating through the use of checkpoints, and dead reckoning, which allows you to predict your course along an intended route. Using a navigation log and filling out a flight plan form are also covered.

DEAD RECKONING
Dead reckoning involves calculating distance, speed, time, and direction as a means of navigating from your departure to your destination.

COURSE
1. In order to determine a magnetic course, you must first find the true course, using a plotter. Then, find the nearest isogonic line to the course. Next, add or subtract the variation. When the variation listed is west, add it to the true course to derive the magnetic course. If the variation is east, you must subtract it.
2. To determine the magnetic heading, you must first determine the true heading by correcting the true course for winds. For this, you'll use the wind side of your flight computer. Then, correct true heading for magnetic variation.

VFR CRUISING ALTITUDES
3. On an easterly course (0° to 179°) above 3,000 feet AGL, VFR cruising altitudes are odd thousands plus 500 feet.
4. On a westerly course (180° to 359°), VFR cruising altitudes are even thousands plus 500 feet.

FUEL REQUIREMENTS
5. For a VFR night flight in an airplane, there must be enough fuel, considering wind and forecast weather conditions, to fly to the first point of intended landing, and, assuming normal cruising speed, 45 minutes beyond that point.
6. For VFR day flight in an airplane, there must be enough fuel to fly to the first point of intended landing, and to fly for 30 minutes after that, assuming normal cruising speed.

9-1   B09
Which cruising altitude is appropriate for a VFR flight on a magnetic course of 135°?

A — Even thousandths.
B — Even thousandths plus 500 feet.
C — Odd thousandths plus 500 feet.

9-2   B09
Which VFR cruising altitude is acceptable for a flight on a Victor Airway with a magnetic course of 175°? The terrain is less than 1,000 feet.

A — 4,500 feet.
B — 5,000 feet.
C — 5,500 feet.

9-1. Answer C. GFDPPM 9-12 (FAR 91.159)
On an easterly magnetic course (0° to 179°) above 3,000 feet AGL, VFR cruising altitudes are odd thousands plus 500 feet. Answers (A) and (B) are wrong because even thousands (plus 500 feet) are used for westbound courses above 3,000 feet AGL.

9-2. Answer C. GFDPPM 9-12 (FAR 91.159)
See explanation for Question 9-1. Answer (C) is correct because it is the only answer with odd thousands plus 500 feet.

9-3   B09

Which VFR cruising altitude is appropriate when flying above 3,000 feet AGL on a magnetic course of 185°?

A — 4,000 feet.
B — 4,500 feet.
C — 5,000 feet.

9-4   B09

Each person operating an aircraft at a VFR cruising altitude shall maintain an odd-thousand plus 500-foot altitude while on a

A — magnetic heading of 0° through 179°.
B — magnetic course of 0° through 179°.
C — true course of 0° through 179°.

9-5   H346

(Refer to figure 21 on page 4-18.) Determine the magnetic course from First Flight Airport (area 5) to Hampton Roads Airport (area 2).

A — 141°.
B — 321°.
C — 331°.

9-6   H346

(Refer to figure 22 on page 4-19.) Determine the magnetic heading for a flight from Mercer County Regional Airport (area 3) to Minot International (Area 1). The wind is from 330° at 25 knots, the true airspeed is 100 knots, and the magnetic variation is 10° east.

A — 002°.
B — 012°.
C — 352°.

3157. Answer B. GFDPPM 9-12 (FAR 91.159)
See explanation for Question 9-1. Because the course is westerly, an even thousands altitude plus 500 feet is used.

3158. Answer B. GFDPPM 9-12 (FAR 91.159)
VFR cruising altitudes on an easterly magnetic course (0° to 179°) are odd-thousands plus 500 feet. Answer (A) is wrong because VFR altitudes are based on course, not heading. Answer (C) is wrong because magnetic course is used, not true course.

9-5. Answer C. GFDPPM 9-11 (PHB)
This question requires finding the magnetic course by determining true course, then correcting for magnetic variation.

1. Determine the true course with a plotter (321°).
2. Locate the nearest isogonic line (10°West).
3. Convert TC to MC by correcting for variation. (Since this is a west variation, it must be added to the true course.)
   TC ± Variation = MC (321° + 10° = 331°)

9-6. Answer C. GFDPPM 9-11 (PHB)
This question requires you to find magnetic heading. This is done by first determining true heading by correcting true course for winds. Then, correct true heading for magnetic variation.

1. Use your plotter to determine true course (012°).
2. Use your flight computer to determine true heading.
   a. Enter wind direction and speed (330° at 25 kts.).
   b. Enter the true course (012°).
   c. Enter the TAS (100 kts.).
   d. TH = 002°.
3. Convert TH to MH by correcting for magnetic variation (10°E). (Since this is an east variation, you must subtract it from the true heading.)
   TH ± Variation = MH (002° − 10° = 352°)

9-7   **H346**

(Refer to figure 23 on page 4-20.) Determine the magnetic heading for a flight from Sandpoint Airport (area 1) to St. Maries Airport (area 4). The wind is from 215° at 25 knots, and the true airspeed is 125 knots.

A — 169°.
B — 349°.
C — 187°.

9-8   **H346**

(Refer to figure 23 on page 4-20.) What is the magnetic heading for a flight from Priest River Airport (area 1) to Shoshone County Airport (area 3)? The wind is from 030° at 12 knots, and the true airspeed is 95 knots.

A — 143°.
B — 118°.
C — 136°.

9-9   **H346**

(Refer to figure 23 on page 4-20.) Determine the magnetic heading for a flight from St. Maries Airport (area 4) to Priest River Airport (area 1). The wind is from 340° at 10 knots, and the true airspeed is 90 knots.

A — 345°.
B — 320°.
C — 327°.

9-7. Answer A. GFDPPM 9-11 (PHB)

This question requires you to find magnetic heading. This is done by first determining true heading by correcting true course for winds. Then, correct true heading for magnetic variation.

1. The plotter is used to measure true course (181°).
2. The flight computer is used to determine true heading.
   a. Enter the wind direction and speed (215° at 25 kts.).
   b. Enter the true course (181°).
   c. Enter the TAS (125 kts.).
   d. Determine true heading (TH = 187°).
3. Convert TH to MH by correcting for magnetic variation (18°E). Since this is an east variation, you must subtract it from the true heading.) TH ± Variation = MH (187° - 18° = 169°).

9-8 Answer B. GFDPPM 9-11 (PHB)

This question requires you to find magnetic heading. This is done by first determining true heading by correcting true course for winds. Then, correct true heading for magnetic variation.

1. The plotter is used to measure true course (143°).
2. The flight computer is used to determine true heading.
   a. Enter the wind direction and speed (030° at 12 kts.).
   b. Enter the true course (143°).
   c. Enter the TAS (95 kts.).
   d. TH = 136°
3. Convert TH to MH by correcting for magnetic variation (18°E). Since this is an east variation, you must subtract it from the true heading.) TH ± Variation = MH (136° - 18° = 118°).

9-9. Answer C. GFDPPM 9-11 (PHB)

This question requires you to find magnetic heading. This is done by first determining true heading by correcting true course for winds. Then, correct true heading for magnetic variation.

1. The plotter is used to measure true course (345°).
2. The flight computer is used to determine true heading.
   a. Enter the wind direction and speed (340° at 10 kts.).
   b. Enter the true course (345°).
   c. Enter the TAS (90 kts.).
   d. TH = 345°
3. Convert TH to MH by correcting for magnetic variation (18°E). Since this is an east variation, you must subtract it from the true heading.) TH ± Variation = MH (345° - 18° = 327°).

9-10   H346
(Refer to figure 24 on page 4-21.) Determine the magnetic heading for a flight from Allendale County
Airport (area 1) to Claxton-Evans County Airport (area
2). The wind is from 090° at 16 knots, and the true airspeed is 90 knots.

A — 208°.
B — 230°.
C — 212°.

9-11   H346
(Refer to figure 24 on page 4-21 and figure 59.)
Determine the compass heading for a flight from
Claxton-Evans County Airport (area 2) to Hampton
Varnville Airport (area 1). The wind is from 280° at 08
knots, and the true airspeed is 85 knots.

A — 033°.
B — 042°.
C — 038°.

9-10. Answer A. GFDPPM 9-11 (PHB)
This question requires you to find magnetic heading.
This is done by first determining true heading by correcting true course for winds. Then, correct true heading for magnetic variation.

1. The plotter is used to measure true course (212°).
2. The flight computer is used to determine true heading.
   a. Enter the wind direction and speed (090° at 16
      kts.).
   b. Enter the true course (212°).
   c. Enter the TAS (90 kts.).
   d. TH = 203°
3. Convert TH to MH by correcting for magnetic variation (5°W). Since this is a west variation, you must
   add it from the true heading.) TH ± Variation = MH
   (203° + 5° = 208°).

9-11. Answer B. GFDPPM 9-11 (PHB)
This question requires you to find the heading, then
correct for variation and deviation to achieve compass
heading.

1. Use plotter to determine true course (044°).
2. Use flight computer to calculate true heading (040°).
3. Add variation (5°W) to TH to get magnetic heading
   (045°).
4. Adjust per compass card (-3°) to determine compass heading (042°).

For	N	30	60	E	120	150
Steer	0	27	56	85	116	148
For	S	210	240	W	300	330
Steer	181	214	244	274	303	332

FIGURE 59.—Compass card.

9-12   **H346**
(Refer to figure 25 on page 4-22.) Determine the magnetic course from Airpark East Airport (area 1) to Winnsboro Airport (area 2). Magnetic variation is 6°30′E.

A — 075°.
B — 082°.
C — 091°.

9-13   **H346**
(Refer to figure 26 on page 4-23.) Determine the magnetic heading for a flight from Fort Worth Meacham (area 4) to Denton Muni (area 1). The wind is from 330° at 25 knots, the true airspeed is 110 knots, and the magnetic variation is 7° east.

A — 003°.
B — 017°.
C — 023°.

9-14   **H346**
(Refer to figure 27 on page 4-24.) Determine the magnetic course from Breckheimer (Pvt) Airport (area 1) to Jamestown Airport (area 4).

A — 180°.
B — 188°.
C — 360°.

9-15   **J15**
(Refer to figure 52 on page 9-6.) If more than one cruising altitude is intended, which should be entered in block 7 of the flight plan?

A — Initial cruising altitude.
B — Highest cruising altitude.
C — Lowest cruising altitude.

9-12. Answer A. GFDPPM 9-11 (PHB)
This question requires you find the magnetic course by determining true course, then correcting it for magnetic variation.

1. Use your plotter to determine True Course (082°).
2. Locate the nearest isogonic line to the course (6°30′E). (Add West, Subtract East variation)
3. Convert TC to MC by correcting for variation. (Since this is an east variation, you must subtract it from true course.)
TC ± Variation = MC (082° - 6°30′ = 075°30′)
The closest answer is 075°.

9-13. Answer A. GFDPPM 9-11 (PHB)
This question requires you to find magnetic heading. This is done by first determining true heading by correcting true course for winds. Then, correct true heading for magnetic variation.

1. Use your plotter to determine true course (021°).
2. Use your flight computer to determine true heading.
   a. Enter the wind direction and speed (330° at 25 kts.).
   b. Enter the true course (021°).
   c. Enter the TAS (110 kts.).
   d. TH = 011°
3. Convert TH to MH by correcting for magnetic variation (7°E). (Since this is an east variation, you must subtract it from the true heading.)
TH ± Variation = MH (011° − 7° = 004°)
The closest answer is 003°.

9-14. Answer A. GFDPPM 9-11 (PHB)
The true course, as measured with a plotter, is 190°. The isogonic line down the right side of the figure indicates a 7° east magnetic variation. Subtract easterly variation to get magnetic course (190° - 7° = 183°). 180° is the nearest answer.

9-15. Answer A. GFDPPM 9-15 (PHB)
The initial cruising altitude should be entered on the flight plan. Any subsequent altitude changes should be requested from the enroute controller. If the highest or lowest cruising altitude (answers B and C) is entered, air traffic control will assume that this altitude is the initial cruising altitude.

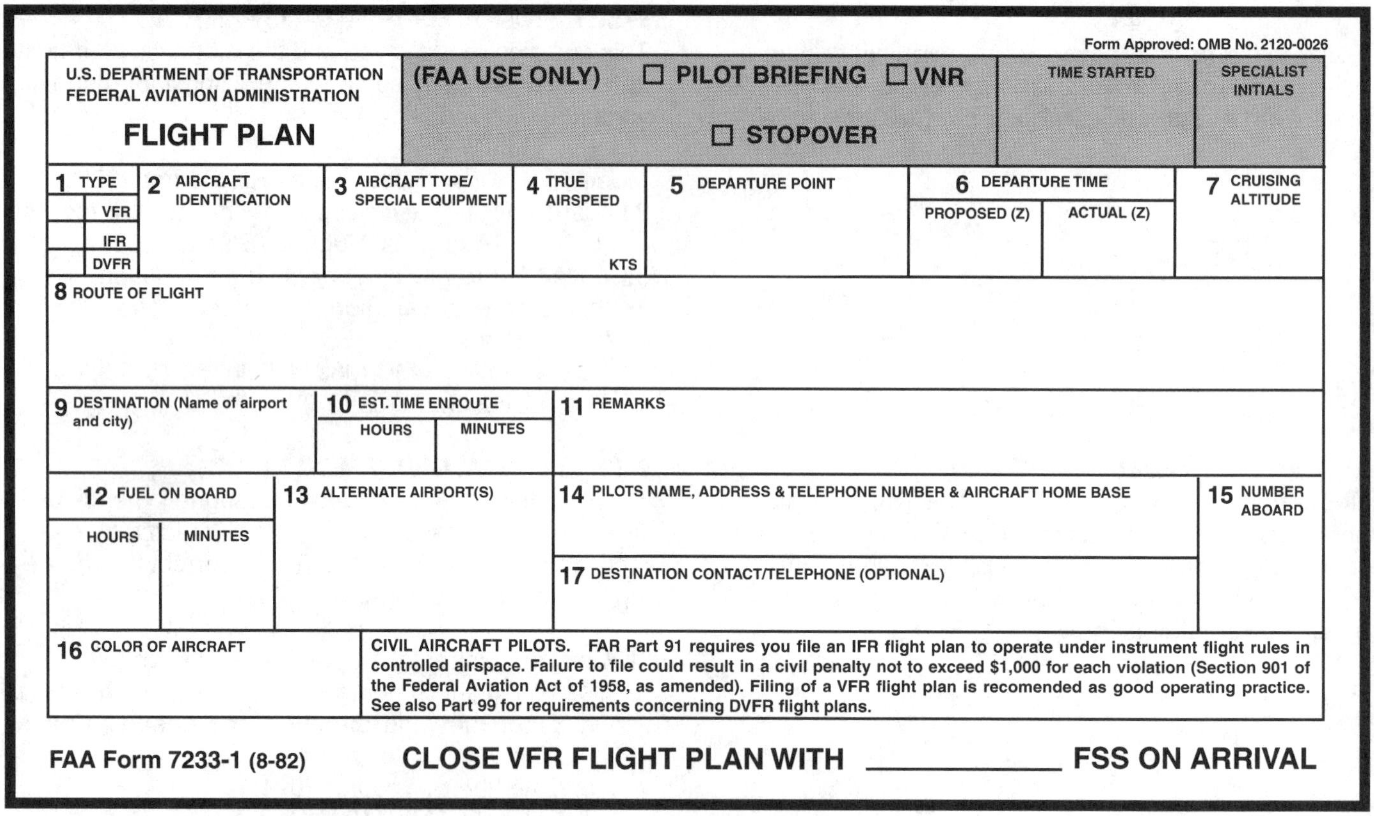

Form Approved: OMB No. 2120-0026

U.S. DEPARTMENT OF TRANSPORTATION
FEDERAL AVIATION ADMINISTRATION

FLIGHT PLAN

(FAA USE ONLY) ☐ PILOT BRIEFING ☐ VNR ☐ STOPOVER | TIME STARTED | SPECIALIST INITIALS

1 TYPE: VFR, IFR, DVFR | 2 AIRCRAFT IDENTIFICATION | 3 AIRCRAFT TYPE/SPECIAL EQUIPMENT | 4 TRUE AIRSPEED KTS | 5 DEPARTURE POINT | 6 DEPARTURE TIME: PROPOSED (Z), ACTUAL (Z) | 7 CRUISING ALTITUDE

8 ROUTE OF FLIGHT

9 DESTINATION (Name of airport and city) | 10 EST. TIME ENROUTE: HOURS, MINUTES | 11 REMARKS

12 FUEL ON BOARD: HOURS, MINUTES | 13 ALTERNATE AIRPORT(S) | 14 PILOTS NAME, ADDRESS & TELEPHONE NUMBER & AIRCRAFT HOME BASE | 15 NUMBER ABOARD

17 DESTINATION CONTACT/TELEPHONE (OPTIONAL)

16 COLOR OF AIRCRAFT

CIVIL AIRCRAFT PILOTS. FAR Part 91 requires you file an IFR flight plan to operate under instrument flight rules in controlled airspace. Failure to file could result in a civil penalty not to exceed $1,000 for each violation (Section 901 of the Federal Aviation Act of 1958, as amended). Filing of a VFR flight plan is recomended as good operating practice. See also Part 99 for requirements concerning DVFR flight plans.

FAA Form 7233-1 (8-82) CLOSE VFR FLIGHT PLAN WITH ________ FSS ON ARRIVAL

FIGURE 52.—Flight Plan Form.

9-16 J15
(Refer to figure 52.) What information should be entered in block 9 for a VFR day flight?

A — The name of the airport of first intended landing.
B — The name of destination airport if no stopover for more than 1 hour is anticipated.
C — The name of the airport where the aircraft is based.

9-16. Answer B. GFDPPM 9-16 (PHB)
FAR 91.153 states that the flight plan shall include the point of first intended landing. However, the AIM says to enter the destination airport. It also recommends that for a stopover of more than 1 hour, a separate flight plan should be filed. Therefore, answer (B) is a correct statement, and we believe it is the best answer. Answer (A) would not be entirely correct for a flight which includes a stopover of less than 1 hour. The aircraft's home base (answer C) is entered in block 14, not block 9.

9-17 J15
(Refer to figure 52.) What information should be entered in block 12 for a VFR day flight?

A — The estimated time en route plus 30 minutes.
B — The estimated time en route plus 45 minutes.
C — The amount of usable fuel on board expressed in time.

9-17. Answer C. GFDPPM 9-15, 16 (PHB)
The fuel on board is the total amount of fuel in hours and minutes (usable fuel is assumed). The estimated time en route (answers A and B) is entered in block 10, not block 12. The reserve fuel (30 minutes VFR, 45 minutes IFR) is not entered on the flight plan; however, the fuel on board should always be at least 30 or 45 minutes greater than the time en route.

9-18   J15

How should a VFR flight plan be closed at the completion of the flight at a controlled airport?

A — The tower will automatically close the flight plan when the aircraft turns off the runway.
B — The pilot must close the flight plan with the nearest FSS or other FAA facility upon landing.
C — The tower will relay the instructions to the nearest FSS when the aircraft contacts the tower for landing.

9-18. Answer B. GFDPPM 9-16 (PHB)

To close a VFR flight plan, you must notify an FSS or other FAA facility. The control tower (answers A and C) does not automatically close VFR flight plans.

SECTION B
VOR NAVIGATION

VOR navigation is the most commonly used system in the country, with over 1,000 installations. VOR navigation is projected to remain central to navigation through the foreseeable future. This section covers the components of the VOR system, including distance measuring equipment (DME), and how to use this equipment in the airplane.

NAVIGATION PROCEDURES

1. To find your position relative to a VOR on the sectional chart, draw a line along a radial until it intersects your position, or the position of the object you wish to locate. Determine the radial using the compass rose depicted on the chart. Measure the distance from the VOR using a plotter.
2. To determine your course to a VOR, find your position along a radial, and find the reciprocal by adding or subtracting 180° from the radial.
3. The magnetic course can be determined by plotting a line from your position or departure point to the VOR. Remember that the radial you read off of the compass rose is the reciprocal of what you would select on the OBS to fly TO the station.
4. You can find your position by triangulation, using two or more VORs. Determine the radial you are on from one VOR, and draw a line from the VOR through the compass rose on that radial. Repeat the procedure with another VOR facility. The intersection point will be your location.
5. Your position is reflected on the VOR receiver by the position of the CDI needle. If the needle is vertical, you are on the radial selected on the OBS. If the needle shows a left or right deflection, you are left or right of course. If the needle is centered with a FROM indication, the heading tuned in on the OBS reflects the radial you are on. Make sure you have the correct radial selected on the OBS; if you have tuned in the reciprocal, the CDI will reverse-sense.
6. If the TO/FROM indicator is blank, you are over the cone of confusion, and the aircraft is either over the station, or on a radial offset 90° from the radial selected on the OBS.
7. When the CDI needle is centered during an omnireceiver check using a VOR test signal (VOT), the OBS and the TO/FROM indicator should read 0° FROM or 180° TO, regardless of the aircraft's position in relation to the VOT.

9-19   H348
(Refer to figure 21 on page 4-18.) What is your approximate position on low altitude airway Victor 1, southwest of Norfolk (area 1), if the VOR receiver indicates you are on the 340° radial of Elizabeth City VOR (area 3)?

A — 15 nautical miles from Norfolk VORTAC.
B — 18 nautical miles from Norfolk VORTAC.
C — 23 nautical miles from Norfolk VORTAC.

9-19. Answer B. GFDPPM 9-27 (PHB)
Using the compass rose of the Elizabeth City VOR, draw a line along the 340° radial until it intersects Victor 1. Measure the distance from this point to the Norfolk VORTAC. The distance is 18 nautical miles. 15 n.m. from Norfolk (answer A) is the intersection of Victor 1 and the 345° radial. 23 n.m. from Norfolk VORTAC (answer C) is the intersection of Victor 1 and the 330° radial. Don't be misled by the number 340 which appears near the 33 on the compass rose. This is the elevation of an obstacle.

9-20   H348
(Refer to figure 21, area 3 on page 4-18; and figure 29 on page 9-9.) The VOR is tuned to Elizabeth City VOR, and the aircraft is positioned over Shawboro. Which VOR indication is correct?

A — 2.
B — 5.
C — 9.

9-20. Answer A. GFDPPM 9-23 (PHB)
Shawboro is on the 030° radial of Elizabeth City VOR. A VOR needle would be centered on 030° with a FROM indication or 210° with a TO indication.

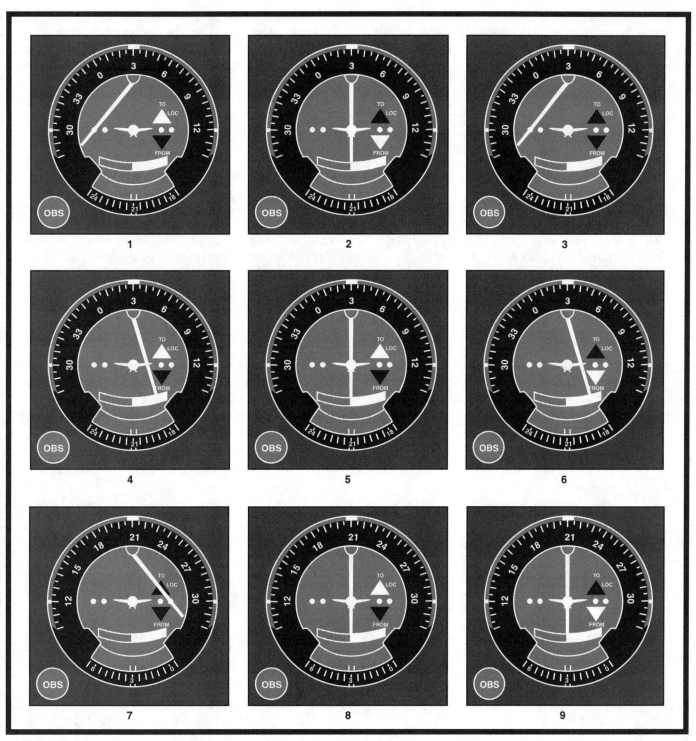

FIGURE 29.—VOR.

9-21   H348
(Refer to figure 22 on page 4-19.) What course should be selected on the omnibearing selector (OBS) to make a direct flight from Mercer County Regional Airport (area 3) to the Minot VORTAC (area 1) with a TO indication?

A — 359°.
B — 179°.
C — 001°.

9-22   H346
(Refer to figure 24 on page 4-19.) What is the approximate position of the aircraft if the VOR receivers indicate the 320° radial of Savannah VORTAC (area 3) and the 184° radial of Allendale VOR (area 1)?

A — Town of Guyton.
B — Town of Springfield.
C — 3 miles east of Marlow.

9-23.   H348
(Refer to figure 24 on page 4-19.) On what course should the VOR receiver (OBS) be set to navigate direct from Hampton Varnville Airport (area 1) to Savannah VORTAC (area 3)?

A — 200°.
B — 183°.
C — 003°.

9-24   H348
(Refer to figure 25 on page 4-22.) What is the approximate position of the aircraft if the VOR receivers indicate the 245° radial of Sulphur Springs VOR-DME (area 5) and the 140° radial of Bonham VORTAC (area 3)?

A — Meadowview Airport.
B — Glenmar Airport.
C — Majors Airport.

9-25   H348
(Refer to figure 25 on page 4-22.) On what radial should the VOR receiver (OBS) be set in order to navigate direct from Majors Airport (area 1) to Quitman VORTAC (area 2)?

A — 101°.
B — 108°.
C — 281°.

9-21. Answer (A). GFDPPM 9-23 (PHB)
The magnetic course can be determined by plotting a line from Mercer County Regional Airport to the Minot VORTAC. The line intersects the Minot VORTAC compass rose at 179°. The reciprocal of 179° is 359°. This is what you would set in the OBS.

9-22. Answer (B). GFDPPM 9-24 (PHB)
The intersection of these two radials places the aircraft near the town of Springfield. The town of Guyton is southwest of Springfield. Three miles east of Marlow is derived from the intersection of the 185° radial of Allendale VOR and the 300° radial of Savannah VOR.

9-23. Answer (B). GFDPPM 9-23 (PHB)
If you draw a line between Hampton Varnville Airport and Savannah VORTAC, it crosses the Savannah compass rose at 003°. To navigate inbound with a "TO" indication, would require the reciprocal of 003°, or 183°, to be set in the OBS.

9-24. Answer B. GFDPPM 9-23 (PHB)
Draw the radials from these VORs. The intersection of these two radials puts the aircraft near the Glenmar Airport. Meadowview and Majors Airports are incorrect because they are both west of the Bonham 140° radial.

9-25. Answer A. GFDPPM 9-27 (PHB)
A direct course from Majors Airport to Quitman VORTAC crosses the compass rose at 283°. The inbound course to be set in the OBS is the reciprocal of 283°, or 103°. The closest answer is 101° (answer A). The inbound course to Quitman VORTAC on Victor 114 is 108° (answer B), but this is not a direct route from Majors Airport. 281° (answer C) is the approximate outbound course from the Quitman VORTAC.

9-26   **H348**
(Refer to figure 25 on page 4-22, and figure 29 on page 9-9.) The VOR is tuned to Bonham VORTAC (area 3), and the aircraft is positioned over the town of Sulphur Springs (area 5). Which VOR indication is correct?

A — 1.
B — 7.
C — 8.

9-27   **H348**
(Refer to figure 26, area 5 on page 4-23.) The VOR is tuned to the Dallas/Fort Worth VORTAC. The omnibearing selector (OBS) is set on 253° with a TO indication, and a right course deviation indicator (CDI) deflection. What is the aircraft's position from the VORTAC?

A — East-northeast.
B — North-northeast.
C — West-southwest.

9-28   **H348**
(Refer to figure 27, areas 4 and 3 on page 4-24; and figure 29 on page 9-9.) The VOR is tuned to Jamestown VOR, and the aircraft is positioned over Cooperstown Airport. Which VOR indication is correct?

A. 9.
B. 6.
C. 2.

9-29   **H348**
(Refer to figure 29, illustration 1 on page 9-9.) The VOR receiver has the indications shown. What is the aircraft's position relative to the station?

A — North.
B — East.
C — South.

9-26. Answer B. GFDPPM 9-28 (PHB)
Sulfur Springs lies near the 120° radial of the Bonham VORTAC. Because all of the VOR indicators in figure 29 have either 030° or 210° set in the OBS, you must determine the position of the aircraft in relation to these settings and the VOR station. Since the 120° radial is perpendicular to the 030°/210° radials, the TO-FROM indicator will indicate "OFF". With the OBS set to 210°, the CDI will be deflected to the right, which is the display on VOR indicator #7. VOR indicators #1 and #8 are incorrect because the TO/FROM indicators indicate "TO" instead of "OFF".

9-27. Answer A. GFDPPM 9-28 (PHB)
A course of 253° will take the aircraft to the station. This means the aircraft is currently on the east side of the station near the 073° radial. A CDI deflection to the right places the aircraft to the left of the 073° radial. East-northeast (answer A) is the best answer given. If the aircraft was north-northeast of the station (answer B), the CDI needle would be deflected to the left. If it was west-southwest of the station (answer C), the TO-FROM indicator would show "FROM."

9-28. Answer C. GFDPPM 9-28 (PHB)
The aircraft is on the 030° radial of the Jamestown VOR. With 030° set, the to-from indicator should be FROM (Number 2). With 210° set, the to-from indicator should read TO. Number 9 reads from, so it is incorrect. Number 6 shows the aircraft left of course with 030° set, so it is also incorrect.

9-29. Answer C. GFDPPM 9-28 (PHB)
With the 030° course selected, a "TO" indication, and a left CDI deflection, the aircraft is right of course, between the 120° and 210° radials. Therefore, south is the correct answer. North and east (answers A and B) are outside the defined quadrant.

9-30   H348
(Refer to figure 29, illustration 3 on page 9-9.) The VOR receiver has the indications shown. What is the aircraft's position relative to the station?

A — East
B — Southeast.
C — West.

9-31   H348
(Refer to figure 29, illustration 8 on page 9-9.) The VOR receiver has the indications shown. What radial is the aircraft crossing?

A — 030°.
B — 210°.
C — 300°.

9-32   J01
When the course deviation indicator (CDI) needle is centered during an omnireceiver check using a VOR test signal (VOT), the omnibearing selector (OBS) and the TO/FROM indicator should read

A — 180° FROM, only if the pilot is due north of the VOT.
B — 0° TO or 180° FROM, regardless of the pilot's position from the VOT.
C — 0° FROM or 180° TO, regardless of the pilot's position from the VOT.

9-30 Answer B. GFDPPM 9-28 (PHB)
Since the TO-FROM indicator is blank, the aircraft is either over the station or on either the 120° or 300° radial. These radials are 90° from the 030° setting. The left CDI deflection puts the aircraft right of the selected radial. Therefore, the correct answer is southeast of the station. If the aircraft was east of the station (answer A), the TO-FROM indicator would show "FROM." If the aircraft was west of the station (answer C), a "TO" indication would be displayed.

9-31. Answer A. GFDPPM 9-28 (PHB)
The selected course of 210° would take the aircraft to the station, as indicated by a "TO" in the TO-FROM window. This places the aircraft northeast of the station on the reciprocal radial of 210°, which is the 030° radial. If the aircraft was on the 210° radial (answer B) with 210° in the OBS, a "FROM" indication would be displayed. If the aircraft was crossing the 300° radial (answer C), the TO-FROM indicator would be blank, because 300° is 90° from 210°.

9-32. Answer C. GFDPPM 9-29 (AIM)
No matter where the aircraft is located in relation to the VOT, the VOR should always read 180° with a "TO" indication or 0° with a "FROM" indication.

SECTION C
ADF NAVIGATION

Another radio navigation system is the Automatic Direction Finder (ADF). ADFs are useful in remote or mountainous locations, where the line of sight nature of the VOR would limit its usefulness. This section covers ADF components, navigation procedures and limitations. The associated ground facilities, called nondirectional radio beacons (NDBs), are also included.

1. When using an ADF receiver, remember that the needle simply points to the station.
2. To find the magnetic bearing to the station, use the following formula: Magnetic Heading + Relative Bearing = Magnetic Bearing.

9-33   H348
(Refer to figure 30, illustration 1 on page 9-14.) Determine the magnetic bearing TO the station.

A — 030°.
B — 180°.
C — 210°.

9-33. Answer C. GFDPPM 9-42 (PHB)
(Note: With a movable-card indicator, the magnetic heading of the aircraft is set under the top index. The bearing pointer indicates the magnetic bearing TO the station, and the tail of the needle indicates the magnetic bearing FROM the station.) In this illustration, the needle is pointing to 210°, which is the magnetic bearing TO the station. The tail of the needle is on 030° (answer A). This is the magnetic bearing FROM the station. 180° (answer B) is not a logical answer.

9-34   H348
(Refer to figure 30, illustration 2 on page 9-14.) What magnetic bearing should the pilot use to fly TO the station?

A — 010°.
B — 145°.
C — 190°.

9-34. Answer C. GFDPPM 9-42 (PHB)
(Refer to the note for Question 9-33 for more details.) The pointer is on the 190° magnetic bearing TO the station. The tail is on the 010° (answer A), which is the magnetic bearing FROM the station. A bearing of 145° TO the station (answer B) is not a logical answer.

9-35   H348
(Refer to figure 30, illustration 2 on page 9-14.) Determine the approximate heading to intercept the 180° bearing TO the station.

A — 040°.
B — 160°.
C — 220°.

9-35. Answer C. GFDPPM 9-42 (PHB)
The tail of the needle is on the 010° magnetic bearing FROM the station. This indicates the aircraft is northeast of the station. To intercept the 180° bearing, which would put the aircraft north of the station, you need to turn toward the southwest. A heading of 220° will provide an intercept of 40°. A heading of 040° (answer A) will not intercept the 180° bearing. Instead it will take the aircraft away from the station to the northeast. A heading of 160° (answer B) will take the aircraft southeast of the station, and the 180° bearing will not be intercepted.

9-36   H348
(Refer to figure 30, illustration 3 on page 9-14.) What is the magnetic bearing FROM the station?

A — 025°.
B — 115°.
C — 295°.

9-36. Answer B. GFDPPM 9-42 (PHB)
(Refer to the note for Question 9-33 for more details.) The tail of the pointer is on the 115° magnetic bearing FROM the station. Answer (A), 025°, is not a logical answer. 295° (answer C) is the magnetic bearing TO the station.

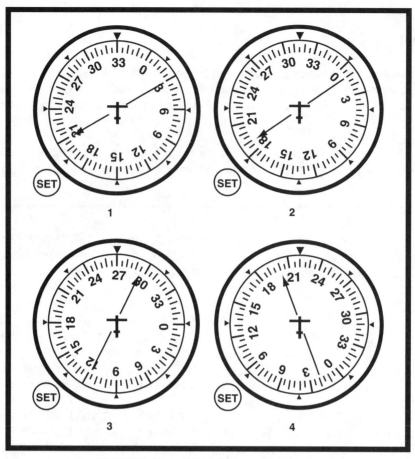

FIGURE 30.—ADF (Moveable Card).

9-37   H348
(Refer to figure 30.) Which ADF indication represents the aircraft tracking TO the station with a right cross-wind?

A — 1.
B — 2.
C — 4.

9-37. Answer C. GFDPPM 9-39, 9-42 (PHB)
To track to the station in a no-wind condition, the head of the bearing pointer would be under the heading index. With a crosswind from the right, the heading would be adjusted a few degrees to the right. Answer (C) is the only correct indication. The ADF indicators for answers (A) and (B) show the aircraft tracking FROM the station.

9-38   H348
(Refer to figure 30, illustration 1.) What outbound bearing is the aircraft crossing?

A — 030°.
B — 150°.
C — 180°.

9-38. Answer A. GFDPPM 9-42 (PHB)
The tail of the needle indicates the magnetic bearing FROM the station, or the outbound bearing. In this case, it is 030°. 150° (answer B) is the reciprocal of the magnetic heading, not the magnetic bearing. Answer (C), 180°, is not a logical choice.

9-39   **H348**
(Refer to figure 31, illustration 1.) The relative bearing TO the station is

A — 045°.
B — 180°.
C — 315°.

9-40   **H348**
(Refer to figure 31, illustration 4.) On a magnetic heading of 320°, the magnetic bearing TO the station is

A — 005°.
B — 185°.
C — 225°.

9-39. Answer C. GFDPPM 9-37 (PHB)
(Note: With a fixed-card indicator, the relative bearing is read directly from the bearing pointer.) In this example, the needle is pointing to 315°. Answer (A), 045°, is the difference between the relative bearing TO the station and 360°. Answer (B), 180°, is not a logical choice.

9-40. Answer B. GFDPPM 9-37 (PHB)
(Note: The relative bearing is the number of degrees between the aircraft's magnetic heading and the magnetic bearing to the station, measured clockwise from the aircraft's heading. The ADF formula is magnetic heading (MH) plus relative bearing (RB) equals magnetic bearing (MB).)

To solve for magnetic bearing use the formula MH + RB = MB. (If the number is higher than 360° subtract 360°.)

In this problem MH = 320° and RB = 225°
320° + 225° = 545° − 360° = 185°.

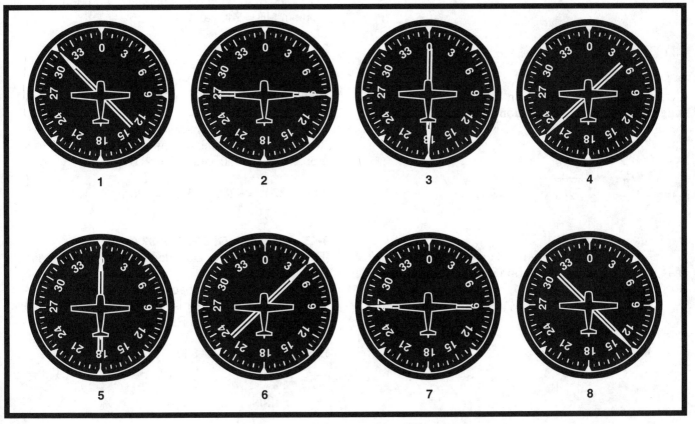

FIGURE 31.—ADF (Fixed Card).

9-41   H348
(Refer to figure 31, illustration 5 on page 9-15.) On a magnetic heading of 035°, the magnetic bearing TO the station is

A — 035°.
B — 180°.
C — 215°.

9-42   H348
(Refer to figure 31, illustration 6 on page 9-15.) On a magnetic heading of 120°, the magnetic bearing TO the station is

A — 045°.
B — 165°.
C — 270°.

9-43   H348
(Refer to figure 31, illustration 6 on page 9-15.) If the magnetic bearing TO the station is 240°, the magnetic heading is

A — 045°.
B — 105°.
C — 195°.

9-44   H348
(Refer to figure 31, illustration 7 on page 9-15.) If the magnetic bearing TO the station is 030°, the magnetic heading is

A — 060°.
B — 120°.
C — 270°.

9-45   H348
(Refer to figure 31, illustration 8 on page 9-15.) If the magnetic bearing TO the station is 135°, the magnetic heading is

A — 135°.
B — 270°.
C — 360°.

9-41. Answer A. GFDPPM 9-37 (PHB)
(Refer to the note for Question 9-40 for more details.)

To solve for magnetic bearing use the formula MH + RB = MB. (If the number is higher than 360° subtract 360°.)

In this problem MH = 035° and RB = 000°
035° + 000° = 035°.

9-42. Answer B. GFDPPM 9-37 (PHB)
(Refer to the note for Question 9-40 for more details.)

To solve for magnetic bearing use the formula MH + RB = MB. (If the number is higher than 360° subtract 360°.)

In this problem MH = 120° and RB = 045°
120° + 045° = 165°.

9-43. Answer C. GFDPPM 9-37 (PHB)
(Note: The relative bearing is the number of degrees between the aircraft's magnetic heading and the magnetic bearing to the station, measured clockwise from the aircraft's heading. The ADF formula is magnetic heading (MH) plus relative bearing (RB) equals magnetic bearing (MB).)

To solve for magnetic heading use the formula MB – RB = MH. (If the number is negative, add 360°.) In this problem MB = 240° and RB = 045°

240° – 045° = 195°.

9-44. Answer B. GFDPPM 9-37 (PHB)
(Refer to the note for Question 9-43 for more details.)

To solve for magnetic heading use the formula MB – RB = MH. (If the number is negative, add 360°.) In this problem MB = 030° and RB = 270°

030° – 270° = –240° + 360° = 120°.

9-45. Answer C. GFDPPM 9-37 (PHB)
(Refer to the note for Question 9-43 for more details.)

To solve for magnetic heading use the formula MB – RB = MH. (If the number is negative, add 360°.) In this problem MB = 135° and RB = 135°

135° – 135° = 000° or 360°.

SECTION D
ADVANCED NAVIGATION

The pace of technological advances has made it possible for astonishingly accurate and versatile navigation radios to be available at a relatively low cost. More and more aircraft are now equipped with long range navigation (LORAN), area navigation (RNAV), and the global positioning system (GPS) receivers. You may also find advanced cockpit management systems, such as radio magnetic indicators (RMIs), horizontal situation indicators (HSIs) and heads-up displays (HUDs).

9-46   J01
How many satellites make up the Global Positioning System (GPS)?

A. 25.
B. 22.
C. 24.

9-47   J01
What is the minimum number of Global Positioning System (GPS) satellites that are observable by a user anywhere on earth?

A. 6.
B. 5.
C. 4.

9-48   J01
How many Global Positioning System (GPS) satellites are required to yield a three dimensional position (latitude, longitude, and altitude) and time solution?

A. 5.
B. 6.
C. 4.

9-46. Answer C. GFDPPM 9-51 (AIM 1-1-21)
GPS is a satellite-based navigation system, consisting of 24 satellites. This satellite constellation is designed so that a minimum of five satellites is always observable anywhere on earth. The GPS receiver needs four satellites to derive a three-dimensional position and time solution.

9-47. Answer B. GFDPPM 9-51 (AIM 1-1-21)
GPS is a satellite-based navigation system, consisting of 24 satellites. This satellite constellation is designed so that a minimum of five satellites is always observable anywhere on earth. The GPS receiver needs four satellites to derive a three-dimensional position and time solution.

9-48. Answer C. GFDPPM 9-51 (AIM 1-1-21)
GPS is a satellite-based navigation system, consisting of 24 satellites. This satellite constellation is designed so that a minimum of five satellites is always observable anywhere on earth. The GPS receiver needs four satellites to derive a three-dimensional position and time solution.

APPLYING HUMAN FACTORS PRINCIPLES

SECTION A
AVIATION PHYSIOLOGY

Humans are designed to be earthbound creatures, but we possess a remarkable ability to adapt to our surroundings. Our bodies can adjust to the demands of aviation to a certain extent, but you should be aware of the limitations to what humans can cope with in the air. This section covers the role that vision plays in flight, and the dangers of spatial disorientation, carbon monoxide poisoning, hypoxia and hyperventilation.

VISION IN FLIGHT
Understanding how your eyes work under different conditions is crucial to safe flying. Night flying brings on specific issues of which you should be aware.

NIGHT VISION
1. The most effective way to look for traffic during night flight is to scan slowly, to permit off-center viewing. Look to the side of an object for the clearest focus.
2. During a night flight, you observe a steady red light and a flashing red light ahead and at the same altitude. The other aircraft is crossing to the left.
3. During a night flight, you observe a steady white light and a flashing red light ahead and at the same altitude. The other aircraft is flying away from you.
4. During a night flight, you observe steady red and green lights ahead and at the same altitude. The other aircraft is approaching head-on.
5. VFR approaches to land at night should be accomplished the same as during the daytime.
6. To adapt the eyes for night flying, the pilot should avoid bright white lights for at least 30 minutes before the flight.

DISORIENTATION
7. A state of temporary confusion resulting from misleading information being sent to the brain by various sensory organs is defined as spatial disorientation.
8. The danger of spatial disorientation during flight in poor visual conditions may be reduced by trusting in the instruments rather than taking a chance on the sensory organs. Pilots are more subject to spatial disorientation if body signals are used to interpret flight attitude.
9. If a pilot experiences spatial disorientation during flight in restricted visibility, the best way to overcome the effect is to rely on the aircraft instrument indications.

RESPIRATION AND ALTITUDE
As humans, we depend on oxygen for our survival. During flight, you may climb to altitudes where oxygen is scarce, and you need to be familiar with the effects that decreased oxygen can have on your body's ability to perform.

HYPOXIA
10. Hypoxia is a state of oxygen deficiency in the body.

CARBON MONOXIDE POISONING
11. Large accumulations of carbon monoxide in the body result in the loss of muscular power.
12. Susceptibility to carbon monoxide poisoning increases as altitude increases.

HYPERVENTILATION

13. Rapid or extra deep breathing while using oxygen can cause a condition known as hyperventilation.

14. Emotional tension, anxiety or fear can cause hyperventilation.

15. A pilot should be able to overcome the symptoms, or avoid future occurrences of hyperventilation, by slowing the breathing rate, breathing into a bag or talking aloud.

10-1   H564

What is the most effective way to use the eyes during night flight?

A — Look only at far away, dim lights.
B — Scan slowly to permit offcenter viewing.
C — Concentrate directly on each object for a few seconds.

10-1. Answer B. GFDPPM 10-4 (AFH)

The rods in the retina are used for night vision. Because they are not located directly behind the pupil, you must use offcenter viewing. Also, in dim light, you might need to move your eyes more slowly to prevent blurring of images than during the day. Answer (A) is impractical since the eyes tend to focus on lights and could miss items of importance. Answer (C) is wrong because if the eye concentrates directly on an object for even a few seconds, the image on the retina begins to fade.

10-2   H564

The best method to use when looking for other traffic at night is to

A — look to the side of the object and scan slowly.
B — scan the visual field very rapidly.
C — look to the side of the object and scan rapidly.

10-2. Answer A. GFDPPM 10-4 (AFH)

The most effective method of night scanning is to use off center vision, which means looking to the side of an object, and to scan slowly to prevent blurring. Rapid scanning (answer B) does not allow the image to focus clearly. Answer (C) is also wrong because scanning should be done slowly, not rapidly.

10-3   H564

The most effective method of scanning for other aircraft for collision avoidance during nighttime hours is to use

A — regularly spaced concentration on the 3-, 9-, and 12-o'clock positions.
B — a series of short, regularly spaced eye movements to search each 30-degree sector.
C — peripheral vision by scanning small sectors and utilizing offcenter viewing.

10-3. Answer C. GFDPPM 10-4 (FTH)

As with the previous questions, scanning should be done slowly, in small sectors, using offcenter (peripheral) vision. Answer (A) is wrong because scanning should not be concentrated in a few specific areas. Both day and night scanning should be done in sectors of 10 degrees, not 30 degrees (answer B).

10-4   H567

During a night flight, you observe a steady red light and a flashing red light ahead and at the same altitude. What is the general direction of movement of the other aircraft?

A — The other aircraft is crossing to the left.
B — The other aircraft is crossing to the right.
C — The other aircraft is approaching head-on.

10-4. Answer A. GFDPPM 10-5 (AFH)

The steady red light is a position light on the left wing and the flashing red light is an anticollision beacon. If you are looking at the left wingtip, the other aircraft would be crossing to the left. If the other aircraft was crossing to the right (answer B), you would see a green light on the wingtip, not a red light. If the other aircraft was approaching head-on (answer C), you would see both red and green wingtip position lights.

10-5   H567

During a night flight, you observe a steady white light and a flashing red light ahead and at the same altitude. What is the general direction of movement of the other aircraft?

A — The other aircraft is flying away from you.
B — The other aircraft is crossing to the left.
C — The other aircraft is crossing to the right.

10-5. Answer A. GFDPPM 10-5 (AFH)

The white position light is on the tail and the flashing red light is the anticollision light. Therefore, you would be looking at the rear of the aircraft, which indicates it is flying away from you. If the aircraft was crossing to the left or to the right (answers B and C), you would be able to see either the steady red or green wingtip position light.

10-6   H567
During a night flight, you observe steady red and green lights ahead and at the same altitude. What is the general direction of movement of the other aircraft?

A — The other aircraft is crossing to the left.
B — The other aircraft is flying away from you.
C — The other aircraft is approaching head-on.

10-6. Answer C. GFDPPM 10-5 (AFH)
In this case, you are seeing both wingtip lights. If there was no white tail light in between them, you would most likely be looking head-on at the aircraft. If the aircraft was crossing to the left (answer A), you would not be able to see the green light on the right wingtip. If the aircraft was flying away from you (answer B), you should be able to see a white tail light. Although the question does not mention which side each light is on, you could tell that an aircraft is approaching head-on if the red light is to your right and the green light is to your left.

10-7   H573
VFR approaches to land at night should be accomplished

A — at a higher speed.
B — with a steeper descent.
C — the same as during daytime.

10-7. Answer C. GFDPPM 10-7 (AFH)
You should try to make night VFR approaches the same as day approaches. Using a higher airspeed (answer A) could result in floating, while using a steeper descent (answer B) could make it difficult to judge altitude when it comes time to flare the airplane for landing.

10-8   J31
Large accumulations of carbon monoxide in the human body result in

A — tightness across the forehead.
B — loss of muscular power.
C — an increased sense of well-being.

10-8. Answer B. GFDPPM 10-15 (AC 20-32)
The key word in this question is "large" accumulations. This condition can produce a loss of muscle power. Answers (A) and (C) describe symptoms of hypoxia.

10-9   J31
Which statement best defines hypoxia?

A — A state of oxygen deficiency in the body.
B — An abnormal increase in the volume of air breathed.
C — A condition of gas bubble formation around the joints or muscles.

10-9. Answer A. GFDPPM 10-13 (AIM)
Hypoxia occurs when the body tissues do not receive enough oxygen. Answer (B) would occur during hyperventilation, when the breathing rate is too fast and too deep. Answer (C) describes decompression sickness, or the "bends," which can occur during and after scuba diving.

10-10   J31
Rapid or extra deep breathing while using oxygen can cause a condition known as

A — hyperventilation.
B — aerosinusitis.
C — aerotitis.

10-10. Answer A. GFDPPM 10-18 (AIM)
Hyperventilation occurs when the breathing rate is too rapid or too deep. It can occur with or without the use of supplemental oxygen. Answer (B), aerosinusitis, is an inflammation of the sinuses. Answer (C), aerotitis, is an inflammation of the middle ear. Both are caused by changes in air pressure.

10-11   J31
Which would most likely result in hyperventilation?

A — Emotional tension, anxiety, or fear.
B — The excessive consumption of alcohol.
C — An extremely slow rate of breathing and insufficient oxygen.

10-11. Answer A. GFDPPM 10-18 (AIM)
Emotional tension, anxiety, and fear can cause the rapid, deep breathing associated with hyperventilation. Excessive consumption of alcohol (answer B), does not cause hyperventilation. Answer (C) is wrong because a slow breathing rate is used to recover from hyperventilation. Also, hyperventilation is caused by insufficient carbon dioxide, not oxygen, in the body.

10-12   J31

A pilot should be able to overcome the symptoms or avoid future occurrences of hyperventilation by

A — closely monitoring the flight instruments to control the airplane.
B — slowing the breathing rate, breathing into a bag, or talking aloud.
C — increasing the breathing rate in order to increase lung ventilation.

10-12. Answer B. GFDPPM 10-18 (AIM)

Slowing the breathing rate is one of the best ways to stop hyperventilation. Also, breathing into a bag and talking out loud are helpful. Answer (A) will not help control the breathing rate. Increasing the breathing rate (answer C) is a cause of hyperventilation, not a cure.

10-13   J31

Susceptibility to carbon monoxide poisoning increases as

A — altitude increases.
B — altitude decreases.
C — air pressure increases.

10-13. Answer A. GFDPPM 10-14, 15 (AC 20-32)

Since carbon monoxide poisoning is a form of hypoxia, its effects are increased with altitude, where there is less oxygen available. As altitude decreases (answer B), oxygen increases, and the effects of CO poisoning are decreased instead of increased. As altitude decreases, air pressure increases (answer C), and the effect is the same as in Answer (B).

10-14   J31

What preparation should a pilot make to adapt the eyes for night flying?

A — Wear sunglasses after sunset until ready for flight.
B — Avoid red lights at least 30 minutes before the flight.
C — Avoid bright white lights at least 30 minutes before the flight.

10-14. Answer C. GFDPPM 10-5 (AIM)

The rods in the human eye can take up to 30 minutes to fully adapt to the dark. Bright lights must be avoided for this amount of time. While sunglasses (answer A) can reduce light intensity, they are not as effective as simply avoiding bright lights for 30 minutes. Avoiding red lights (answer B) is not correct, since red cockpit lighting preserves night vision.

10-15   J31

The danger of spatial disorientation during flight in poor visual conditions may be reduced by

A — shifting the eyes quickly between the exterior visual field and the instrument panel.
B — having faith in the instruments rather than taking a chance on the sensory organs.
C — leaning the body in the opposite direction of the motion of the aircraft.

10-15. Answer B. GFDPPM 10-9 (AIM)

To avoid spatial disorientation, a pilot must rely on the instruments in the cockpit and not the feelings from the sensory organs. Answer (A) is wrong because when visual conditions are poor, scanning outside is not very effective. Shifting the eyes quickly will only add to spatial disorientation. Answer (C) is not a good option, as it would tend to increase spatial disorientation.

10-16   J31

A state of temporary confusion resulting from misleading information being sent to the brain by various sensory organs is defined as

A — spatial disorientation.
B — hyperventilation.
C — hypoxia.

10-16. Answer A. GFDPPM 10-8 (AC 67-2)

Spatial disorientation occurs when the brain receives conflicting messages from the sensory organs. Answer (B), hyperventilation, is a breathing rate that is too rapid or too deep. Answer (C), hypoxia, is a state of oxygen deficiency in the blood.

10-17   J31

Pilots are more subject to spatial disorientation if

A — they ignore the sensations of muscles and inner ear.
B — body signals are used to interpret flight attitude.
C — eyes are moved often in the process of cross-checking the flight instruments.

10-18   J31

If a pilot experiences spatial disorientation during flight in a restricted visibility condition, the best way to overcome the effect is to

A — rely upon the aircraft instrument indications.
B — concentrate on yaw, pitch, and roll sensations.
C — consciously slow the breathing rate until symptoms clear and then resume normal breathing rate.

10-17. Answer B. GFDPPM 10-11 (AC 67-2)
Spatial disorientation is more likely to occur when a pilot believes the signals from the body's sensory organs. Answer (A) is wrong because pilots are more subject to spatial disorientation if they rely on the body's sensations. Answer (C), moving the eyes often, is wrong because the key is to focus on the instruments, rely on them, and avoid rapid head movements.

10-18. Answer A. GFDPPM 10-9 (AIM)
Since the brain receives confusing messages from the body's senses, the pilot must rely on the aircraft's instruments. Concentrating on pitch, roll, and yaw sensations (answer B) will cause or increase spatial disorientation. Slowing the breathing rate (answer C) will reduce hyperventilation, but by itself will not overcome the effects of spatial disorientation.

SECTION B
AERONAUTICAL DECISION MAKING

As pilot in command, you are presented with a continuous stream of decisions to make during each flight. Although you can't prepare specifically for every situation you'll encounter, you can be prepared to make effective decisions when these situations arise. Good aeronautical decision making is central to flying safely; however, the FAA test asks no specific questions pertaining to this section.

10-19   L05

What is it often called when a pilot pushes his or her capabilities and the aircraft's limits by trying to maintain visual contact with the terrain in low visibility and ceiling?

A — Scud running.
B — Mind set.
C — Peer pressure.

10-20   L05

What is the antidote when a pilot has a hazardous attitude, such as "Antiauthority"?

A — Rules do not apply in this situation.
B — I know what I am doing.
C — Follow the rules.

10-21   L05

What is the antidote when a pilot has a hazardous attitude, such as "Impulsivity"?

A — It could happen to me.
B — Do it quickly to get it over with.
C — Not so fast, think first.

10-19. Answer A. (AC 60-22)
Scud running is one of the operational pitfalls, describing a pilot that tries to maintain visual contact with the surface in low visibility and ceiling. Mind set is another operational pitfall that describes the inability to recognize and cope with changes in the situation different from those anticipated or planned. Peer pressure is an operational pitfall that describes poor decision making based upon emotional response to peers, rather than evaluating a situation objectively.

10-20. Answer C. GFDPPM 1-54 (AC 60-22)
The antidote for the hazardous attitude, "Antiauthority" is: Follow the rules, they are usually right. "Rules do not apply in this situation" and "I know what I am doing" are not antidotes to any of the hazardous attitudes.

10-21. Answer C. GFDPPM 1-54 (AC 60-22)
The antidote for the hazardous attitude, "Impulsivity" is: Not so fast, think first. "It could happen to me" and "Do it quickly to get it over with" are not antidotes to any of the hazardous attitudes.

10-22   L05
What is the antidote when a pilot has a hazardous attitude, such as "Invulnerability"?

A — It will not happen to me.
B — It can not be that bad.
C — It could happen to me.

10-23   L05
What is the antidote when a pilot has a hazardous attitude, such as "Macho"?

A — I can do it.
B — Taking chances is foolish.
C — Nothing will happen.

10-24   L05
What is the antidote when a pilot has a hazardous attitude, such as "Resignation"?

A — What is the use.
B — Someone else is responsible.
C — I am not helpless.

10-25   L05
Who is responsible for determining whether a pilot is fit to fly for a particular flight, even though he or she holds a current medical certificate?

A — The FAA.
B — The medical examiner.
C — The pilot.

10-26   L05
What is the one common factor which affects most preventable accidents?

A — Structural failure.
B — Mechanical malfunction.
C — Human error.

10-27   L05
What often leads to spatial disorientation or collision with ground/obstacles when flying under Visual Flight Rules (VFR)?

A — Continual flight into instrument conditions.
B — Getting behind the aircraft.
C — Duck-under syndrome.

10-28   L05
What is one of the neglected items when a pilot relies on short and long-term memory for repetitive tasks?

A — Checklists.
B — Situation awareness.
C — Flying outside the envelope.

10-22. Answer C. GFDPPM 1-54 (AC 60-22)
The antidote for the hazardous attitude, "Invulnerability" is: It could happen to me. "It will not happen to me" and "It can not be that bad" are not antidotes to any of the hazardous attitudes.

10-23. Answer B. GFDPPM 1-54 (AC 60-22)
The antidote for the hazardous attitude, "Macho" is: Taking chances is foolish. "I can do it" and "Nothing will happen" are not antidotes to any of the hazardous attitudes.

10-24. Answer C. GFDPPM 1-54 (AC 60-22)
The antidote for the hazardous attitude, "Resignation" is: I am not helpless. "What is the use" and "Someone else is responsible" are not antidotes to any of the hazardous attitudes.

10-25. Answer C. GFDPPM 10-29 (AC 60-22)
You, the pilot, are always responsible for determining if you are fit to fly for a particular flight. The FAA and medical examiners determine if you are fit to hold a medical certificate.

10-26. Answer C. GFDPPM 1-52 (AC 60-22)
Most preventable accidents have one common factor: human error rather than a mechanical malfunction or structural failure. According to NTSB statistics gathered from 1992 to 1996, the pilot was the general cause or a contributing factor in 49% of the accidents. Whereas the aircraft only accounted for 19% of the accidents.

10-27. Answer A. GFDPPM 10-11 (AC 60-22)
Continuing flight under VFR into instrument conditions often leads to spatial disorientation or collision with ground/obstacles. Getting behind the aircraft does not normally result in spatial disorientation or collision with the ground. Although duck-under syndrome often leads to impact with the ground, it normally does not result in spatial disorientation.

10-28. Answer A. (AC 60-22)
Pilots that rely on their memory for repetitive tasks, do not normally use checklists.

CHAPTER 11

FLYING CROSS-COUNTRY

SECTION A
THE FLIGHT PLANNING PROCESS

Thorough preflight planning has made cross-country flight much safer since the early days. Preflight planning utilizes the knowledge and skills that you have acquired during the course of your training. This section covers aspects of preflight protocol, including airworthiness, preflight inspection, route selection, weather considerations, completing a navigation log and cockpit management.

PREFLIGHT INSPECTION
1. Each pilot in command shall, before beginning a flight, become familiar with all available information concerning that flight.
2. Preflight action, as required for all flights away from the vicinity of an airport, shall include an alternate course of action if the flight cannot be completed as planned.
3. In addition to the other preflight actions for a VFR flight away from the vicinity of the departure airport, regulations specifically require the pilot in command to determine runway lengths at airports of intended use and the aircraft's takeoff and landing distance data.

AIRWORTHINESS
4. The Airworthiness Certificate of an airplane remains valid as long as the aircraft is maintained and operated as required by Federal Aviation Regulations.
5. The owner or operator of an aircraft is responsible for ensuring that an aircraft is maintained in an airworthy condition.

WALK-AROUND INSPECTION
6. The pilot in command is responsible for determining if an aircraft is in condition for safe flight.
7. In regard to preflighting an aircraft, the minimum expected of a pilot prior to every flight is to perform a walk-around inspection.
8. The use of a written checklist is recommended for preflight inspection and engine start to ensure that all necessary items are checked in a logical sequence.
9. After an aircraft has been stored for an extended period of time, the pilot should make a special check for damage or obstructions caused by animals, birds, or insects.

11-1   B13
How long does the Airworthiness Certificate of an aircraft remain valid?

A — As long as the aircraft has a current Registration Certificate.

B — Indefinitely, unless the aircraft suffers major damage.

C — As long as the aircraft is maintained and operated as required by Federal Aviation Regulations.

11-1. Answer C. GFDPPM 11-11 (PHB)
The Airworthiness Certificate remains valid only as long as the aircraft is maintained and operated in accordance with the FARs. Answer (A) is incorrect because the Airworthiness Certificate is dependent on the maintenance and operation of the aircraft, not the registration. Obviously, answer (B) is wrong because the Airworthiness Certificate is valid only as long as the aircraft is properly maintained and operated. Minor damage could make an Airworthiness Certificate invalid.

11-2   H311

During the preflight inspection who is responsible for determining the aircraft is safe for flight?

A — The owner or operator.
B — The certificated mechanic who performed the annual inspection.
C — The pilot in command.

11-2. Answer C. GFDPPM 11-11 (PHB)
The owner or operator is generally responsible to make sure that the required maintenance and inspections are performed. These tasks may be assigned to a certificated maintenance technician, but the responsibility for compliance remains with the owner or operator. Preflight inspection is the responsibility of the pilot in command (PIC). Prior to every flight, the PIC is required to accomplish a thorough and systematic preflight to ensure that the aircraft is safe for flight. The preflight inspection should be completed according to procedures recommended by the manufacturer. Normally, this means the PIC should use a checklist for the preflight inspection.

11-3   H311

How should an aircraft preflight inspection be accomplished for the first flight of the day?

A — Thorough and systematic means recommended by the manufacturer.
B — Quick walk around with a check of gas and oil.
C — Any sequence as determined by the pilot-in-command.

11-3. Answer A. GFDPPM 11-11 (PHB)
See explanation for Question 11-2.

11-4   H311

Who is primarily responsible for maintaining an aircraft in airworthy condition?

A — Pilot-in-command.
B — Owner or operator.
C — Mechanic.

11-4. Answer B. GFDPPM 11-12 (PHB)
See explanation for Question 11-2.

SECTION B
THE FLIGHT

Not every flight follows the carefully laid plans you've set during the flight planning process. However, this preparation allows you to better deal with any contingency that might arise. Although no FAA test questions specifically relate to this section, Chapter 11 of the *Private Pilot Manual* contains a valuable, detailed model of a typical cross-country flight.

FEDERAL AVIATION REGULATIONS

SECTION A
PART 1—DEFINITIONS AND ABBREVIATIONS

As a private or recreational pilot, you should have a working understanding of Parts 1, 61, 91, and NTSB 830 of the Federal Aviation Regulations (FARs). Although some information regarding FARs is included in the *Private Pilot Manual*, you should include a current publication of the FARs in your test preparation, to ensure that you learn all appropriate flight regulations. A FAR/AIM book and CD-ROM, published by Jeppesen Sanderson, are available along with other private pilot training materials. These books include a recommended study list, along with exercises to assist you in preparing for the computer test. This section covers pertinent definitions and abbreviations from Part 1.

NIGHT
1. The definition of nighttime is the time between the end of evening civil twilight and the beginning of morning civil twilight.

V-SPEEDS
2. V_{FE} represents the maximum flap operating speed.
3. V_{LE} represents the maximum landing gear extended speed.
4. V_{NO} is defined as the maximum structural cruising speed.
5. V_{SO} is defined as the stalling speed or minimum steady flight speed in the landing configuration.

PREVENTIVE MAINTENANCE
6. Preventive maintenance includes such items as servicing landing gear wheel bearings and replenishing hydraulic fluid.

12-1   A01
The definition of nighttime is

A — sunset to sunrise.
B — 1 hour after sunset to 1 hour before sunrise.
C — the time between the end of evening civil twilight and the beginning of morning civil twilight.

12-2   A02
Which V-speed represents maximum flap extended speed?

A — V_{FE}.
B — V_{LOF}.
C — V_{FC}.

12-1. Answer C. (FAR 1.1)
Night is the time between the end of evening civil twilight and the beginning of morning civil twilight. Answer (A) describes the time during which aircraft lights must be used according to FAR 91.209. Answer (B) reflects the night experience currency requirements found in FAR 61.57.

12-2. Answer A. (FAR 1.2)
V_{FE} is defined as maximum flap extended speed. Answer (B) represents lift-off speed. Answer (C) is used to describe maximum speed for stability characteristics.

12-3   A02

Which V-speed represents maximum landing gear extended speed?

A — V_{LE}.
B — V_{LO}.
C — V_{FE}.

12-4   A02

V_{NO} is defined as the

A — normal operating range.
B — never-exceed speed.
C — maximum structural cruising speed.

12-5   A02

V_{S0} is defined as the

A — stalling speed or minimum steady flight speed in the landing configuration.
B — stalling speed or minimum steady flight speed in a specified configuration.
C — stalling speed or minimum takeoff safety speed.

12-6   A16

Which operation would be described as preventive maintenance?

A — Servicing landing gear wheel bearings.
B — Alteration of main seat support brackets.
C — Engine adjustments to allow automotive gas to be used.

12-7   A16

Which operation would be described as preventive maintenance?

A — Repair of landing gear brace struts.
B — Replenishing hydraulic fluid.
C — Repair of portions of skin sheets by making additional seams.

12-3. Answer A. (FAR 1.2)
V_{LE} is defined as maximum landing gear extended speed. Answer (B) is maximum landing gear operating speed. Answer (C) represents maximum flap extended speed.

12-4. Answer C. (FAR 1.2)
V_{NO} is defined as maximum structural cruising speed. Answer (A) is not defined by any V-speed. Answer (B), never-exceed speed, is represented by V_{NE}.

12-5. Answer A. (FAR 1.2)
V_{S0} is stalling speed or minimum steady flight speed in a landing configuration. Answer (B) is represented by V_{S1}. Answer (C) has two V-speeds. Stalling speed is V_S and minimum takeoff safety speed is $V_{2\,min}$.

12-6. Answer A. (FAR 1.1, FAR 43 — APPENDIX A)
Preventive maintenance involves simple or minor preservation operations. Servicing landing gear is an example of preventive maintenance listed in FAR Part 43, Appendix A. Answers (B) and (C) are alterations, and are not listed in Appendix A.

12-7. Answer B. (FAR 1.1, FAR 43 — APPENDIX A)
Replenishing hydraulic fluid is listed as preventive maintenance in FAR Part 43, Appendix A. Answers (A) and (C) are not listed in Appendix A and they are considered as repair work.

SECTION B
PART 61—CERTIFICATION: PILOTS, FLIGHT INSTRUCTORS, AND GROUND INSTRUCTORS

As a pilot, you'll need to know the Part 61 requirements for obtaining certificates and ratings, and the privileges and limitations associated with your license.

PILOT DOCUMENTS
1. While operating an aircraft as pilot in command, you must have both your medical certificate and your pilot certificate in your personal possession.
2. Each person who holds a pilot certificate or a medical certificate shall present it for inspection upon the request of the Administrator, the National Transportation Safety Board, or any federal, state, or local law enforcement officer.

MEDICAL CERTIFICATES
3. A third-class medical certificate is good until the end of the 24th calendar month after the date of examination, if the pilot is age 40 or over.
4. A third-class medical is good until the end of the 36th calendar month after the date of examination, if the pilot is under age 40.
5. To exercise the privileges of a commercial pilot, a second-class medical is good until the end of the 12th calendar month after the date of examination. For private pilot operations, a second-class medical is good until the end of the 24th calendar month after the date of examination, if over age 40, and until the end of the 36th month after the date of examination, if under age 40.
6. To exercise the privileges of an ATP, a first-class medical is good until the end of the 6th calendar month after the date of examination. At that point, the medical allows for second-class privileges, such as those requiring a commercial certificate, until the end of the 12th calendar month following the date of examination. After that, the certificate is good for third class privileges, such as those allowed by a private pilot certificate, until the end of the 24th calendar month after the date of examination, if the pilot is over age 40. If the pilot is under age 40, third-class privileges are available until the end of the 36th calendar month after the date of examination.

TYPE RATINGS
7. The pilot in command is required to hold a type rating for the operation of aircraft having a gross weight of more than 12,500 pounds.

HIGH-PERFORMANCE AIRCRAFT
8. The definition of a high-performance airplane is an airplane with more than 200 horsepower, or retractable landing gear, flaps and a controllable propeller.
9. Before a person holding a private pilot certificate may act as pilot in command of a high-performance airplane, that person must have received flight instruction from an authorized flight instructor, who then endorses that person's logbook. The instruction must be given in an aircraft that has more than 200 horsepower, or has retractable landing gear, flaps, and a controllable propeller.

FLIGHT REVIEW
10. To act as pilot in command of an aircraft carrying passengers, a pilot must show by logbook endorsement the satisfactory completion of a flight review or completion of a pilot proficiency check within the preceding 24 calendar months.

RECENCY OF FLIGHT EXPERIENCE
11. If recency of experience requirements for night flight are not met, the latest time passengers may be carried is 1 hour after official sunset. The three takeoffs and landings required to act as pilot in command at night must be done during the time period from 1 hour after sunset to 1 hour before sunrise.
12. To act as pilot in command of an aircraft carrying passengers, the pilot must have made at least three takeoffs and three landings in an aircraft of the same category and class, and if a type rating is required, of the same type, within the preceding 90 days.

13. The takeoffs and landings required to meet the recency of flight experience requirements for carrying passengers in a tailwheel airplane must be to a full stop.
14. To meet the recency of experience requirements to act as pilot in command carrying passengers at night, a pilot must have made at least three takeoffs and three landings to a full stop within the preceding 90 days in the same category and class of aircraft to be used.

CHANGE OF ADDRESS
15. If a certificated pilot changes permanent mailing address and fails to notify the FAA Airmen Certification Branch of the new address, the pilot is entitled to exercise the privileges of the pilot certificate for a period of only 30 days after the date of the move.

GLIDER TOWING
16. A certificated pilot may not act as pilot in command of an aircraft towing a glider unless there is entered in the pilot's logbook a minimum of 100 hours of pilot flight time in powered aircraft.
17. To act as pilot in command of an aircraft towing a glider, a person is required to have made within the preceding 12 months at least three actual or simulated glider tows while accompanied by a qualified pilot.

RECREATIONAL PILOTS
18. A recreational pilot acting as pilot in command must have in his/her personal possession the current and appropriate pilot and medical certificates while aboard the aircraft.
19. A third-class medical, appropriate to exercise the privileges of a recreational pilot, expires at the end of the 36th calendar month after the date of examination, if the pilot is under age 40.
20. To act as pilot in command of an aircraft, a recreational pilot must have completed a biennial flight review within the preceding 24 calendar months.
21. A recreational pilot may carry one passenger.
22. A recreational pilot may share the pro rata share of the operating expenses of the flight with a passenger.
23. A recreational pilot may only act as pilot in command within 50 nautical miles of the airport/heliport at which they received instruction.
24. A recreational pilot may not act as pilot in command of an aircraft that is certificated for more than four occupants.
25. A recreational pilot may not act as pilot in command of an aircraft in furtherance of a business, or for a donation to a charitable organization.
26. The earliest time that a recreational pilot may take off is at sunrise, and the latest time a flight may terminate is at sunset.
27. A recreational pilot may operate to and from an airport that lies within Class C airspace for the purpose of obtaining an additional certificate or rating while under the supervision of an authorized flight instructor.
28. A recreational pilot may operate from an airport that lies within Class D airspace, and that has a part-time control tower, when the tower is closed, the ceiling is at least 1000 feet, and the visibility is at least 3 miles.
29. During daytime, the minimum flight or surface visibility required for recreational pilots in Class G airspace below 10,000 feet is 3 miles. The same visibility holds for flight within controlled airspace.
30. The recreational pilot may not demonstrate an aircraft in flight to a prospective buyer.
31. The recreational pilot may not act as pilot in command of an aircraft towing a banner.
32. A recreational pilot must have a pilot-in-command flight check if the pilot has less than 400 total flight hours and has not flown as pilot in command in an aircraft within the preceding 180 days.
33. A recreational pilot may fly as the sole occupant of an aircraft at night while under the supervision of a flight instructor, provided the flight or surface visibility is at least 5 miles.

PRIVATE PILOT LIMITATIONS
34. A private pilot may share the pro rata share of the operating expenses of the flight with a passenger.
35. A private pilot may act as pilot in command of an aircraft used in a passenger-carrying airlift sponsored by a charitable organization, and for which the passengers make a donation to the organization.

12-8   A20
What document(s) must be in our personal possession or readily accessible in the aircraft while operating as pilot in command of an aircraft?

A — A pilot certificate with an endorsement showing accomplishment of an annual flight review and a pilot logbook showing recency of experience.
B — Certificates showing accomplishment of a checkout in the aircraft and a current biennial flight review.
C — An appropriate pilot certificate and an appropriate current medical certificate if required.

12-9   A20
When must a current pilot certificate be in the pilot's personal possession or readily accessible in the aircraft?

A — When acting as a crew chief during launch and recovery.
B — Only when passengers are carried.
C — Anytime when acting as pilot in command or as a required crewmember.

12-10   A20
A recreational or private pilot acting as pilot in command, or in any other capacity as a required pilot flight crewmember, must have in his or her personal possession or readily accessible in the aircraft a current

A — endorsement on the pilot certificate to show that a flight review has been satisfactorily accomplished.
B — medical certificateif required and an appropriate pilot certificate.
C — logbook endorsement to show that a flight review has been satisfactorily accomplished.

12-11   A20
Each person who holds a pilot certificate or a medical certificate shall present it for inspection upon the request of the Administrator, the National Transportation Safety Board, or any

A — authorized representative of the Department of Transportation.
B — person in a position of authority.
C — federal, state, or local law enforcement officer.

12-8. Answer C. (FAR 61.3)
Both an appropriate pilot certificate and an appropriate medical certificate if required, must be in your personal possession or readily accessible in the aircraft in order to act as pilot in command of an aircraft. Answers (A) and (B) are incorrect because there are no regulations requiring pilots to have proof of currency in their personal possession.

12-9. Answer C. (FAR 61.3)
You must have a current pilot certificate in your personal possession or readily accessible in the aircraft whenever you are pilot in command or acting as a required pilot flight crewmember. Answer (A) is incorrect because a crew chief is not a required pilot flight crewmember. Answer (B) is wrong because it makes no difference whether you are carrying passengers or not.

12-10. Answer B. (FAR 61.3)
You must have both the medical certificate if required, and the pilot certificate in your personal possession or readily accessible in the aircraft. Answers (A) and (C) are incorrect because you are not required to have proof of flight reviews in your personal possession.

12-11. Answer C. (FAR 61.3)
By regulation you, as the pilot, are required to present your pilot certificate upon request of the administrator, an authorized representative of the National Transportation Safety Board (NTSB) or any Federal, State, or local law enforcement officer. Answers (A) and (B) are incorrect because a representative of the Department of Transportation or a person in a position of authority could mean someone other than an administrator, NTSB representative, or law enforcement officer.

12-12   A20
A Third-Class Medical Certificate is issued to a 36-year old pilot on August 10, this year. To exercise the privileges of a Private Pilot Certificate, the medical certificate will be valid until midnight on

A — August 10, 2 years later.
B — August 31, 3 years later.
C — August 31, 2 years later.

12-13   A20
A Third-Class Medical Certificate is issued to a 51-year old pilot on May 3, this year. To exercise the privileges of a Private Pilot Certificate, the medical certificate will be valid until midnight on

A — May 3, 1 year later.
B — May 31, 1 year later.
C — May 31, 2 years later.

12-14   A20
For private pilot operations, a Second-Class Medical Certificate issued to a 42-year old pilot on July 15, this year, will expire at midnight on

A — July 15, 2 years later.
B — July 31, 1 year later.
C — July 31, 2 years later.

12-15   A20
For private pilot operations, a First-Class Medical Certificate issued to a 23-year old pilot on October 21, this year, will expire at midnight on

A — October 21, 2 years later.
B — October 31, next year.
C — October 31, 3 years later.

12-12. Answer B. (FAR 61.23)
A third-class medical is good until the end of the 36th calendar month after the date of examination, if under age 40. Answer (A) is wrong because a medical certificate expires at the end of the month. Answer (C) is wrong because a third-class medical certificate for a pilot under age 40 is good for three years.

12-13. Answer C. (FAR 61.23)
A third-class medical is good until the end of the 24th calendar month after the date of examination, if age 40 and over. Answer (A) is wrong because a third-class medical expires at the end of the month and is good for more than one year. Answer (B) is wrong because a third-class medical certificate is good for two years, if age 40 and over.

12-14. Answer C. (FAR 61.23)
To exercise the privileges of a commercial pilot, a second-class medical is good until the end of the 12th calendar month after the date of examination. For private pilot operations, a second-class medical is good until the end of the 24th calendar month after the date of examination, if age 40 and over. Answer (A) is wrong because a medical certificate expires at the end of the month. Answer (B) is incorrect because a second-class medical certificate expires at the end of one year for commercial pilot operations, not private pilot operations.

12-15. Answer C. (FAR 61.23)
To exercise the privileges of an ATP, a first-class medical is good until the end of the 6th calendar month after the date of examination. Between the beginning of the 7th month and the end of the 12th month, the first-class medical carries 2nd class privileges. From the beginning of the 13th month to the end of the 36th calendar month if under age 40, a first-class medical is good only for operations requiring a 3rd class medical. Answer (A) is wrong because a medical certificate expires at the end of the month. Answer (B) is incorrect because a first-class medical expires at the end of six months for an ATP, one year for a commercial pilot, and two or three years for a private pilot.

12-16   A20

The pilot in command is required to hold a type rating in which aircraft?

A — Aircraft involved in ferry flights, training flights, or test flights.

B — Aircraft having a gross weight of more than 12,500 pounds.

C — Aircraft operating under an authorization issued by the Administrator.

12-16. Answer B. (FAR 1.1, 61.5, 61.31)

FAR 61.31 indicates that a type rating is required for a large aircraft. FAR 1.1 defines large aircraft as having a gross weight greater than 12,500 pounds. Answers (A) and (C) are incorrect because a type rating is not required for either kind of operation.

12-17   A20

What is the definition of a high-performance airplane?

A — An airplane with 180 horsepower, or retractable landing gear, flaps, and a fixed-pitch propeller.

B — An airplane with a normal cruise speed in excess of 200 knots.

C — An airplane with an engine of more than 200 horsepower.

12-17. Answer C. (FAR 61.31)

A high-performance airplane is defined as an airplane with an engine of more than 200 horsepower. Answer (A) is incorrect because it lists 180 horsepower as being high-performance. Answer (B) is incorrect because the definition of high-performance has nothing to do with a speed.

12-18   A20

Before a person holding a private pilot certificate may act as pilot in command of a high-performance airplane, that person must have

A — passed a flight test in that airplane from an FAA inspector.

B — an endorsement in that person's logbook that he or she is competent to act as pilot in command.

C — received ground and flight instruction from an authorized flight instructor who then endorses that person's logbook.

12-18 Answer C. (FAR 61.31)

In order to act as pilot in command of a high-performance airplane, you must have received ground and flight instruction from an authorized flight instructor who then endorses that person's logbook. Answer (A) is incorrect because a flight test is not required for a high-performance endorsement. Answer (B) is incomplete because it does not mention flight and ground instruction.

12-19   A20

In order to act as pilot in command of a high-performance airplane, a pilot must have

A — received and logged ground and flight instruction in an airplane that has more than 200 horsepower.

B — made and logged three solo takeoffs and landings in a high-performance airplane.

C — passed a flight test in a high-performance airplane.

12-19. Answer A. (FAR 61.31)

No person may act as pilot in command of a high-performance airplane (an airplane with an engine of more than 200 horsepower) unless that person has received ground and flight instruction from an authorized flight instructor in a high-performance airplane and received a one-time endorsement in that person's logbook showing proficiency. Answers (B) and (C) are incorrect because there are no solo or flight test requirements for high-performance airplanes.

12-20   A20

To act as pilot in command of an aircraft carrying passengers, a pilot must show by logbook endorsement the satisfactory completion of a flight review or completion of a pilot proficiency check within the preceding

A — 6 calendar months.

B — 12 calendar months.

C — 24 calendar months.

12-20. Answer C. (FAR 61.56)

To act as pilot in command of any aircraft, whether you are carrying passengers or not, you must have, within the preceding 24 calendar months, complied with the flight review requirements. Answers (A) and (B) are the wrong time frames for flight review requirements.

12-21   A20
If recency of experience requirements for night flight are not met and official sunset is 1830, the latest time passengers may be carried is

A — 1829.
B — 1859.
C — 1929.

12-22   A20
To act as pilot in command of an aircraft carrying passengers, the pilot must have made at least three takeoffs and three landings in an aircraft of the same category, class, and if a type rating is required, of the same type, within the preceding

A — 90 days.
B — 12 calendar months.
C — 24 calendar months.

12-23   A20
To act as pilot in command of an aircraft carrying passengers, the pilot must have made three takeoffs and three landings within the preceding 90 days in an aircraft of the same

A — make and model.
B — category and class, but not type.
C — category, class, and type, if a type rating is required.

12-24   A20
The takeoffs and landings required to meet the recency of experience requirements for carrying passengers in a tailwheel airplane

A — may be touch and go or full stop.
B — must be touch and go.
C — must be to a full stop.

12-25   A20
The three takeoffs and landings that are required to act as pilot in command at night must be done during the time period from

A — sunset to sunrise.
B — 1 hour after sunset to 1 hour before sunrise.
C — the end of evening civil twilight to the beginning of morning civil twilight.

12-21. Answer C. (FAR 61.57)
No person may act as pilot in command of an aircraft carrying passengers during the period beginning 1 hour after sunset and ending 1 hour before sunrise, unless that person meets night experience requirements. Answers (A) and (B) are wrong because the times are less than one hour after sunset.

12-22. Answer A. (FAR 61.57)
To meet recent flight experience requirements for carrying passengers, the pilot in command must have, within the preceding 90 days, made three takeoffs and landings (to a full stop for night currency requirements). Answers (B) and (C) are incorrect because they exceed the 90 day time period.

12-23. Answer C. (FAR 61.57)
To meet the recency of experience requirements for carrying passengers, FAR 61.57(c) states that you must have made three takeoffs and landings within the preceding 90 days in an aircraft of the same category and class, and if a type rating is required, of the same type. Answer (A) is wrong because make and model is more restrictive than category and class. Answer (B) is incorrect because currency requirements must be met for each aircraft requiring a type rating.

12-24. Answer C. (FAR 61.57)
FAR 61.57(c) states that to meet the recency of experience requirement in a tailwheel airplane, the landings must have been made to a full stop. Answers (A) and (B) are incorrect because a touch and go is not an option for meeting currency requirements in a tailwheel airplane.

12-25. Answer B. (FAR 61.57)
To act as pilot in command of an aircraft carrying passengers between one-hour after sunset and one-hour before sunrise, the pilot must have, within the preceding 90 days, made three takeoffs and landings to a full stop. Answer (A) is not applicable because this is the time period when aircraft lights must be used. Answer (C) is wrong because this is the definition of night, not the time period in the recent flight experience regulation.

12-26   A20
To meet the recency of experience requirements to act as pilot in command carrying passengers at night, a pilot must have made at least three takeoffs and three landings to a full stop within the preceding 90 days in

A — the same category and class of aircraft to be used.
B — the same type of aircraft to be used.
C — any aircraft.

12-27   A20
If a certificated pilot changes permanent mailing address and fails to notify the FAA Airmen Certification Branch of the new address, the pilot is entitled to exercise the privileges of the pilot certificate for a period of only

A — 30 days after the date of the move.
B — 60 days after the date of the move.
C — 90 days after the date of the move.

12-28   A21
A certificated private pilot may not act as pilot in command of an aircraft towing a glider unless there is entered in the pilot's logbook a minimum of

A — 100 hours of pilot-in-command time in the aircraft category, class, and type, if required, that the pilot is using to tow a glider.
B — 200 hours of pilot-in-command time in the aircraft category, class, and type, if required, that the pilot is using to tow a glider.
C — 100 hours of pilot flight time in any aircraft, that the pilot is using to tow a glider.

12-29   A21
To act as pilot in command of an aircraft towing a glider, a pilot is required to have made within the preceding 12 months

A — at least three flights in a powered glider.
B — at least three flights as observer in a glider being towed by an aircraft.
C — at least three actual or simulated glider tows while accompanied by a qualified pilot.

12-26. Answer A. (FAR 61.57)
No person may act as pilot in command of an aircraft carrying passengers at night unless that person has made three takeoffs and three landings to a full stop within the preceding 90 days. The takeoffs and landings must be at night and in the same category and class of aircraft that is to be used for the carriage of passengers.

12-27. Answer A. (FAR 61.60)
As a pilot, you may not exercise the privileges of your certificate after 30 days from the date of your permanent mailing address change unless you notify the FAA's Airman Certificate Branch in writing of the new address. Answers (B) and (C) are incorrect because the time specified exceeds the 30 day limitation.

12-28. Answer A. (FAR 61.69)
No person may act as pilot in command for towing a glider unless that person has logged at least 100 hours of pilot-in-command time in the aircraft category, class, and type, if required, that the pilot is using to tow a glider. Answer (B) is incorrect because the 200 hours of pilot-in-command time is a combination of powered and other-than-powered aircraft and is only required for a pilot who does not have at least 100 hours of pilot-in-command time in airplanes. Answer (C) is incorrect because the 100 hours must be flown in the aircraft category, class, and type, if required.

12-29. Answer C. (FAR 61.69)
The pilot in command of an aircraft towing a glider must have, within the preceding 12 months, made at least three actual or simulated glider tows while accompanied by a qualified pilot, or made at least three flights as PIC of a glider towed by an aircraft. Answer (A) is wrong because the requirement applies to a glider, not a powered glider. Answer (B) is incorrect because the requirement is for three flights as PIC in a glider, not as an observer.

12-30   A29
A recreational pilot acting as pilot in command must have in his or her personal possession while aboard the aircraft

A — a current logbook endorsement to show that a flight review has been satisfactorily accomplished.
B — the pilot logbook to show recent experience requirements to serve as pilot in command have been met.
C — a current logbook endorsement that permits flight within 50 nautical miles from the departure airport.

12-31   A20
A third-class medical certificate was issued to a 19-year old pilot on August 10, this year. To exercise the privileges of a recreational or private pilot certificate, the medical certificate will expire at midnight on

A — August 31, 3 years later.
B — August 31, 2 years later.
C — August 10, 2 years later.

12-32   A20
If a recreational or private pilot had a flight review on August 8, this year, when is the next flight review required?

A — August 31, next year.
B — August 8, 2 years later.
C — August 31, 2 years later.

12-33   A20
Each recreational or private pilot is required to have

A — an annual flight review.
B — a biennial flight review.
C — a semiannual flight review.

12-34   A20
If a recreational or private pilot had a flight review on August 8, this year, when is the next flight review required?

A — August 31, 2 years later.
B — August 31, 1 year later.
C — August 8, next year.

12-30. Answer C. (FAR 61.3)
A recreational pilot may act as pilot in command of an aircraft on a flight that is within 50 nautical miles of the departure airport, provided that person has received a current logbook endorsement from an authorized instructor, and that endorsement is carried on the person's possession in the aircraft. Answers (A) and (B) are incorrect because there are no regulatory requirements for pilots to have proof of currency in their personal possession.

12-31. Answer A. (FAR 61.23)
A third-class medical, which is appropriate to exercise the privileges of a recreational pilot or a private pilot, expires at the end of the 36th calendar month after the date of examination, if under the age of 40. Answer (B) is wrong because it indicates two years instead of three years. Answer (C) is incorrect because a medical certificate expires at the end of the month.

12-32. Answer C. (FAR 61.56)
To act as pilot in command of an aircraft, a recreational or private pilot must have, within the preceding 24 calendar months, complied with the biennial flight review (BFR) requirement. (Calendar month means the review is good until the end of the month in which it expires.) Answer (A) is wrong because there is no requirement for an annual (12 calendar months) flight review. Answer (B) is incorrect because that date is not the last day of the 24th month.

12-33. Answer B. (FAR 61.56)
In order for any pilot to act as pilot in command of an aircraft, that person must have, within the preceding 24 calendar months, complied with the biennial flight review (BFR) requirements. Answer (A) is wrong because an annual flight review is not required. Answer (C) is incorrect because semiannual means six months, not two years.

12-34. Answer A. (FAR 61.56)
To act as pilot in command of an aircraft, a recreational or private pilot must have, within the preceding 24 calendar months, complied with the biennial flight review (BFR) requirement. (Calendar month means the review is good until the end of the month in which it expires.) Answer (B) is wrong because there is no requirement for an annual (12 calendar months) flight review. Answer (C) is incorrect because that date is neither the end of the month nor is it the 24th month.

12-35   A29

How many passengers is a recreational pilot allowed to carry on board?

A — One.
B — Two.
C — Three.

12-36   A29

According to regulations pertaining to privileges and limitations, a recreational pilot may

A — not be paid in any manner for the operating expenses of a flight.
B — be paid for the operating expenses of a flight.
C — not pay less than the pro rata share of the operating expenses of a flight with a passenger.

12-37   A29

In regard to privileges and limitations, a recreational pilot may

A — not pay less than the pro rata share of the operating expenses of a flight with a passenger.
B — fly for compensation or hire within 50 nautical miles from the departure airport with a logbook endorsement.
C — not be paid in any manner for the operating expenses of a flight from a passenger.

12-38   A29

When may a recreational pilot act as pilot in command on a cross-country flight that exceeds 50 nautical miles from the departure airport?

A — After receiving ground and flight instructions on cross-country training and a logbook endorsement.
B — After attaining 100 hours of pilot-in-command time and a logbook endorsement.
C — 12 calendar months after receiving his or her recreational pilot certificate and a logbook endorsement.

12-39   A29

A recreational pilot may act as pilot in command of an aircraft that is certificated for a maximum of how many occupants?

A — Three.
B — Two.
C — Four.

12-35. Answer A. (FAR 61.101)
According to the limitations specified in FAR 61.101(a)(1), a recreational pilot may not carry more than one passenger. Answers (B) and (C) are incorrect because they both exceed the passenger limit for recreational pilots.

12-36. Answer C. (FAR 61.101)
A person who holds a recreational pilot certificate may not pay less than the pro rata share of the operating expenses of a flight with a passenger, provided the expenses involve only fuel, oil, airport expenses, or aircraft rental fees. Answer (A) is incorrect because it indicates that a recreational pilot cannot share operating expenses of a flight in any manner. Answer (B) is wrong because it indicates that the recreational pilot will be paid for all operating expenses and will not share in the cost.

12-37. Answer A. (FAR 61.101)
A person who holds a recreational pilot certificate may not pay less than the pro rata share of the operating expenses of a flight with a passenger, provided the expenses involve only fuel, oil, airport expenses, or aircraft rental fees. Answer (B) is incorrect because a recreational pilot cannot fly for hire under any circumstances. Answer (C) is incorrect because it indicates that a recreational pilot cannot share the operating expenses of the flight.

12-38. Answer A. (FAR 61.101)
A person who holds a recreational pilot certificate may act as pilot in command of an aircraft on a flight that exceeds 50 nautical miles from the departure airport, provided that person has received ground and flight training from an authorized instructor on cross-country training and received a logbook endorsement which is carried on that person's possession in the aircraft. Answer (B) is wrong because the regulations do not specify 100 hours of pilot-in-command time as a requirement. Answer (C) is incorrect because the regulations do not specify a time period requirement such as 12 calendar months.

12-39. Answer C. (FAR 61.101)
This regulation states that a recreational pilot may not act as pilot in command of an aircraft that is certificated for more than four occupants. Answers (A) and (B) are wrong because they are less than the maximum occupancy limit for recreational pilots.

12-40   A29
A recreational pilot may act as pilot in command of an aircraft with a maximum engine horsepower of

A — 160.
B — 180.
C — 200.

12-41   A29
What exception, if any, permits a recreational pilot to act as pilot in command of an aircraft carrying a passenger for hire?

A — If the passenger pays no more than the operating expenses.
B — If a donation is made to a charitable organization for the flight.
C — There is no exception.

12-42   A29
May a recreational pilot act as pilot in command of an aircraft in furtherance of a business?

A — Yes, if the flight is only incidental to that business.
B — Yes, providing the aircraft does not carry a person or property for compensation or hire.
C — No, it is not allowed.

12-43   A29
With respect to daylight hours, what is the earliest time a recreational pilot may take off?

A — One hour before sunrise.
B — At sunrise.
C — At the beginning of morning civil twilight.

12-44   A29
If sunset is 2021 and the end of evening civil twilight is 2043, when must a recreational pilot terminate the flight?

A — 2021.
B — 2043.
C — 2121.

12-40. Answer B. (FAR 61.101)
A recreational pilot may not act as pilot in command of an aircraft that is certificated with more than 180 horsepower. Answer (A) is incorrect because it is less than the maximum horsepower limit for recreational pilots. Answer (C) is wrong because it exceeds the 180 maximum horsepower limit for recreational pilots.

12-41. Answer C. (FAR 61.101)
A recreational pilot may only share operating expenses with a passenger, there are no exceptions. Answer (A) is wrong because it implies that the passenger is permitted to pay all of the operating expenses. Answer (B) is incorrect because recreational pilots are specifically prohibited from being a participant in a passenger-carrying airlift sponsored by a charitable organization.

12-42. Answer C. (FAR 61.101)
The regulation specifically states that a recreational pilot is prohibited from flying in furtherance of a business. Answer (A) is incorrect because, even if the flight is incidental to business, it is still considered in the furtherance of business. Answer (B) is incorrect because, even if the flight is not conducted for compensation or hire, the intended purpose is still considered for the furtherance of business.

12-43. Answer B. (FAR 61.101)
A recreational pilot may not act as pilot in command of an aircraft between sunset and sunrise. Therefore the earliest takeoff time is sunrise. Answer (A) refers to night as defined for currency purposes under FAR 61.57. Answer (C) is also incorrect. It is part of the definition of night under FAR 1.1.

12-44. Answer A. (FAR 61.101)
As indicated in the previous answer, a recreational pilot may not act as pilot in command of an aircraft between sunset and sunrise. Answers (B) and (C) are incorrect because both of these times are after 2021.

12-45   A29

When may a recreational pilot operate to or from an airport that lies within Class C airspace?

A — Anytime the control tower is in operation.
B — When the ceiling is at least 1,000 feet and the surface visibility is at least 3 miles.
C — For the purpose of obtaining an additional certificate or rating while under the supervision of an authorized flight instructor.

12-46   A29

Under what conditions may a recreational pilot operate at an airport that lies within Class D airspace and that has a part-time control tower in operation?

A — Any time when the tower is in operation, the ceiling is at least 3,000 feet, and the visibility is more than 1 mile.
B — Between sunrise and sunset when the tower is in operation, the ceiling is at least 2,500 feet, and the visibility is at least 3 miles.
C — Between sunrise and sunset when the tower is closed, the ceiling is at least 1,000 feet, and the visibility is at least 3 miles.

12-47   A29

When may a recreational pilot fly above 10,000 feet MSL?

A — When 2,000 feet AGL or below.
B — When 2,500 feet AGL or below.
C — When outside of controlled airspace.

12-48   A29

During daytime, what is the minimum flight or surface visibility required for recreational pilots in Class G airspace below 10,000 feet MSL?

A — 1 mile.
B — 3 miles.
C — 5 miles.

12-45. Answer C. (FAR 61.101)

A recreational pilot may operate in airspace, such as Class C airspace, that requires communication with air traffic control only when such operations are conducted for the purpose of obtaining additional certificates or ratings. These operations must be under the supervision of an authorized flight instructor. Answer (A) is incorrect because it does not state that the operation is for the purpose of obtaining an additional certificate or rating. Answer (B) is incorrect because it implies that as long as visibility minimums are maintained, a recreational pilot may enter Class C airspace.

12-46. Answer C. (FAR 61.101, 91.155)

A recreational pilot may not operate in airspace in which communications are required with ATC. An example is within Class D airspace. However, Class D airspace is only valid when the tower is operational. When the tower is closed, this airspace becomes Class E. If the ceiling is at least 1,000 feet AGL, and the visibility is at least three miles, a recreational pilot may legally operate at an airport in Class E airspace under visual flight rules (VFR). A recreational pilot is also limited to flight between sunrise and sunset. Answers (A) and (B) are wrong because the tower is operational, which makes the airspace Class D.

12-47. Answer A. (FAR 61.101)

A recreational pilot cannot fly above an altitude of 10,000 feet MSL, unless the aircraft is within 2,000 feet of the ground. Answer (B) is wrong because a recreational pilot may fly above 10,000 feet when at 2,000 feet AGL, or less, not 2,500 feet above the surface. Answer (C) is incorrect because whether the airspace is controlled or uncontrolled, a recreational pilot is not authorized to fly above 10,000 feet MSL unless the aircraft is within 2,000 feet AGL.

12-48. Answer B. (FAR 61.101)

A recreational pilot may not act as pilot in command of an aircraft when the flight or surface visibility is less than three statute miles. Answer (A) is wrong; the minimum daytime visibility requirement is three statute miles, not one. Answer (C) is incorrect because the minimum daytime flight or surface visibility for a recreational pilot in either controlled or uncontrolled airspace is three, not five, statute miles.

12-49   A29
During daytime, what is the minimum flight visibility required for recreational pilots in controlled airspace below 10,000 feet MSL?

A — 1 mile.
B — 3 miles.
C — 5 miles.

12-49. Answer B. (FAR 61.101)
This question and the answer choices are almost identical to the previous question (12-48). A recreational pilot may not act as pilot in command of an aircraft when the flight or surface visibility is less than three statute miles. Answer (A) is less than the recreational pilot's minimum and therefore is incorrect. Answer (C) is incorrect because it corresponds to either the visibility minimum above 10,000 MSL, or the night visibility minimum that applies to a student pilot.

12-50   A29
Under what conditions, if any, may a recreational pilot demonstrate an aircraft in flight to a prospective buyer?

A — The buyer pays all the operating expenses.
B — The flight is not outside the United States.
C — None.

12-50. Answer C. (FAR 61.101)
FAR 61.101(b)(12) specifically prohibits recreational pilots from demonstrating an aircraft in flight to prospective buyers. Answers (A) and (B) are obviously incorrect because there are no conditions under which a recreational pilot can demonstrate an aircraft, in flight, to a prospective buyer.

12-51   A29
When, if ever, may a recreational pilot act as pilot in command in an aircraft towing a banner?

A — If the pilot has logged 100 hours of flight time in powered aircraft.
B — If the pilot has an endorsement in his/her pilot logbook from an authorized flight instructor.
C — It is not allowed.

12-51. Answer C. (FAR 61.101)
FAR 61.101(b)(14) specifically prohibits recreational pilots from towing any object. Answers (A) and (B) are eliminated with selection of answer (C).

12-52   A29
When must a recreational pilot have a pilot-in-command flight check?

A — Every 400 hours.
B — Every 180 days.
C — If the pilot has less than 400 total flight hours and has not flown as pilot in command in an aircraft within the preceding 180 days.

12-52. Answer C. (FAR 61.101)
A recreational pilot who has logged fewer than 400 flight hours and who has not logged pilot-in-command time in an aircraft within the preceding 180 days may not act as pilot in command of an aircraft until the pilot receives flight instruction from an authorized flight instructor who certifies in the pilot's logbook that the recreational pilot is competent to act as pilot in command. Answers (A) and (B) are incomplete and incorrect.

12-53   A29
A recreational pilot may fly as sole occupant of an aircraft at night while under the supervision of a flight instructor provided the flight or surface visibility is at least

A — 3 miles.
B — 4 miles.
C — 5 miles.

12-53. Answer C. (FAR 61.101)
For the purpose of obtaining additional certificates or ratings, while under the supervision of an authorized flight instructor, a recreational pilot may fly as sole occupant of an aircraft between sunset and sunrise, provided the flight or surface visibility is at least five statute miles. Answers (A) and (B) are less than the required minimum.

12-54   A23

In regard to privileges and limitations, a private pilot may

A — not be paid in any manner for the operating expenses of a flight.

B — not pay less than the pro rata share of the operating expenses of a flight with passengers provided the expenses involve only fuel, oil, airport expenditures, or rental fees.

C — act as pilot in command of an aircraft carrying a passenger for compensation if the flight is in connection with a business or employment.

12-55   A23

According to regulations pertaining to privileges and limitations, a private pilot may

A — not pay less than the pro rata share of the operating expenses of a flight with passengers provided the expenses involve only fuel, oil, airport expenditures, or rental fees.

B — not be paid in any manner for the operating expenses of a flight.

C — be paid for the operating expenses of a flight if at least three takeoffs and three landings were made by the pilot within the preceding 90 days.

12-56   A23

What exception, if any, permits a private pilot to act as pilot in command of an aircraft carrying passengers who pay for the flight?

A — If the passengers pay all the operating expenses.

B — If a donation is made to a charitable organization for the flight.

C — There is no exception.

12-54. Answer B. (FAR 61.113)

A private pilot may not pay less than the pro rata share of the operating expenses of a flight with passengers, provided the expenses involve only fuel, oil, airport expenditures, or rental fees. Answer (A) is wrong because it says that a private pilot cannot share the operating expenses of the flight. Answer (C) is incorrect because when a private pilot receives compensation for a flight that is in connection with a business or employment, the flight must be incidental to that business and the aircraft must not carry any passengers or property for compensation or hire.

12-55. Answer A. (FAR 61.113)

A private pilot may not pay less than the pro rata share of the operating expenses of a flight with passengers, provided the expenses involve only fuel, oil, airport expenditures, or rental fees. Answer (B) is wrong because it indicates that a private pilot cannot share the operating expenses of the flight. Answer (C) is incorrect because it indicates that the private pilot will be paid for all operating expenses and will not share in the cost.

12-56. Answer B. (FAR 61.113)

Paragraph 61.113 of the FARs indicates a private pilot may act as pilot in command of an aircraft used in a passenger-carrying airlift sponsored by a charitable organization, and for which the passengers make a donation to the organization. Answer (A) is incorrect because it indicates that the private pilot will be paid for all operating expenses and will not share in the cost. Answer (C) is incorrect because it applies to recreational pilots.

SECTION C
PART 91—GENERAL OPERATING AND FLIGHT RULES

As a pilot, you must be familiar with the "rules of the sky" in order to operate safely in the National Airspace System. The regulations covered in this section are an important part of your aeronautical knowledge.

PREVENTIVE MAINTENANCE
1. When preventive maintenance has been performed on an aircraft, the signature, certificate number, and kind of certificate held by the person approving the work must be entered in the aircraft maintenance records.

PILOT IN COMMAND
2. The pilot in command is the final authority as to the operation of an aircraft.
3. The pilot in command is directly responsible for the pre-launch briefing of the passengers for a flight.
4. If an in-flight emergency requires immediate action, the pilot in command may deviate from the FARs to the extent required to meet that emergency. A written report is not required unless requested by the FAA.

DROPPING OBJECTS
5. Objects may be dropped from an aircraft if precautions are taken to avoid injury or damage to persons or property on the surface.

DRUGS AND ALCOHOL
6. A pilot may allow a person who is obviously under the influence of drugs to be carried aboard the aircraft in an emergency, or if the person is a medical patient under proper care.
7. A person may not act as a crewmember of a civil aircraft if alcoholic beverages have been consumed within the preceding 8 hours.
8. No person may act as a crewmember of a civil aircraft with .04 percent by weight or more alcohol in the blood.

SAFETY BELTS
9. Flight crewmembers are required to keep their safety belts and shoulder harnesses fastened during takeoffs and landings. Safety belts must stay fastened while en route.
10. The pilot in command must brief the passengers on the use of safety belts and notify them to fasten their safety belts during taxi, takeoff and landing. Passengers must have their safety belts fastened during taxi, takeoffs and landings.

FORMATION FLIGHT
11. No person may operate an aircraft in formation flight except by prior arrangement with the pilot in command of each aircraft.

SEAPLANES
12. When an aircraft, or an aircraft and a vessel, are on crossing courses, the aircraft or vessel to the other's right has the right-of-way.

AIRSPEED
13. Unless otherwise authorized, the maximum indicated airspeed at which a person may operate an aircraft below 10,000 feet MSL is 250 knots. This is also the maximum indicated airspeed within Class B airspace.
14. Under Class B airspace, or in a VFR corridor through a Class B area, no person shall operate at an indicated airspeed of more than 200 knots.

ATC CLEARANCES
15. When an ATC clearance has been obtained, no pilot may deviate from that clearance, unless that pilot obtains an amended clearance. The exception to this regulation is in an emergency.
16. A pilot who deviates from a clearance, and is given priority by ATC because of that emergency, shall submit a detailed report of that emergency within 48 hours to the manager of that facility, if requested by ATC.

TRAFFIC PATTERNS

17. The correct traffic pattern procedure to use at a noncontrolled airport is to comply with any FAA traffic pattern established for the airport.

AIRCRAFT DOCUMENTS

18. In addition to a valid Airworthiness Certificate, operating limitations and the registration certificate must also be on board an aircraft during flight.

ELTS

19. When the ELT has been in use for more than 1 cumulative hour, or if 50 percent of the useful life the batteries expires, the batteries must be replaced or recharged.

POSITION LIGHTS

20. During sunset to sunrise, except in Alaska, lighted position lights must be displayed on an aircraft.

SUPPLEMENTAL OXYGEN

21. When operating an aircraft at cabin pressure altitudes above 12,500 feet MSL up to and including 14,000 feet MSL, supplemental oxygen shall be used, by required crewmembers, during that flight time in excess of 30 minutes at those altitudes.
22. Unless each person is provided with supplemental oxygen, no person may operate a civil aircraft of US registry above a maximum cabin pressure altitude of 15,000 feet MSL.

ACROBATIC FLIGHT

23. No person may operate an aircraft in acrobatic flight when over any congested area of a city, town or settlement.
24. Acrobatic flight is prohibited in Class D airspace, and Class E airspace designated for Federal Airways.
25. The lowest altitude permitted for acrobatic flight is 1500 feet AGL. In-flight visibility must be at least 3 miles.

PARACHUTES

26. A chair-type parachute must have been packed by a certificated and appropriately rated parachute rigger within the preceding 120 days.
27. With certain exceptions, each occupant must wear an approved parachute when intentionally pitching the nose of the aircraft up or down more than 30° or exceeding 60° of bank.

RESTRICTED/EXPERIMENTAL AIRCRAFT

28. Flight over densely populated areas is prohibited in restricted category aircraft.
29. Unless specifically authorized, no person may operate an aircraft that has an experimental certificate over a densely populated area or in a congested airway.

MAINTENANCE

30. The responsibility for ensuring that maintenance personnel make the appropriate entries in the aircraft maintenance records, indicating the aircraft has been approved for return to service, lies with the owner or operator.
31. Completion of an annual inspection and the return of the aircraft to service should always be indicated by an appropriate notation in the aircraft maintenance records.
32. If an alteration or repair substantially affects an aircraft's operation in flight, that aircraft must be flown by an appropriately rated private pilot and approved for return to service before being operated with passengers aboard.
33. No person may operate an aircraft unless, within the preceding 12 calendar months, it has had an annual inspection.
34. To determine the expiration date of the last annual inspection, a person should refer to the aircraft maintenance records.
35. The required inspections for rental aircraft that are used for flight instruction are annual and 100-hour inspections.
36. No person may operate an aircraft carrying any person for hire, or give flight instruction for hire in an aircraft, which that person provides, unless within the preceding 100 hours of time in service, the aircraft has received an annual or 100-hour inspection. The aircraft may be flown beyond the 100 hours if it is being transported to a place where service can be completed. However, the next 100 hour inspection must be completed within 100 hours of the original expiration time.

37. The owner or operator of an aircraft shall keep a record of current status of applicable airworthiness directives in the aircraft maintenance records.

TRANSPONDERS

38. An ATC transponder must be inspected, tested, and found to comply with standards every 24 calendar months.
39. All operations within Class C airspace must be in an aircraft equipped with a 4096-code transponder with Mode C encoding capability.

12-57   A13
What should an owner or operator know about Airworthiness Directives (AD's)?

A — For Informational purposes only.
B — They are mandatory.
C — They are voluntary.

12-58   A13
May a pilot operate an aircraft that is not in compliance with an Airworthiness Directive (AD)?

A — Yes, under VFR conditions only.
B — Yes, AD's are only voluntary.
C — Yes, if allowed by the AD.

12-59   A15
Preventive maintenance has been performed on an aircraft. What paperwork is required?

A — A full, detailed description of the work done must be entered in the airframe logbook.
B — The date the work was completed, and the name of the person who did the work must be entered in the airframe and engine logbook.
C — The signature, certificate number, and kind of certificate held by the person approving the work and a description of the work must be entered in the aircraft maintenance records.

12-60   A15
What regulation allows a private pilot to perform preventive maintenance?

A.   14 CFR Part 91.403.
B.   14 CFR Part 43.7.
C.   14 CFR Part 61.113.

12-61   A15
Who may perform preventive maintenance on an aircraft and approve it for return to service?

A.   Private or Commercial pilot.
B.   Student or Recreational pilot.
C.   None of the above.

12-57. Answer B. (FAR 39)
ADs are published as part of the FARs. You may not operate an aircraft to which an airworthiness directive applies, except in accordance with that airworthiness directive.

12-58. Answer C. (FAR 39)
ADs are published as part of the FARs. You may not operate an aircraft to which an airworthiness directive applies, except in accordance with that airworthiness directive.

12-59. Answer C. (FAR 91.417, FAR Part 43.9)
FAR 91.417 states that records of preventive maintenance must include a description of the work performed, the date of completion, and the signature and certificate number of the person approving the aircraft for return to service. In addition, FAR 43.9 also indicates that the kind of certificate held by the person approving the work must be included in the record. Answers (A) and (B) are incorrect because if there are separate logbooks for the engine, propeller, and airframe normally only that kind of work would be recorded in the appropriate logbook.

12-60. Answer B. (FAR 43.7)
14 CFR Part 43 covers preventive maintenance. If you hold at least a private pilot certificate, you may perform preventive maintenance such as replacing and servicing batteries, replacing spark plugs, servicing wheel bearings, etc.

12-61. Answer A. (FAR 43.7)
14 CFR Part 43 covers preventive maintenance. If you hold at least a private pilot certificate, you may perform preventive maintenance such as replacing and servicing batteries, replacing spark plugs, servicing wheel bearings, etc.

12-62   B07
The final authority as to the operation of an aircraft is the

A — Federal Aviation Administration.
B — pilot in command.
C — aircraft manufacturer.

12-63   B07
The person directly responsible for the pre-launch briefing of passengers for a flight is the

A — safety officer.
B — pilot in command.
C — ground crewmember.

12-64   B07
If an in-flight emergency requires immediate action, the pilot in command may

A — deviate from the FAR's to the extent required to meet the emergency, but must submit a written report to the Administrator within 24 hours.
B — deviate from the FAR's to the extent required to meet that emergency.
C — not deviate from the FAR's unless prior to the deviation approval is granted by the Administrator.

12-65   B07
When must a pilot who deviates from a regulation during an emergency send a written report of that deviation to the Administrator?

A — Within 7 days.
B — Within 10 days.
C — Upon request.

12-66   B07
Who is responsible for determining if an aircraft is in condition for safe flight?

A — A certificated aircraft mechanic.
B — The pilot in command.
C — The owner or operator.

12-67   B07
Under what conditions may objects be dropped from an aircraft?

A — Only in an emergency.
B — If precautions are taken to avoid injury or damage to persons or property on the surface.
C — If prior permission is received from the Federal Aviation Administration.

12-62. Answer B. (FAR 91.3)
As clearly indicated in the regulation, the pilot in command of an aircraft is directly responsible for, and is the final authority as to, the operation of that aircraft. Therefore (B) is the only correct answer.

12-63. Answer B. (FAR 91.3)
The pilot in command of an aircraft is directly responsible for operation of that aircraft. Therefore, the pilot in command is responsible for pre-launch passenger briefing on safety belts according to FAR 91.107, as well as other pertinent information. Answers (A) and (C) normally do not apply to private pilot operations.

12-64. Answer B. (FAR 91.3)
In an in-flight emergency requiring immediate action, the pilot in command may deviate from any rule to the extent required to meet that emergency. Answer (A) is incorrect because a written report is not required unless it is requested from the FAA. Answer (C) is incorrect because it is not practicable (if not impossible) to get prior permission to deviate from a FAR in an actual emergency situation.

12-65. Answer C. (FAR 91.3)
The regulations clearly indicate that a written report is not required, unless a report is requested from the FAA. Answers (A) and (B) are incorrect because they indicate that a written report must automatically be submitted upon deviation of the FARs during an emergency.

12-66. Answer B. (FAR 91.7)
The pilot in command of a civil aircraft is responsible, and has final authority, for determining whether that aircraft is in condition for safe flight. Answers (A) and (C) indicate that the pilot in command does not make the final determination.

12-67. Answer B. (FAR 91.15)
Objects can be dropped from an aircraft in flight, if reasonable precautions are taken to avoid injury or damage to persons or property. Answer (A) is incorrect because it indicates that objects are always prohibited from being dropped. Answer (C) is incorrect because there is no requirement for FAA notification.

12-68   B07
A person may not act as a crewmember of a civil aircraft if alcoholic beverages have been consumed by that person within the preceding

A — 8 hours.
B — 12 hours.
C — 24 hours.

12-69   B07
Under what condition, if any, may a pilot allow a person who is obviously under the influence of drugs to be carried aboard an aircraft?

A — In an emergency or if the person is a medical patient under proper care.
B — Only if the person does not have access to the cockpit or pilot's compartment.
C — Under no condition.

12-70   B07
No person may attempt to act as a crewmember of a civil aircraft with

A —.008 percent by weight or more alcohol in the blood.
B —.004 percent by weight or more alcohol in the blood.
C — .04 percent by weight or more alcohol in the blood.

12-71   B07
Which preflight action is specifically required of the pilot prior to each flight?

A —Check the aircraft logbooks for appropriate entries.
B — Become familiar with all available information concerning the flight.
C — Review wake turbulence avoidance procedures.

12-72   B07
Preflight action, as required for all flights away from the vicinity of an airport, shall include

A — the designation of an alternate airport.
B — a study of arrival procedures at airports/heliports of intended use.
C — an alternate course of action if the flight cannot be completed as planned.

12-73   B07
In addition to other preflight actions for a VFR flight away from the vicinity of the departure airport, regulations specifically require the pilot in command to

A — review traffic control light signal procedures.
B — check the accuracy of the navigation equipment and the emergency locator transmitter (ELT).
C — determine runway lengths at airports of intended use and the aircraft's takeoff and landing distance data.

12-68. Answer A. (FAR 91.17)
A common saying used in aviation for this regulation is "eight hours from bottle to throttle." In other words, no person may act or attempt to act as a crewmember of a civil aircraft within eight hours after the consumption of any alcoholic beverage.

12-69. Answer A. (FAR 91.17)
Except in an emergency, no pilot of a civil aircraft may allow a person who appears to be intoxicated or who demonstrates by manner or physical indications that the individual is under the influence of drugs (except a patient under proper care) to be carried in that aircraft. Answer (B) is incorrect because there are no provisions for limiting passenger access to the cockpit. Answer (C) is incorrect because a person under medical care can be under the influence of drugs.

12-70. Answer C. (FAR 91.17)
No person may act or attempt to act as a crewmember of a civil aircraft while having .04 percent by weight or more alcohol in the blood. Answers (A) and (B) are incorrect because the alcohol blood contents are far below the limit set by the regulations.

12-71. Answer B. (FAR 91.103)
Each pilot in command shall, before beginning a flight, become familiar with all available information concerning that flight. Answer (A) is incorrect because it addresses only the aircraft preflight inspection. Answer (C) is wrong because not all of the available information concerning the flight is utilized.

12-72. Answer C. (FAR 91.103)
The preflight action for flights away from the vicinity of an airport include checking weather reports and forecasts, fuel requirements, alternatives available if the flight cannot be completed as planned, and any known traffic delays. Answer (A) is incorrect because alternate airports are only a requirement for instrument flight rules. Answer (B) is not a specific requirement under FAR 91.103 and is incorrect because the pilot is not using all of the available information concerning the flight.

12-73. Answer C. (FAR 91.103)
For any flight, a pilot must determine runway lengths at airports of use and the airplane's takeoff and landing distance data. Answers (A) and (B) are not specific to FAR 91.103.

12-74   B07
Flight crewmembers are required to keep their safety belts and shoulder harnesses fastened during

A — takeoffs and landings.
B — all flight conditions.
C — flight in turbulent air.

12-75   B07
Which best describes the flight conditions under which flight crewmembers are specifically required to keep their safety belts and shoulder harnesses fastened?

A — Safety belts during takeoff and landing; shoulder harnesses during takeoff and landing.
B — Safety belts during takeoff and landing; shoulder harnesses during takeoff and landing and while en route.
C — Safety belts during takeoff and landing and while en route; shoulder harnesses during takeoff and landing.

12-76   B07
With respect to passengers, what obligation, if any, does a pilot in command have concerning the use of safety belts?

A — The pilot in command must instruct the passengers to keep safety belts fastened for the entire flight.
B — The pilot in command must brief the passengers on the use of safety belts and notify them to fasten their safety belts during taxi, takeoff, and landing.
C — The pilot in command has no obligation in regard to passengers' use of safety belts.

12-77   B07
With certain exceptions, safety belts are required to be secured about passengers during

A — taxi, takeoffs, and landings.
B — all flight conditions.
C — flight in turbulent air.

12-78   B07
Safety belts are required to be properly secured about which persons in an aircraft and when?

A — Pilots only, during takeoffs and landings.
B — Passengers, during taxi, takeoffs, and landings only.
C — Each person on board the aircraft during the entire flight.

12-74. Answer A. (FAR 91.105)
According to the regulation, safety belts are required during takeoff and landing and while enroute. In addition, shoulder harnesses are required during takeoff and landing, unless the seat of the crewmembers' stations are not equipped with shoulder harnesses, or the crewmembers are not able to perform their duties with the shoulder harness fastened. Answers (B) and (C) are incorrect because shoulder harnesses are only required during takeoff and landing.

12-75. Answer C. (FAR 91.105)
During takeoff and landing, and while enroute, each required flight crewmember shall keep the safety belt fastened while at the crewmember station. In addition, each required flight crewmember shall, during takeoff and landing, keep the shoulder harness fastened while at the crewmember station. Answer (A) is wrong because safety belts are required while enroute. Answer (B) is incorrect because shoulder harnesses are not required while enroute.

12-76. Answer B. (FAR 91.107)
The pilot in command must ensure that each person on board is briefed on how to fasten and unfasten the safety belt and shoulder harness, as well as ensure all persons on board are notified to fasten their safety belt (and shoulder harness, if installed) during taxi, takeoff, or landing. Answer (A) is incorrect because safety restraints are only required for passengers during taxi, takeoff, and landings. Answer (C) is incorrect because FAR 91.107 specifically puts the responsibility and obligation on the pilot in command.

12-77. Answer A. (FAR 91.107)
Passengers are only required to have safety belts (and shoulder harnesses, if installed) fastened during taxi, takeoff, and landing. Answers (B) and (C) are incorrect because safety restraints are not required at all times, nor are they required during turbulent air conditions.

12-78. Answer B. (FAR 91.107)
Passengers are required to have safety belts (and shoulder harnesses, if installed) fastened during taxi, takeoff, and landing. Answer (A) is incorrect because pilots must wear restraints while enroute and while at their stations. Answer (C) is incorrect because safety restraints are not required at all times for passengers or crewmembers when they are not at their station.

12-79   B08
No person may operate an aircraft in formation flight

A — over a densely populated area.
B — in Class D airspace under special VFR.
C — except by prior arrangement with the pilot in
      command of each aircraft.

12-80   B08
A seaplane and a motorboat are crossing courses. If the motorboat is to the left of the seaplane, which has the right-of-way?

A — The motorboat.
B — The seaplane.
C — Both should alter course to the right.

12-81   B08
Unless otherwise authorized, what is the maximum indicated airspeed at which a person may operate an aircraft below 10,000 feet MSL?

A — 200 knots.
B — 250 knots.
C — 288 knots.

12-82   B08
Unless otherwise authorized, the maximum indicated airspeed at which aircraft may be flown when at or below 2,500 feet AGL and within four nautical miles of the primary airport of Class C airspace is

A — 200 knots.
B — 230 knots.
C — 250 knots.

12-83   B08
When flying in the airspace underlying Class B airspace, the maximum speed authorized is

A — 200 knots.
B — 230 knots.
C — 250 knots.

12-79. Answer C. (FAR 91.111)
No person may operate an aircraft in formation flight except by arrangement with the pilot in command of each aircraft in the formation. Answers (A) and (B) are incorrect because there are no special restrictions concerning formation flight over densely populated areas or in Class D airspace.

12-80. Answer B. (FAR 91.115)
When an aircraft, or an aircraft and a vessel, are on crossing courses, the aircraft or vessel to the other's right has the right-of-way. Answer (A) is incorrect because the aircraft is to the right of the motorboat and has the right-of-way. Answer (C) is wrong because it applies only to vehicles approaching head on.

12-81. Answer B. (FAR 91.117)
Unless otherwise authorized by the Administrator, no person may operate an aircraft below 10,000 feet MSL at an indicated airspeed of more than 250 knots. Answer (A) is incorrect because this airspeed limitation applies when operating below 2,500 feet above the surface when within four nautical miles of the primary airport of a Class C or D airspace area. It is also the airspeed limitation for operating within the airspace underlying a Class B airspace area, or in a VFR corridor designated through such a Class B airspace area. Answer (C) is incorrect because the correct answer is 288 mph not 288 knots.

12-82. Answer A. (FAR 91.117)
The maximum indicated airspeed inside or within 4 n.m. of the primary airport in Class C airspace is 200 knots. Answer (B) is incorrect because this is the speed in miles per hour, not knots. Answer (C) is the allowable speed within Class B, not C, airspace.

12-83. Answer A. (FAR 91.117)
No person may operate an aircraft in the airspace underlying a Class B airspace area, or in a VFR corridor designated through a Class B airspace area, at an indicated airspeed of more than 200 knots. Answer (B) is wrong because the correct answer is 230 mph not 230 knots. Answer (C) is incorrect because this speed applies to either the speed restriction below 10,000 feet MSL, or the speed restriction for operations within a Class B airspace area.

12-84   B08

When flying in a VFR corridor designated through Class B airspace, the maximum speed authorized is

A — 180 knots.
B — 200 knots.
C — 250 knots.

12-84. Answer B. (FAR 91.117)

No person may operate an aircraft in a VFR corridor designated through a Class B airspace area, or in the airspace underlying a Class B airspace area, at an indicated airspeed of more than 200 knots. Answer (A) is wrong because 180 knots does not apply to any airspeed restriction. Answer (C) is incorrect because this speed applies to either the speed restriction below 10,000 feet MSL, or the speed restriction for operations within a Class B airspace area.

12-85   B08

When an ATC clearance has been obtained, no pilot in command may deviate from that clearance, unless that pilot obtains an amended clearance. The one exception to this regulation is

A — when the clearance states "at pilot's discretion."
B — an emergency.
C — if the clearance contains a restriction.

12-85. Answer B. (FAR 91.123)

According the FAR 91.23(a), when an ATC clearance has been obtained, no pilot in command may deviate from that clearance, except in an emergency, unless an amended clearance is obtained. Answer (A) is incorrect because "at pilot's discretion" means that the pilot must still comply with the clearance. Answer (C) is incorrect because a clearance restriction has no bearing on complying with ATC instructions.

12-86   B08

When would a pilot be required to submit a detailed report of an emergency which caused the pilot to deviate from an ATC clearance?

A — When requested by ATC.
B — Immediately.
C — Within 7 days.

12-86. Answer A. (FAR 91.3, 91.123)

According to FAR 91.123(d), a pilot in command who deviates from a clearance and then is given priority by ATC because of that emergency, shall submit a detailed report of that emergency within 48 hours to the manager of that ATC facility, if requested by ATC. Answer (B) is incorrect because you are allowed 48 hours to submit the report. Answer (C) is a specification found for reporting an overdue aircraft under NTSB 830.15(a).

12-87   B08

What action, if any, is appropriate if the pilot deviates from an ATC instruction during an emergency and is given priority?

A — Take no special action since you are pilot in command.
B — File a detailed report within 48 hours to the chief of the appropriate ATC facility, if requested.
C — File a report to the FAA Administrator, as soon as possible.

12-87. Answer B. (FAR 91.123)

A pilot in command who is given priority by ATC because of an emergency, shall submit a detailed report of that emergency within 48 hours to the manager of that ATC facility, if requested by ATC. Answer (A) is incorrect because of the above reason. Answer (C) is incorrect because according to FAR 91.3, you must file a report with an FAA administrator (not ATC) when an FAR was violated, as a result of an emergency, and a report is requested from the administrator.

12-88   B08

Which is the correct traffic pattern departure procedure to use at a noncontrolled airport?

A — Depart in any direction consistent with safety, after crossing the airport boundary.
B — Make all turns to the left.
C — Comply with any FAA traffic pattern established for the airport.

12-88. Answer C. (FAR 91.127)

Each person operating an aircraft to or from an airport without an operating control tower shall, in the case of an aircraft departing the airport, comply with any traffic patterns established for that airport in Part 93. Answers (A) and (B) are incorrect because they will not always comply with established traffic patterns.

12-89   B09

What is the specific fuel requirement for flight under VFR during daylight hours in an airplane?

A — Enough to complete the flight at normal cruising speed with adverse wind conditions.
B — Enough to fly to the first point of intended landing and to fly after that for 30 minutes at normal cruising speed.
C — Enough to fly to the first point of intended landing and to fly after that for 45 minutes at normal cruising speed.

12-90   B09

What is the specific fuel requirement for flight under VFR at night in an airplane?

A — Enough to complete the flight at normal cruising speed with adverse wind conditions.
B — Enough to fly to the first point of intended landing and to fly after that for 30 minutes at normal cruising speed.
C — Enough to fly to the first point of intended landing and to fly after that for 45 minutes at normal cruising speed.

12-91   B09

What minimum visibility and clearance from clouds are required for a recreational pilot in Class G airspace at 1,200 feet AGL or below during daylight hours?

A — 1 mile visibility and clear of clouds.
B — 3 miles visibility and clear of clouds.
C — 3 miles visibility, 500 feet below the clouds.

12-92   B09

Outside controlled airspace, the minimum flight visibility requirement for a recreational pilot flying VFR above 1,200 feet AGL and below 10,000 feet MSL during daylight hours is

A — 1 mile.
B — 3 miles.
C — 5 miles.

12-93   B11

In addition to a valid Airworthiness Certificate, what documents or records must be aboard an aircraft during flight?

A — Aircraft engine and airframe logbooks, and owner's manual.
B — Radio operator's permit, and repair and alteration forms.
C — Operating limitations and Registration Certificate.

12-89. Answer B. (FAR 91.151)

For day VFR flight in an airplane, there must be enough fuel (considering wind and forecast weather conditions) to fly to the first point of intended landing, and, assuming normal cruising speed, 30 minutes thereafter. Answer (A) is incorrect because the fuel required is based on forecasted weather, not adverse winds. Answer (C) is incorrect because it is based on night VFR.

12-90. Answer C. (FAR 91.151)

For night VFR flight in an airplane, there must be enough fuel (considering wind and forecast weather conditions) to fly to the first point of intended landing, and assuming normal cruising speed, 45 minutes thereafter. Answer (A) is incorrect because the fuel required is based on forecasted weather, not adverse winds. Answer (B) is incorrect because it is based on day VFR.

12-91. Answer B. (FAR 61.101, 91.155)

VFR minimums for uncontrolled airspace at 1,200 feet AGL, or below, is one mile visibility and clear of clouds. However, recreational pilots must have at least three miles visibility. Answer (A) is incorrect because it only applies to private, commercial, and ATP pilots. Answer (C) is incorrect because the aircraft only has to remain clear of clouds when within 1,200 feet AGL, or below, in uncontrolled airspace.

12-92. Answer B. (FAR 61.101, 91.155)

For recreational pilots, the visibility minimum below 10,000 feet MSL, is three miles. Answer (A) is wrong because it is the visibility minimum for uncontrolled airspace at or below 1,200 feet AGL and is not applicable to recreational pilots. Answer (C) is incorrect because it is the visibility minimum for airspace above 1,200 feet AGL and above 10,000 feet MSL.

12-93. Answer C. (FAR 91.9, 91.203)

An acronym commonly used by pilots for remembering the required certificates and documents is ARROW. The ARROW acronym means AIRWORTHINESS certificate; aircraft REGISTRATION; RADIO station permit; OPERATING limitations; and WEIGHT and balance. Answer (A) is incorrect because engine and airframe logbooks are not required to be in the aircraft. Answer (B) is incorrect because repair and alteration forms are not required to be in the aircraft.

12-94   B11
When must batteries in an emergency locator transmitter (ELT) be replaced or recharged, if rechargeable?

A — After any inadvertent activation of the ELT.
B — When the ELT has been in use for more than 1 cumulative hour.
C — When the ELT can no longer be heard over the airplane's communication radio receiver.

12-95   B11
When are non-rechargeable batteries of an emergency locator transmitter (ELT) required to be replaced?

A — Every 24 months.
B — When 50 percent of their useful life expires.
C — At the time of each 100-hour or annual inspection.

12-96   B11
Except in Alaska, during what time period should lighted position lights be displayed on an aircraft?

A — End of evening civil twilight to the beginning of morning civil twilight.
B — 1 hour after sunset to 1 hour before sunrise.
C — Sunset to sunrise.

12-97   B11
When operating an aircraft at cabin pressure altitudes above 12,500 feet MSL up to and including 14,000 feet MSL, supplemental oxygen shall be used during

A — the entire flight time at those altitudes.
B — that flight time in excess of 10 minutes at those altitudes.
C — that flight time in excess of 30 minutes at those altitudes.

12-98   B11
Unless each occupant is provided with supplemental oxygen, no person may operate a civil aircraft of U.S. registry above a maximum cabin pressure altitude of

A — 12,500 feet MSL.
B — 14,000 feet MSL.
C — 15,000 feet MSL.

12-99   B12
No person may operate an aircraft in acrobatic flight when

A — flight visibility is less than 5 miles.
B — over any congested area of a city, town, or settlement.
C — less than 2,500 feet AGL.

12-94. Answer B. (FAR 91.207)
Batteries used in the emergency locator transmitters must be replaced (or recharged, if the battery is rechargeable) when the transmitter has been in use for more than one cumulative hour. Answer (A) is incorrect because the ELT can be reset after an inadvertent activation well before one cumulative hour has occurred. Answer (C) is incorrect because it is well past the one cumulative hour specification.

12-95. Answer B. (FAR 91.207)
Non-rechargeable batteries used in the ELT must be replaced when 50 percent of their useful life, as established by the manufacturer, has expired. Answer (A) is incorrect because the useful half life of the ELT battery is not fixed, and it may vary from manufacturer to manufacturer. Answer (C) is wrong because a 100-hour or annual inspection could occur well before or well after the time an ELT battery needs to be replaced or recharged.

12-96. Answer C. (FAR 91.209)
No person may, during the period from sunset to sunrise, operate an aircraft unless it has lighted position lights. Answer (A) is wrong because it reflects the FAR 1.1 definition for night, which is used for logging time. Answer (B) is incorrect because it is the terminology used to define currency requirements for carrying passengers.

12-97. Answer C. (FAR 91.211)
Between cabin pressure altitudes of 12,500 feet MSL and 14,000 feet MSL, the required minimum flight crew is required to use supplemental oxygen for any duration of the flight past 30 minutes. Answers (A) and (B) greatly exceed the oxygen requirements.

12-98. Answer C. (FAR 91.211)
At cabin pressure altitudes above 15,000 feet MSL, each occupant of the aircraft must be provided with supplemental oxygen. Answers (A) and (B) are incorrect because at those altitudes, only required crewmembers must use oxygen for any portion of the flight past 30 minutes.

12-99. Answer B. (FAR 91.303)
No person may operate an aircraft in acrobatic flight over any congested area of a city, town, or settlement. Answer (A) is incorrect because the minimum visibility for acrobatic flight is three miles. Answer (C) is incorrect because minimum altitude above the ground for acrobatic flight is 1,500 feet AGL.

12-100   B12

In which class of airspace is acrobatic flight prohibited?

A — Class G airspace above 1,500 AGL.
B — Class E airspace below 1,5000 feet AGL.
C — Class E airspace not designated for Federal
     Airways above 1,500 feet AGL.

12-100. Answer B. (FAR 91.303)
No person may operate an aircraft in acrobatic flight within class B, C, or D airspace, class E airspace designated for an airport, or within 4 NM of the centerline of any Federal Ariway. Acrobatic flight is also prohibited below 1,500 feet AGL and when the flight visibility is less than 3 statute miles.

12-101   B12

What is the lowest altitude permitted for acrobatic flight?

A — 1,000 feet AGL.
B — 1,500 feet AGL.
C — 2,000 feet AGL.

12-101. Answer B. (FAR 91.303)
No person may operate an aircraft in acrobatic flight below an altitude of 1,500 feet above the surface.

12-102   B12

No person may operate an aircraft in acrobatic flight when the flight visibility is less than

A — 3 miles.
B — 5 miles.
C — 7 miles.

12-102. Answer A. (FAR 91.303)
No person may operate an aircraft in acrobatic flight when flight visibility is less than three statute miles. Answers (B) and (C) are greater than the required minimum.

12-103   B12

A chair-type parachute must have been packed by a certificated and appropriately rated parachute rigger within the preceding

A — 60 days.
B — 90 days.
C — 120 days.

12-103. Answer C. (FAR 91.307)
No pilot of a civil aircraft may allow a parachute that is available for emergency use to be carried in that aircraft unless it is an approved type, and if a chair type (canopy in back), it has been packed by a certificated and appropriately rated parachute rigger within the preceding 120 days. Answers (A) and (B) are less than the required 120 days.

12-104   B12

An approved chair-type parachute may be carried in an aircraft for emergency use if it has been packed by an appropriately rated parachute rigger within the preceding

A — 120 days.
B — 180 days.
C — 365 days.

12-104. Answer A. (FAR 91.307)
No pilot of a civil aircraft may allow a parachute that is available for emergency use to be carried in that aircraft unless it is an approved type, and if a chair type (canopy in back), it has been packed by a certificated and appropriately rated parachute rigger within the preceding 120 days. Answers (B) and (C) are longer than the required maximum of 120 days.

12-105   B12

With certain exceptions, when must each occupant of an aircraft wear an approved parachute?

A — When a door is removed from the aircraft to
     facilitate parachute jumpers.
B — When intentionally pitching the nose of the air-
     craft up or down 30° or more.
C — When intentionally banking in excess of 30°.

12-105. Answer B. (FAR 91.307)
Unless each occupant of the aircraft is wearing an approved parachute, no pilot of a civil aircraft, carrying any person (other than a crewmember) may execute any intentional maneuver that exceeds a nose-up or nose-down attitude of 30 degrees relative to the horizon.

12-106   **B12**
Which is normally prohibited when operating a restricted category civil aircraft?

A — Flight under instrument flight rules.
B — Flight over a densely populated area.
C — Flight within Class D airspace.

12-107   **B12**
Unless otherwise specifically authorized, no person may operate an aircraft that has an experimental certificate

A — beneath the floor of Class B airspace.
B — over a densely populated area or in a congested airway.
C — from the primary airport within Class D airspace.

12-108   **B13**
The responsibility for ensuring that an aircraft is maintained in an airworthy condition is primarily that of the

A — pilot in command.
B — owner or operator.
C — mechanic who performs the work.

12-109   **B13**
The airworthiness of an aircraft can be determined by a preflight inspection and a

A — statement from the owner or operator that the aircraft is airworthy.
B — log book endorsement from a flight instructor.
C — review of the maintenance records.

12-110   **B13**
The responsibility for ensuring that maintenance personnel make the appropriate entries in the aircraft maintenance records indicating the aircraft has been approved for return to service lies with the

A — owner or operator.
B — pilot in command.
C — mechanic who performed the work.

12-111   **B13**
Who is responsible for ensuring appropriate entries are made in maintenance records indicating the aircraft has been approved for return to service?

A — Owner or operator.
B — Certified mechanic.
C — Repair station.

12-106. Answer B. (FAR 91.313)
No person may operate a restricted category civil aircraft within the United States over a densely populated area. Answer (A) is incorrect because there currently are no restrictions for operating a restricted aircraft under IFR. Answer (C) is terminology found in the FAR regulating acrobatic flight and is not applicable to restricted category civil aircraft.

12-107. Answer B. (FAR 91.319)
Unless otherwise authorized by the Administrator in special operating limitations, no person may operate an aircraft that has an experimental certificate over a densely populated area or in a congested airway. Answers (A) and (C) are incorrect because there are no restrictions specific to the airspace listed.

12-108. Answer B. (FAR 91.403)
The owner or operator of an aircraft is primarily responsible for maintaining that aircraft in an airworthy condition. Answer (A) is incorrect because the pilot in command is only responsible for determining if the aircraft is in an airworthy condition. Answer (C) is incorrect because the certified mechanic is only responsible for the work he/she performs.

12-109. Answer C. (FAR 91.403)
The maintenance records document whether all of the required inspections have been completed, and whether all of the airworthiness directives (ADs) have been complied with.

12-110. Answer A. (FAR 91.405)
Each owner or operator of an aircraft shall ensure that maintenance personnel make appropriate entries in the aircraft maintenance record. Answers (B) and (C) are incorrect because it is not the responsibility of the pilot in command or mechanic to make sure the appropriate entries have been made.

12-111. Answer A. (FAR 91.405)
Each owner or operator of an aircraft shall ensure that maintenance personnel make appropriate entries in the aircraft maintenance records indicating the aircraft has been approved for return to service.

12-112   B13
Who is responsible for ensuring Airworthiness Directives (AD's) are complied with?

A — Owner or operator.
B — Repair station.
C — Mechanic with inspection authorization (IA).

12-113   B13
Completion of an annual inspection and the return of the aircraft to service should always be indicated by

A — the relicensing date on the Registration Certificate.
B — an appropriate notation in the aircraft maintenance records.
C — an inspection sticker placed on the instrument panel that lists the annual inspection completion date.

12-114   B13
If an alteration or repair substantially affects an aircraft's operation in flight, that aircraft must be test flown by an appropriately-rated pilot and approved for return to service prior to being operated

A — by any private pilot.
B — with passengers aboard.
C — for compensation or hire.

12-115   B13
Before passengers can be carried in an aircraft that has been altered in a manner that may have appreciably changed its flight characteristics, it must be flight tested by an appropriately-rated pilot who holds at least a

A — Commercial Pilot Certificate with an instrument rating.
B — Private Pilot Certificate.
C — Commercial Pilot Certificate and a mechanic's certificate.

12-116   B13
An aircraft's annual inspection was performed on July 12, this year. The next annual inspection will be due no later than

A — July 1, next year.
B — July 13, next year.
C — July 31, next year.

12-112. Answer A. (FAR 91.403)
The owner or operator of an aircraft is primarily responsible for maintaining that aircraft in an airworthy condition, including compliance with 14 CFR Part 39 (ADs).

12-113. Answer B. (FAR 91.409)
No person may operate an aircraft unless, within the preceding 12 calendar months it has had an annual inspection by a person authorized to do that type of inspection and is entered as an annual inspection in the required maintenance records. Answer (A) is incorrect because an annual is either entered in maintenance records, or in the issuance of an airworthiness certificate. Answer (C) is wrong because it does not meet the requirement for recording an annual inspection.

12-114. Answer B. (FAR 91.407)
Before any person (other than a crewmember) can fly in an aircraft that has been maintained, rebuilt, or altered in a manner that may have appreciably changed its flight characteristics or substantially affected the operation in flight, an appropriately rated pilot with at least a private pilot certificate must first conduct a test flight and log the flight in aircraft records. Answer (A) is wrong because a private pilot is a required crewmember. Answer (C) is incorrect because flying the aircraft for compensation or hire may not involve carrying passengers.

12-115. Answer B. (FAR 91.407)
An appropriately rated pilot with at least a private pilot certificate is authorized to flight test the aircraft. Answers (A) and (C) are incorrect because a commercial pilot with either an instrument rating or a mechanic rating is not the minimum requirement for the pilot.

12-116. Answer C. (FAR 91.409)
No person may operate an aircraft unless, within the preceding 12 calendar months, it has had an annual inspection. The term "calendar month" is defined as to the end of the month. Answer (A) is incorrect because it is less than 12 months. Answer (B) is incorrect because it is less than 12 calendar months.

12-117   B13
To determine the expiration date of the last annual aircraft inspection, a person should refer to the

A — Airworthiness Certificate.
B — Registration Certificate.
C — aircraft maintenance records.

12-118   B13
What aircraft inspections are required for rental aircraft that are also used for flight instruction?

A — Annual and 100-hour inspections.
B — Biannual and 100-hour inspections.
C — Annual and 50-hour inspections.

12-119   B13
An aircraft had a 100-hour inspection when the tachometer read 1259.6. When is the next 100-hour inspection due?

A — 1349.6 hours.
B — 1359.6 hours.
C — 1369.6 hours.

12-120   B13
A 100-hour inspection was due at 3302.5 hours on the tachometer. The 100-hour inspection was actually done at 3309.5 hours. When is the next 100-hour inspection due?

A — 3312.5 hours.
B — 3402.5 hours.
C — 3409.5 hours.

12-121   B13
Maintenance records show the last transponder inspection was performed on September 1, 1993. The next inspection will be due no later than

A — September 30, 1994.
B — September 1, 1995.
C — September 30, 1995.

12-117. Answer C. (FAR 91.417)
The registered owner or operator shall keep records of the maintenance, preventive maintenance, alterations, records of the 100-hour, annual, progressive, and other required or approved inspections, as appropriate, for each aircraft. This information is found in the aircraft's maintenance records. Answers (A) and (B) are incorrect because a record of maintenance is not kept on the airworthiness certificate or registration certificate.

12-118. Answer A. (FAR 91.409)
No person may operate an aircraft carrying any person (other than a crewmember) for hire, or give flight instruction for hire in an aircraft, which that person provides, unless within the preceding 100-hours of time in service, the aircraft has received an annual or 100-hour inspection. Answer (B) is incorrect because a biannual inspection is not in compliance with the annual inspection requirement. Answer (C) is incorrect because 50-hour inspections are not required for all rented aircraft.

12-119. Answer B. (FAR 91.409)
No person may operate an aircraft carrying any person (other than a crewmember) for hire, or give flight instruction for hire in an aircraft, which that person provides, unless within the preceding 100-hours of time in service, the aircraft has received an annual or 100-hour inspection. Answer (A) is at 90 hours and is incorrect. Answer (C) is at 110 hours and is incorrect. An aircraft can go 10 hours over the 100 hour inspection as long as it is enroute to a place where the inspection can be done. If an aircraft does go over 100 hours, that time must be subtracted from the next 100 hours.

12-120. Answer B. (FAR 91.409)
The 100-hour limitation may be exceeded by not more than 10 hours while enroute to reach a place where the inspection can be done. However, the excess time used to reach a place must be included in computing the next 100 hours of time in service. Answer (A) is incorrect because although an aircraft can go 10 hours over the 100 hour inspection, it is due at the 100 hour time. Answer (C) is incorrect because any time over 10 hours that is used to get an aircraft to a place of inspection, is counted against the next 100 hour inspection.

12-121. Answer C. (FAR 91.413)
No person may use an ATC transponder unless, within the preceding 24 calendar months, that transponder has been tested and found to comply with the appropriate standards listed in Appendix F of Part 43. The term "calendar month" is defined as to the end of the month. Answers (A) and (B) are incorrect because they are less than 24 calendar months.

12-122   B13

Which records or documents shall the owner or operator of an aircraft keep to show compliance with an applicable Airworthiness Directive?

A — Aircraft maintenance records.
B — Airworthiness Certificate and Pilot's Operating Handbook.
C — Airworthiness and Registration Certificates.

12-123   J08

All operations within Class C airspace must be in

A — accordance with instrument flight rules.
B — compliance with ATC clearances and instructions.
C — an aircraft equipped with a 4096-code transponder with Mode C encoding capability.

12-122. Answer A. (FAR 91.417)

The owner or operator of an aircraft shall keep a record of current status of applicable airworthiness directives (ADs) in the appropriate aircraft maintenance records. Answers (B) and (C) are not appropriate maintenance records.

12-123. Answer C. (FAR 91.215, 91.130)

All aircraft must have an altitude encoding transponder in order to operate within Class C airspace. Answer (B) is not entirely correct because the regulations state that in order to enter Class C airspace, all you need is two-way radio contact with ATC. However, per FAR 91.123, once you receive a clearance from ATC, you cannot deviate from that clearance except in an emergency. Answer (A) is not correct because an IFR clearance is not a requirement for operations within Class C airspace.

SECTION D
NTSB 830—AIRCRAFT ACCIDENT AND INCIDENT REPORTING

Pilots need to be familiar with the procedures and requirements for reporting aircraft accidents, incidents and overdue aircraft to the National Transportation Safety Board (NTSB).

ACCIDENTS
1. If an aircraft is involved in an accident which results in substantial damage to the aircraft, the nearest NTSB field office should be notified immediately.
2. Aircraft wreckage may be moved prior to the time the NTSB takes custody, but only to protect the wreckage from further damage.
3. The owner of an aircraft that has been involved in an accident is required to file an accident report within 10 days.

INCIDENTS
4. A flight control system malfunction or failure, and an in flight fire are two incidents that require immediate notification to the nearest NTSB field office.
5. An overdue aircraft that is believed to be involved in an accident must be immediately reported to the nearest NTSB field office.
6. The operator of an aircraft that has been involved in an incident is required to submit a report to the nearest NTSB field office when requested.

12-124   G11
If an aircraft is involved in an accident which results in substantial damage to the aircraft, the nearest NTSB field office should be notified

A — immediately.
B — within 48 hours.
C — within 7 days.

12-124. Answer A. (NTSB 830.5)
The operator of an aircraft shall immediately, and by the most expeditious means available, notify the nearest National Transportation Safety Board field office when an aircraft accident occurs. Answer (B) does not comply with notification requirements. Answer (C) is terminology found in NTSB 830.15 for filing reports and statements.

12-125   G11
Which incident requires an immediate notification to the nearest NTSB field office?

A — A forced landing due to engine failure.
B — Landing gear damage, due to a hard landing.
C — Flight control system malfunction or failure.

12-125. Answer C. (NTSB 830.5)
The operator of an aircraft shall immediately, and by the most expeditious means available, notify the nearest National Transportation Safety Board field office when a flight control system malfunction or failure occurs. Answers (A) and (B) do not require immediate notification.

12-126   G11
Which incident would necessitate an immediate notification to the nearest NTSB field office?

A — An in-flight generator/alternator failure.
B — An in-flight fire.
C — An in-flight loss of VOR receiver capability.

12-126. Answer B. (NTSB 830.5)
The operator of an aircraft shall immediately, and by the most expeditious means available, notify the nearest National Transportation Safety Board field office when a fire in flight occurs. Answers (A) and (C) do not require immediate notification.

12-127   G11
Which incident requires an immediate notification be made to the nearest NTSB field office?

A — An overdue aircraft that is believed to be involved in an accident.
B — An in-flight radio communications failure.
C — An in-flight generator or alternator failure.

12-127. Answer A. (NTSB 830.5)
The operator of an aircraft shall immediately, and by the most expeditious means available, notify the nearest National Transportation Safety Board field office when an overdue aircraft is believed to be involved in an accident. Answers (B) and (C) do not require immediate notification.

12-128   G12

May aircraft wreckage be moved prior to the time the NTSB takes custody?

A — Yes, but only if moved by a federal, state, or local law enforcement officer.
B — Yes, but only to protect the wreckage from further damage.
C — No, it may not be moved under any circumstances.

12-128. Answer B. (NTSB 830.10)

Prior to the time the Board or its authorized representative takes custody of aircraft wreckage, mail, or cargo, such wreckage may not be disturbed or moved except to the extent necessary to protect the wreckage from further damage.

12-129   G13

The operator of an aircraft that has been involved in an accident is required to file an accident report within how many days?

A — 5.
B — 7.
C — 10.

12-129. Answer C. (NTSB 830.15)

The operator of an aircraft shall file a report within 10 days after an accident, or after 7 days if an overdue aircraft is still missing. Answer (A) is less than the required 10 days. Answer (B) is wrong because it applies to aircraft that are overdue and still missing.

12-130   G13

The operator of an aircraft that has been involved in an incident is required to submit a report to the nearest field office of the NTSB

A — within 7 days.
B — within 10 days.
C — when requested.

12-130. Answer C. (NTSB 830.15)

A report on an incident for which notification is required by 830.5(a) shall be filed only when requested by an authorized representative of the Board.

SUBJECT MATTER KNOWLEDGE CODES

APPENDIX 1

To determine the knowledge area in which a particular question was incorrectly answered, compare the subject matter code(s) on the Federal Aviation Administration Airmen Computer Test Report to the following subject matter outline. The total number of test items missed may differ from the number of subject matter codes shown on the test report, since you may have missed more than one question in a certain subject matter code.

Title 14 of the Code of Federal Regulations (14 CFR) part 1-Definitions and Abbreviations

A01 General Definitions
A02 Abbreviations and Symbols

14 CFR part 21-Certification Procedures forProducts and Parts

A100 General
A102 Type Certificates
A104 Supplemental Type Certificates
A108 Airworthiness Certificate
A110 Approval of Materials, Part, Processes, and Appliances
A112 Export Airworthiness Approvals
A114 Approval of Engines, Propellers, Materials, Parts, and Appliances Import
A117 Technical Standard Order Authorizations

14 CFR part 23-Airworthiness Standards: Normal, Utility, Acrobatic, and Commuter Category Aircraft

A150 General
A151 Flight
A152 Structure
A153 Design and Construction
A154 Powerplant
A155 Equipment
A157 Operating Limitations and Information
A159 Appendix G: Instructions for Continued Airworthiness

14 CFR part 27-Airworthiness Standards: Normal Category Rotorcraft

A250 General
A253 Flight
A255 Strength Requirements
A257 Design and Construction
A259 Powerplant
A261 Equipment

A263 Operating Limitations and Information
A265 Appendix A: Instructions for Continued Airworthiness

14 CFR part 39-Airworthiness Directives

A13 General
A14 Airworthiness Directives

14 CFR part 45-Identification and Registration Marking

A400 General
A401 Identification of Aircraft and Related Products
A402 Nationality and Registration Marks

14 CFR part 61-Certification: Pilots, Flight Instructors, and Ground Instructors

A20 General
A21 Aircraft Ratings and Pilot Authorizations
A22 Student Pilots
A23 Private Pilots
A24 Commercial Pilots
A25 Airline Transport Pilots
A26 Flight Instructors
A27 Ground Instructors
A29 Recreational Pilot

14 CFR part 71-Designation of Class A, Class B, Class C, Class D, and Class E Airspace Areas; Airways; Routes; and Reporting Points

A60 General-Class A Airspace
A61 Class B Airspace
A64 Class C Airspace
A65 Class D Airspace
A66 Class E Airspace

14 CFR part 91-General Operating and Flight Rules

B07	General
B08	Flight Rules-General
B09	Visual Flight Rules
B10	Instrument Flight Rules
B11	Equipment, Instrument, and Certificate Requirements
B12	Special Flight Operations
B13	Maintenance, Preventive Maintenance, and Alterations
B14	Large and Turbine-powered Multiengine Airplanes
B15	Additional Equipment and Operating Requirements for Large and Transport Category Aircraft
B16	Appendix A-Category II Operations: Manual, Instruments, Equipment, and Maintenance
B17	Foreign Aircraft Operations and Operations of U.S.-Registered Civil Aircraft Outside of the U.S.

14 CFR part 97-Standard Instrument Approach Procedures

B97	General

14 CFR part 105-Parachute Jumping

C01	General
C02	Operating Rules
C03	Parachute Equipment

14 CFR part 119-Certification: Air Carriers and Commercial Operators

C20	General
C21	Applicability of Operating Requirements to Different Kinds of Operations Under Parts 121, 125, and 135
C22	Certification, Operations Specifications, and Certain Other Requirements for Operations Conducted Under Parts 121 or 135

14 CFR part 121-Operating Requirements: Domestic, Flag, and Supplemental Operations

D01	General
D02	Certification Rules for Domestic and Flag Air Carriers
D03	Certification Rules for Supplemental Air Carriers and Commercial Operators
D04	Rules Governing all Certificate Holders Under This Part
D05	Approval of Routes: Domestic and Flag Air Carriers
D06	Approval of Areas and Routes for Supplemental Air Carriers and Commercial Operators
D07	Manual Requirements
D08	Aircraft Requirements
D09	Airplane Performance Operating Limitations
D10	Special Airworthiness Requirements
D11	Instrument and Equipment Requirements
D12	Maintenance, Preventive Maintenance, and Alterations
D13	Airman and Crewmember Requirements
D14	Training Program
D15	Crewmember Qualifications
D16	Aircraft Dispatcher Qualifications and Duty Time Limitations: Domestic and Flag Air Carriers
D17	Flight Time Limitations and Rest Requirements: Domestic Air Carriers
D18	Flight Time Limitations: Flag Air Carriers
D19	Flight Time Limitations: Supplemental Air Carriers and Commercial Operators
D20	Flight Operations
D21	Dispatching and Flight Release Rules
D22	Records and Reports
D23	Crewmember Certificate: International
D24	Special Federal Aviation Regulation SFAR No. 14

NTSB 830-Rules Pertaining to the Notification and Reporting of Aircraft Accidents or Incidents and Overdue Aircraft, and Preservation of Aircraft Wreckage, Mail, Cargo, and Records

G10	General
G11	Initial Notification of Aircraft Accidents, Incidents, and Overdue Aircraft
G12	Preservation of Aircraft Wreckage, Mail, Cargo, and Records
G13	Reporting of Aircraft Accidents, Incidents, and Overdue Aircraft

AC 61-13-Basic Helicopter Handbook

H70	General Aerodynamics
H71	Aerodynamics of Flight
H72	Loads and Load Factors
H73	Function of the Controls
H74	Other Helicopter Components and Their Functions
H75	Introduction to the Helicopter Flight Manual
H76	Weight and Balance
H77	Helicopter Performance
H78	Some Hazards of Helicopter Flight
H79	Precautionary Measures and Critical Conditions

H80 Helicopter Flight Maneuvers
H81 Confined Area, Pinnacle, and Ridgeline Operations
H82 Glossary

FAA-H-8083-1-Aircraft Weight and Balance Handbook

H100 Why is Weight and Balance Important?
H101 Weight Control
H102 Effects of Weight
H103 Weight Changes
H104 Stability and Balance Control
H105 Weight and Balance Theory
H106 Weight and Balance Documents
H107 Requirements
H108 Equipment for Weighing
H109 Preparation for Weighing
H110 Determining the Center of Gravity
H111 Empty-Weight Center of Gravity Formulas
H112 Determining the Loaded Weight and CG
H113 Multiengine Airplane Weight and Balance Computations
H114 Determining the Loaded CG
H115 Equipment List
H116 Weight and Balance Revision Record
H117 Weight Changes Caused by a Repair or Alteration
H118 Empty-Weight CG Range
H119 Adverse-Loaded CG Checks
H120 Ballast
H121 Weighing Requirements
H122 Locating and Monitoring Weight and CG Location
H123 Determining the Correct Stabilizer Trim Setting
H124 Determining CG Changes Caused by Modifying the Cargo
H125 Determining Cargo Pallet Loads with Regard to Floor Loading Limits
H126 Determining the Maximum Amount of Payload That Can Be carried
H127 Determining the Landing Weight
H128 Determining the Minutes of Fuel Dump Time
H129 Weight and Balance of Commuter Category Airplanes
H130 Determining the Loaded CG of a Helicopter
H131 Using an Electronic Calculator to Solve Weight and Balance Problems
H132 Using an E6-B Flight Computer to Solve Weight and Balance Problems
H133 Using a Dedicated Electronic Computer to Solve Weight and Balance Problems
H134 Typical Weight and Balance Problems
H135 Glossary

FAA-H-8083-9-Aviation Instructor Handbook

H200 Learning Theory
H201 Definition of Learning
H202 Characteristics of Learning
H203 Principles of Learning
H204 Level of Learning
H205 Learning Physical Skills
H206 Memory
H207 Transfer of Learning
H208 Control of Human Behavior
H210 Human Needs
H211 Defense Mechanisms
H212 The Flight Instructor as a Practical Psychologists
H213 Basic Elements
H214 Barriers of Effective Communication
H215 Developing Communications Skills
H216 Preparation
H217 Presentation
H218 Application
H219 Review and Evaluation
H220 Organizing Material
H221 Lecture Method
H222 Cooperative or Group Learning Method
H223 Guided Discussion Method
H224 Demonstration-Performance Method
H225 Computer-Based Training Method
H226 The Instructor as a Critic
H227 Evaluation
H228 Instructional Aid Theory
H229 Reasons for Use of Instructional Aids
H230 Guidelines for Use of Instructional Aids
H231 Types of Instructional Aids
H232 Test Preparation Material
H233 Aviation Instructor Responsibilities
H234 Flight Instructor Responsibilities
H235 Professionalism
H236 The Telling-and-Doing Technique
H237 Integrated Flight Instruction
H238 Obstacles to Learning During Flight Instruction
H239 Positive Exchange of Flight Controls
H240 Use of Distractions
H241 Aeronautical Decision Making
H242 Factors Affecting Decision Making
H243 Operational Pitfalls
H244 Evaluating Student Decision Making
H245 Course of Training
H246 Blocks of Learning
H247 Training Syllabus
H248 Lesson Plans
H249 Growth and Development
H250 Sources of Material
H251 Appendix A-Sample Test Items
H252 Appendix B-Instructor Endorsements
H253 Glossary

AC 61-23-Pilot's Handbook of Aeronautical Knowledge

H300 Forces Acting on the Airplane in Flight
H301 Turning Tendency (Torque Effect)
H302 Airplane Stability
H303 Loads and Load Factors
H304 Airplane Structure
H305 Flight Control Systems
H306 Electrical System
H307 Engine Operation
H308 Propeller
H309 Starting the Engine
H310 Exhaust Gas Temperature Gauge
H311 Aircraft Documents, Maintenance, and Inspections
H312 The Pitot-Static System and Associated Instruments
H313 Gyroscopic Flight Instruments
H314 Magnetic Compass
H315 Weight Control
H316 Balance, Stability, and Center of Gravity
H317 Airplane Performance
H318 Observations
H319 Service Outlets
H320 Weather Briefings
H321 Nature of the Atmosphere
H322 The Cause of Atmospheric Circulation
H323 Moisture and Temperature
H324 Air Masses and Fronts
H325 Aviation Weather Reports, Forecasts, and Weather Charts
H326 Types of Airports
H327 Sources for Airport Data
H328 Airport Markings and Signs
H329 Airport Lighting
H330 Wind Direction Indicators
H331 Radio Communications
H332 Air Traffic Services
H333 Wake Turbulence
H334 Collision Avoidance
H335 Controlled Airspace
H336 Uncontrolled Airspace
H337 Special Use Airspace
H338 Other Airspace Areas
H339 Aeronautical Charts
H340 Latitude and Longitude
H341 Effect of Wind
H342 Basic Calculations
H343 Pilotage
H344 Dead Reckoning
H345 Flight Planning
H346 Charting the Course
H347 Filing a VFR Flight Plan
H348 Radio Navigation
H349 Obtaining a Medical Certificate
H350 Health Factors Affecting Pilot Performance
H351 Environmental Factors which Affect Pilot Performance

FAA-H-8083-11-Balloon Flying Handbook

H400 History
H401 Physics
H402 Basic Balloon Terms
H403 Balloon Components
H404 Support Equipment
H405 Choosing a Balloon
H406 Flight Planning
H407 Preflight Operations
H408 Checklists
H409 Crew
H410 Chase
H411 Inflation
H412 Launch
H413 Approach to Landing
H414 Landing
H415 Standard Burn
H416 Level Flight
H417 Use of Instruments
H418 Ascents and Descents
H419 Maneuvering
H420 Winds Above
H421 Winds Below
H422 Contour Flying
H423 Radio Communications
H424 Deflation
H425 Preparing for Pack-up
H426 Legal Considerations
H427 Propane Management and Fueling
H428 Tethering
H429 Emergency Procedures
H430 Regulations
H431 Maintenance
H432 Earning a Pilot Certificate
H433 Practical Test Standards
H434 Skill Development
H435 What is a Good Instructor
H436 Aeronautical Decision Making
H437 Types of Decisions
H438 Effectiveness of ADM
H439 Glossary

FAA-H-8083-3-Airplane Flying Handbook

H501 Choosing a Flight School
H502 Instructor/Student Relationship
H503 Role of the FAA
H504 Flight Standards District Offices (FSDOís)
H505 Study Habits
H506 Study Materials
H507 Collision Avoidance
H509 Pilot Assessment
H510 Preflight Preparation and Flight Planning
H511 Airplane Preflight Inspection
H512 Minimum Equipment Lists (MELís) and Operations with Inoperative Equipment
H513 Cockpit Management

H514 Use of Checklists
H515 Ground Operations
H516 Taxiing
H517 Taxi Clearances at Airports with an
      Operating Control Tower
H518 Before Takeoff Check
H519 After-landing
H520 Postflight
H522 Terms and Definitions
H523 Prior to Takeoff
H524 Normal Takeoff
H525 Crosswind Takeoff
H526 Short-field Takeoff and Climb
H527 Soft-field Takeoff and Climb
H528 Rejected Takeoff
H529 Noise Abatement
H531 Integrated Flight Instruction
H532 Attitude Flying
H533 Straight-and-level Flight
H534 Turns
H535 Climbs
H536 Descents
H538 Slow Flight
H539 Stalls
H540 Spins
H541 Spin Procedures
H542 Aircraft Limitations
H543 Weight and Balance Requirements
H545 Maneuvering by Reference to Ground
      Objects
H546 Performance Maneuvers
H548 Airport Traffic Patterns and Operations
H549 Normal Approach and Landing
H550 Crosswind Approach and Landing
H551 Short-field Approach and Landing
H552 Soft-field Approach and Landing
H553 Power-off Accuracy Approaches
H554 Faulty Approaches and Landings
H555 Final Approaches
H556 Roundout (Flare)
H557 Touchdown
H559 Basic Instrument Training
H560 Basic Instrument Flight
H561 Use of Navigation Systems
H562 Use of Radar Services
H564 Night Vision
H565 Night Illusions
H566 Pilot Equipment
H567 Airplane Equipment and Lighting
H568 Airport and Navigation Lighting Aids
H569 Preparation and Preflight
H570 Starting, Taxiing, and Runup
H571 Takeoff and Climb
H572 Orientation and Navigation
H573 Approaches and Landings
H574 Night Emergencies
H576 VOR Navigation
H577 VOR/DME RNAV

H578 LORAN-C Navigation
H579 Global Positioning System (GPS)
H580 Radar Services
H582 Systems and Equipment Malfunctions
H583 Emergency Approaches and Landings
      (Actual)
H585 Airplane Systems
H586 Pressurized Airplanes
H587 Oxygen Systems
H588 Physiological Altitude Limits
H589 Regulatory Requirements
H591 Multiengine Performance Characteristics
H592 The Critical Engine
H593 Vmc for Certification
H594 Performance
H595 Factors in Takeoff Planning
H596 Accelerates/Stop Distance
H597 Propeller Feathering
H598 Use of Trim Tabs
H599 Preflight Preparation
H600 Checklist
H601 Taxiing
H602 Normal Takeoffs
H603 Crosswind Takeoffs
H604 Short-field or Obstacle Clearance Takeoff
H605 Stalls
H606 Emergency Descent
H607 Approaches and Landings
H608 Crosswind Landings
H609 Short-field Landing
H610 Go-around Procedure
H611 Engine Inoperative Emergencies
H612 Engine Inoperative Procedures
H613 Vmc Demonstrations
H614 Engine Failure Before Lift-off (Rejected
      Takeoff)
H615 Engine Failure After Lift-off
H616 Engine Failure En Route
H617 Engine Inoperative Approach and Landing
H618 Types of Decisions
H619 Effectiveness of ADM

Understanding the Gyroplane -The Abbott Co.

H650 Magic of Rotor Blades
H651 Behind the Power Curve
H652 Beating P.I.O.

FAA-H-8083-21-Rotorcraft Flying Handbook

H700 Glossary
Helicopter
H701 Introduction to the Helicopter
H702 General Aerodynamics
H703 Aerodynamics of Flight
H704 Autorotation
H705 Helicopter Flight Controls
H706 Helicopter Systems

H707 Engines
H708 Transmission System
H709 Main Rotor System
H710 Fuel Systems
H711 Electrical Systems
H712 Hydraulics
H713 Stability Augmentations Systems
H714 Autopilot
H715 Environmental Systems
H716 Anti-Icing Systems
H717 Rotorcraft Flight Manual
H718 Operating Limitations
H719 Weight and Balance
H720 Performance
H721 Performance Charts
H722 Basic Flight Maneuvers
H723 Minimum Equipment Lists
H724 Rotor Safety Considerations
H725 Vertical Takeoff to a Hover
H726 Hovering
H727 Taxiing
H728 Turns
H729 Normal Takeoff
H730 Ground Reference Maneuvers
H731 Traffic Patterns
H732 Approaches
H733 Go-Around
H734 Noise Abatement Procedures
H735 Advance Flight Maneuvers
H736 Reconnaissance Procedures
H737 Maximum Performance Takeoff
H738 Running/Rolling Takeoff
H739 Rapid Deceleration (Quick Stop)
H740 Steep Approach to a Hover
H741 Shallow Approach and Running/Roll-On
      Landing
H742 Slope Operations
H743 Confined Area Operations
H744 Pinnacle and Ridgeline Operations
H745 Helicopter Emergencies
H746 Autorotation
H747 Height/Velocity Diagram
H748 Retreating Blade Stall
H749 Ground Resonance
H750 Dynamic Rollover
H751 Low G Conditions and Mast Bumping
H752 Low Rotor RPM and Blade Stall
H753 Recovery From Low Rotor RPM
H754 Systems Flight Diversion Malfunctions
H755 Lost Procedures
H756 Emergency Equipment and Survival Gear
H757 Attitude Instrument Flying
H758 Flight Instruments
H759 Night Operations
H760 Aeronautical Decision Making
      Gyroplanes
H761 Introduction to the Gyroplane
H762 Aerodynamics of the Gyroplane

H763 Autorotations
H764 Rotor Disc Regions
H765 Retreating Blade Stall
H766 Rotor Force
H767 Stability
H768 Horizontal Stabilizer
H769 Propeller Thrust Line
H770 Gyroplane Flight Controls
H771 Cyclic Control
H772 Gyroplanes Systems
H773 Semirigid Rotor Systems
H774 Fully Articulated Rotor System
H775 Prerotator
H776 Rotorcraft Flight Manual
H777 Weight and Balance
H778 Performance
H779 Height/Velocity Diagram
H780 Gyroplane Flight Operations
H781 Taxi
H782 Blade Flap
H783 Takeoff
H784 Jump Takeoff
H785 Basic Flight Maneuvers
H786 Ground Reference Maneuvers
H787 Flight at Slow Airspeeds
H788 High Rate of Descent
H789 Landings/Crosswind
H790 Go Around
H791 Gyroplane Emergencies
H792 Aborted Takeoff
H793 Lift-Off at Low Airspeed and High Angle of
      Attack
H794 Pilot-Induced Oscillation (PIO)
H795 Buntover (Power Pushover)
H796 Ground Reference
H797 Emergency Approach and Landing
H798 Aeronautical Decision Making

FAA-H-8083-15-Instrument Flying Handbook

Human Factors
H800 Sensory Systems
H801 Spatial Disorientation
H802 Optical Illusions
H803 Physiological and Psychological Factors
H804 Medical Factors
H805 Aeronautical Decision Making
H806 Crew/Cockpit Resource Management
      Aerodynamics
H807 Basic Aerodynamics
Flight Instruments
H808 Pitot Static
H809 Compass
H810 Gyroscopic
H811 Flight Director
H812 Systems Preflight
Airplane Attitude Instrument Flying
H813 Fundamental Skills

Airplane Basic Flight Maneuvers
H814 Straight-and-level Flight
H815 Straight Climbs and Descents
H816 Turns
H817 Approach to Stall
H818 Unusual Attitude Recoveries
H819 Instrument Takeoff
H820 Instrument Flight Patterns
Helicopter Attitude Instrument Flying
H821 Instrument Flight
H822 Straight-and-level
H823 Straight Climbs
H824 Straight Descents
H825 Turns
H826 Unusual Attitude Recoveries
H827 Emergencies
H828 Instrument Takeoff
Navigation Systems
H829 Basic Radio Principals
H830 Nondirectional Beacon (NDB)
H831 Very High Frequency Omnidirectional
      Range
(VOR)
H832 Distance Measuring Equipment (DME)
H833 Area Navigation (RNAV)
H834 Long Range Navigation (LORAN)
H835 Global Positioning System (GPS)
H836 Inertia Navigation System (INS)
H837 Instrument Landing System (ILS)
H838 Microwave Landing System (MLS)
H839 Flight Management Systems (FMS)
H840 Head-up Display (HUD)
H841 Radar Navigation (Ground Based)
National Airspace System
H842 IFR Enroute Charts
H843 U.S. Terminal Procedures Publications
H844 Instrument Approach Procedures
Air Traffic Control Systems
H845 Communications Equipment
H846 Communications Procedures
H847 Communications Facilities
IFR Flight
H848 Planning
H849 Clearances
H850 Departures
H851 Enroute
H852 Holding
H853 Arrival
H854 Approaches
H855 Flying Experience
H856 Weather Conditions
H857 Conducting an IFR Flight
Emergency Operations
H858 Unforecast Adverse Weather
H859 Aircraft System Malfunction
H860 Communication/Navigation System
      Malfunction
H861 Loss of Situational Awareness

Glossary
H862 Glossary

Gyroplane Flight Training Manual-Jean-Pierre Harrison

H660 General Aerodynamics
H661 Aerodynamics of Flight
H662 Rotor RPM During Autorotations
H663 Function of the Controls
H664 Some Hazards of Gyroplane Flight
H665 Precautionary Measures and Critical
      Conditions
H666 Gyroplane Flight Maneuvers

AC 61-27-Instrument Flying Handbook

I01 Training Considerations
I02 Instrument Flying: Coping with Illusions in
    Flight
I03 Aerodynamic Factors Related to
    Instrument Flying
I04 Basic Flight Instruments
I05 Attitude Instrument Flying-Airplanes
I06 Attitude Instrument Flying-Helicopters
I07 Electronic Aids to Instrument Flying
I08 Using the Navigation Instruments
I09 Radio Communications Facilities and
    Equipment
I10 The Federal Airways System and
    Controlled Airspace
I11 Air Traffic Control
I12 ATC Operations and Procedures
I13 Flight Planning
I14 Appendix: Instrument Instructor Lesson
    Guide-Airplanes
I15 Segment of En Route Low Altitude Chart

AC 00-6-Aviation Weather

I20 The Earthís Atmosphere
I21 Temperature
I22 Atmospheric Pressure and Altimetry
I23 Wind
I24 Moisture, Cloud Formation, and
    Precipitation
I25 Stable and Unstable Air
I26 Clouds
I27 Air Masses and Fronts
I28 Turbulence
I29 Icing
I30 Thunderstorms
I31 Common IFR Producers
I32 High Altitude Weather
I33 Arctic Weather
I34 Tropical Weather
I35 Soaring Weather
I36 Glossary of Weather Terms

AC 00-45-Aviation Weather Services

I54	The Aviation Weather Service Program
I55	Aviation Routine Weather Report (METAR)
I56	Pilot and Radar Reports, Satellite Pictures, and Radiosonde Additional Data (RADATs)
I57	Aviation Weather Forecasts
I58	Surface Analysis Chart
I59	Weather Depiction Chart
I60	Radar Summary Chart
I61	Constant Pressure Analysis Charts
I62	Composite Moisture Stability Chart
I63	Winds and Temperatures Aloft Chart
I64	Significant Weather Prognostic Charts
I65	Convective Outlook Chart
I66	Volcanic Ash Advisory Center Products
I67	Turbulence Locations, Conversion and Density Altitude Tables, Contractions and Acronyms, Station Identifiers, WSR-88D Sites, and Internet Addresses

AIM-Aeronautical Information Manual

J01	Air Navigation Radio Aids
J02	Radar Services and Procedures
J03	Airport Lighting Aids
J04	Air Navigation and Obstruction Lighting
J05	Airport Marking Aids and Signs
J06	AirspaceóGeneral
J07	Class G Airspace
J08	Controlled Airspace
J09	Special Use Airspace
J10	Other Airspace Areas
J11	Service Available to Pilots
J12	Radio Communications Phraseology and Techniques
J13	Airport Operations
J14	ATC Clearance/Separations
J15	Preflight
J16	Departure Procedures
J17	En Route Procedures
J18	Arrival Procedures
J19	Pilot/Controller Roles and Responsibilities
J20	National Security and Interception Procedures
J21	Emergency ProceduresóGeneral
J22	Emergency Services Available to Pilots
J23	Distress and Urgency Procedures
J24	Two-Way Radio Communications Failure
J25	Meteorology
J26	Altimeter Setting Procedures
J27	Wake Turbulence
J28	Bird Hazards, and Flight Over National Refuges, Parks, and Forests
J29	Potential Flight Hazards
J30	Safety, Accident, and Hazard Reports

J31	Fitness for Flight
J32	Type of Charts Available
J33	Pilot Controller Glossary

Other Documents

J34	Airport/Facility Directory
J35	En Route Low Altitude Chart
J36	En Route High Altitude Chart
J37	Sectional Chart
J39	Terminal Area Chart
J40	Instrument Departure Procedure Chart
J41	Standard Terminal Arrival (STAR) Chart
J42	Instrument Approach Procedures
J43	Helicopter Route Chart

ADDITIONAL ADVISORY CIRCULARS

K01	AC 00-24, Thunderstorms
K02	AC 00-30, Atmospheric Turbulence Avoidance
K03	AC 00-34, Aircraft Ground Handling and Servicing
K04	AC 00-54, Pilot Wind Shear Guide
K05	AC 00-55, Announcement of Availability: FAA Order 8130.21A
K06	AC 43-4, Corrosion Control for Aircraft
K11	AC 20-34, Prevention of Retractable Landing Gear Failures
K12	AC 20-32, Carbon Monoxide (CO) Contamination in Aircraft-Detection and Prevention
K13	AC 20-43, Aircraft Fuel Control
K20	AC 20-103, Aircraft Engine Crankshaft Failure
K23	AC 20-121, Airworthiness Approval of Airborne Loran-C Navigation Systems for Use in the U.S. National Airspace System
K26	AC 20-138, Airworthiness Approval of Global Positioning System (GPS) Navigation Equipment for Use as a VFR and IFR Supplemental Navigation System
K40	AC 25-4, Inertial Navigation Systems (INS)
K45	AC 39-7, Airworthiness Directives
K46	AC 43-9, Maintenance Records
K47	AC 43.9-1, Instructions for Completion of FAA Form 337
K48	AC 43-11, Reciprocating Engine Overhaul Terminology and Standards
K49	AC 43.13-1, Acceptable Methods, Techniques, and PracticesóAircraft Inspection and Repair
K50	AC 43.13-2, Acceptable Methods, Techniques, and PracticesóAircraft Alterations
K80	AC 60-4, Pilot's Spatial Disorientation
L05	AC 60-22, Aeronautical Decision Making
L10	AC 61-67, Stall Spin Awareness Training

L15   AC 61-107, Operations of Aircraft at Altitudes Above 25,000 Feet MSL and/or MACH numbers (Mmo) Greater Than .75

L25   FAA-G-8082-11, Inspection Authorization Knowledge Test Guide

L34   AC 90-48, Pilots' Role in Collision Avoidance

L42   AC 90-87, Helicopter Dynamic Rollover

L44   AC 90-94, Guidelines for Using Global Positioning System Equipment for IFR En Route and Terminal Operations and for Nonprecision Instrument Approaches in the U.S. National Airspace System

L45   AC 90-95, Unanticipated Right Yaw in Helicopters

L50   AC 91-6, Water, Slush, and Snow on the Runway

L52   AC 91-13, Cold Weather Operation of Aircraft

L53   AC 91-14, Altimeter Setting Sources

L57   AC 91-43, Unreliable Airspeed Indications

L59   AC 91-46, Gyroscopic InstrumentsóGood Operating Practices

L61   AC 91-50, Importance of Transponder Operation and Altitude Reporting

L62   AC 91-51, Effect of Icing on Aircraft Control and Airplane Deice and Anti-Ice Systems

L70   AC 91-67, Minimum Equipment Requirements for General Aviation Operations Under FAR Part 91

L80   AC 103-4, Hazard Associated with Sublimation of Solid Carbon Dioxide (Dry Ice) Aboard Aircraft

L90   AC 105-2, Sport Parachute Jumping

M01   AC 120-12, Private Carriage Versus Common Carriage of Persons or Property

M02   AC 120-27, Aircraft Weight and Balance Control

M08   AC 120-58, Pilot Guide for Large Aircraft Ground Deicing

M13   AC 121-195-1, Operational Landing Distances for Wet Runways; Transport Category Airplanes

M35   AC 135-17, Pilot Guide-Small Aircraft Ground Deicing

M51   AC 20-117, Hazards Following Ground Deicing and Ground Operations in Conditions Conducive to Aircraft Icing

M52   AC 00-2, Advisory Circular Checklist Soaring Flight ManualóJeppesen Sanderson, Inc.

N20   Sailplane Aerodynamics

N21   Performance Considerations

N22   Flight Instruments

N23   Weather for Soaring

N24   Medical Factors

N25   Flight Publications and Airspace

N26   Aeronautical Charts and Navigation

N27   Computations for Soaring

N28   Personal Equipment

N29   Preflight and Ground Operations

N30   Aerotow Launch Procedures

N31   Ground Launch Procedures

N32   Basic Flight Maneuvers and Traffic

N33   Soaring Techniques

N34   Cross-Country Soaring

Flight Instructor Manual-Balloon Federation of America

O10   Flight Instruction Aids

O11   Human Behavior and Pilot Proficiency

O12   The Flight Check and the Designated Examiner

Balloon Digest-Balloon Federation of America

O150   Balloon-Theory and Practice

O155   Structure of the Modern Balloon

O160   Lift-off to Landing

O165   Weather for the Balloonist

O170   Propane and Fuel Management

O171   Chemical and Physical Properties

O172   Tanks

O173   Burners

O174   Hoses

O175   Refueling

O176   Fuel Contamination

O177   Heat Tapes (Coils)

O178   Nitrogen Pressurization

O179   Repairs and Maintenance

Powerline Excerpts-Balloon Federation of America

O30   Excerpts

Balloon Ground School-Balloon Publishing Co.

O220   Balloon Operations

How To Fly A Balloon-Balloon Publishing Co.

O250   Basic Terminology

O251   History

O252   Physics

O253   Equipment

O254   Checklists

O255   Flight Planning

O256   Preflight Operations

O257   The Standard Burn

O258   Inflation

O259   Launch

O260   Level Flight

O261   Ascents and Descents

O262   Contour Flying

O263 Maneuvering
O264 Approach to Landing
O265 Landings
O266 Deflation
O267 The Chase
O268 Landowners Relations
O269 Recovery and Pack-up
O270 Propane: Management and Fueling
O271 Tethering
O272 Emergency Procedures
O273 Skill Development
O274 Crew
O275 What is a Good Instructor
O276 Regulations
O277 Maintenance
O278 Earning a Pilot Certificate
O279 Radio Communications
O280 Appendix 1: Glossary

Goodyear Airship Operations Manual

P01 Buoyancy
P02 Aerodynamics
P03 Free Ballooning
P04 Aerostatics
P05 Envelope
P06 Car
P07 Powerplant
P08 Airship Ground Handling
P11 Operating Instructions
P12 History
P13 Training

The Parachute Manual-Para Publishing

P31 Regulations
P32 The Parachute Rigger Certificate
P33 The Parachute Loft
P34 Parachute Materials
P35 Personnel Parachute Assemblies
P36 Parachute Component Parts
P37 Maintenance, Alteration, and
     Manufacturing Procedures
P38 Design and Construction
P39 Parachute Inspecting and Packing
P40 Glossary/Index

The Parachute Manual, Vol. II-Para Publishing

P51 Parachute Regulations
P52 The Parachute Riggerís Certificate
P53 The Parachute Loft
P54 Parachute Materials
P55 Personnel Parachute Assemblies
P56 Parachute Component Parts
P57 Maintenance, Alteration, and
     Manufacturing
P58 Parachute Design and Construction

P59 Parachute Inspection and Packing
P60 Appendix
P61 Conversion Tables
P62 Product/ManufactureróIndex
P63 Name and ManufactureóIndex
P64 Glossary-Index

FAA Accident Prevention Program Bulletins

V01 FAA-P-8740-2, Density Altitude
V02 FAA-P-8740-5, Weight and Balance
V03 FAA-P-8740-12, Thunderstorms
V04 FAA-P-8740-19, Flying Light Twins Safely
V05 FAA-P-8740-23, Planning your Takeoff
V06 FAA-P-8740-24, Tips on Winter Flying
V07 FAA-P-8740-25, Always Leave Yourself
     an Out
V08 FAA-P-8740-30, How to Obtain a Good
     Weather Briefing
V09 FAA-P-8740-40, Wind Shear
V10 FAA-P-8740-41, Medical Facts for Pilots
V11 FAA-P-8740-44, Impossible Turns
V12 FAA-P-8740-48, On Landings, Part I
V13 FAA-P-8740-49, On Landings, Part II
V14 FAA-P-8740-50, On Landings, Part III
V15 FAA-P-8740-51, How to Avoid a Midair
     Collision
V16 FAA-P-8740-52, The Silent Emergency

FTP-Flight Theory for Pilots-Jeppesen Sanderson, Inc.

W01 Introduction
W02 Air Flow and Airspeed Measurement
W03 Aerodynamic Forces on Airfoils
W04 Lift and Stall
W05 Drag
W06 Jet Aircraft Basic Performance
W07 Jet Aircraft Applied Performance
W08 Prop Aircraft Basic Performance
W09 Prop Aircraft Applied Performance
W10 Helicopter Aerodynamics
W11 Hazards of Low Speed Flight
W12 Takeoff Performance
W13 Landing Performance
W14 Maneuvering Performance
W15 Longitudinal Stability and Control
W16 Directional and Lateral Stability and Control
W17 High Speed Flight

Fly the Wing-Iowa State University Press/Ames, Second Edition

X01 Basic Aerodynamics
X02 High-Speed Aerodynamics
X03 High-Altitude Machs
X04 Approach Speed Control and Target
     Landings

X05   Preparation for Flight Training
X06   Basic Instrument Scan
X07   Takeoffs
X08   Rejected Takeoffs
X09   Climb, Cruise, and Descent
X10   Steep Turns
X11   Stalls
X12   Unusual Attitudes
X14   Maneuvers At Minimum Speed
X15   Landings: Approach Technique and Performance
X16   ILS Approaches
X17   Missed Approaches and Rejected Landings
X18   Category II and III Approaches
X19   Nonprecision and Circling Approaches
X20   Weight and Balance
X21   Flight Planning
X22   Icing
X23   Use of Anti-ice and Deice
X24   Winter Operation
X25   Thunderstorm Flight
X26   Low-Level Wind Shear

Practical Test Standards

Z01   FAA-S-8081-6, Flight Instructor Practical Test Standards for Airplane
Z02   FAA-S-8081-7, Flight Instructor Practical Test Standards for Rotorcraft
Z03   FAA-S-8081-8, Flight Instructor Practical Test Standards for Glider

NOTE: AC 00-2, Advisory Circular Checklist, transmits the status of all FAA advisory circulars (ACís), as well as FAA internal publications and miscellaneous flight information, such as Aeronautical

Information Manual, Airport/Facility Directory, knowledge test guides, practical test standards, and other material directly related to a certificate or rating. To obtain a free copy of AC 00-2, send your request to:

U.S. Department of Transportation
Subsequent Distribution Office, SVC-121.23
Ardmore East Business Center
3341 Q 75 Ave.
Landover, MD 20785

APPENDIX 2

LEGEND INFORMATION

2

DIRECTORY LEGEND
SAMPLE

①   ③ ④ ⑤   ⑥   ⑦

CITY NAME
AIRPORT NAME   (ORL)   4 E   UTC–5(–4DT)   N28°32.72' W81°21.17'   **JACKSONVILLE**
200   B   S4   **FUEL**   100. JET A   OX 1, 2,3   TPA—1000(800)   AOE   ARFF Index A   Not insp.   **COPTER**
                                                         H–4G, L–19C
 ⑨ ⑩ ⑪   ⑫   ⑬   ⑭   ⑮ ⑯   ⑰   **IAP**
                                                              ⑧

⑱→ **RWY 07-25:** H6000X150 (ASPH-PFC)   S–90, D–160, DT–300–PCN 80 R/B/W/T   HIRL   CL   0.4% up E
     RWY 07: ALSF1. Trees.   **RWY 25:** REIL. Rgt tfc.
     RWY 13-31: H4620X100 (ASPH)   HIRL
     RWY 13: SAVASI(S2L)—GA 3.3° TCH 89'. Pole.   **RWY 31:** PAPI(P2L)—GA 3.1° TCH 36'. Tree. Rgt tfc.
     RUNWAY DECLARED DISTANCE·INFORMATION
     RWY 07:   TORA–6000   TODA–6700   ASDA–5700   LDA–5500
     RWY 25:   TORA–6000   TODA–6000   ASDA–6000   LDA–5700
⑲→ **AIRPORT REMARKS:** Special Air Traffic Rules—Part 93, see Regulatory Notices. Attended 1200-0300Z‡. Parachute
     Jumping. CAUTION cattle and deer on arpt. Acft 100,000 lbs or over ctc Director of Aviation for approval
     305–894-9831. Fee for all airline charters, travel clubs and certain revenue producing acft. Flight Notification
     Service (ADCUS) available.
⑳→ **WEATHER DATA SOURCES:** AWOS-1 120.3 (202) 426-8000. LLWAS.
㉑→ **COMMUNICATIONS:** ATIS 127.25   UNICOM 122.95
     NAME FSS (ORL) on arpt. 123.65 122.65 122.2. TF 1-800-WX-BRIEF. NOTAM FILE ORL.   ←②
  ® **NAME APP/DEP CON** 128.35 (1200-0400Z‡)
     TOWER 118.7   **GND CON** 121.7   **CLNC DEL** 125.55   **PRE TAXI CLNC** 125.5
㉒→ **AIRSPACE: CLASS B** See VFR Terminal Area Chart.
㉓→ **RADIO AIDS TO NAVIGATION:** NOTAM FILE MCO. VHF/DF ctc FSS.
     (H) ABVORTAC 112.2   MCO   Chan 59   N28°32.55' W81°20.12'   at fld.   1110/8E.
       TWEB avbl 1300-0100Z‡. VOR unusable 050°–060° beyond 15 NM below 5000'.
     HERNY NDB (LOM) 221   OR   N28°30.40' W81°26.05'   067° 5.4 NM to fld.
     ILS 109.9   I-ORL   Rwy 07.   LOM HERNY NDB.
     ASR/PAR (1200–0400Z‡)
㉔→ **COMM/NAVAID REMARKS:** Emerg frequency 121.5 not available at tower.
    •
     HELIPAD H1: H100X75 (ASPH)
     HELIPAD H2: H60X60 (ASPH)   ↘①
     HELIPORT REMARKS: Helipad H1 lctd on general aviation side and H2 lctd on air carrier side of arpt.
    •
     187   TPA 1000(813)
     WATERWAY 13-31: 5000X300 (WATER)
     SEAPLANE REMARKS: Birds roosting and feeding areas along river banks. Seaplanes operating adjacent to NE side of
     arpt not visible from twr and are required to ctc twr.

D AIRPORT NAME   (MCO)   6 SE   UTC–5(–4DT)   N28°25.88' W81°19.48'   **JACKSONVILLE**
96   B   **FUEL** 100, JET A, MOGAS   LRA   **H–4G, L–19C**
RWY 18R-36L: H12004X300 (CONC-GRVD)   S–100, D–200, DT–400   HIRL   **IAP**
     RWY 18R: ALSF1. REIL. Rgt tfc.   0.3% up.   **RWY 36L:** ALSF1.   0.4% down.
RWY 18L-36R: H12004X200 (ASPH)   S–165, D–200, DT–400   HIRL
     RWY 18L: LDIN. ALSF1. TDZL. REIL. VASI(V4L)—GA 3.5° TCH 36'. Thld dsplcd 300'. Trees. Rgt tfc. Arresting device.
AIRPORT REMARKS: Attended 1200-0300Z‡. ACTIVATE HIRL Rwy 18L–36R—CTAF.
COMMUNICATIONS: CTAF 124.3   ATIS 127.75   UNICOM 122.8
     NAME FSS (MCO) TF 1-800-WX-BRIEF. LC 894-0869. NOTAM FILE MCO.
     NAME RCO 122.4 112.2T 122.1R (NAME FSS)
  ® **APP CON** 124.8 (337°–179°)   120.1 (180°–336°)   **DEP CON** 120.15
     TOWER 124.3 NFCT (1200–0400Z‡)   **GND CON** 121.85   **CLNC DEL** 134.7
AIRSPACE: CLASS D svc 1200–0400Z‡ other times CLASS E.
RADIO AIDS TO NAVIGATION: NOTAM FILE MCO.
     (H) VORTAC 112.2   MCO   Chan 59   N28°32.55' W81°20.12'   173° 5.7 NM to fld. 1110/8E.   **HIWAS.**
     MLS   Chan 514   Rwy 36R.

All Bearings and Radials are Magnetic unless otherwise specified.
All mileages are nautical unless otherwise noted.
All times are UTC except as noted.
The horizontal reference datum of this publication is North American Datum of 1983 (NAD83), which for charting purposes
is considered equivalent to World Geodetic System 1984 (WGS 84).

LEGEND 2.—Airport/Facility Directory.

DIRECTORY LEGEND
3
LEGEND

This Directory is an alphabetical listing of data on record with the FAA on all airports that are open to the public, associated terminal control facilities, air route traffic control centers and radio aids to navigation within the conterminous United States, Puerto Rico and the Virgin Islands. Airports are listed alphabetically by associated city name and cross referenced by airport name. Facilities associated with an airport, but with a different name, are listed individually under their own name, as well as under the airport with which they are associated.

The listing of an airport in this directory merely indicates the airport operator's willingness to accommodate transient aircraft, and does not represent that the facility conforms with any Federal or local standards, or that it has been approved for use on the part of the general public.

The information on obstructions is taken from reports submitted to the FAA. It has not been verified in all cases. Pilots are cautioned that objects not indicated in this tabulation (or on charts) may exist which can create a hazard to flight operation.

Detailed specifics concerning services and facilities tabulated within this directory are contained in Aeronautical Information Manual, Basic Flight Information and ATC Procedures.

The legend items that follow explain in detail the contents of this Directory and are keyed to the circled numbers on the sample on the preceding page.

① CITY/AIRPORT NAME

Airports and facilities in this directory are listed alphabetically by associated city and state. Where the city name is different from the airport name the city name will appear on the line above the airport name. Airports with the same associated city name will be listed alphabetically by airport name and will be separated by a dashed rule line. All others will be separated by a solid rule line. (Designated Helipads and Seaplane Landing Areas (Water) associated with a land airport will be separated by a dotted line.)

② NOTAM SERVICE

All public use landing areas are provided NOTAM "D" (distant dissemination) and NOTAM "L" (local dissemination) service. Airport NOTAM file identifier is shown following the associated FSS data for individual airports, e.g. "NOTAM FILE IAD". See AIM, Basic Flight Information and ATC Procedures for detailed description of NOTAM's.

③ LOCATION IDENTIFIER

A three or four character code assigned to airports. These identifiers are used by ATC in lieu of the airport name in flight plans, flight strips and other written records and computer operations.

④ AIRPORT LOCATION

Airport location is expressed as distance and direction from the center of the associated city in nautical miles and cardinal points, i.e., 4 NE.

⑤ TIME CONVERSION

Hours of operation of all facilities are expressed in Coordinated Universal Time (UTC) and shown as "Z" time. The directory indicates the number of hours to be subtracted from UTC to obtain local standard time and local daylight saving time UTC−5(−4DT). The symbol ‡ indicates that during periods of Daylight Saving Time effective hours will be one hour earlier than shown. In those areas where daylight saving time is not observed that (−4DT) and ‡ will not be shown. All states observe daylight savings time except Arizona, Hawaii and that portion of Indiana in the Eastern Time Zone and Puerto Rico and the Virgin Islands.

⑥ GEOGRAPHIC POSITION OF AIRPORT

Positions are shown in degrees, minutes and hundredths of a minute and represent the approximate center of mass of all usable runways.

⑦ CHARTS

The Sectional Chart and Low and High Altitude Enroute Chart and panel on which the airport or facility is located. Helicopter Chart locations will be indicated as, i.e., COPTER.

⑧ INSTRUMENT APPROACH PROCEDURES

IAP indicates an airport for which a prescribed (Public Use) FAA Instrument Approach Procedure has been published.

⑨ ELEVATION

The highest point of an airport's usable runways measured in feet from mean sea level. When elevation is sea level it will be indicated as (00). When elevation is below sea level a minus (−) sign will precede the figure.

⑩ ROTATING LIGHT BEACON

B indicates rotating beacon is available. Rotating beacons operate dusk to dawn unless otherwise indicated in AIRPORT REMARKS.

⑪ SERVICING

S1: Minor airframe repairs.
S2: Minor airframe and minor powerplant repairs.
S3: Major airframe and minor powerplant repairs.
S4: Major airframe and major powerplant repairs.

LEGEND 3.—Airport/Facility Directory.

4 DIRECTORY LEGEND

⑫ FUEL

CODE	FUEL	CODE	FUEL
80	Grade 80 gasoline (Red)	B	Jet B—Wide-cut turbine fuel, freeze point-50° C.
100	Grade 100 gasoline (Green)		
100LL	100LL gasoline (low lead) (Blue)	B+	Jet B—Wide-cut turbine fuel with icing inhibitor, freeze point-50° C.
115	Grade 115 gasoline		
A	Jet A—Kerosene freeze point-40° C.	MOGAS	Automobile gasoline which is to be used as aircraft fuel.
A1	Jet A-1—Kerosene freeze point-50°C.		
A1+	Jet A-1—Kerosene with icing inhibitor, freeze point-50° C.		

NOTE: Automobile Gasoline. Certain automobile gasoline may be used in specific aircraft engines if a FAA supplemental type cetificate has been obtained. Automobile gasoline which is to be used in aircraft engines will be identified as "MOGAS", however, the grade/type and octane rating will not be published.

Data shown on fuel availability represents the most recent information the publisher has been able to acquire. Because of a variety of factors, the fuel listed may not always be obtainable by transient civil pilots. Confirmation of availability of fuel should be made directly with fuel dispensers at locations where refueling is planned.

⑬ OXYGEN

OX 1   High Pressure
OX 2   Low Pressure
OX 3   High Pressure—Replacement Bottles
OX 4   Low Pressure—Replacement Bottles

⑭ TRAFFIC PATTERN ALTITUDE

Traffic Pattern Altitude (TPA)—The first figure shown is TPA above mean sea level. The second figure in parentheses is TPA above airport elevation.

⑮ AIRPORT OF ENTRY, LANDING RIGHTS, AND CUSTOMS USER FEE AIRPORTS

U.S. CUSTOMS USER FEE AIRPORT—Private Aircraft operators are frequently required to pay the costs associated with customs processing.

AOE—Airport of Entry—A customs Airport of Entry where permission from U.S. Customs is not required, however, at least one hour advance notice of arrival must be furnished.

LRA—Landing Rights Airport—Application for permission to land must be submitted in advance to U.S. Customs. At least one hour advance notice of arrival must be furnished.

NOTE: Advance notice of arrival at both an AOE and LRA airport may be included in the flight plan when filed in Canada or Mexico, where Flight Notification Service (ADCUS) is available the airport remark will indicate this service. This notice will also be treated as an application for permission to land in the case of an LRA. Although advance notice of arrival may be relayed to Customs through Mexico, Canadian, and U.S. Communications facilities by flight plan, the aircraft operator is solely responsible for insuring that Customs receives the notification. (See Customs, Immigration and Naturalization, Public Health and Agriculture Department requirements in the International Flight Information Manual for further details.)

⑯ CERTIFICATED AIRPORT (FAR 139)

Airports serving Department of Transportation certified carriers and certified under FAR, Part 139, are indicated by the ARFF index; i.e., ARFF Index A, which relates to the availability of crash, fire, rescue equipment.

FAR—PART 139 CERTIFICATED AIRPORTS
INDICES AND AIRCRAFT RESCUE AND FIRE FIGHTING EQUIPMENT REQUIREMENTS

Airport Index	Required No. Vehicles	Aircraft Length	Scheduled Departures	Agent + Water for Foam
A	1	<90'	≥1	500#DC or HALON 1211 or 450#DC + 100 gal H$_2$O
B	1 or 2	≥90', <126'	≥5	Index A + 1500 gal H$_2$O
		≥126', <159'	<5	
C	2 or 3	≥126', <159'	≥5	Index A + 3000 gal H$_2$O
		≥159', <200'	<5	
D	3	≥159', <200'	≥5	Index A + 4000 gal H$_2$O
		>200'	<5	
E	3	≥200'	≥5	Index A + 6000 gal H$_2$O

> Greater Than; < Less Than; ≥ Equal or Greater Than; ≤ Equal or Less Than; H$_2$O—Water; DC—Dry Chemical.

NOTE: The listing of ARFF index does not necessarily assure coverage for non-air carrier operations or at other than prescribed times for air carrier. ARFF Index Ltd.—indicates ARFF coverage may or may not be available, for information contact airport manager prior to flight.

LEGEND 4.—Airport/Facility Directory.

DIRECTORY LEGEND

5

(17) FAA INSPECTION

All airports not inspected by FAA will be identified by the note: Not insp. This indicates that the airport information has been provided by the owner or operator of the field.

(18) RUNWAY DATA

Runway information is shown on two lines. That information common to the entire runway is shown on the first line while information concerning the runway ends are shown on the second or following line. Lengthy information will be placed in the Airport Remarks.

Runway direction, surface, length, width, weight bearing capacity, lighting, slope and appropriate remarks are shown for each runway. Direction, length, width, lighting and remarks are shown for sealanes. The full dimensions of helipads are shown, i.e., 50X150.

RUNWAY SURFACE AND LENGTH

Runway lengths prefixed by the letter "H" indicate that the runways are hard surfaced (concrete, asphalt). If the runway length is not prefixed, the surface is sod, clay, etc. The runway surface composition is indicated in parentheses after runway length as follows:

(AFSC)—Aggregate friction seal coat	(GRVD)—Grooved	(RFSC)—Rubberized friction seal coat
(ASPH)—Asphalt	(GRVL)—Gravel, or cinders	(TURF)—Turf
(CONC)—Concrete	(PFC)—Porous friction courses	(TRTD)—Treated
(DIRT)—Dirt	(PSP)—Pierced steel plank	(WC)—Wire combed

RUNWAY WEIGHT BEARING CAPACITY

Runway strength data shown in this publication is derived from available information and is a realistic estimate of capability at an average level of activity. It is not intended as a maximum allowable weight or as an operating limitation. Many airport pavements are capable of supporting limited operations with gross weights of 25-50% in excess of the published figures. Permissible operating weights, insofar as runway strengths are concerned, are a matter of agreement between the owner and user. When desiring to operate into any airport at weights in excess of those published in the publication, users should contact the airport management for permission. Add 000 to figure following S, D, DT, DDT, AUW, etc., for gross weight capacity:

S—Single-wheel type landing gear. (DC–3), (C–47), (F–15), etc.

D—Dual-wheel type landing gear. (DC–6), etc.

T—Twin-wheel type landing gear. (DC–6), (C–9A), etc.

ST—Single-tandem type landing gear. (C–130).

SBTT—Single-belly twin tandem landing gear (KC–10).

DT—Dual-tandem type landing gear, (707), etc.

TT—Twin-tandem type (includes quadricycle) landing gear (707), (B–52), (C–135), etc.

TRT—Triple-tandem landing gear, (C–17)

DDT—Double dual-tandem landing gear. (E4A/747).

TDT—Twin delta-tandem landing gear. (C–5, Concorde).

AUW—All up weight. Maximum weight bearing capacity for any aircraft irrespective of landing gear configuration.

SWL—Single Wheel Loading. (This includes information submitted in terms of Equivalent Single Wheel Loading (ESWL) and Single Isolated Wheel Loading). SWL figures are shown in thousands of pounds with the last three figures being omitted.

PSI—Pounds per square inch. PSI is the actual figure expressing maximum pounds per square inch runway will support, e.g., (SWL 000/PSI 535).

Quadricycle and dual-tandem are considered virtually equal for runway weight bearing consideration, as are single-tandem and dual-wheel. Omission of weight bearing capacity indicates information unknown.

The ACN/PCN System is the ICAO method of reporting pavement strength for pavements with bearing strengths greater than 12,500 pounds. The Pavement Classification Number (PCN) is established by an engineering assessment of the runway. The PCN is for use in conjunction with an Aircraft Classification Number (ACN). Consult the Aircraft Flight Manual or other appropriate source for ACN tables or charts. Currently, ACN data may not be available for all aircraft. If an ACN table or chart is available, the ACN can be calculated by taking into account the aircraft weight, the pavement type, and the subgrade category. For runways that have been evaluated under the ACN/PCN system, the PCN will be shown as a five part code (e.g. PCN 80 R/B/W/T). Details of the coded format are as follows:

(1) The PCN NUMBER—The reported PCN indicates that an aircraft with an ACN equal or less than the reported PCN can operate on the pavement subject to any limitation on the tire pressure.

(2) The type of pavement:

    R — Rigid

    F — Flexible

(3) The pavement subgrade category:

    A — High

    B — Medium

    C — Low

    D — Ultra-low

(4) The maximum tire pressure authorized for the pavement:

    W — High, no limit

    X — Medium, limited to 217 psi

    Y — Low, limited to 145 psi

    Z — Very low, limited to 73 psi

(5) Pavement evaluation method:

    T — Technical evaluation

    U — By experience of aircraft using the pavement

NOTE: Prior permission from the airport controlling authority is required when the ACN of the aircraft exceeds the published PCN or aircraft tire pressure exceeds the published limits.

LEGEND 5.—Airport/Facility Directory.

6   DIRECTORY LEGEND

RUNWAY LIGHTING

Lights are in operation sunset to sunrise. Lighting available by prior arrangement only or operating part of the night only and/or pilot controlled and with specific operating hours are indicated under airport remarks. Since obstructions are usually lighted, obstruction lighting is not included in this code. Unlighted obstructions on or surrounding an airport will be noted in airport remarks. Runway lights nonstandard (NSTD) are systems for which the light fixtures are not FAA approved L-800 series: color, intensity, or spacing does not meet FAA standards. Nonstandard runway lights, VASI, or any other system not listed below will be shown in airport remarks.

Temporary, emergency or limited runway edge lighting such as flares, smudge pots, lanterns or portable runway lights will also be shown in airport remarks. Types of lighting are shown with the runway or runway end they serve.

NSTD—Light system fails to meet FAA standards.
LIRL—Low Intensity Runway Lights
MIRL—Medium Intensity Runway Lights
HIRL—High Intensity Runway Lights
RAIL—Runway Alignment Indicator Lights
REIL—Runway End Identifier Lights
CL—Centerline Lights
TDZL—Touchdown Zone Lights
ODALS—Omni Directional Approach Lighting System.
AF OVRN—Air Force Overrun 1000' Standard
    Approach Lighting System.
LDIN—Lead-In Lighting System.
MALS—Medium Intensity Approach Lighting System.
MALSF—Medium Intensity Approach Lighting System with
    Sequenced Flashing Lights.
MALSR—Medium Intensity Approach Lighting System with
    Runway Alignment Indicator Lights.

SALS—Short Approach Lighting System.
SALSF—Short Approach Lighting System with Sequenced
    Flashing Lights.
SSALS—Simplified Short Approach Lighting System.
SSALF—Simplified Short Approach Lighting System with
    Sequenced Flashing Lights.
SSALR—Simplified Short Approach Lighting System with
    Runway Alignment Indicator Lights.
ALSAF—High Intensity Approach Lighting System with
    Sequenced Flashing Lights
ALSF1—High Intensity Approach Lighting System with Se-
    quenced Flashing Lights, Category I, Configuration.
ALSF2—High Intensity Approach Lighting System with Se-
    quenced Flashing Lights, Category II, Configuration.
VASI—Visual Approach Slope Indicator System.

NOTE: Civil ALSF-2 may be operated as SSALR during favorable weather conditions.

VISUAL GLIDESLOPE INDICATORS

APAP—A system of panels, which may or may not be lighted, used for alignment of approach path.

PNIL	APAP on left side of runway	PNIR	APAP on right side of runway

PAPI—Precision Approach Path Indicator

P2L	2-identical light units placed on left side of runway	P4L	4-identical light units placed on left side of runway
P2R	2-identical light units placed on right side of runway	P4R	4-identical light units placed on right side of runway

PVASI—Pulsating/steady burning visual approach slope indicator, normally a single light unit projecting two colors.

PSIL-	PVASI on left side of runway	PSIR-	PVASI on right side of runway

SAVASI—Simplified Abbreviated Visual Approach Slope Indicator

S2L	2-box SAVASI on left side of runway	S2R	2-box SAVASI on right side of runway

TRCV—Tri-color visual approach slope indicator, normally a single light unit projecting three colors.

TRIL	TRCV on left side of runway	TRIR	TRCV on right side of runway

VASI—Visual Approach Slope Indicator

V2L	2-box VASI on left side of runway	V6L	6-box VASI on left side of runway
V2R	2-box VASI on right side of runway	V6R	6-box VASI on right side of runway
V4L	4-box VASI on left side of runway	V12	12-box VASI on both sides of runway
V4R	4-box VASI on right side of runway	V16	16-box VASI on both sides of runway

NOTE: Approach slope angle and threshold crossing height will be shown when available; i.e., –GA 3.5° TCH 37'.

PILOT CONTROL OF AIRPORT LIGHTING

Key Mike	Function
7 times within 5 seconds	Highest intensity available
5 times within 5 seconds	Medium or lower intensity (Lower REIL or REIL-Off)
3 times within 5 seconds	Lowest intensity available (Lower REIL or REIL-Off)

Available systems will be indicated in the Airport Remarks, as follows:

ACTIVATE MALSR Rwy 07, HIRL Rwy 07–25–122.8 (or CTAF).
        or
ACTIVATE MIRL Rwy 18–36–122.8 (or CTAF).
        or
ACTIVATE VASI and REIL, Rwy 07–122.8 (or CTAF).

Where the airport is not served by an instrument approach procedure and/or has an independent type system of different specification installed by the airport sponsor, descriptions of the type lights, method of control, and operating frequency will be explained in clear text. See AIM, ''Basic Flight Information and ATC Procedures,'' for detailed description of pilot control of airport lighting.

RUNWAY SLOPE

Runway slope will be shown only when it is 0.3 percent or more. On runways less than 8000 feet: When available the direction of the slope upward will be indicated, ie., 0.3% up NW. On runways 8000 feet or greater: When available the slope will be shown on the runway end line, ie., RWY 13: 0.3% up., RWY 21: Pole. Rgt tfc. 0.4% down.

RUNWAY END DATA

Lighting systems such as VASI, MALSR, REIL; obstructions; displaced thresholds will be shown on the specific runway end. ''Rgt tfc''—Right traffic indicates right turns should be made on landing and takeoff for specified runway end.

LEGEND 6.—Airport/Facility Directory.

DIRECTORY LEGEND

RUNWAY DECLARED DISTANCE INFORMATION

7

TORA—Take-off Run Available
TODA—Take-off Distance Available
ASDA—Accelerate-Stop Distance Available
LDA—Landing Distance Available

⑲ AIRPORT REMARKS

Landing Fee indicates landing charges for private or non-revenue producing aircraft. In addition, fees may be charged for planes that remain over a couple of hours and buy no services, or at major airline terminals for all aircraft.
Remarks—Data is confined to operational items affecting the status and usability of the airport.
Parachute Jumping.—See ''PARACHUTE'' tabulation for details.
Unless otherwise stated, remarks including runway ends refer to the runway's approach end.

⑳ WEATHER DATA SOURCES

ASOS—Automated Surface Observing System. Reports the same as an AWOS-3 plus precipitation identification and intensity, and freezing rain occurrence (future enhancement).
AWOS—Automated Weather Observing System

AWOS-A—reports altimeter setting.
AWOS-1—reports altimeter setting, wind data and usually temperature, dewpoint and density altitude.
AWOS-2—reports the same as AWOS-1 plus visibility.
AWOS-3—reports the same as AWOS-1 plus visibility and cloud/ceiling data.
See AIM, Basic Flight Information and ATC Procedures for detailed description of AWOS.

HIWAS—See RADIO AIDS TO NAVIGATION
LAWRS—Limited Aviation Weather Reporting Station where observers report cloud height, weather, obstructions to vision, temperature and dewpoint (in most cases), surface wind, altimeter and pertinent remarks.
LLWAS—indicates a Low Level Wind Shear Alert System consisting of a center field and several field perimeter anemometers.
SAWRS—identifies airports that have a Supplemental Aviation Weather Reporting Station available to pilots for current weather information.
SWSL—Supplemental Weather Service Location providing current local weather information via radio and telephone.

㉑ COMMUNICATIONS

Communications will be listed in sequence in the order shown below:
Common Traffic Advisory Frequency (CTAF), Automatic Terminal Information Service (ATIS) and Aeronautical Advisory Stations (UNICOM) along with their frequency is shown, where available, on the line following the heading ''COMMUNICATIONS.'' When the CTAF and UNICOM is the same frequency, the frequency will be shown as CTAF/UNICOM freq.
Flight Service Station (FSS) information. The associated FSS will be shown followed by the identifier and information concerning availability of telephone service, e.g., Direct Line (DL), Local Call (LC-384-2341), Toll free call, dial (TF 800-852-7036 or TF 1-800-227-7160), Long Distance (LD 202-426-8800 or LD 1-202-555-1212) etc. The airport NOTAM file identifier will be shown as ''NOTAM FILE IAD.'' Where the FSS is located on the field it will be indicated as ''on arpt'' following the identifier. Frequencies available will follow. The FSS telephone number will follow along with any significant operational information. FSS's whose name is not the same as the airport on which located will also be listed in the normal alphabetical name listing for the state in which located. Remote Communications Outlet (RCO) providing service to the airport followed by the frequency and name of the Controlling FSS.
FSS's provide information on airport conditions, radio aids and other facilities, and process flight plans. Local Airport Advisory Service is provided on the CTAF by FSS's located at non-tower airports or airports where the tower is not in operation.
(See AIM, Par. 157/158 Traffic Advisory Practices at airports where a tower is not in operation or AC 90 - 42C.)
Aviation weather briefing service is provided by FSS specialists. Flight and weather briefing services are also available by calling the telephone numbers listed.
Remote Communications Outlet (RCO)—An unmanned air/ground communications facility, remotely controlled and providing UHF or VHF communications capability to extend the service range of an FSS.
Civil Communications Frequencies—Civil communications frequencies used in the FSS air/ground system are now operated simplex on 122.0, 122.2, 122.3, 122.4, 122.6, 123.6; emergency 121.5; plus receive-only on 122.05, 122.1, 122.15, and 123.6.

   a. 122.0 is assigned as the Enroute Flight Advisory Service channel at selected FSS's.
   b. 122.2 is assigned to most FSS's as a common enroute simplex service.
   c. 123.6 is assigned as the airport advisory channel at non-tower FSS locations, however, it is still in commission at some FSS's collocated with towers to provide part time Local Airport Advisory Service.
   d. 122.1 is the primary receive-only frequency at VOR's. 122.05, 122.15 and 123.6 are assigned at selected VOR's meeting certain criteria.
   e. Some FSS's are assigned 50 kHz channels for simplex operation in the 122-123 MHz band (e.g. 122.35). Pilots using the FSS A/G system should refer to this directory or appropriate charts to determine frequencies available at the FSS or remoted facility through which they wish to communicate.

Part time FSS hours of operation are shown in remarks under facility name.

Emergency frequency 121.5 is available at all Flight Service Stations, Towers, Approach Control and RADAR facilities. unless indicated as not available.
Frequencies published followed by the letter ''T'' or ''R'', indicate that the facility will only transmit or receive respectively on that frequency. All radio aids to navigation frequencies are transmit only.

LEGEND 7.—Airport/Facility Directory.

8   DIRECTORY LEGEND

TERMINAL SERVICES

CTAF—A program designed to get all vehicles and aircraft at uncontrolled airports on a common frequency.

ATIS—A continuous broadcast of recorded non-control information in selected areas of high activity.

UNICOM—A non-government air/ground radio communications facility utilized to provide general airport advisory service.

APP CON —Approach Control. The symbol Ⓡ indicates radar approach control.

TOWER—Control tower

GND CON—Ground Control

DEP CON—Departure Control. The symbol Ⓡ indicates radar departure control.

CLNC DEL—Clearance Delivery.

PRE TAXI CLNC—Pre taxi clearance

VFR ADVSY SVC—VFR Advisory Service. Service provided by Non-Radar Approach Control.
   Advisory Service for VFR aircraft (upon a workload basis) ctc APP CON.

TOWER, APP CON and DEP CON RADIO CALL will be the same as the airport name unless indicated otherwise.

㉒ AIRSPACE

CLASS B—Radar Sequencing and Separation Service for all aircraft in CLASS B airspace

TRSA—Radar Sequencing and Separation Service for participating VFR Aircraft within a Terminal Radar Service Area

Class C, D, and E airspace described in this publication is that airspace usually consisting of a 5 NM radius core surface area that begins at the surface and extends upward to an altitude above the airport elevation (charted in MSL for Class C and Class D).

When CLASS C airspace defaults to CLASS E, the core surface area becomes CLASS E. This will be formatted as: **AIRSPACE: CLASS C** svc ''times'' ctc **APP CON** other times CLASS E.

When Class C airspace defaults to Class G, the core surface area becomes Class G up to but not including the overlying controlled airspace. There are Class E airspace areas beginning at either 700' or 1200' AGL used to transition to/from the terminal or enroute environment. This will be formatted as: **AIRSPACE: CLASS C** svc ''times'' ctc **APP CON** other times CLASS G. CLASS E 700' (or 1200') AGL & abv.

NOTE: AIRSPACE SVC EFF ''TIMES'' INCLUDE ALL ASSOCIATED EXTENSIONS. Arrival extensions for instrument approach procedures become part of the primary core surface area. These extensions may be either Class D or Class E airspace and are effective concurrent with the times of the primary core surface area.

(See CLASS AIRSPACE in the Aeronautical Information Manual for further details)

㉓ RADIO AIDS TO NAVIGATION

The Airport Facility Directory lists by facility name all Radio Aids to Navigation, except Military TACANS, that appear on National Ocean Service Visual or IFR Aeronautical Charts and those upon which the FAA has approved an Instrument Approach Procedure. All VOR, VORTAC ILS and MLS equipment in the National Airspace System has an automatic monitoring and shutdown feature in the event of malfunction. Unmonitored, as used in this publication for any navigational aid, means that FSS or tower personnel cannot observe the malfunction or shutdown signal. The NAVAID NOTAM file identifier will be shown as ''NOTAM FILE IAD'' and will be listed on the Radio Aids to Navigation line. When two or more NAVAIDS are listed and the NOTAM file identifier is different than shown on the Radio Aids to Navigation line, then it will be shown with the NAVAID listing. NOTAM file identifiers for ILS's and their components (e.g., NDB (LOM) are the same as the identifiers for the associated airports and are not repeated. Hazardous Inflight Weather Advisory Service (HIWAS) will be shown where this service is broadcast over selected VOR's.

NAVAID information is tabulated as indicated in the following sample:

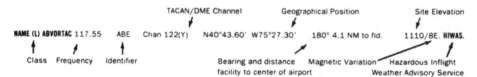

VOR unusable 020°-060° beyond 26 NM below 3500'

Restriction within the normal altitude/range of the navigational aid (See primary alphabetical listing for restrictions on VORTAC and VOR/DME).

   Note: Those DME channel numbers with a (Y) suffix require TACAN to be placed in the ''Y'' mode to receive distance information.

HIWAS—Hazardous Inflight Weather Advisory Service is a continuous broadcast of inflight weather advisories including summarized SIGMETs, convective SIGMETs, AIRMETs and urgent PIREPs. HIWAS is presently broadcast over selected VOR's and will be implemented throughout the conterminous U.S.

ASR/PAR—Indicates that Surveillance (ASR) or Precision (PAR) radar instrument approach minimums are published in the U.S. Terminal Procedures. Only part-time hours of operation will be shown.

LEGEND 8.—Airport/Facility Directory.

DIRECTORY LEGEND   9

RADIO CLASS DESIGNATIONS

VOR/DME/TACAN Standard Service Volume (SSV) Classifications

SSV Class	Altitudes	Distance (NM)
(T) Terminal	1000' to 12,000'	25
(L) Low Altitude	1000' to 18,000'	40
(H) High Altitude	1000' to 14,500'	40
	14,500' to 18,000'	100
	18,000' to 45,000'	130
	45,000' to 60,000'	100

NOTE: Additionally, (H) facilities provide (L) and (T) service volume and (L) facilities provide (T) service. Altitudes are with respect to the station's site elevation. Coverage is not available in a cone of airspace directly above the facility.

The term VOR is, operationally, a general term covering the VHF omnidirectional bearing type of facility without regard to the fact that the power, the frequency protected service volume, the equipment configuration, and operational requirements may vary between facilities at different locations.

AB	Automatic Weather Broadcast
DF	Direction Finding Service.
DME	UHF standard (TACAN compatible) distance measuring equipment.
DME(Y)	UHF standard (TACAN compatible) distance measuring equipment that require TACAN to be placed in the ''Y'' mode to receive DME.
H	Non-directional radio beacon (homing), power 50 watts to less than 2,000 watts (50 NM at all altitudes).
HH	Non-directional radio beacon (homing), power 2,000 watts or more (75 NM at all altitudes).
H-SAB	Non-directional radio beacons providing automatic transcribed weather service.
ILS	Instrument Landing System (voice, where available, on localizer channel).
ISMLS	Interim Standard Microwave Landing System.
LDA	Localizer Directional Aid.
LMM	Compass locator station when installed at middle marker site (15 NM at all altitudes).
LOM	Compass locator station when installed at outer marker site (15 NM at all altitudes).
MH	Non-directional radio beacon (homing) power less than 50 watts (25 NM at all altitudes).
MLS	Microwave Landing System
S	Simultaneous range homing signal and/or voice.
SABH	Non-directional radio beacon not authorized for IFR or ATC. Provides automatic weather broadcasts.
SDF	Simplified Direction Facility.
TACAN	UHF navigational facility-omnidirectional course and distance information.
VOR	VHF navigational facility-omnidirectional course only.
VOR/DME	Collocated VOR navigational facility and UHF standard distance measuring equipment.
VORTAC	Collocated VOR and TACAN navigational facilities.
W	Without voice on radio facility frequency.
Z	VHF station location marker at a LF radio facility.

LEGEND 9.—Airport/Facility Directory.

JeppPrep Online

JeppPrep is Jeppesen's latest innovation in FAA test preparation. With JeppPrep you can study from the latest FAA questions, continuously updated in our database. JeppPrep is an easy way to ensure you are ready to take an FAA exam.

With the purchase of JeppPrep, you will receive a 60-day period of unlimited study for a particular FAA knowledge exam. If necessary, you can renew for another 30-days for an additional charge.

JeppPrep Features: • Study actual FAA questions at your own pace, on your own time • Review answers and explanations to actual FAA questions • Take sample tests that emulate actual FAA knowledge tests • Efficiently review the results of your practice tests • Compare your performance on several tests • Work with the most current FAA questions • View or print the FAA figures and legends for FAA questions • Private, Instrument, Commercial

Order on the web at: www.jeppesen.com or call 800.621.5377

WB100500 JeppPrep Initial Order – Valid for 60 days $29.95
WB100543 JeppPrep 30-day Renewal $19.95

FAR/AIM Manual (paper)

An excellent study or reference source, the new, larger format includes 14 CFR 135 with complete pilot/controller glossary. Changes are conveniently indicated. Including FAR Parts 1, 43, 61, 67, 71, 73, 91, 97, 119, 133, 135, 141, 142, HMR 175 and NTSB 830, the *FAR/AIM* uses special study lists to direct students to the appropriate FARs. You can check your understanding of the FARs with exercise questions tailored for Private, Instrument, Commercial, and Helicopter. A free Update Summary is available on the internet at www.jeppesen.com.   JS314550 $17.95

Expanded FAR/AIM CD-ROM (includes *FARs Explained*)

The Federal Aviation Regulations are an integral part of aeronautical training. This CD contains applicable portions of Parts 1, 13, 21, 23, 27, 33, 34, 35, 39, 43, 45, 47, 61, 67, 71, 73, 91, 97, 119, 125, 133, 135, 141, 142, 145 (new and old), 147, 183, HMR 175 and NTSB 830. You can search the regulations by part, keyword, or phrase. The FAR/AIM CD-ROM contains: the FARs, FARs Explained by Kent Jackson, FAR Exercises, the AIM and the Pilot Controller Glossary. It also includes SFARs and Maintenance Advisory Circulars as well as FAA-G-8082-11. Both Pilot and Maintenance Regulations are included. Available with a revision service that includes two updated FAR/AIM CD-ROMs following the FAA AIM revisions (two per year). System requirements: PC with 486 or faster processor, 2x CD-ROM drive, Windows 95. Free update summary available on www.jeppesen.com.   JS206350 $29.95

Aviation Weather

This award-winning, 480-page hardcover textbook is extensively updated with the latest METAR, TAF, and Graphic Weather Products from AC00-45E, Aviation Weather Services. Over 500 full-color illustrations and photographs present detailed material in an uncomplicated way. International weather considerations are included as well as accident/incident information to add relevance to the weather data. *Aviation Weather*, by Peter F. Lester, features comprehensive coverage of icing, weather hazards, and flight planning, as well as review questions with answers at the end of the book. The appendices cover common conversions, weather reports, forecasts, and charts, as well as domestic and international METAR, TAF, and graphic weather products.
JS319010 $57.95

Both Bags feature removable headset bags!

B

A

A. The Captain Bag

Contains two detachable headset bags, which can be connected together to form a separate bag. Other features include: Removable Transceiver/GPS • 4-way adjustable divider that holds up to 4 Jeppesen binders • Exterior front pocket • Two large zippered storage pockets • 600 denier poly in black or blue. 12"x22¹/₂"x8"
JS621214 (black) $139.95
JS621251 (blue) $139.95

The Navigator Bag

he ultimate choice for convenience and exibility. Contains two detachable headset bags, which can be connected together to form a eparate bag. Other features include: Two exterior ockets • 4-way adjustable divider that holds up o 4 Jeppesen binders • Exterior front pocket 600 denier poly in black or blue. 12"x22¹/₂"x8"
S621213 (black) $99.95 JS621250 (blue) $99.95

C. The Student Pilot

A great first bag for the student pilot. Features include: Outside pockets • Removable shoulder strap • Double zipper opening • Reinforced bottom • PVC backed 600 denier poly. 10"x5¹/₂"x17" JS621212 (black only) $41.95

D. The Aviator Bag

Spacious enough for all of your flight materials. Features include: exterior front pocket • detachable headset and transceiver cases PVC backed 600 denier poly. 15"x6¹/₂"x12"
JS621252 (black only) $79.95

D

C

E

E. The Protector Headset Bags

Features include: Padded 600 denier poly • Snap-On handle grip • Fits ANR headsets • Single and dual configuration. 12"x2³/₄"x8"
JS621220 Single (black only) $17.95
JS621219 Dual (black only) $35.95

Visit Your Jeppesen Dealer or Call 1.800.621.5377
Make sure to check out our web page at http://www.jeppesen.com
Prices subject to change.

almost

real.

TechStar® Pro

The TechStar Pro combines a 7-function aviation computer and 8-function personal organizer, all in one compact handheld unit. In addition to basic and advanced arithmetic functions, TechStar Pro is designed with 7 main aviation operating modes and 8 organizer modes which offer quick and simple use including:

• Time/Speed/Distance • Altitude/Airspeed • Wind • Weight and Balance • Latitude/Longitude • Timer • Conversions • Telephone/Address • Personal Memo/To Do • Daily Scheduler • Trip Expense Log • Monthly Calendar • Local Time • World Time (128 cities + Zulu time conversions) • Calculator • Approved for use on FAA Knowledge Examinations
JS505000 $89.95

Fuel Tester

Made of clear butyrate plastic to resist cracking, breaking and yellowing. Works with both pin and petcock actuators. Removable splash guard attaches to side for storage. Solid bronze rod actuator prevents breaking and pushing down. Includes hard-tempered, reversible phillips and slotted bit.   JS628855 $13.95

JeppShades

IFR flip-up training glasses replace bulky instrument training hoods. Improved design allows better student/instructor interaction and works conveniently under headsets, while reducing pressure on ears and temples. Flip-up, impact-resistant lens allows convenient IFR/VFR flight transition.
JS404311 $24.95

VFR/IFR Kneeboard

Holds charts, flight computers/plotters, flashlight, pen, pilot notes and more. Features an elastic leg strap with a Velcro closure. The metal clipboard has an additional strap allowing you to use the clipboard independent of the kneeboard.
Kneeboard/Clipboard JS626003 $36.95
Clipboard only with Leg Strap JS626001 $16.95

FREE
Flight Planning Charts
Included! *$6.95 Value!*

Chart Training Videos and DVD

Chart Series Professionally designed and produced, the FlighTime Chart Series Videos and DVD cover Jeppesen enroute charts and approach charts, as well as SIDs and STARs. JS200251 Videos $99.95   JS200300 DVD $79.95

Approach Charts includes a detailed introduction of Jeppesen's approach charts, featuring the Briefing Strip™ format. RNAV and GPS procedures are also covered. JS273268 $37.95

Enroute Charts features Jeppesen four-color enroute charts and is based primarily on US-LO series charts. JS273269 $37.95

Departures and Arrivals presents the unique characteristics of SID and STAR charts. JS273270 $37.95

Now Available on **NEW INTERACTIVE** **DVD!**

FliteLog® Electronic LogBook
A traditional paper logbook feel *(modeled after our Professional Pilot Logbook)*, with the flexibility of a computer program. Available for Windows only. JM301592 $89.00

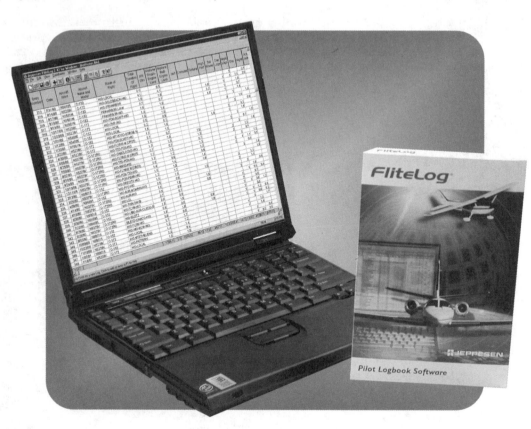